Get

What You Pay For
Or
Don't Pay at All

Get
What You Pay For
Or
Don't Pay at All

Donna McCrohan

Crown Trade Paperbacks

New York

This book is a guide to effective ways of protecting your rights in various consumer situations. It is not a guarantee. Phone numbers and addresses are subject to change; laws also are subject to change and vary from state to state. You must carefully assess your position and exercise reasonable judgment in each case.

Copyright © 1994 by Donna McCrohan

Published by Crown Trade Paperbacks, 201 East 50th Street, New York, New York 10022. Member of the Crown Publishing Group.

Random House, Inc. New York, Toronto, London, Sydney, Auckland

CROWN TRADE PAPERBACKS and colophon are trademarks of Crown Publishers, Inc.

Manufactured in the United States of America

Design by Lenny Henderson

Library of Congress Cataloging-in-Publication Data
McCrohan, Donna.
    Get what you pay for—or don't pay at all / Donna McCrohan. —
1st ed.
        p.   cm.
    Includes index.
    1. Consumer protection.   2. Consumer education.   I. Title.
HC79.C63M39   1994
381.3—dc20   93-23498
                                                                  CIP

ISBN 0-517-88048-2

10 9 8 7 6 5 4 3 2 1

First Edition

To Mary Duane Hoffman,
whose examples taught me a lot.

Contents

Acknowledgments

My heartfelt gratitude goes to every community service representative, salesperson, or clerk who ever took the time to respond fairly to a customer's question. I know they're overworked and underpaid. Their kindness has not gone unnoticed.

My thanks, too, to Denise Marcil and Ruth McDaniel for urging me to write this book; to Aneta Corsaut, Carolyn Gilbert, Patricia Kaczynski, Karen Keenan, Ilene Klinghoffer-Goldfarb, Muriel Kruger, Jane Ray Lawton, and Mark Schiavone for their ideas and insights; to Joe Setaro for his desk; and to Ron Keenan for his office.

Irene Prokop, my editor, has been a particular treasure. I value her patience and guidance and can think of few people with whom I'd rather swap hair-raising tales of consumer justice.

Introduction

IT'S YOUR DEAL

Did you buy a toaster that doesn't toast? Then you're entitled to a repair, a replacement, or a refund—not an argument. Does your expensive investment broker ignore your instructions and erode your resources? Then insist on an investigation, full credit for your investment, and a new broker. Has the hospital billing officer charged you for "room and board" and meals as well? Then drag this person kicking and screaming into awareness that "board" means "meals."

Believe me, it can be done. As a free-lance writer, I've often found myself shelling out major money on a project for which the advance is months away. Frankly, I can't afford to ignore other people's apparent obsession with pillaging my bankroll—and it kills me to see them hide behind words that they're using wrong in the first place. A guarantee is a guarantee. A contract is a contract. My money is my money until *I* decide that it's theirs.

I've been at the mercy of airlines, hotels, and cabdrivers who thought I wouldn't notice the absence of advertised services. I noticed, and in the end was compensated with free rooms, free airfare, and cash refunds. I've had similar experiences with department, appliance, and grocery stores. I've had particular fun with manufacturers—sometimes they can be their own worst enemies.

Some years ago, I spent a week in Beverly Hills to complete a series of interviews. Friday arrived and I still hadn't been able to do the most important interview, but my subject promised to phone me during the day to arrange something for that evening. Because I had a lunchtime interview to conduct and wanted to do it in the hotel restaurant, I spoke to the assistant manager of the hotel and got his firm guarantee that he'd page me for every call. I said several times, "If you can't make this promise, tell me and I'll do the interview from my room. It will be awkward, but I'll do it unless I can be certain that you'll remember that I must be paged."

I was assured and reassured, so I went to lunch. When I returned to my room—naturally—the phone light told me I had a message. The message was that the party had called, wouldn't be anywhere I could reach by phone, and had reluctantly been left with no choice but to cancel our interview.

I phoned the assistant manager who had made the original promise. He said, "Oops, I forgot." I reminded him that I'd had his guarantee. He said, "I'm sorry. I accept full responsibility." I asked what this full responsibility entailed and he said, "I'm extending my sincerest apology."

Thinking perhaps he could do better, I pressed on: "But you accept full responsibility?"

He insisted he did.

I then said, "Okay. As a result of your error, I will have to spend another night in this hotel, pay for a few more meals, and dump $80 for cabfare on a round trip to Walnut, California, to do this interview tomorrow. I don't see where you get to say you're sorry and I get to dig $300 out of my pocket when you're *fully responsible.*"

He said, "Gurgle . . ."

Soon I had a free room for the night, and the hotel issued me a check for meals plus the $80 cabfare.

I'm obstinate. I'll force myself to pursue a refund or replacement through whatever maze of photocopies, phone calls, and pickleheads they throw at me. I'll usually win.

Be obstinate and you can win too. Just never let yourself forget that all consumerism boils down to one deal—*your* deal—and it's this: A product or service is portrayed to you in some way that persuades you to buy it.

- **You start with a choice.**
- **The choice is based on what the seller tells you.**
- **If the seller misinforms you, it shouldn't cost you more.**
- **The seller is entitled to your money only if the terms of the deal are met.**
- **If the terms aren't met, you should have the option to call off or renegotiate the deal.**

I don't expect you to sit down and read this book cover to cover. But if you just read Part I, you'll come away with a general approach to handling grievances. Then when you have any specific problem you can turn to the appropriate section of Part II for ways of proceeding in that situation.

I can't tell you that everything in this book will work every time. I also can't give legal advice, if only because so much consumer law varies from jurisdiction to jurisdiction.

But I can give you a really comprehensive list of resources. For instance, it's extremely difficult to get redress from hospitals and doctors that have done you wrong and very easy to get runarounds. I can't swear the runarounds will stop. But I can name organizations that agree with you that you deserve fair treatment and that want to help you get it.

And I can give you a basic philosophy that's worked for me. A philosophy is vital, because this is a people issue. You deal in facts, but you deal with people. Each case is going to be a little dif-

ferent from every other. You can study one of the checklists from Part II and follow it to the letter, but be hitting all the wrong people down the line. This will affect your chances. So you have to read personalities, have an eye for strategy, detect nuances.

Let's start with the obvious. Assume you've got a valid complaint. Perhaps the seller knows you're right. Maybe the seller admits you're right. You say, "Now I get the refund?" The seller says, "NO."

A person who has your money or your car and says NO probably feels it's a terrific way to keep your car and your money. The speaker may not have the support of management and may be dead wrong, but still has the power to utter the word NO, which, once uttered, is a bigger stumbling block than "Yes" or "I'll try" or even "We're not set up to do what you want."

NO isn't what you want to hear. NO goes nowhere. One of your biggest negotiating skills will be to avoid hearing NO or at the very least to forestall hearing it as long as possible.

Often, the resistant seller is counting on wearing you down. Repeated NOs are intended to cost you so much time that you drop the matter in despair. It's true that you don't want to be drawn into a long process. But neither does the seller. No one does. Turn that fact to your advantage.

Of course, many customer service people believe it's their job to promise whatever it takes to make you go away. They don't get around to saying NO until you come to collect.

Consider it a challenge, and no matter how much it pains you, be reasoning, not rude. You can be firm. But don't be insulting. Calling a person stupid is a bad plan. It's a bad plan if you're just venting frustration. It's a worse plan if the person actually is stupid, because people ill suited for their jobs are understandably defensive about keeping them.

Threatening is another bad plan, unless as an absolute last resort. If it's a big threat, you probably won't get around to following through, and your adversary knows it. If you do make good, the payoff will be a long time coming. You'll encounter salespeople who will routinely and automatically dismiss your complaints. The fact that you can have their businesses swamped with paperwork from investigative agencies, or fined, or closed, doesn't faze them because they don't believe you will follow through. Reconcile yourself to the fact that you won't get satisfaction from such people. Go over their heads.

You will get eventual satisfaction if you make it your business to illustrate to stonewalling salespeople how very uncomfortable they will be when their business is targeted by investigative agencies, fined, and closed. But if you threaten and don't follow through, you'll simply reinforce their conviction that disgruntled consumers can't touch them. If you follow through, they'll learn.

One way or another, unyielding sellers refuse you when they decide to stop listening (or were never listening in the first place). They conclude that you don't have a case, or can't make one, or can't make it stick. They feel they don't have to accommodate you because there's nothing to make them do it. Ultimately, smiling or not, they say NO.

This leads to your other negotiating skill: You've got to find a reason to make them want to do what you want them to do. More than anything, that's what this book is about.

Part 1

The Theory

A Matter of Principles

A Short History of Shopping

Tradition has it that merchants and service providers used to take pride in their work, with occasional spells when they didn't.

One of the more famous spells occurred in the late 1950s, when some industries perceived that defective merchandise is more lucrative because customers have to pay for it over and over (once to buy it, then every few years to replace it). This was coupled with the realization that people in general were becoming lost in the crowd—codified and I.D.-numbered—relinquishing their individuality in the eyes of the institutions that served them.

There followed a tremendous national awareness of the importance of consumer protection and individual assertiveness. Shoppers, groups, and governments became involved, establishing countless consumer protection and advocacy agencies into the sixties.

But in the seventies and eighties, over-the-counter consumer awareness took a backseat to flashier monetary concerns, such as how to get the best pension, how to invest wisely, how to shelter income, and how to strike a sound bargain with the neighborhood S&L. Too many shoppers seemed to accept that time was more important than money—that it was better to let oneself be cheated out of a few dollars or even a few hundred dollars than to waste time going after it—and droves of sellers happily abandoned traditional values.

If shoppers complained at all, they complained to friends and neighbors, but never to the guilty company because it wasn't "worth the bother." According to the Washington-based Technical Assistance Research Programs, only 4 percent of dissatisfied customers let a business know when they were unhappy with a product or service.

Having sent the message that we were too preoccupied to insist on a fair deal, we marched head-long into a recession that left us counting our nickels. Suddenly we were anxious to get our consumer rights back. But businesses were less able than ever to oblige. Besides having succumbed to bad habits, they were cutting corners every which way. Staffs were sized down. Customer relations departments frequently existed in name only because it was considered simply too expensive to treat customers right. Worse, the recession often forced overqualified workers to take semiskilled jobs—perhaps to stand behind a counter when a year ago they'd run a company—and these employees may not have been in the best of moods to hear other people's complaints. And if we actually complained to the consumer protection agencies, we discovered that they too had been sized down and hardly had the resources (or desire) to pressure any money-making, tax-paying enterprise.

We reacted by belatedly venting steam. Books and articles related incendiary anecdotes to illustrate the thesis that a consumer uprising is overdue. It's true. If we want our rights again, we've got to demand them. But we can't content ourselves with lip service to storming Frankenstein's castle. We consumer townsfolk have got to follow the road maps that take us there.

This means not just buying books about getting our rights. It means putting the principles into action. If you read the books without following through, you haven't joined the fray. Arm yourself with persistence, research, and a variety of approaches. Review your options. Be flexible. Your objective is to reeducate sellers, teach them that your money isn't theirs without your consent. If they've cheated to get your money, don't let them keep it.

Because sellers are not particularly eager to hear you, you've got to choose your audience. You can have every fact in your favor and state your case with brilliant lucidity, but you still have to express it to somebody. Look for somebody able and willing to comprehend. People can be remarkably obtuse if they think you'll lose interest and go away. Find someone who can grasp the notion that you're not going anywhere. If one employee in the shop doesn't care, poke around for another who does. If nobody in the shop cares, call in the agencies and advocacy groups.

You can do it, and you can win.

Showing Them You Mean Business

Visualize the complaint process as an upward ladder. You may have to climb it rung by rung on up to the top, but it's definitely a solid structure for getting you where you want to go.

Rung One: Both Feet on the Ground

If you're in the store or office when the difficulty occurs, your initial defense is to talk to someone about it. Be reasonable, not rude. If you can't get resolution, seek out someone better equipped (or authorized) to help—perhaps a supervisor or customer service representative. Take notes of what you're told and who tells you.

Maybe you're conducting your transaction in a confused setting—for instance, a luncheonette that doubles as the ticket office for a long-distance bus company. Your questions are entirely legitimate and you may not be able to call back later (because you have to make your connection in the next ten minutes). A waitress may be the only employee there and may not have your answers. You're entitled to want information and to appeal to her better nature to help you get it, but if she draws a blank, it may not be her fault. Yet you've got nobody else to ask.

It could be that her boss set things up so thoughtlessly that helping you isn't anybody's job. For this, blame the boss (and in this case, file a report with the bus company and Chamber of Commerce). But don't take it out on the waitress.

Even in the absence of a formal Serviceperson's Bill of Rights, you do yourself and your argument a favor by bearing in mind that the individual:

- **Has the right to be assumed intelligent.**
- **Has feelings.**
- **May have a difficult or irrational boss.**
- **May be aware of a stupid policy yet be forced to observe it.**
- **Has a personal life just as you do, complete with sick loved ones, career disappointments, and bad days.**

Rung Two: Time to Move Up

If you get nowhere, you accomplish nothing by repeating yourself ad infinitum to the same people. If you can find somebody of greater authority, terrific. If you can persuade the highest-ranking employee there to phone a regional representative, or if you can call an 800 number for a consumer service supervisor who will take your side, excellent. If you can do anything that will increase your leverage, go for it.

But if you can't, say pleasantly that it's perfectly clear no progress is being made. You don't have the time for an extended discussion, any more than the employees do. So you would now like to pursue the matter on another level. Request the name and address of the regional manager, owner, house counsel, or whatever title strikes you as appropriate to the situation. Confirm that you have the correct spellings—of their names, and the names of the employees who spoke to you already.

Another time to beat a retreat is when you're wearing your scrungiest clothes. However unfairly, people form opinions. They can be wrong about what they conclude, but that doesn't stop them from thinking what they want to think. This snap judgment is likely to reflect on what they believe to be the value of keeping you as a customer and the legitimacy of your complaint.

If you look like a mess, you're at a disadvantage in any face-to-face confrontation. Accordingly, you may not want to pursue the matter at the instant of transaction. It might help your case more if you'd phone, or write a neatly typed, brilliantly persuasive letter to the supervisor, manager, or customer service department when you get home.

Rung Three: The Telephone

Sometimes matters can be resolved by phone. Other times, calling may only get you a request to write a letter. But at least you'll be able to ask questions and confirm complaint procedures if you phone first.

If you'll actually be disputing by phone, be ready with your facts. Run them through in your head. Rehearse them. Know what you're going to say, and come to the point. If you're phoning a large operation (a credit card carrier, a utility company), have your account number handy and give it before you go into your story. The representative may not be able to do another thing with you until your file comes up on the computer, and the account number is needed to access your file.

If you're calling a smaller company, be alert to telltale signs of the speaker's environment: a phone that rings many times before it's answered, phones ringing one after another in the immediate background, or someone who speaks very fast as though in a panic to get off the phone.

A small company could be little different from the luncheonette described above, with one recep-

tionist answering calls of every conceivable nature. That person may also be exclusively responsible for addressing 200 envelopes by hand within the hour—"Oh, and if the phone rings, answer it . . . but finish those envelopes, *or else*"—and is therefore under great pressure. But the representative you need is on vacation, or your problem doesn't fall under anybody's job description. So the receptionist is stuck with you, and sounds harried. Don't take it personally, and don't pick a fight. A quarrel might exhaust what little time the receptionist can spare to speak to you.

Ask whom you might call at a later time, or whether tomorrow would be a better time to call. If calling is discouraged, get the name of the boss and/or owner, and write a letter.

No matter who answers the phone, if the person answers by giving a name, write it down immediately. If the conversation develops into a less than cordial one, the speaker may hang up before you get another chance.

When you finally speak to the right party, state your problem and what resolution you expect. Write down what you're told and who tells you. If the person agrees to do something for you, ask how long it will take. If you're given a time frame, reply, "Okay. If I don't hear from you by then, I'll follow up with another phone call to you."

If the time frame seems unduly long, ask why. Perhaps certain checks are only processed on a monthly basis, and you just missed the deadline. This is sensible, although you can certainly ask, "Why can't you make an exception and cut the check sooner?"

Unfortunately, some matters take a long time because they have to travel to several desks, and they're low-priority for everyone who has to handle them. These steps probably can be rushed along. Ask who is responsible for the process and talk to that person.

If you're trying to nail down company policy and are told, "I don't know," suggest that the individual consult the corporate handbook or company policy manual.

If the policy materializes, or if you're given an answer that will resolve your complaint—"We'll cancel the charge," or "Come in before the end of the month and we'll give you a replacement"—ask to have it in writing. If the individual won't write a letter, follow up with a letter of your own in which you summarize the conversation.

Rung Four: The Letter

Letters have three very special advantages:

1. If confrontations fluster you, you can avoid them with a letter. (Writing the letter may fluster you too, but you can fiddle with it until you get it into shape.)
2. You can compose your thoughts carefully, and you can advance your entire case without interruption. But don't make your letter so wordy that your reader is in pain wading through it.
3. You have a record of what you said and when you said it. (*Always* keep copies of your complaint letters.) Conversations can be denied. But a clerk could not very well contend that your letter came but was missing the third paragraph.

A typed letter is preferable, because people will read it more easily and with greater comprehension than one that's handwritten. Whether you type or write by hand, be neat, for the same reason. The more easily the letter can be read, the more clearly your points will stand out.

Be as brief as you can be without sacrificing accuracy. Name the people who spoke to you, and explain why you aren't satisfied with what they said. Include photocopies of material such as receipts and copies of ads and refer to them in the letter. Indicate what it will take to satisfy you. Don't leave it up to the reader to guess. Proofread whatever you send, because you'll feel foolish if a typo obscures the issue. Reread it as though you

don't know what it's going to say. If your meaning no longer seems clear, rewrite. If you need help making it clear, ask a friend for input. Keep photocopies of what you send. And keep them where you can find them if someone phones you.

Here's a sample:

Sample Complaint Letter

[Your address]
[City, state, ZIP]
[Phone number—optional]
[Date]

[Name of contact person]
[Title, department]
[Company name]
[Street address]
[City, state, ZIP]

Re: [account number, invoice number, serial number, or some identifying code or description]

Dear [contact person]:

Last week [or whenever, but be specific] I purchased [or had repaired, etc.] the above-captioned item [or name other service performed]. I made this purchase at [location, date, and other important details of transaction].

Unfortunately, your [product or service] was unsatisfactory because [state the problem; if you can quote from a printed guarantee or offer that was not fulfilled, so much the better]. I brought this to the attention of [name and position of employee], who [referred me to you; lacked the authority to take action; whatever]. I am therefore asking you to resolve this without further delay.

Enclosed are copies of my records [receipts, correspondence, canceled checks, etc.]. To solve the problem, I would appreciate [what? Do you want a replacement? A refund? A statement or credit memo showing a charge has been removed from your account?].

I am looking forward to your prompt reply and resolution of my problem. Please contact me at the above address by return mail. [If you give a phone number and ask for a return call, you may get your satisfaction sooner. But if you get a call, ask for the caller to confirm the conversation with a letter to you.]

Very truly yours,

[Your signature]
[Your name printed/typed]

CC: [Company president by name?]
      [Consumer protection agency?]

Initially you write your letter to a salesman or representative. If you don't get results, your next forum is the company's consumer service department. From there, you write to the consumer service supervisor or the individual's department manager.

Write any follow-up letter so that it will be fully comprehensible to people who haven't read your earlier letters. Enclose copies of past correspondence. If the first few letters don't do the trick, start using CC. In other words, send copies (CC originally stood for "carbon copy") to the company president, house counsel, CEO, and/or appropriate consumer protection agencies, indicating these additional recipients of the letter with a CC followed by their names at the bottom of your complaint. Make a photocopy of each letter plus attachments for each recipient. Mail each. You don't need to do separate cover letters unless you want to. Keep photocopies.

When you send letters, receipts, and claim forms to large organizations, your envelope may be dumped into a bin of mail that is worked on in the order in which it emerges. If you later phone to inquire if the letter was at least received, the representative may have no idea because it's buried under a pile of similar envelopes.

A strategy for avoiding this is to send such a letter in a colored envelope (unless the company insists that you use one provided by the company). The mailroom employees may wonder about your sanity when they see the Day-Glo green. But when you speak to your claims rep, you can say, "I understand that you receive thousands of pieces of mail. But mine is bright green. I'll wait until you've had a chance to look for it and you can tell me you have it."

Whenever it's important to prove that you sent something, or sent it by a certain date, invest a few extra dollars in mailing it certified or registered, return receipt requested.

Rung Five: The Paper Trail

If correspondence is ongoing, your blood pressure may be rising, but you're compiling impressive evidence of your sincere attempt to play fair. You're also demonstrating that you're not one to be dismissed: that employees will have to expend time and energy on you until you get the answer you deserve.

If you must take your correspondence beyond initial stages, you may want to compose brief cover letters to go with one or more of the CCs. For example, if a company president has recently gone public with a mission statement or commitment to service, refer to it in your cover letter to the president. No person whose name is associated with a promise in advertising and publicity releases wants the company's negligence to make him or her a liar.

Companies don't mean to mislead you most of the time. However, once they've made the error, they may try to avoid the annoyance of correcting it. If a company has violated the terms of a printed contract or solicitation that was the basis of your spending money, try its legal department. Lawyers understand the ramifications of misrepresentation through interstate mail; the Federal Trade Commission (FTC) and the U.S. Postal Inspector take a dim view of the practice.

If the legal department doesn't care, doesn't exist, or would have no reason to be involved, take your case to the Better Business Bureau, consumer protection agencies, the Direct Marketing Association, the Postmaster General, or one of the hotlines listed elsewhere in this book.

Another suggestion: As well as complaining to the company that sold you an unsatisfactory item, you can complain to the company that made it. In economically depressed times, suppliers may be cutting corners, and manufacturers may be blissfully unaware of it. When this happens with the result that you've bought a faulty product, the manufacturer is likely to be delighted to hear from you, particularly if you identify the product fully and give the inspector number and/or the serial number. Force yourself to write or call even when you have no time. You owe it to yourself and others.

Rung Six: Credit Cards

If you made the purchase by credit card, watch your monthly statements. If the charge appears but you're disputing the item with the store or service provider, write your credit card company at the address indicated on the statement. Explain your dilemma. Include photocopies of receipts and correspondence. Request a credit or charge-back (*see* CREDIT CARDS).

Occasionally a business operation will decide you owe money and simply present the charge to your credit card company without getting your prior authorization. As a rule, the credit card company will pay, and won't delete the charge until you call attention to it. For instance, a friend once purchased a $70 item for $20 plus a $50 gift certificate. The clerk accepted the $20, then guessed at the way to write up the sale. The slip submitted to his card company—but never presented to him for his signature—showed $70 − $20 = $50, then billed his credit card company for the "unpaid" balance. When he explained what had happened *and* provided a photocopy of the gift certificate plus its serial number, VISA immediately deleted the $50.

Incidentally, some card companies offer added protection or extended warranties as a bonus when you sign up. Phone the service number on the statement to determine what extra help may be due you.

Rung Seven: Enlist Allies

There are two kinds of troops: the troops you know, and the troops you don't.

It helps if a friend is on the board of an advocacy group, or is a member of the Chamber of Commerce, or serves in an elected capacity—not because you want to corrupt anybody, but simply because this person knows you to be fair and honorable. Furthermore, the person is more likely to accept a call from you directly, rather than channeling it through a subordinate. If what you want can be achieved by this person's interceding on your behalf with a phone call or quick letter, your request is more likely to go to the top of the "to do" pile.

If you don't know anybody in an appropriate position, consider widening your sphere of acquaintances. Can you volunteer to stuff envelopes for a nearby elected official? Does the Chamber of Commerce need help with its next spring fair? Do you belong to a community service organization such as Rotary, Kiwanis, or Pilot International? There are many opportunities to rub shoulders deliberately with people you might otherwise never meet, people whose professions nicely complement the contacts you already have.

If you have no contacts, don't despair. You still have the telephone directory. Businesses are listed, as are government agencies (look under "United States Government" and under the name of your state, county, and city or town). Some cities and states have an "ombudsman," whose function is to help citizens who are having trouble with city and state agencies. Note that U.S. Government entries aren't usually for Washington, D.C., but for regional branches of federal departments.

Besides the phone book and 800 information (*see* 800 NUMBERS in Part II), you have your area library, county and state Cooperative Extension Services, and your local, state, and federal elected officials (selectmen/women, assemblymen/women, congressmen/women, senators, etc.). An inquiry directed to any of these should result in, at the very least, helpful referrals.

Your library probably has a copy of *National Trade and Professional Associations of the United States,* which lists nearly 40,000 associations that represent businesses and professions ranging from manufacturers to lawyers. These associations have several consumer functions, and some have programs for resolving consumer complaints. Many of the most useful ones are listed throughout this book in the appropriate chapters.

Rung Eight: Call Out the Troops

If one disgruntled letter doesn't worry a local merchant, perhaps fifty will—and if the merchant's attitude annoys you, it ought to have the same effect on others in your community. Organize a letter-writing campaign, or a boycott. Fifty letters stating "I won't buy toys for my children at your store because you don't give refunds when your merchandise breaks" can easily turn the hardest heart into one of buttery softness, out of necessity. You can also request letters from organizations with some tie to the problem. For example, the PTA may be happy to protest a situation that endangers children.

You can bring the matter to a community action group, or, if you're sufficiently provoked, you can form one. To get it off the ground quickly, contact the local media, particularly a small local paper that might do a whole story on you. Take out an ad in the paper, inviting others who share your concern to join you. Print official letterhead stationery and use it, even if you have only three members. Never lie, but don't overlook the impact of an appearance of strength. If you

can do a letterhead, why not a brochure? If you're handy with desktop publishing, you can do one on your computer. Repeat, *don't lie.* Don't say you have 200 members unless it's an accurate statement. But feel free to enumerate the objectives of your organization, for instance, "To encourage, through united community effort, a consumer-sensitive environment in every enterprise in our neighborhood." Then present it to the merchant next time you go to complain. Okay, it's a bluff. It may fall flat. Or it may succeed. Or droves of people may join your group, eager to march with the dedication of an army.

Pickets are tricky. They can be extremely impressive, attracting shoppers' attention as well as the media's. But before you do anything, be sure that you're acting within the law. Contact the local police department to see what permission you need and what security measures may be appropriate.

If the troops won't march, a lone picket can occasionally work wonders. Comedienne Elayne Boosler once hassled with a New York City bedding store. She had paid $1,200 for a comforter, but felt she was sent a cheaper version for the same money. She returned it for a replacement, but didn't like the next shipment any better. When she returned *it,* nobody rebated her money. So she picketed the store and handed out flyers. In the end she won a full refund.

Rung Nine: Arbitration, Mediation, Litigation

Some contracts stipulate that any disputes that arise be submitted to binding arbitration. In fact, signing such an agreement can mean waiving access to a court case. So don't sign that sort of deal unless you're comfortable with what you're doing (although the provisions, even if signed by all parties, can occasionally be overturned).

But don't be afraid of arbitration, either. It's faster and cheaper than a lawsuit, and presumably impartial. The local Better Business Bureau or your state or city department of consumer affairs may offer arbitration between consumers and sellers. If neither is listed in the directory for your area, ask your library or local elected official for ideas. Or you can seek out the assistance of organizations such as the American Arbitration Association (AAA), 140 West 51st Street, New York, NY 10020-1203; 212-484-4000.

Services of the American Arbitration Association are available for a small fee to nonmembers as well as members, and to consumers as well as businesses. Disputes can be about defects in new cars, medical malpractice, employer-employee disputes, construction, insurance, securities, and any number of consumer issues. When a party contacts the AAA (main or regional office), other parties named in the demand are advised. If they agree to arbitration, a list of impartial arbitrators is provided (with biographical data). The parties mutually select their panel from the list. The decision is considered binding.

Some people object to arbitration when they can review biographies but not question panelists in advance on their backgrounds and possible biases. There are alternatives such as mediation (a mediator hears both sides and gives an opinion, but resolution is left to the parties themselves), med-arb (combining voluntary resolution and binding judgment), and mini-trial (essentially a nonbinding exchange of information).

There are roughly 400 community mediation programs throughout the United States, operating through colleges, churches, and other institutions. Police departments frequently refer people to mediation, or you can consult your telephone directory (try looking under "Mediation" in the business listings) or the local bar association.

If you feel you have to go to court—that is, resort to litigation—you don't necessarily need a lawyer. Or if you get a lawyer, you may not have to go to court. Your lawyer may simply be able to call your nemesis and win your case by phone. It happens. But don't count on it.

Rung Ten: Small-Claims Court

You don't need a lawyer if you take your dispute to small-claims court. For amounts under a certain limit ($1,000, $2,000, etc.; different states have different rules), you can sue in small-claims court over, for instance, faulty repairs, or a neighbor who backs a truck over your lawnmower but won't pay to replace it. If you sue in small-claims court you may waive the right to later taking the matter to another court; and if you file to bring somebody to small-claims court, the party may have the right to move the case to a regular civil court.

If you want to bring a case to small-claims court, call ahead to determine what you'll have to do (check the government listings in your phone book, both state and city, and subheads such as "Courts" and "Law" or "Judicial Departments"; or get a number from your state or city department of consumer affairs). There will be a procedure for filing, and a small fee. When you actually appear in court, arrive early, because the case may be dismissed if you're not there when it's time to begin. Bring your documentation (bills, receipts, canceled checks, photographs) and witnesses if applicable. It may be possible to subpoena a witness unwilling to come. If you have to do this, ask about the procedure; it will involve another fee.

If you win the judgment, the court won't collect for you, but you may be able to go back to the court clerk for assistance with the next step. You might get a wage execution, allowing you to have money deducted from your antagonist's paycheck, or you may get the money from a property sale or bank account. But the court won't make your arrangements. You'll probably have to work through a sheriff or constable, and don't be surprised if there's another fee.

Rung Eleven: Class-Action Suit

When you go against big corporations, you have your rights, but they have their lawyers.

Their strategy may be to stall you, run up the number of hours your lawyer has to bill you for, and eventually force you to give up.

A way around this may be to have a large organization bring a class-action suit—that is, to sue on behalf of you and others in your position. For instance, your state attorney general is, in a sense, the top lawyer in your state. His or her office has the power to enforce laws and review complaints to determine what action can be taken in the name of the people of the state. The attorney general can sue on behalf of the public interest, but won't litigate your personal dispute. Yet a ruling against your adversary may give you immense satisfaction. When the attorney general's office won't prosecute, a staff member may attempt to mediate for you, or refer you to an agency equipped to solve your problems.

Other large organizations potentially willing to use your complaint as the basis for a class-action suit include various advocacy groups. For example, if your case involves a violation of civil rights, you might be able to interest the American Civil Liberties Union in pursuing it.

An independent attorney can also litigate a class-action suit. The attorney applies to the court (or a panel of judges) for permission to represent the entire class (of people injured by a particular product, or subjected to hazardous conditions, or discriminated against, etc.). If the court grants permission, the decision is usually binding on the whole class (although in some cases individuals can "opt out" and sue as individuals).

Class-action suits are a practical means of wrapping up thousands of individual suits without taking thousands of years to do it, yet some people feel they impinge on individual rights. If you sustained an unusually severe injury, you might not appreciate having your case settled by people who never met or saw you or examined the extent of your loss.

Most of the time, you'll feel that your consumer gripes don't warrant a class-action suit. Yet the *threat* of a class-action suit can be enough to persuade a business or corporation. If a contractor thinks seventy people in the neighborhood are about to sue him for inferior work, he may settle with you to forestall a whole class action. Members of a class are often sought by means of newspaper ads. No business enjoys seeing its name in such an ad.

If the action continues, the corporation loses good will, employee hours, and often considerable money. Even though each individual might get only 4 cents in the mail, the expense to the corporation is enormous. Suggest this to a corporate house counsel if you find yourself considering such a dispute. Speedy satisfaction may ensue.

If you're aware of a class-action suit that applies to you but you haven't been contacted, write to the clerk of the court that has jurisdiction over the case. Indicate that you want to be included in the class. If you don't receive a reply after a reasonable wait, write again, or phone.

Rung Twelve: Your Elected Officials

You've got elected officials on local, state, and national levels. Appointed ones, too. Newspapers will frequently publish current lists of their names, business addresses, and phone numbers. If you see a list, clip it out and keep it. If you don't, phone the League of Women Voters, the board of elections, or the library, if there is one in your area.

Politicians often print and distribute newsletters of their activities. If you read them and pay attention to the news, you'll know who stands on which side of a question and who serves on which committees, and you'll also know how to contact the politicians.

The offices of local politicians are frequently a good source of advice or referrals. Remember, this is why they're in office: to represent you. Sometimes they can get information for you. Sometimes they'll intercede on your behalf. If your concern is the concern of a great many voters, expect your politicians to be alert to what you say—because you are the people who will elect or reject them at the polls.

You can phone the offices of local, state, and U.S. politicians, or you can write. If you phone, be courteous. If you write, write neatly or type your letter. Avoid using a form letter or postcard if at all possible. Use the proper form of address, such as "The Honorable So-and-So" (such forms are listed in the appendices of most dictionaries). If your comments are about pending legislation—such as a health care or cable bill—give the name and number of the bill, if you know it, to establish yourself as an informed constituent. Ask for a reply. Sign the letter; if you write anonymously, you lose credibility. It's appropriate to follow up whether the reply is positive or negative. Because there's strength in numbers, try to mobilize friends and people who share your convictions to write letters too. Be assured, letters are read *and* tallied—how many for, how many against.

If an issue is coming up for a vote—a hike in transit fares, or a new landlord-tenant law—ask your representative if a public hearing is scheduled. If it is, try to attend. Request the agenda in advance, and if it looks as if the public's voice will be shoved off to the wee hours, press for the public's right to comment first. If the hearing seems to be scheduled at an impossible time for the public to attend, ask your local politicians to insist on a more realistic hour or day.

Though it's difficult to arrange, you may be able to testify at a congressional hearing if you have significant expertise about a point of view not familiar to legislators. Write to the committee chairman, stating your position and qualifications, and including a detailed summary of what you expect to say. You can call your state representatives for guidance with this procedure, or you can check the *Congressional Directory,* which is available in most libraries.

Rung Thirteen: Tell the Media

If you think it's unlucky to call the media from the thirteenth rung of your imaginary ladder, do it sooner. Or delight in knowing that your media

alert will be bad luck for your target. A letter to the editor of a local newspaper is one way to start. Or you can invite TV news cameras to the site of a picket, or to photograph your house sinking into a hole left by the pool-repair fellow. Or contact the *National Enquirer* or the *Star.* These publications love to make someone look ridiculous, and they need stories. Your tale may not appear right away, but you will probably feel vindicated when it does. And you will have reinforced the valuable lesson that consumer complaints cannot be dismissed.

Of course, it isn't earth-shattering news if the plumber charged $200 to ruin your pipes, but your neighbors will appreciate the warning. Call area newspapers and radio and TV stations about your story. Many have consumer action reporters, or segments like *Shame on You* devoted to exposing people who cheat consumers.

Rung Fourteen: The Creative End Run

If your adversary has survived every other assault, be creative. Assuming you're right, you must have leverage somehow. Study your problem from new angles. What's its "selling point"? Where's the tragic flaw?

A few years ago, a number of RICO suits were brought by the Eastern District of Pennsylvania against several very visible manufacturers. RICO (the Racketeer Influenced and Corrupt Organizations Act of 1970) makes it unlawful "for any person through a pattern of racketeering activity . . . to acquire or maintain . . . an interest in or control of any enterprise." The purpose of this legislation was to eliminate the infiltration by organized crime into legitimate business. But Pennsylvania consumer activists maintained that the use of the mails and telephones to convey false advertising violated federal mail and wire fraud statutes and thereby constituted racketeering, and if the profits from these activities were invested in maintaining the enterprises, the conditions for RICO had been met.

Needless to say, these companies were no racketeers. But attorneys who pressed the case believed that the companies had consistently engaged in unfair advertising practices with no fear of consumer reprisal. By detecting and attacking an unprotected flank, the attorneys made their point. Most of the cases were settled expensively out of court because the companies didn't want the public misreading reports of their "involvement with organized crime."

Another creative end run occurred in New York City. A woman lived in public housing and had five children, one with cerebral palsy and seizures so severe that his life depended on being able to get to the hospital in a hurry. But the building's elevator rarely functioned. When the woman's repeated efforts with the usual agencies failed, she borrowed a few hundred dollars from friends to buy a fancy dress and a ticket to a $150-a-plate dinner, which Mayor Dinkins would be attending.

She buttonholed the mayor after dinner, getting his ear as well as tremendous publicity, and was promised a better building or at the least an apartment on the ground floor.

Rung Fifteen: Play Fair or Fall off the Ladder

All this assumes a certain level of honesty:

That companies will honestly advertise their policies, and honestly attempt to fulfill them.

That employees will deal honestly with customers.

And that customers in turn will be honest in their representations to companies and employees.

As long as you play fair, you're right to demand fairness. Even if it takes every trick in the book (this book) to show what fairness is.

Major Consumer Organizations

Certain operations exist to improve the lives of consumers: Chambers of Commerce, Better Business Bureaus, departments of consumer protection or consumer affairs, and the Federal Trade Commission (FTC), to name the best-known. To differing degrees, each will provide brochures and referrals, clarify complaint procedures and consumer laws, attempt mediation or arbitration, investigate, and fine violators. To determine what these organizations can do for you, call or write. If your area doesn't have organizations by these names, ask your library for the local equivalents.

Chambers of Commerce

Chambers of Commerce are confederations of area (or town, or city) professional people who band together with a view to improving conditions for themselves and for consumers. They work closely (and sometimes at loggerheads) with elected and appointed officials. They may be involved in increasing the number of parking spaces downtown, or designing campaigns to attract more shoppers to Main Street. In a small town, you may be able to persuade a Chamber member to talk to the guy in the used car lot who cheated you on a repair. In a large metropolitan city, don't necessarily expect such personal service, but you can still interest the Chamber of Commerce in any problem that hurts business in general—such as a total lack of security at a popular tourist spot.

Better Business Bureaus

Approximately 200 Better Business Bureaus (BBBs) operate in the United States. These nonprofit organizations provide services ranging from safety reports to arbitration to a history of complaints filed against a given company. They are fact-finding operations that review and compile reports filed with them by consumers, to develop a data base of companies' selling and advertising practices.

Some you can call free. Others require a toll charge—even a 900-number call—for information. But the answers you get tend to be well worth the price. Some publish directories that list members who have agreed to meet BBB standards. Contact your area BBB to determine if such a directory is available to you. Following are the addresses and phone numbers of the Council of Better Business Bureaus, Inc., and local BBBs in the United States, courtesy of the U.S. Department of Consumer Affairs.

National Headquarters

Council of Better Business
  Bureaus, Inc.
4200 Wilson Boulevard
Arlington, VA 22203
703-276-0100

Local Bureaus

Alabama

P.O. Box 55268
Birmingham, AL 35255-5268
205-558-2222

118 Woodburn Street
Dothan, AL 36301
205-792-3804

P.O. Box 383
Huntsville, AL 35801
205-533-1640

707 Van Antwerp Building
Mobile, AL 36602
205-433-5494, 5495

Commerce Street, Suite 806
Montgomery, AL 36104
205-262-5606

Alaska

3380 C Street, Suite 103
Anchorage, AK 99503
907-562-0704

Arizona

4428 North 12th Street
Phoenix, AZ 85014-4585
602-264-1721

50 West Drachman Street,
  Suite 103
Tucson, AZ 85705
602-622-7651 (inquiries)
602-622-7654 (complaints)

Arkansas

1415 S. University
Little Rock, AR 72204
501-664-7274

California

705 Eighteenth Street
Bakersfield, CA 93301-4882
805-322-2074

P.O. Box 970
Colton, CA 92324-0522
714-825-7280

6101 Ball Rd., Suite 309
Cypress, CA 90630
714-527-0680

1398 West Indianapolis, Suite 102
Fresno, CA 93705
209-222-8111

494 Alvarado Street, Suite C
Monterey, CA 93940
408-372-3149

510 16th Street
Oakland, CA 94612
415-839-5900

400 S Street
Sacramento, CA 95814
916-443-6843

3111 Camino del Rio North,
  Suite 600
San Diego, CA 92108-1729
619-281-6422

33 New Montgomery St. Tower
San Francisco, CA 94105
415-243-9999

1505 Meridian Avenue
San Jose, CA 95125
408-978-8700

P.O. Box 294
San Mateo, CA 94401
415-696-1240

P.O. Box 746
Santa Barbara, CA 93102
805-963-8657

300 B Street
Santa Rosa, CA 95401
707-577-0300

1111 North Center Street
Stockton, CA 95202-1383
209-948-4880, 4881

Colorado

P.O. Box 7970
Colorado Springs, CO 80933
719-636-1155

1780 South Bellaire, Suite 700
Denver, CO 80222
303-758-2100 (inquiries)
303-758-2212 (complaints)

1730 S. College Ave., Suite 303
Fort Collins, CO 80525
303-484-1348

119 West 6th Street, Suite 203
Pueblo, CO 81003-3119
719-542-6464

Connecticut

2345 Black Rock Turnpike
Fairfield, CT 06430
203-374-6161

2080 Silas Deane Highway
Rocky Hill, CT 06067-2311
203-529-3575

100 South Turnpike Road
Wallingford, CT 06492-4395
203-269-2700 (inquiries)
203-269-4457 (complaints)

Delaware

2055 Limestone Road, Suite 200
Wilmington, DE 19808
302-996-9200

District of Columbia

1012 14th Street, N.W.
14th Floor
Washington, DC 20005-3410
202-393-8000

Florida

*In addition to the Better Business
Bureaus, Florida has a number of
Better Business Councils which are
affiliated with local Chambers of*

Commerce throughout the state. The Better Business Councils are listed following the Better Business Bureaus.

Bureaus:

P.O. Box 7950
Clearwater, FL 34618-7950
813-535-5522

2976-E Cleveland Avenue
Fort Myers, FL 33901
813-334-7331

3100 University Blvd. South, Suite 239
Jacksonville, FL 32216
904-721-2288

2605 Maitland Center Parkway
Maitland, FL 32751-7147
407-660-9500

16291 Northwest 57th Avenue
Miami, FL 33014-6709
305-625-0307 (inquiries for Dade County)
305-625-1302 (complaints for Dade County)
305-524-2803 (inquiries for Broward County)
305-527-1643 (complaints for Broward County)

P.O. Box 1511
Pensacola, FL 32597-1511
904-433-6111

1950 SE Port St. Lucie Blvd., Suite 211
Port St. Lucie, FL 34952
407-878-2010
407-337-2083 (Martin County)

2247 Palm Beach Lakes Blvd., Suite 211
West Palm Beach, FL 33409
407-686-2200

Councils:

P.O. Box 3607
Lakeland, FL 33802-3607
813-680-1030 (Polk County)

P.O. Box 492426
Leesburg, FL 32749-2426
904-326-0770 (Lake County)

400 Fortenberry Road
Merritt Island, FL 32952
407-452-8869 (Central Brevard County)

13000 South Tamiami Trail, Suite 111
North Port, FL 34287
813-426-8744

4100 Dixie Highway, NE
Palm Bay, FL 32905
407-984-8454 (South Brevard County)

1819 Main Street, Suite 240
Sarasota, FL 34236
813-366-3144

P.O. Drawer 2767
Titusville, FL 32781-2767
407-268-2822 (North Brevard County)

257 Tamiami Trail, North
Venice, FL 34285-1534
813-485-3510

Georgia

1319-B Dawson Road
Albany, GA 31707
912-883-0744
1-800-868-4222

100 Edgewood Avenue, Suite 1012
Atlanta, GA 30303
404-688-4910

P.O. Box 2085
Augusta, GA 30903
404-722-1574

P.O. Box 2587
Columbus, GA 31902
404-324-0712

1765 Shurling Drive
Macon, GA 31211
912-742-7999

P.O. Box 13956
Savannah, GA 31416-0956
912-354-7521

Hawaii

1600 Kapiolani Boulevard, Suite 714
Honolulu, HI 96814
808-942-2355

Idaho

1333 West Jefferson
Boise, ID 83702
208-342-4649
208-467-5547 (Canyon County)

545 Shoup Avenue, Suite 210
Idaho Falls, ID 83402
208-523-9754

Illinois

211 W. Wacker Drive
Chicago, IL 60606
312-444-1188 (inquiries)
312-346-3313 (complaints)

3024 West Lake
Peoria, IL 61615
309-688-3741

810 East State Street, 3rd Floor
Rockford, IL 61104
815-963-2222

Indiana

P.O. Box 405
Elkhart, IN 46515-0405
219-262-8996

4004 Morgan Avenue, Suite 201
Evansville, IN 47715
812-473-0202

1203 Webster Street
Fort Wayne, IN 46802
219-423-4433

4231 Cleveland Street
Gary, IN 46408
219-980-1511

Victoria Centre
22 East Washington Street,
 Suite 200
Indianapolis, IN 46204
317-637-0197

Marion, IN
1-800-552-4631 (in IN)

Consumer Education Council
 (non-BBB)
BSW WB 150
Muncie, IN 47306
317-285-5668

52303 Emmons Road, Suite 9
South Bend, IN 46637
219-277-9121

Iowa

852 Middle Road, Suite 290
Bettendorf, IA 52722-4100
319-355-6344

615 Insurance Exchange Building
Des Moines, IA 50309
515-243-8137

318 Badgerow Building
Sioux City, IA 51101
712-252-4501

Kansas

501 Jefferson, Suite 24
Topeka, KS 66607-1190
913-232-0454

300 Kaufman Building
Wichita, KS 67202
316-263-3146

Kentucky

311 West Short Street
Lexington, KY 40507
606-259-1008

844 South 4th Street
Louisville, KY 40203-2186
502-583-6546

Louisiana

1605 Murray St., Suite 117
Alexandria, LA 71301
318-473-4494

2055 Wooddale Boulevard
Baton Rouge, LA 70806-1519
504-926-3010

501 East Main Street
Houma, LA 70360
504-868-3456

P.O. Box 30297
Lafayette, LA 70593-0297
318-981-3497

P.O. Box 1681
Lake Charles, LA 70602
318-433-1633

141 De Siard Street, Suite 808
Monroe, LA 71201-7380
318-387-4600, 8421

1539 Jackson Avenue
New Orleans, LA 70130-3400
504-581-6222

1401 North Market Street
Shreveport, LA 71107-6525
318-221-8352

Maine

812 Stevens Avenue
Portland, ME 04103
207-878-2715

Maryland

2100 Huntingdon Avenue
Baltimore, MD 21211-3215
301-347-3990

Massachusetts

20 Park Plaza, Suite 820
Boston, MA 02116-4404
617-426-9000

Framingham, MA
1-800-422-2811 (in MA)

78 North Street, Suite 1
Hyannis, MA 02601-3808
508-771-3022

Lawrence, MA
1-800-422-2811 (in MA)

293 Bridge Street, Suite 320
Springfield, MA 01103
413-734-3114

P.O. Box 379
Worcester, MA 01601
508-755-2548

Michigan

620 Trust Building
Grand Rapids, MI 49503
616-774-8236

30555 Southfield Road, Suite 200
Southfield, MI 48076-7751
313-644-1012 (inquiries)
313-644-9136 (complaints)
313-644-9152 (Auto Line)
1-800-955-5100 (nationwide Auto
 Line)

Minnesota

2706 Gannon Road
St. Paul, MN 55116
612-699-1111

Mississippi

460 Briarwood Drive, Suite 340
Jackson, MS 39206-3088
601-956-8282
1-800-274-7222 (in MS)
601-957-2886 (automotive complaints only)

Missouri

306 East 12th Street, Suite 1024
Kansas City, MO 64106-2418
816-421-7800

5100 Oakland Avenue, Suite 200
St. Louis, MO 63110
314-531-3300

205 Park Central East, Suite 509
Springfield, MO 65806
417-862-9231

Nebraska

719 North 48th Street
Lincoln, NE 68504-3491
402-467-5261

1613 Farnam Street, Room 417
Omaha, NE 68102-2158
402-346-3033

Nevada

1022 E. Sahara Avenue
Las Vegas, NV 89104-1515
702-735-6900, 1969

P.O. Box 21269
Reno, NV 89515-1269
702-322-0657

New Hampshire

410 South Main Street
Concord, NH 03301
603-224-1991

New Jersey

494 Broad Street
Newark, NJ 07102
201-642-INFO

2 Forest Avenue
Paramus, NJ 07652
201-845-4044

1721 Route 37, East
Toms River, NJ 08753-8239
201-270-5577

1700 Whitehorse
Hamilton Square, Suite D-5
Trenton, NJ 08690
609-588-0808 (Mercer County)

P.O. Box 303
Westmont, NJ 08108-0303
609-854-8467

New Mexico

4600-A Montgomery NE, Suite 200
Albuquerque, NM 87109
505-884-0500
1-800-445-1461 (in NM)

308 North Locke
Farmington, NM 87401
505-826-6501

2407 W. Picacho, Suite B-2
Las Cruces, NM 88005
505-524-3130

New York

346 Delaware Avenue
Buffalo, NY 14202
716-856-7180

266 Main Street
Farmingdale, NY 11735
516-420-0500
1-800-955-5100 (Auto Line)

257 Park Avenue South
New York, NY 10010
1-900-463-6222 (85 cents per
minute)

1122 Sibley Tower
Rochester, NY 14604-1084
716-546-6776

847 James Street, Suite 200
Syracuse, NY 13203
315-479-6635

1211 Route 9
Wappingers Falls, NY 12590
914-297-6550
1-800-955-5100 (Auto Line)

30 Glenn Street
White Plains, NY 10603
914-428-1230, 1231
1-800-955-5100 (Auto Line)

North Carolina

801 BB&T Building
Asheville, NC 28801
704-253-2392

1130 East Third Street, Suite 400
Charlotte, NC 28204-2626
704-332-7151

3608 West Friendly Avenue
Greensboro, NC 27410
919-852-4240, 4241, 4242

P.O. Box 1882
Hickory, NC 28603
704-464-0372

3120 Poplarwood Court, Suite 101
Raleigh, NC 27604-1080
919-872-9240

2110 Cloverdale Avenue, Suite 2-B
Winston-Salem, NC 27103
919-725-8348

Ohio

222 West Market Street
Akron, OH 44303-2111
216-253-4590

1434 Cleveland Avenue, NW
Canton, OH 44703
216-454-9401

898 Walnut Street
Cincinnati, OH 45202
513-421-3015

2217 East 9th St., Suite 200
Cleveland, OH 44115-1299
216-241-7678

527 South High Street
Columbus, OH 43215
614-221-6336

40 West Fourth Street, Suite 1250
Dayton, OH 45402
513-222-5825
1-800-521-8357 (in OH)

P.O. Box 269
Lima, OH 45802
419-223-7010

130 West 2nd Street
Mansfield, OH 44902-1915
419-522-1700

425 Jefferson Avenue, Suite 909
Toledo, OH 43604-1055
419-241-6276

345 N. Market, Suite 202
Wooster, OH 44691
216-263-6444

P.O. Box 1495
Youngstown, OH 44501-1495
216-744-3111

Oklahoma

17 South Dewey
Oklahoma City, OK 73102
405-239-6860 (inquiries)
405-239-6081 (inquiries)
405-239-6083 (complaints)

6711 S. Yale, Suite 230
Tulsa, OK 74136-3327
918-492-1266

Oregon

610 S.W. Alder St., Suite 615
Portland, OR 97205
503-226-3981
1-800-488-4166 (in OR)

Pennsylvania

528 North New Street
Bethlehem, PA 18018
215-866-8780

6 Marion Court
Lancaster, PA 17602
717-291-1151
717-232-2800 (Harrisburg)
717-846-2700 (York County)
717-394-9318 (Auto Line)

P.O. Box 2297
Philadelphia, PA 19103-0297
215-496-1000

610 Smithfield Street
Pittsburgh, PA 15222
412-456-2700

P.O. Box 993
Scranton, PA 18501
717-342-9129, 655-0445

Puerto Rico

Condominium Olimpo Plaza,
   Suite 208
1002 Munoz Rivera Avenue
Rio Piedras, PR 00927
809-756-5400
809-767-0446

Rhode Island

Bureau Park
P.O. Box 1300
Warwick, RI 02887-1300
401-785-1212 (inquiries)
401-785-1213 (complaints)

South Carolina

1830 Bull Street
Columbia, SC 29201
803-254-2525

311 Pettigru Street
Greenville, SC 29601
803-242-5052

1310-G Azalea Court
Myrtle Beach, SC 29577
803-497-8667

Tennessee

P.O. Box 1178 TCAS
Blountville, TN 37617
615-323-6311

1010 Market Street, Suite 200
Chattanooga, TN 37402-2614
615-266-6144 (also serves Whitfield
   and Murray counties in GA)
615-479-6096 (Bradley County
   only)

900 East Hill Avenue, Suite 165
Knoxville, TN 37915-2525
615-522-2552

P.O. Box 750704
Memphis, TN 38175-0704
901-795-8771

Sovran Plaza, Suite 1830
Nashville, TN 37239
615-254-5872

Texas

3300 S. 14th St., Suite 307
Abilene, TX 79605
915-691-1533

P.O. Box 1905
Amarillo, TX 79105-1905
806-379-6222

708 Colorado, Suite 720
Austin, TX 78701-3028
512-476-1616

P.O. Box 2988
Beaumont, TX 77704-2988
409-835-5348

202 Varisco Building
Bryan, TX 77803
409-823-8148, 8149

4535 S. Padre Island Drive,
   Suite 28
Corpus Christi, TX 78411
512-854-2892

2001 Bryan Street, Suite 850
Dallas, TX 75201
214-220-2000
1-800-442-1456 (in TX)

5160 Montana, Lower Level
El Paso, TX 79903
915-772-2727

512 Main Street, Suite 807
Fort Worth, TX 76102
817-332-7585

2707 North Loop West, Suite 900
Houston, TX 77008
713-868-9500

P.O. Box 1178
Lubbock, TX 79408-1178
806-763-0459

P.O. Box 60206
Midland, TX 79711-0206
915-563-1880
1-800-592-4433 (in 915 area code)

P.O. Box 3366
San Angelo, TX 76902-3366
915-949-2989

1800 Northeast Loop 410,
　Suite 400
San Antonio, TX 78217
512-828-9441

P.O. Box 6652
Tyler, TX 75711-6652
903-581-5704

P.O. Box 7203
Waco, TX 76714-7203
817-772-7530

P.O. Box 69
Weslaco, TX 78596-0069
512-968-3678

1106 Brook Street
Wichita Falls, TX 76301-5079
817-723-5526

Utah

1588 South Main Street
Salt Lake City, UT 84115
801-487-4656

Virginia

4022B Plank Road
Fredericksburg, VA 22407
703-786-8397

3608 Tidewater Drive
Norfolk, VA 23509-1499
804-627-5651

701 East Franklin Street, Suite 712
Richmond, VA 23219
804-648-0016

31 W. Campbell Avenue
Roanoke, VA 24011-1301
703-342-3455

Washington

127 West Canal Drive
Kennewick, WA 99336-3819
509-582-0222

2200 Sixth Avenue, Suite 828
Seattle, WA 98121-1857
206-448-8888
206-448-6222 (24-hour business
　reporting system)

South 176 Stevens
Spokane, WA 99204-1393
509-747-1155

P.O. Box 1274
Tacoma, WA 98401-1274
206-383-5561

P.O. Box 1584
Yakima, WA 98907-1584
509-248-1326

Wisconsin

740 North Plankinton Avenue
Milwaukee, WI 53203
414-273-1600 (inquiries)
414-273-0123 (complaints)

Wyoming

BBB/Idaho Falls
(*serves Teton, Park, and Lincoln
　counties*)
545 Shoup Avenue, Suite 210
Idaho Falls, ID 83402
208-523-9754

BBB/Fort Collins
(*serves all other counties*)
1730 South College Avenue,
　Suite 303
Fort Collins, CO 80525
1-800-873-3222 (in WY)

State and Local Consumer Affairs Departments

State and local consumer affairs, or consumer protection, departments explain and administer certain complaint procedures, disperse buying tips by means of brochures, by mail, and over the phone, and often are empowered to enforce consumer protection laws. They may be prepared to advise consumers if a company is the target of a lawsuit, but generally they don't go into the same detail as a BBB with regard to the company's history of settling complaints. Check the government listings, both state and local, of your phone directory. In general, become more familiar with your phone directory. Is there a general information number at the beginning of the state listings? If there's no Attorney General, try Secretary of State, or call your local library or telephone information number for direction.

Federal Trade Commission

The Federal Trade Commission (FTC) educates the public and investigates and prosecutes on behalf of the nation's consumers. It won't litigate individual complaints, but it relies on consumers' reports to uncover abuses. If evidence mounts against a company or industry, the FTC can act in any number of ways, including by holding hearings, creating new rulings, or enforcing those already on the books. Write the FTC to report your complaint: Correspondence Branch, Room 692, FTC, 6th Street and Pennsylvania Avenue, Washington, DC 20580. For more specific information on a particular area of FTC jurisdiction, phone:

- **Advertising practices: 202-326-3131.**
- **Credit practices (including credit cards, elec-**tronic fund transfer, and debt collection): 202-326-3758.
- **Mail and telephone order practices: 202-326-3768.**
- **Marketing practices (including rebate coupons): 202-326-3128.**

For general information, or to request brochures or a list of publications, contact the Public Reference Branch, Room 130, FTC, Washington, DC 20580, or phone 202-326-2222, or contact the nearest regional office (listed below).

FTC Headquarters

6th & Pennsylvania Avenue, N.W.
Washington, DC 20580
202-326-2222
202-326-2502 (TDD)

FTC Regional Offices

1718 Peachtree Street, N.W.,
  Suite 1000
Atlanta, GA 30367
404-347-4836

101 Merrimac Street
Boston, MA 02114
617-424-5960

55 East Monroe Street, Suite 1437
Chicago, IL 60603
312-353-4423

668 Euclid Avenue, Suite 520-A
Cleveland, OH 44114
216-522-4207

100 N. Central Expressway,
  Suite 500
Dallas, TX 75201
214-767-5501

1405 Curtis Street, Suite 2900
Denver, CO 80202-2393
303-844-2271

11000 Wilshire Boulevard,
  Suite 13209
Los Angeles, CA 90024
310-575-7575

150 William Street, Suite 1300
New York, NY 10038
212-264-1207

901 Market Street, Suite 570
San Francisco, CA 94103
415-744-7920

2806 Federal Bldg., 915 Second
  Ave.
Seattle, WA 98174
206-220-6363

Other U.S. Government Agencies

The FTC is only one of the U.S. Government's enforcement and/or complaint-handling federal agencies. Here are a variety of others that field inquiries and grievances from the general public, adapted from a list courtesy of the U.S. Department of Consumer Affairs.

Commission on Civil Rights

Look in your telephone directory under "U.S. Government, Civil Rights Commission." Or contact:
Commission on Civil Rights
1121 Vermont Avenue, N.W.,
Suite 800

Washington, DC 20425
1-800-552-6843 (complaint referral
  outside DC)
202-376-8512 (complaint referral in
  DC)
202-376-8116 (TDD—nationwide
  complaint referral)
202-376-8105 (publications)
202-376-8312 (public affairs)

Commodity Futures Trading Commission (CFTC)

2033 K Street, N.W.
Washington, DC 20581
202-254-3067 (complaints only)
202-254-8630 (information)

Consumer Information Center (CIC)

Pueblo, CO 81009
You can obtain a free Consumer Information Catalog by writing to the above address or by calling 719-948-4000.

Department of Agriculture (USDA)

Agricultural Marketing Service
Department of Agriculture
Washington, DC 20250
202-447-8998

Animal and Plant Health Inspection Service
Public Information
Department of Agriculture
Federal Building, Room 700
6505 Belcrest Road
Hyattsville, MD 20782
301-436-7799

Cooperative Extension Service
Department of Agriculture
Washington, DC 20250
202-447-3029
202-755-2799 (TDD)
Or consult county or city government listings in your local telephone directory for the number of your local Cooperative Extension Service office.

Farmers Home Administration
Department of Agriculture
Washington, DC 20250
202-447-4323

Food and Nutrition Service
Department of Agriculture
3101 Park Center Drive
Alexandria, VA 22302
703-756-3276

Human Nutrition Information Service
Department of Agriculture
Federal Building
Rooms 360 and 364
6505 Belcrest Road
Hyattsville, MD 20782
301-436-8617, 7725

Inspector General's Hotline
Office of the Inspector General
Department of Agriculture
P.O. Box 23399
Washington, DC 20026
1-800-424-9121

Meat and Poultry Hotline Food Safety and Inspection Service
Department of Agriculture
Washington, DC 20250
202-447-3333 (voice/TDD)
1-800-535-4555 (voice/TDD outside DC)

Office of the Consumer Advisor
Department of Agriculture
Washington, DC 20250
202-382-9681

Office of Public Affairs
Visitor Information Center
Department of Agriculture
Washington, DC 20250
202-447-2791

Department of Commerce

Office of Consumer Affairs
Department of Commerce
Room 5718
Washington, DC 20230
202-377-5001

National Institute of Standards and Technology
Office of Weights and Measures
Department of Commerce
Washington, DC 20234
301-975-4004

National Marine Fisheries Service
Office of Trade and Industry Services
Department of Commerce
1335 East-West Highway
Silver Spring, MD 20910
301-427-2355 (inspection and safety)
301-427-2358 (nutrition information)

Department of Defense

Office of National Ombudsman
National Committee for Employer Support of the Guard and Reserve
1555 Wilson Boulevard, Suite 200
Arlington, VA 22209-2405
703-696-1400
1-800-336-4590 (outside DC metropolitan area)
Provides assistance with employer/employee problems for members of the Guard and Reserve and their employers.

Department of Education

Clearinghouse on Disability Information
OSERS
Department of Education
330 C Street, S.W.
Washington, DC 20202-2524
202-205-8241 (voice/TTY)

Consumer Affairs Staff
OIIA
Department of Education
Room 3061
Washington, DC 20202
202-401-3679

Federal Student Financial Aid Programs
Public Documents
Distribution Center
31451 United Avenue
Pueblo, CO 81009-8109
202-708-8391

National Clearinghouse on Bilingual Education Hotline
Department of Education
1118 22nd Street, N.W.
Washington, D.C. 20037
202-467-0867
1-800-321-NCBE (outside DC)

Office of Public Affairs
Department of Education
400 Maryland Avenue, S.W.
Washington, DC 20202
202-401-3020

Center for Choice in Education
400 Maryland Avenue, S.W.,
Room 3077
Washington, DC 20202
1-800-442-PICK

Department of Energy

*For information about conservation
and renewable energy:*
**National Appropriate Technology
Assistance Service**
Department of Energy
P.O. Box 2525
Butte, MT 59702-2525
1-800-428-1718 (in MT)
1-800-428-2525 (outside MT)

**Conservation and Renewable
Energy Inquiry and Referral
Service**
Department of Energy
P.O. Box 8900
Silver Spring, MD 20907
1-800-523-2929

**Office of Scientific and Technical
Information**
Department of Energy
P.O. Box 62
Oak Ridge, TN 37831
Written inquiries only.

**Office of Consumer and Public
Liaison**
Department of Energy
Washington, DC 20585
202-586-5373

**Office of Conservation and Renew-
able Energy**
Weatherization assistance inquiries:
Department of Energy
Washington, DC 20585
202-586-2204

Department of Health and Human Services (HHS)

AIDS Hotline
**Acquired Immune Deficiency
Syndrome**
1-800-342-AIDS

Cancer Hotline
1-800-4-CANCER
*During daytime hours, callers in
California, Florida, Georgia, Illi-
nois, northern New Jersey, New
York, and Texas may ask for
Spanish-speaking staff members.*

**Food and Drug Administration
(FDA)**
*Look in your telephone directory
under "U.S. Government, Health
and Human Services Department,
Food and Drug Administration." Or
contact:* **Consumer Affairs and
Information Staff**
Food and Drug Administration
(HFE-88)
Department of Health and Human
  Services
5600 Fishers Lane, Room 16-85
Rockville, MD 20857
301-443-3170

**Division of Beneficiary Services
Health Care Financing Administration (HCFA)**
Department of Health and Human
  Services
6325 Security Boulevard
Baltimore, MD 21207
1-800-638-6833 (Taped answering
service; a specialist will return your
call.)

**Hill-Burton Free Hospital Care
Hotline**
1-800-492-0359 (in MD)
1-800-638-0742 (outside MD)

**Inspector General's Hotline
HHS/OIG/Hotline**
P.O. Box 17303
Baltimore, MD 21203-7303
1-800-368-5779

**National Center on Child Abuse
and Neglect**
Department of Health and Human
  Services
330 C Street, S.W.
Washington, DC 20201
202-245-0586

National Health Information Center
Department of Health and Human
  Services
P.O. Box 1133
Washington, DC 20013-1133
301-565-4167 (Washington Metro
  Area)
1-800-336-4797

National Runaway Switchboard
1-800-621-4000

**Office of Child Support
Enforcement**
Department of Health and Human
  Services
Washington, DC 20201
202-401-9387

Office for Civil Rights
Department of Health and Human
  Services
Washington, DC 20201
202-245-6671
1-800-863-0100 (outside DC)
202-368-1019 (TDD)

Office of Prepaid Health Care
Operations and Oversight
HCFA
Department of Health and Human
  Services
Washington, DC 20201
202-619-3555

Second Surgical Opinion Program
Department of Health and Human
  Services
Washington, DC 20201
1-800-838-6833 (outside DC)

Social Security Administration
1-800-SSA-1213

Department of Housing and Urban Development (HUD)

HUD Fraud Hotline
202-708-4200
1-800-347-3735 (outside DC)

Interstate Land Sales Registration Division
Department of Housing and
   Urban Development
Room 6278
Washington, DC 20410
202-708-0502

Manufactured Housing and Construction Standards Division
Department of Housing and
   Urban Development
Room 9158
Washington, DC 20410
202-708-2210

Office of Fair Housing and Equal Opportunity
Department of Housing and
   Urban Development
Room 5100
Washington, DC 20410
202-708-4252
1-800-424-8590 (outside DC)

Office of Single Family Housing
Department of Housing and
   Urban Development
Room 9282
Washington, DC 20410
202-708-3175

Office of Urban Rehabilitation
Department of Housing and
   Urban Development
Room 7168
Washington, DC 20410
202-708-2685

Title I Insurance Division
Department of Housing and
   Urban Development
Room 9156
Washington, DC 20410
202-708-1590

Department of the Interior

Consumer Affairs Administrator
Office of the Secretary
Department of the Interior
Washington, DC 20240
202-208-5521

Department of Justice

Antitrust Division
Department of Justice
Washington, DC 20530
202-514-2401

Civil Rights Division
*Look in your telephone directory
under "U.S. Government, Justice
Department, Civil Rights Division."
Or contact:*
Civil Rights Division
Department of Justice
Washington, DC 20530
202-514-2151
202-514-0716 (TDD)

Drug Enforcement Administration (DEA)
*Look in your telephone directory
under "U.S. Government, Justice
Department, Drug Enforcement
Administration." Or contact:*
Drug Enforcement Administration
Department of Justice
Washington, DC 20537
202-307-8000

Federal Bureau of Investigation (FBI)
*Look inside the front cover of your
telephone directory for the number
of the nearest FBI office. If it does
not appear, look under "U.S. Government, Justice Department, Federal Bureau of Investigation." Or
contact:*
Federal Bureau of Investigation
Department of Justice
Washington, DC 20535
202-324-3000

Immigration and Naturalization Service (INS)
*Look in your telephone directory
under "U.S. Government, Justice
Department, Immigration and Naturalization Service." Or contact:*
Immigration and Naturalization Service
Department of Justice
425 I Street, N.W.

Washington, DC 20536
202-514-4316

Department of Labor

Bureau of Labor-Management Relations and Cooperative Programs
Department of Labor
Washington, DC 20210
202-523-6098

Coordinator of Consumer Affairs
Department of Labor
Washington, DC 20210
202-523-6060 (general inquiries)

Employment and Training Administration
*Look in your telephone directory
under "U.S. Government, Labor
Department, Employment and
Training Administration." Or
contact:*
Employment and Training Administration
Director, Office of Public Affairs
Department of Labor
Washington, DC 20210
202-523-6871

Employment Standards Administration
Office of Public Affairs
Department of Labor
Washington, DC 20210
202-523-8743

Mine Safety and Health Administration
Office of Information and Public
   Affairs
Department of Labor
Ballston Towers #3
Arlington, VA 22203
703-235-1452

Occupational Safety and Health Administration (OSHA)
*Look in your telephone directory
under "U.S. Government, Labor
Department, Occupational Safety
and Health Administration." Or
contact:*

**Occupational Safety and Health
Administration**
Office of Information and
  Consumer Affairs
Department of Labor
Washington, DC 20210
202-523-8151

**Office of the Assistant Secretary
for Veterans' Employment and
Training**
Department of Labor
Washington, DC 20210
202-523-9116
1-800-442-2VET (Veterans' Job
  Rights Hotline)

**Office of Labor-Management
Standards**
Department of Labor
Washington, DC 20210
202-523-7343

**Pension and Welfare Benefits
Administration**
Office of Program Services
Department of Labor
Washington, DC 20210
202-523-8776

**Women's Bureau
The Work and Family Clearinghouse**
Department of Labor
Washington, DC 20210
1-800-827-5335
*Employers may contact this office
for information about dependent care
(child and/or elder care) policies.*

**Women's Bureau
The Workforce Quality
Clearinghouse**
Department of Labor
Washington, DC 20210
202-523-8913
1-800-523-0525 (outside DC)
*Employers may contact this office
for information about workplace
quality resources, e.g., employee
training and skills development.*

Department of State

Overseas Citizen Services
Department of State
Washington, DC 20520
202-647-3666 (nonemergencies)
202-647-5225 (emergencies)

**Passport Services
Washington Passport Agency**
1425 K Street, N.W.
Washington, DC 20524
202-647-0518

Visa Services
Department of State
Washington, DC 20520
202-647-0510

Department of Transportation (DOT)

Air safety:
**Federal Aviation Administration
(FAA)**
Community and Consumer Liaison
  Division
FAA (APA-200)
Washington, DC 20591
202-267-3479, 8592
1-800-FAA-SURE (outside DC)

Airline service complaints:
**Office of Intergovernmental and
Consumer Affairs (I-25)**
Department of Transportation
400 Seventh Street S.W.
Washington, DC 20590
202-366-2220

Auto safety hotline:
**National Highway Traffic Safety
Administration (NHTSA)
(NEF-11)**
Department of Transportation
Washington, DC 20690
202-366-0123
202-755-8919 (TDD)
1-800-424-9393 (outside DC)
1-800-424-9153 (TDD outside DC)

Boating safety classes:
United States Coast Guard Office

of Boating, Public and Consumer
Affairs (G-NAB-5)
Department of Transportation
Washington, DC 20593
202-267-0972

Boating safety hotline:
United States Coast Guard
Department of Transportation
Washington, DC 20593
202-267-0780
1-800-368-5647

Oil and chemical spills:
National Response Center
United States Coast Guard
Headquarters, G-TGC-2
Department of Transportation
Washington, DC 20593
202-267-2675
1-800-424-8802 (outside DC)

Railway safety:
Federal Railroad Administration
Office of Safety (RRS-20)
Department of Transportation
Washington, DC 20590
202-366-0522

Department of the Treasury

Bureau of the Public Debt
Public Affairs Officer
Office of the Commissioner
Department of the Treasury
999 E Street, N.W., Room 553
Washington, DC 20239-0001
202-376-4302

Comptroller of the Currency
*The Comptroller of the Currency
handles complaints about national
banks, i.e., banks that have the
word "National" in their names or
the initials "N.A." after their
names. For assistance, look in your
telephone directory under "U.S.
Government, Treasury Department,
Comptroller of the Currency." Or
contact:*
Comptroller of the Currency
Director, Compliance Policy

Department of the Treasury
250 E Street, S.W.
Washington, DC 20219
202-874-4820

Financial Management Service
Office of Legislative and Public
  Affairs
Department of the Treasury
401 14th Street, S.W., Room 555
Washington, DC 20227
202-287-0669

Internal Revenue Service (IRS)
*Look in your telephone directory
under "U.S. Government, Treasury
Department, Internal Revenue
Service."*

Office of Thrift Supervision
*The Office of Thrift Supervision
(formerly Federal Home Loan
Bank Board) handles complaints
about savings and loan associations
and savings banks. For assistance
contact:*
Office of Thrift Supervision
Consumer Affairs
1700 G Street, N.W.
Washington, DC 20552
202-906-6237
1-800-842-6929 (outside DC)

United States Customs Service
*Look in your telephone directory
under "U.S. Government, Treasury
Department, U.S. Customs
Service."*

*To report fraudulent import prac-
tices, call U.S. Customs Service's*
Fraud Hotline:
1-800-USA-FAKE

*To report drug-smuggling activity,
call U.S. Customs Service's*
Narcotics Hotline:
1-800-BE-ALERT

United States Mint
Customer Relations Division
Department of the Treasury
10001 Aerospace Road

Lanham, MD 20706
301-436-7400

**United States Savings Bonds
Division**
Office of Public Affairs
Department of the Treasury
Washington, DC 20220
202-634-5389
1-800-US-BONDS (recording)

Department of Veterans Affairs (VA)

*For information about VA medical
care or benefits, write, call, or visit
your nearest VA facility. Your telephone directory will list a VA medical center or regional office under
"U.S. Government, Department of
Veterans Affairs," or under "U.S.
Government, Veterans Administration." You may also contact the
offices listed below.*

For information about benefits:
**Veterans Benefits Administration
(27)**
Department of Veterans Affairs
810 Vermont Avenue, N.W.
Washington, DC 20420
202-233-2576

For information about medical care:
**Veterans Health Administration
(184C)**
810 Vermont Avenue, N.W.
Washington, DC 20420
202-535-7208

*For information about burials,
headstones or markers, and presi-
dential memorial certificates:*
National Cemetery System (40H)
Department of Veterans Affairs
810 Vermont Avenue, N.W.
Washington, DC 20420
202-535-7856

*For consumer information or gen-
eral assistance:*
Consumer Affairs Service
Department of Veterans Affairs

810 Vermont Avenue, N.W.
Washington, DC 20420
202-535-8962

Environmental Protection Agency (EPA)

Asbestos Action Program
202-382-3949

**Emergency Planning and
Community Right-to-Know
Information Hotline**
Environmental Protection Agency
Washington, DC 20460
202-479-2449
1-800-535-0202 (outside AK and
DC)

**Inspector General's Whistle Blower
Hotline**
202-382-4977
1-800-424-4000 (outside DC)

**National Pesticides Telecommunica-
tions Network (NPTN)**
806-743-3091
1-800-858-PEST (outside TX)

Office of External Relations
Environmental Protection Agency
Washington, DC 20460
202-382-4454

Public Information Center
PIC (PM-211B)
Environmental Protection Agency
Washington, DC 20460
202-382-2080 (general information)

**Resource Conservation and
Recovery Act**
RCRA/Superfund Hotline
Environmental Protection Agency
Washington, DC 20460
703-920-9810
1-800-424-9346 (outside DC)

Safe Drinking Water Hotline
202-382-5533
1-800-426-4791 (outside DC)

**Toxic Substances Control Act
Assistance Information Service**
Environmental Protection Agency
Washington, DC 20024
202-554-1404

Equal Employment
Opportunity Commission

*Look in your telephone directory
under "U.S. Government, Equal
Employment Opportunity Commission." Or contact:*
**Office of Communications and
Legislative Affairs**
Equal Employment Opportunity
   Commission
1801 L Street, N.W.
Washington, DC 20507
202-663-4900
202-663-4494 (TDD)
1-800-USA-EEOC
1-800-800-3302 (TDD)

Federal Communications
Commission (FCC)

Complaints about telephone systems:
Common Carrier Bureau
Informal Complaints Branch
Federal Communications
   Commission
2025 M Street, N.W., Room 6202
Washington, DC 20554
202-632-7553
202-634-1855 (TDD)

General information:
**Consumer Assistance and Small
Business Office**
Federal Communications
   Commission
1919 M Street, N.W., Room 254
Washington, DC 20554
202-632-7000
202-632-6999 (TDD)

Complaints about radio or television:
Mass Media Bureau
Complaints and Investigations
Federal Communications
   Commission
2025 M Street, N.W., Room 8210

Washington, DC 20554
202-632-7048

Federal Deposit Insurance
Corporation (FDIC)

*FDIC handles questions about
deposit insurance coverage and
complaints about FDIC-insured
state banks which are not members
of the Federal Reserve System. For
assistance, look in your telephone
directory under "U.S. Government,
Federal Deposit Insurance Corporation." Or contact:*
Office of Consumer Affairs
Federal Deposit Insurance
   Corporation
550 17th Street, N.W.
Washington, DC 20429
202-898-3536
202-898-3535 (voice/TDD)
1-800-424-5488 (outside DC)

Federal Emergency
Management Agency

*Look in your telephone directory
under "U.S. Government, Federal
Emergency Management Agency."
Or contact:*
**Emergency Preparedness and
Response**
Office of the External Affairs
   Directorate
Federal Emergency Management
   Agency
Washington, DC 20472
202-646-4000

Federal Insurance Administration
Federal Emergency Management
   Agency
Washington, DC 20472
202-646-2781
1-800-638-6620

**Office of Disaster Assistance
Programs**
Federal Emergency Management
   Agency
Washington, DC 20472
202-646-3615

U.S. Fire Administration
Federal Emergency Management
   Agency
NETC
16825 South Seton Avenue
Emmitsburg, MD 21727
301-447-1080
202-646-2449

Federal Maritime
Commission

**Office of Informal Inquiries and
Complaints**
1100 L Street, N.W.
Washington, DC 20573
202-523-5807

Federal Reserve System

*The Board of Governors handles
consumer complaints about state-
chartered banks and trust compa-
nies which are members of the
Federal Reserve System. For assis-
tance, look in your telephone direc-
tory under "U.S. Government,
Federal Reserve System, Board of
Governors," or "Federal Reserve
Bank." Or contact:*
**Board of Governors of the Federal
Reserve System**
Division of Consumer and
   Community Affairs
Washington, DC 20551
202-452-3667
202-452-3544 (TDD)

Federal Savings and Loans
Office of Community Investment
Federal Home Loan Bank Board
1700 G Street, N.W. (5th Floor)
Washington, DC 20552
202-377-6237

Government Printing
Office (GPO)

Government Publications:
Publications Service Section
Government Printing Office
Washington, DC 20402
202-275-3050

Subscriptions to government periodicals:
Subscription Research Section
Government Printing Office
Washington, DC 20402
202-275-3054

Interstate Commerce Commission (ICC)

Office of Compliance and Consumer Assistance
Washington, DC 20423
202-927-5500

National Credit Union Administration

Look in your telephone directory under "U.S. Government, National Credit Union Administration." Or contact:
National Credit Union Administration
1755 Duke Street
Alexandria, VA 22314
703-518-6300

National Labor Relations Board

Office of the Executive Secretary
1717 Pennsylvania Ave., N.W., Room 701
Washington, DC 20570
202-254-9430

Nuclear Regulatory Commission (NRC)

Office of Governmental and Public Affairs
Washington, DC 20555
301-492-0240

Pension Benefit Guaranty Corporation

2020 K Street, N.W.
Washington, DC 20006-1860
202-778-8800
202-778-8859 (TDD)

Postal Rate Commission

Office of the Consumer Advocate
Postal Rate Commission
1333 H Street, N.W., Suite 300
Washington, DC 20268
202-789-6830

President's Committee on Employment of People with Disabilities

1111 20th Street, N.W., Suite 636
Washington, DC 20036-3470
202-653-5044
202-653-5050 (TDD)

Railroad Retirement Board

844 Rush Street
Chicago, IL 60611
312-751-4500

Securities and Exchange Commission (SEC)

Office of Filings, Information and Consumer Services
450 5th Street, N.W.
(Mail Stop 2-6)
Washington, DC 20549
202-272-7440 (investor complaints)
202-272-7450 (filings by corporations and other regulated entities)
202-272-5624 (SEC Information Line—general topics and sources of assistance)

Small Business Administration (SBA)

Office of Consumer Affairs
409 Third Street, S.W.
Washington, DC 20416
202-205-6948 (complaints only)
1-800-U-ASK-SBA (information)

U.S. Consumer Product Safety Commission (CPSC)

To report a hazardous product or a product-related injury, or to inquire about product recalls, call or write:
Product Safety Hotline
U.S. Consumer Product Safety Commission
Washington, DC 20207
1-800-638-CPSC
1-800-638-8270 (TDD outside MD)
1-800-492-8104 (TDD in MD)

United States Postal Service

If you experience difficulty when ordering merchandise or conducting business transactions through the mail, or suspect that you have been the victim of a mail fraud or misrepresentation scheme, contact your postmaster or local Postal Inspector. Look in your telephone directory under "U.S. Government, Postal Service U.S." for these local listings. If they do not appear, contact:
Chief Postal Inspector
United States Postal Service
Washington, DC 20260-2100
202-268-4267

For consumer convenience, all post offices and letter carriers have postage-free Consumer Service Cards available for reporting mail problems and submitting comments and suggestions. If the problem cannot be resolved using the Consumer Service Card or through direct contact with the local post office, write or call:
Consumer Advocate
United States Postal Service
Room 5910
Washington, DC 20260-6720
202-268-2284
202-268-2310 (TDD)

P a r t   2

Giving Them the Business—
Business by Business

Airlines

Though it's true that most areas of the air-line industry are subject to some measure of federal regulation, all U.S. carriers don't share a single policy, and foreign carriers may not be bound by U.S. guidelines in matters such as fares. Policies are described fully in the "contract of carriage" on file in airline offices, and are summarized on the backs of tickets and in ads promoting new fares. But promotional and other terms only last until new ones are concocted. Then the rules can change.

1. Your best best is to study the printed policy on each ticket. If you book a nonrefundable ticket over the phone and have it sent to you, it will already be issued and therefore nonrefundable when you receive it. If you then find the restrictions are a problem, you're on thin ice.

2. Consequently, if you book a ticket over the phone, have the agent declare all terms to you, including itinerary and billing details. Do I get a meal? Do I change planes? Do I change airlines? What are the restrictions? Write them down. Note your confirmation number, the date of the call, and the name of the agent, and ask for his or her agency code.

3. To be doubly prudent, call again. State your confirmation number and run through all the specifics you were given. If the second agent concurs with the first, note the date, the name of the agent, and the agency code. If not, ask for the supervisor and explain that a ticket being processed for you was booked on the basis of wrong information. Find out what can be done to set it right.

4. If two agents have agreed on terms but you receive a ticket that contradicts the terms previously declared to you, call the airline and protest to a supervisor. If the supervisor can't help, ask how you can contact the airline's customer service department.

5. If the customer service agent tells you he or she is very sorry but the nonrefundability (or whatever) restrictions still apply, explain that the only information you had was what was disclosed to you by more than one of the airline's employees over the phone. If the airline's employees were wrong, why are you responsible? What authority or control do you have over their discharge of their function? What is the point of asking questions of designated personnel if you're not supposed to believe the answers? You did more than could be reasonably expected to confirm that the information was correct. If the airline's employees lied to you to part you from your money, the airline really does have every obligation to try to rectify the situation. If they didn't lie but either didn't actually know or weren't paying attention, this is the airline's human resources problem, which it probably ought to deal with after it has arranged for a correction in your ticket or billing. If you stick to your guns, satisfaction is a real possibility.

6. Another reason to require precise information from the first agent and to confirm it with a second is that terms are sometimes unclear, even to an airline's own personnel. For instance, "direct flight" has yet to be legally defined. Depending on the circumstances, a direct flight

can entail a change of planes or even a change of airlines. (However, "nonstop" does mean the plane won't stop except for an emergency.)

7. If the rates for the flight go down after you've purchased your nonrefundable ticket, call the airline or your travel agent. You may be allowed to exchange your ticket for an identical ticket at the lower rate.

8. Once you've booked the ticket, consult an airline guide or travel agent for the next three flights on the same route. If you get to the airport but your plane can't leave on time, you'll have a fallback position.

9. There are now ways for people with on-line computer services to check schedules and rates and to book tickets themselves. If you decide to go this route, remember that any mistakes you make will be your responsibility. If you book yourself to Oakland instead of Oklahoma, you may find a sympathetic supervisor willing to exchange your ticket, or you may be treating ticket agents to a good laugh at your expense.

If You Cancel or Have to Change Arrangements

1. Cancellation shouldn't be a problem for fully refundable tickets. That's one of the reasons you pay a premium price for them. Trip cancellation coverage and travel insurance policies may cover you if your tickets are nonrefundable or partially refundable. Other coverage can include lost or stolen baggage, delays, or emergency medical care. Before you travel, know what coverage you have and decide if you want more.

2. If your reason for cancellation is illness stemming from a preexisting condition, you may not be covered anyway.

3. Airlines used to grant refunds on nonrefundable tickets if presented with a doctor's note stating you were too sick to travel. Some still recognize illness waivers, others don't, or they impose a cancellation fee.

4. Other reasons that might justify cancellation are illness of your traveling companion, a loved one's critical illness or death, or a natural disaster. The only way to find out for sure is to raise the question.

5. The same reasons may enable you to change the return on your flight. If the airline agent won't help you, try pleading your cause with a supervisor or the customer service department. If the airline is still reluctant and you're a traveler whose company does business with the airline, explain that you will certainly recommend that your company take its high-volume business to a less rigid carrier.

6. As a rule, arbitrary reasons for cancellation or change won't wash. If you merely change your mind, that's your hard luck.

7. Certain airlines have modified their restrictions on nonrefundable tickets, allowing passengers to reschedule departures and/or returns for a fee in the neighborhood of $10 to $75. With some, if the ticket isn't used within a year, it can be exchanged for a voucher good on another flight. Ask if your airline has any such policies.

8. When you get to the airport—even if your seat is already assigned and your boarding pass is in hand—check in with the gate agent. Failure to do so may cost you a seat or a voucher if the flight is overbooked.

When You're Delayed

1. Some travel insurance policies pay if flights are so late that you miss your connections—for instance, if you miss your cruise because the plane was six hours late.

2. Depending on the airline's policy and the length of the delay, you may be entitled to meal and hotel vouchers. If nobody offers, ask.

3. You may be able to persuade the gate agent to give you an FIM (flight interruption manifest), which, even if your ticket is restricted or nonrefundable, will enable you to make your connection on another plane without additional charge.

4. If you belong to one of the frequent flyer elite clubs that have special lounges in designated airports, if you're in one of the airports that has such a lounge, and if you won't be jeopardizing your entitlements by leaving the boarding area, see what sort of privileges the host or hostess can arrange. Bear in mind that you pay for this membership, and explain that you consider it much more valuable to be helped in these instances than to be given a free drink. If nothing else, you're more likely to have the airline staff's ear than if you were crowding around the boarding area with a hundred other passengers trying equally hard to be heard.

When You're Bumped

1. Airlines overbook because passengers overbook. The proportion of no-shows for a flight can be as high as 20 percent. (The kinder, gentler policies governing nonrefundable tickets seem to have increased the number of people who change plans at the last minute.) The industry tries to reduce the loss by accepting more reservations than it has seats. Occasionally, gate agents announce that some people will have to relinquish their space. First they ask for volunteers, who, for their cooperation, are put on the next flight and rewarded with vouchers toward future travel.

2. If a sufficient number of passengers don't volunteer and you're willing, offer to be bumped in exchange for an extra voucher or one worth more money.

3. If you agree to be bumped, you will be asked to surrender your ticket and wait until the flight leaves. It may turn out that when everyone else is aboard, there's still room for you. If you're instructed at the last minute to dash onto the plane and take any seat, you should point out that if you don't get the seat you booked, then you've still relinquished your ticket. If you are told, "We were so busy that we weren't paying attention to who sat where," explain that you don't fault them

for being busy, but a deal's a deal. You went to the trouble of booking a window seat or an aisle seat or whatever you booked; then you went to the additional trouble of agreeing to surrender your ticket and to wait until the last minute to see if you were in fact taking the plane or not. And you don't appreciate being rewarded with a cramped middle seat for your troubles. Why should you be penalized for advance planning and a cooperative spirit? If you're scolded, "Get on the plane now or it leaves without you and you don't get a replacement ticket," get on the plane—then get the name of the person who ordered you onto the flight and follow up with the airline when you get home.

4. If there aren't enough volunteers, passengers can be bumped against their will. If this happens to you on a domestic flight (not on many commuter planes, nor on international flights originating overseas), current federal law requires that you receive compensation.

5. If being bumped means you'll have to stay overnight, the airline will provide the hotel room, transportation to it, and a breakfast voucher. So if it's late and you'd just as soon get some sleep, and if there are unquestionably more passengers than there are seats, offer to be bumped in exchange for the stated privileges, but insist that you don't want to be held at the airport for another two hours while they decide whom else to bump. Otherwise, you could be the first and only volunteer, and then have to sit on a bench while they bump another fifty people; then all fifty-one people are led to the ground transportation area to line up for the complimentary van to the hotel (it can only accommodate twelve people at a time); then it's 1:00 A.M. when you finally check in; and the van must pick you up at 6:00 A.M. the next morning in order to catch your new flight.

6. If you're bumped from a flight leaving a European Community airport—Belgium, Denmark, England, France, Germany, Greece, Italy, Luxembourg, the Netherlands, Portugal, or Spain—and are not put on another flight within

two hours, the Association of European Airlines directs that you be given hotel accommodations, meals, and phone calls (if appropriate) and cash or cash vouchers.

7. If you belong to one of the elite frequent flyer clubs with a lounge (as noted above), see what support the host or hostess will provide.

8. Although bumping policy is generally spelled out on the back of your ticket, the 9th U.S. Circuit Court of Appeals ruled in 1990 that "airlines can be sued for damages for selling tickets that are subject to bumping when flights are overbooked" and that a passenger isn't precluded from suing under ordinary state law for harm caused by airline practices. This is far from the last word. But if you have an overwhelming reason for needing to be on a flight and the airline turns a deaf ear, citing this bit of information might improve your chances of getting aboard.

9. If your plane is canceled, it's not the same as your being bumped, and, unfortunately, you don't have the same favorable rights as a bumped passenger. The rationale is that flights are canceled essentially for safety reasons—such as a mechanical malfunction or bad weather—and the airline's primary responsibility is to deliver passengers safely to their destination.

10. If the flight is canceled, the airline will most likely book you on the next available flight. If it's more expensive than the original flight, ask the airline to absorb the difference.

Aboard the Flight

Being a passenger on an airplane can sometimes feel like living under martial law. The flight attendants are in charge. They can be lovely, or they can be arbitrary, mean-spirited, and reminiscent of the crankiest schoolteacher you ever had. If you feel that one is denying you proper service or due courtesy:

1. Ask for the "A." The A is the attendant in charge of the other attendants on a given flight

and has additional authority. This allows you to voice your complaint to someone other than the offending party.

2. If the A won't help, note the name of the attendant and the A and write to the airline about both of them when you return home.

Following Up with the Airline

1. If you book a ticket over the phone and discover after you receive it that it was inaccurately described to you at the time of purchase, or if you had difficulties on the flight and need to report it afterward, contact the airline at its 800 number. Explain that you have a problem and would like to be put through to someone who can help you.

2. Perhaps the first person you speak to can provide the solution. More likely, the first person who hears you out will be unable to help, or will give you an unsatisfactory answer. Ask to speak to the supervisor.

3. Explain yourself to the supervisor. If you were misinformed or improperly treated, give names and dates.

4. If the supervisor can't help, ask for a customer service number at the head office. If it's a toll number, ask if there's an 800 number.

5. If the only number is a toll number, inquire as to the least busy time to call. You want to avoid being put on hold and listening to music on a customer service number while the minutes tick away into more money.

6. If you call a toll number, your first words when a human voice answers should be: "I prefer not to pay for a toll call. Will you ring me back at this number?" With any luck, the airline representative will comply.

7. Provide names, dates, and accurate information.

8. If the matter can't be resolved over the phone, you may be asked to write a letter. Again, provide names, dates, and accurate information. CC the airline's president.

9. If the airline can't resolve your complaint (or can't locate your missing luggage, or has engaged in deceptive practices), contact the Department of Transportation (DOT), Office of Intergovernmental and Consumer Affairs, I-25, 400 Seventh, S.W., Washington, DC 20590; 202-366-2220.

10. Another tack is to write a letter to Ombudsman, *Condé Nast Traveler,* 360 Madison Avenue, New York, NY (or fax it to 212-880-2190). This excellent travel advice column will print inquiries of special interest, answer them intelligently, and attempt to negotiate with the offending airline on your behalf.

If the Airline Goes Under

1. Airlines have been known to declare bankruptcy yet remain in business after filing for Chapter 11 protection. In other words, just because the airline is bankrupt doesn't mean your plane won't fly.

2. If you've paid for the ticket on your credit card and there wasn't any flight, you can request the credit card company to remove the charge from your statement.

3. Problem airlines will occasionally set up funds to back unusable tickets in the event their planes stop flying. If you have doubts about the longevity of your airline, inquire when making your reservation if protection is automatically available.

4. If you paid cash, you may file for a refund with the bankruptcy court. The DOT, the airline's 800 number, or a travel agent can tell you how to proceed.

5. Other carriers often honor the tickets of failed airlines when they have space on their flights.

6. Don't assume that travel insurance will cover you if the airline goes out of business before or during your trip. For instance, many policies won't apply if the airline had already applied for bankruptcy protection when you bought the ticket. If you want to know for sure before you leave, read the policy.

7. If you have frequent flyer miles logged with the airline, your best hope is that it will be taken over by a company that automatically transfers the credits to its own program.

8. If you know the airline is in trouble, you might want to use up your free miles while you still have them.

When You're a Possible Claimant in a Class-Action Suit

1. If you've suffered serious injury aboard an airline, consult a lawyer. If you are in an airline disaster involving many passengers, talk to your attorney, who will in turn advise you with respect to other lawyers who wish to contact you. A class-action suit may be instituted. (*See* RUNG ELEVEN: CLASS-ACTION SUITS, in Part I.)

2. But not all class-action suits have to do with pain and suffering. For instance, a suit was instituted against a number of airlines for alleged price-fixing. Large numbers of travelers who might have claims were identified by computer and were mailed forms to file. Newspaper articles in travel and business sections alerted others of their potential status and told them how to be listed as members of the class. Although claimants were paid in vouchers (with any cash going toward legal fees), vouchers could be applied toward future travel. The way to find out about such matters is to be an informed consumer. Read the papers. Watch TV news.

3. Like most vouchers, such vouchers will contain restrictions. Read the instructions before attempting to use them.

Speaking of Lawsuits

Travel law is a specialty. If you're keen on taking your airline to court, you might be wise to seek out a specialist.

About Vouchers and Special Promotions

1. The less a ticket costs, the more restrictive its terms tend to be. Investigate the rules before attempting to use the ticket.

2. If you want to book a certain flight using a special ticket or voucher but are told the space reserved for those deals is sold out, ask whether space is available at full price. If it is, speak to a supervisor. Supervisors have the authority to release unsold seats. Explain the circumstances that earned you the voucher—for instance, that you agreed to be bumped on a previous flight at great inconvenience to yourself—and request that the airline find a way to oblige you.

Luggage Lost or Misrouted

1. If you wait until the last minute to check your luggage, it may miss the plane, and the airline may charge you if the luggage has to be delivered to your hotel. Otherwise, if the airline misroutes your belongings, the airline is responsible for delivering it without charge to the place where you will be staying.

2. If your luggage is missing, report it before you leave the premises. Request that a missing luggage report be filed. Ask for a copy. Keep your luggage tag to identify your property until it's returned to you.

3. The airline has to compensate you for the value of lost luggage (with some exceptions).

4. If you are deprived of misrouted luggage while away from home, the airline is supposed to compensate you for replacement of items you may need quickly, such as toiletries and a change of clothes. Ask the baggage supervisor for cash. If you're refused, make the necessary purchases, save the receipts, and complain to the airline when you get home.

5. Credit card protection and homeowner's policies may cover lost and stolen baggage and items contained in it. Read the agreements to determine if you're covered. Some credit card companies offer optional baggage insurance that covers theft, loss, damage, and delay. It may also be available as a rider on your homeowner's policy.

6. To be on the safe side, pack valuables and necessities in your carry-on bag. Then keep your eye on the bag.

Airport Thefts

Your luggage, or the contents of your luggage, can be stolen by professional airport thieves, local crooks, and even unethical airport employees. The fact that you arrive home or at your hotel with all your luggage doesn't rule out the possibility that it was opened and pillaged en route. A vigilant attitude is your best ally, along with these precautions:

1. Have your luggage tagged, not only on the outside but also on the inside. If bags can't be identified, they are subject to sale at auction. If your bags are lost and can't be traced, you can ask what happens to unidentified belongings, and in a worst-case scenario, try to intercept them at the other end of their journey.

2. It's a poor idea to have the address of your vacant home displayed on the outside of (or even inside) your luggage. Thieves know that if you're traveling, you're probably not home. They don't even have to steal your valise to read the address on the tag. When leaving home, you might consider using the address of your hotel, a relative, a business, or whomever you'll be visiting. On your return trip, ask permission to use the address of neighbors or your building superintendent. If the baggage is lost and returned to them, you'll still get it back, without having revealed that your home was empty for two weeks.

3. Don't leave your things unattended. Don't trust a stranger to watch your property.

4. Not everyone in a uniform is an official red-cap. Be alert to the possibility that a crook in costume may be offering to help you with your bags.

5. Be alert to airport ploys and scams. People working in teams, stopping you for information or on another pretext, can fleece you while you're distracted.

6. If you believe your property was stolen, not simply misplaced, report the incident to airport police. Call your airline. Follow up with your airline's missing baggage desk.

7. Even though you fly on a particular airline or combination of airlines, airports operate under their own authority. If you're complaining about *any matter* that involves the airport itself, write to airport management as well as contacting the airlines in question. The executive office and business address of the airport should be listed in the business section of your telephone directory.

If You Transport a Pet

1. Know exactly what coverage the airline is prepared to provide. Request a written statement and study it carefully.

2. In a recent ruling, it was determined that although a dog had struggled horribly and then died in the overheated baggage compartment of an airplane, the pet had to be considered as property. The owner was found to be entitled only to the compensation he would have received for a lost piece of luggage.

A Final Word

Capitol Hill is aware that voters fly, and that airlines often give the distinct impression of not caring how abominably passengers are treated. As a result, further consumer's rights legislation is in the works. When it will take off and where it will land remain open to conjecture.

▲ *See also* CREDIT CARDS, TOURS.

Appliances

Your best defense against defective appliances is being careful when you buy, but even after you've paid your money you aren't without recourse.

Precautions When You Purchase

1. Know the store, in person or by reputation.

2. Without fail, inquire about return and repair policies, guarantees, and warranties. Look around to see if any signs are posted concerning such matters.

3. If you're purchasing a gift that won't be opened for several weeks and the store policy is "no refund after ten days," see if you can get the refund period extended.

4. If the salesperson wants to sell you an expensive piece of merchandise such as a fax or computer, ask if the store has a policy of loaners when the original has to be repaired. Most stores don't, but the moment of purchase is a good time to try to negotiate the arrangement. You won't lose anything by asking; some stores do have such policies, and some stores would initiate them if pressed.

5. If you're replacing an old appliance—for example, an answering machine that isn't as modern as it might be—*keep it as a backup* until you're certain the new one works. As soon as you throw the old one away, you relinquish the luxury of time you would otherwise have to wait out satisfactory repair or exchange terms. Without any backup, you may find yourself desperate enough to settle for mediocre service.

6. Whatever anybody tells you, ask to have it in writing if it sounds too good to be true or even a little out of the ordinary.

7. Whatever promises are made to you at the time of purchase, at least get the name and title of the person making the sale.

8. If a no-refund policy is posted, realize that you increase your vulnerability if the merchandise turns out to be defective.

9. Particularly if the store operates under a no-return policy, open the box and inspect the merchandise. See if assembly is required and, if there are instructions, if you can follow them. If the surface is scratched, if parts are missing, if the item seems to have been used and damaged by a previous party—whatever the flaw—refuse the item and ask to see another box.

10. Bear in mind that if you purchase an appliance in a store far from home—for instance, while you're on vacation—you deprive yourself of the possibility of a face-to-face return or exchange, unless you're willing to travel back to the scene to negotiate.

11. It's definitely a bad habit to overextend yourself on your credit card and to make more purchases than you can pay off without running up interest charges on unpaid balances—but if you make your purchase on a credit card, you have the leverage of challenging the charge if the purchase turns out to be defective. Additionally,

some credit cards include certain extended warranties and similar protection.

12. Be sure that you've found, completed, and mailed the guarantee or warranty card before discarding the box your merchandise came in. (Remember that some companies request you to keep the original packaging, to be used in case you have to return the item for replacement or repair.) And be sure to use every feature and establish its good working condition before the warranty expires.

If the Item Is Defective

1. If the store has a refund counter, you know where to start. If not, speak to the first person willing to engage you, but be prepared to talk to the manager, because not every employee is authorized to handle an exchange or return. Not every employee unable to help you will refer you to the manager, either, so be prepared to make the suggestion yourself. You may be told the manager isn't in. If so, get the manager's name, ask when he or she will be in, and ask to talk to whoever is in charge in the manager's absence.

2. If talking gets you nowhere because you've attempted a return or replacement based on promises that nobody seems prepared to honor, you are in a position to paraphrase some or all of the following sentiment (depending on the level of resistance you meet):

"So-and-so specifically told me that this was your policy. Under no circumstance would I have made the purchase without that assurance. If it isn't true, the salesperson was lying to make a deal, was trying to get rid of me and move on to the next customer, or was misinformed. I cannot be held responsible for the behavior of your employees until I am given the power to hire and fire them. Until then, it isn't fair to penalize me for believing that your employees give accurate answers to direct questions. I made the purchase

in good faith. I certainly believed the employee to be acting in good faith. I would appreciate your abiding by the assurances I was given."

3. Saturdays can be bad days to attempt this, because they tend to be more hectic than weekdays, and because managers may be off for the weekend.

4. If talking fails, write a letter to the store manager, giving specific details such as the date of purchase, the salesclerk who spoke to you and the assurances you were given, the nature of your complaint, the steps you took to resolve the matter in person, and what reparation you expect to see. You may wish to include your phone number. Enclose a photocopy of your receipt.

5. If the store doesn't get back to you, follow up by phone.

6. If the discussion is unsatisfactory and if the store belongs to a chain, try contacting the customer service department by phone or by mail.

7. Even if the store posts a no-return policy, you're entitled to complain if you were blatantly misled at the point of purchase—for instance, if it became apparent after you brought the item home that it had already been returned as defective by someone else. If the store contends that "no returns" means "no returns," you may have to contact your state or local consumer affairs department.

8. If you purchased by credit card, contact your credit card company (using the 800 number if there is one) and determine what coverage you have. Meanwhile, ask for a chargeback or credit until the matter is resolved.

9. The above guidelines apply if your quarrel is with the store. Even if you can be convinced that the defect in question was not the store's fault, ask that the merchandise be replaced and suggest that the store return the defective article to the manufacturer for credit.

10. If the store can't or won't do this, or the item misfunctions after you've used it for a short period, check your warranty or guarantee to see what steps you can take.

11. If these steps aren't sufficient, phone or write the manufacturer's corporate headquarters for redress.

12. If you purchased a major appliance (such as a refrigerator, oven, dishwasher, or air conditioner) and all else has failed, contact the MACAP: Major Appliance Consumer Action Panel, 20 North Wacker Drive, Chicago, IL 60606; 1-800-621-0477. The MACAP, funded by the appliance industry, will determine the validity of your complaint. If the complaint is properly documented and appears to be reasonable, the MACAP will approach the manufacturer on your behalf.

13. If the manufacturer won't cooperate, the MACAP will draw its own conclusions and recommend a solution.

14. MACAP decisions aren't binding, but most manufacturers participate in the program and will be swayed by the findings.

Product Liability Laws

For more details on this, *see* PRODUCT LIABILITY AND RECALLS. For the moment, bear the following points in mind—and be prepared to mention them to dealers and manufacturers:

1. The Consumer Product Safety Act of 1972 protects consumers against dangerous products.
2. The Consumer Product Safety Commission has established mandatory safety standards for consumer products sold in this country. It has the power to enforce them with fines, penalties, and time in jail.
3. The commission can require the recall, repair, or replacement of products found to be dangerous. It can require refunds for them. It can ban them.
4. It's bad enough for a consumer to be sold a hazardous product. But a dealer or manufacturer who, having done so, refuses responsibility *may be in violation of federal law.*

▲ *See also* CREDIT CARDS; GUARANTEES; MAIL ORDERS; RETAIL SHOPPING; WARRANTIES.

Automated Teller Machines (ATMs)

Some consumers can no longer imagine what life was like before automated tellers, back when it was impossible to withdraw money when in another town, or after a bank had closed for the day.

Banks are happy too, because automated tellers reduce the workload on personnel, leaving human tellers free to handle more complicated transactions.

If only ATMs could be perfect. But they're not, and when they disappoint you, they're made more frustrating by the fact that there's usually not a human employee around to resolve complaints.

You've got two main strategies for beating the hassle: advance precautions, and fast follow-ups.

Advance Precautions

1. If your bank has an automated teller system, find out how versatile your ATM card is going to be. Determine how many different networks it works with, and how available these networks are in the places you expect to be.

2. What will each transaction cost you? Some banks allow you free transactions from the bank's own ATMs, but assess a service charge when you use the machines at other banks.

3. Compare these charges with what you'd pay at the window. Among banks that charge for ATM transactions, these charges may nonetheless be lower than what you'd pay inside.

4. Can you make withdrawals from every terminal on the system? Can you deposit to every terminal, or only those belonging to your bank?

5. When are transactions posted to your account? Are withdrawals immediate? Is there a waiting period on deposits?

6. Are there limitations on the frequency or dollar amounts of transactions?

7. Even when you get ATM receipts for deposits, the accuracy of the information depends solely on what you enter. If you deposit $100 and enter $1,000, the receipt will read $1,000, but it will be subject to verification by the bank. Find out how quickly the bank will advise you about this kind of error.

8. By the same token, the bank may make an error in verifying. For instance, you might deposit three checks at the ATM and type in the numbers accurately, but one of the checks may somehow go astray. If so, your correct receipt isn't proof that you deposited the check the way a receipt from a human teller would be. Ask exactly what the bank's procedure is for collecting ATM deposits. To what degree is it foolproof? What steps can you take in the unlikely event that an ATM-deposited check is misplaced?

9. Make a note of this information, with date and name of the person who gave it to you. If you later have a problem, cite the assurances you were given by a person who, after all, spoke on the bank's behalf in accepting responsibility for your money.

10. You may find yourself reminding the bank that the terminal is an ATM, not a slot machine, and that you didn't think you were gambling when you conducted your transaction. But it will very occasionally happen that the wrong denomination of bills will be loaded into the machine, and when, for example, you request $20, you'll get maybe $5 or $50. Whether you make a profit or take a loss, report it immediately. Chances are that if it happens to you, it will happen to others. The true amounts will be tracked and posted to your account. Any loss will be made up—and the real amount of the withdrawal, if it is more than you requested, will be subtracted from your balance.

11. Is there a phone at the ATM, set up for you to call support personnel if a problem arises? Does it provide twenty-four-hour service? Weekends and holidays too?

12. Under what circumstances could your ATM card be voided? How and how soon would you be notified? It's one thing to acknowledge that misunderstandings can occur, but quite another to be counting on withdrawing $100 before catching a plane out of town and discovering that your card was voided a week ago.

13. Whatever answers you're given, write them down with name and date. If you do have a problem of this sort, you'll want to resolve it to your satisfaction without delay.

14. Examine the ATM locations you're most likely to use. Are you comfortable with the security? Are they open and well lighted? Are there surveillance cameras?

15. Some people feel safer if their ATMs are inside a locked area accessible only to account holders with ATM cards. Others may feel trapped, fearing they could be backed into a corner. One study has shown that outdoor units are no more susceptible to crime than indoor units.

16. If you use indoor ATMs, look first to see whether shady characters might be in hiding under counters or behind obstructions. Is the lighting bright? Are there mirrors to expose someone lurk-ing in the shadows? Is there an unobstructed view of the area from the street?

17. Ask your bank what security policies apply to its ATMs.

18. Ask your state banking commission (in the phone directory, look in the government listings for your state) what laws cover ATMs and electronic transfers of funds.

19. Some municipal laws require a specific level of security for ATMs. Your local police department, elected officials, or municipal governing authority (see the government listings for your city or town) can provide further details. Learn what the laws are. Take a few minutes to see if your bank observes them.

20. If not, bring it to the attention of a bank officer, service representative, or branch manager. If you aren't satisfied with the response, alert the police department.

21. Under the federal Electronic Fund Transfer (EFT) Act, your bank is required to give you a disclosure statement summarizing the bank's and your liability for unauthorized transfers. It must also indicate the telephone number and address of the person to be notified when you believe an unauthorized transfer has been made or may be made, along with a statement of the institution's "business days." This information will tell you the number of days you have to report suspected unauthorized transfers.

22. As soon as you get your ATM card, sign it.

Fast Follow-ups

1. If you lose your card, spot an error, whatever—act fast! Though the bank may not respond as quickly as you'd like, your best protection every time is to report problems as soon as you notice them.

2. Federal law says you're entitled to a periodic statement for each statement cycle in which an electronic transfer is made. It must include a telephone number and address to be used for inquiries.

3. You're entitled to a quarterly statement even if you made no electronic transfers in the quarter.

4. Read your statements when you get them. Compare them with your receipts and records of transactions. If you spot an error, report it immediately.

5. Be sure to read any notices accompanying your statement. They may be informing you of new transaction charges or other changes.

6. In the event of errors, the EFT Act says you have sixty days from the date a problem or error appears on your periodic statement or terminal receipt to notify your financial institution.

7. The best way to protect yourself in such cases is to notify the issuer by certified letter, return receipt requested. Keep a copy of the letter for your records.

8. The institution has ten business days to investigate and notify you of the results.

9. If the institution needs more time to investigate, it can take up to forty-five days, but only if the money is returned to your account in the interim.

10. If no error is found, the bank may take back the money, but not without giving you a written explanation.

11. Under federal law, the institution has no obligation to conduct an investigation if you miss the sixty-day deadline.

12. If your ATM card is lost or stolen, report it immediately to the issuer. Make a record of the time, date, and person you spoke to. The EFT Act says you can't be held liable for any unauthorized withdrawals made after the report.

13. If you report the loss within two days of discovering that your card is missing, and if the card has been used without authorization, you should not be held responsible for more than $50.

14. If you fail to make your report within two business days, you can lose as much as $500 for an unauthorized withdrawal.

15. If you don't report an unauthorized transfer or withdrawal within sixty days after your statement is mailed to you, you risk unlimited loss.

16. If there are extenuating reasons why you were unable to report—severe illness, lengthy travel—ask your bank to extend your time period.

17. If state law or your contract imposes lower limits on your liability, those lower limits apply instead of the limits in the federal EFT Act.

18. Though you aren't liable for transactions that occur after you've reported a theft or loss, continue to read your statements carefully, and continue to report any discrepancies.

19. Check for irregularities in the area each time you use your ATM card. Is the place still well lighted and clearly visible from the street? If not, report the changes immediately—to the bank and, if its administrators don't care, to the police department and the governing authority that oversees your ATM security laws. CC the bank's branch manager.

20. If you're the victim of crime at an ATM site, the bank may be responsible (depending on your local laws). If the surveillance camera was operating, there should be a record of the incident. If the camera was broken or out of film, the bank may have defaulted on a legal responsibility.

21. Notify the bank and the police immediately. It's an important step in crime prevention, and besides, it affords you certain coverage under the law.

22. If you were forced to make a withdrawal and the film backs you up—or if film is unavailable because the bank was negligent—you have coverage for the loss. Under the federal EFT Act, "the amount of a consumer's liability for an unauthorized electronic funds transfer . . . shall not exceed $50."

23. If the bank was negligent, insist that it credit the $50 to your account from its own funds.

To Complain

1. Complaints about sloppy ATM service can be addressed to the local branch manager.

2. If poor service isn't improved, write the branch manager again. CC "Director of Consumer Banking" and "Director of Marketing Services and Product Management" at the bank's headquarters office, which is likely to have executives with those or similar titles.

3. If inadequate security is an issue, CC the above-named as well as the captain (or person in charge of) your local police department, and the local government department whose laws govern ATM security.

4. If you believe the institution that issued your ATM card has failed to fulfill its responsibilities to you under the EFT Act, you might contact the federal agency below that has enforcement jurisdiction over the issuer:

State Member Banks of Federal Reserve System

Board of Governors of the Federal
   Reserve System
Division of Consumer and
   Community Affairs
20th & C Streets, N.W.
Washington, DC 20551
202-452-3667

Nonmember Federally Insured Banks

Office of Consumer Affairs
Federal Deposit Insurance
Corporation
550 17th Street, N.W.
Washington, DC 20429
202-898-3536
1-800-424-5488 (outside DC)

National Banks

Director, Consumer Protection
Office of the Comptroller of the
   Currency
Washington, DC 20219
202-874-5219
Also: Director, Compliance Policy
Department of the Treasury
250 E Street, S.W.
Washington, DC 20219
202-874-4820

Federal Credit Unions

National Credit Union
   Administration
1775 Duke Street
Alexandria, VA 22314
703-518-6300

Federal Savings and Loans

Office of Thrift Supervision
1700 G Street, N.W. (Fifth Floor)
Washington, DC 20552
202-906-6000

▲ *See also* BANKING; CREDIT RATINGS; ELECTRONIC FUND TRANSFERS.

Automobiles

NEW, LEASED, USED—AND FINDING A MECHANIC

At least in theory, automakers show signs of embracing the current consumer movement, having occasionally instructed their dealers that a satisfied customer is better than one who's been humiliated, sweated, and double-talked into a deal. Some manufacturers have instituted customer-service schools, while the National Automobile Dealers Association (NADA) has begun a certification course for salespeople.

One dealer lends beepers to service customers so that mechanics can contact them throughout the day with estimates and questions. Sweeping changes may not be far behind—including non-negotiable sticker prices that allow a reasonable profit for dealerships but spare consumers the agony and confusion of high-pressure sales tactics.

"Getting most auto dealers to treat customers well will take some structural changes," observed a 1992 issue of *Business Week* magazine. But remember that automobile defects virtually sparked the consumer movement of the sixties with Ralph Nader's inspiring and highly effective attacks, and keep telling yourself that any effort—theirs or yours—is certainly better than none.

Whether You Buy or Lease

1. You'll want to consider the obvious features—cost, style, fuel efficiency, safety, environmental considerations, and more.

2. You'll weigh the relative value *to you* of special orders and factory options such as antilock brakes, airbags, air conditioning, and power windows.

3. You'll take a test drive.

4. All this means research, research, research. Most libraries are well stocked with invaluable publications for the would-be car buyer. For instance, *Consumer Reports* periodically rates cars on numerous criteria.

5. Many useful consumer hotlines and services are at your disposal, for free or for a modest fee.

6. Consumer Reports Auto Price Service, 101 Truman Avenue, Yonkers, NY 10703-1052; 914-378-2000, will provide comparison information.

7. AAA Auto Pricing Services offers instant comparison information to members: 1-800-933-7700 (not available in Alaska or Hawaii).

8. The Auto Safety Hotline of the National Highway Traffic Safety Administration, Department of Transportation (1-800-424-9393, or 1-800-424-9153 for people who are hearing-impaired, or 202-366-0123 in Washington, DC), can tell you the recall history of the models you have in mind, their highway safety record, etc. Also, ask for referrals to sources of other information.

9. The Insurance Institute for Highway Safety Communications Department, 1005 North Glebe Road, Suite 800, Arlington, VA 22201, 703-247-1500, will tell you about the crashworthiness and theft histories of various makes and models.

10. IntelliChoice's ArmChair Compare, 1-800-227-2665, will use preferences you supply to analyze the cost of your contemplated purchase, taking into account such factors as license and registration fees, taxes, estimated repair and maintenance costs, and the terms of your loan to purchase the car.

11. Contact your state department of consumer affairs (see government listings for your state in your phone directory) to determine whether it keeps a record of consumers' disputes with manufacturers, of manufacturers' compliance with decisions, and of the number of refunds and replacements ordered.

12. *Gas Mileage Guides,* prepared by the Federal Energy Administration and the Environmental Protection Agency, list mileage for new cars as rated by a series of standardized tests. By law, a copy should be on hand in all new car dealer showrooms. Or you can get your own copy by writing Fuel Economy, Pueblo, CO 81009.

If You Buy

1. Base your decision on your research, recommendations of friends, and comparisons between dealerships.

2. Take your friends' misgivings about a dealership seriously. For a purchase as important as an automobile, you can always go to the next town if you have doubts about the dealer closest to you.

3. Confirm the reputation of the dealership with the Better Business Bureau, your local Chamber of Commerce, or your state's department of consumer affairs.

4. Don't be bullied when negotiating a price. High-pressure tactics are well known but not universal. In any event, your best defense is to be clear on what you want and suspicious of sudden revelations.

5. In negotiating a price, ask to see the car dealer's invoice from the manufacturer—in other words, what the car costs the dealer. Then bargain up from the invoice price ("base price") instead of bargaining down from the sticker price.

6. If you see the initials ADP, ADM, or AMV, compare the sticker with a reputable price guide, because these stand for Additional Dealer Profit, Additional Dealer Markup, and Additional Market Value.

7. Don't buy extras you don't need. For example, if the manufacturer provides a warranty against rust or if corrosion resistance is engineered into the car, the charge for optional rustproofing may simply be intended to part you from your money.

8. Though you may want dealer-installed options such as a luggage rack, it may be cheaper to get them from a nearby garage after you buy the car.

9. Customers with disabilities may require adaptive equipment to be added or installed. Some automakers arrange rebates when this is done. For more information, contact GM's Mobility Assistance Center (1-800-323-9935, or 1-800-833-9935 for TDD users) or Chrysler's Physically Challenged Resource Center (1-800-255-9877).

10. Take a good look at the contract. If the car arrives damaged, can you refuse it and recoup your down payment? If not, don't sign the contract until such wording is included.

11. What if you discover defects shortly after you get the car home? Will the dealer pick it up for servicing? (Get it in writing.) Will the dealer give you a loaner? Are there specific conditions that apply? (Get *them* in writing.)

12. Look for items you've never discussed. Is there a "destination charge" (shipping cost)? Don't wait for it to turn up on the bill. Ask about it in advance, and negotiate.

13. What warranties are offered? A basic warranty ought to come with the vehicle, and you may be offered an extended warranty at an additional cost.

14. Compare the basic warranties of the different cars you're considering buying. Do they

include deductibles (costs you must bear before coverage kicks in) and special conditions?

15. If you opt for an extended warranty, who provides it? The manufacturer, the dealer, or an independent third party? Whom will you have to go to when somebody has to honor the deal?

16. Salespeople might tell you that service not provided by the dealer and parts not made by the manufacturer will void the warranty. But this isn't legal under the Magnuson-Moss Warranty Act (*see* WARRANTIES). By law, manufacturers can't make a warranty conditional on the use of a specific product or service part unless you can obtain the product free of charge, or unless the FTC has stipulated that only a certain part can be used.

17. But see what your warranty does require— such as regular preventive maintenance. Is it spelled out? If not, have it clarified in writing.

18. When the maintenance is performed, keep records, bills, and receipts. You may need them later to prove that you kept up your end of the deal, or to demonstrate that malfunctions aren't the result of your carelessness.

19. Report complaints against a dealership to your state department of motor vehicles (look in the government listings for your state in your phone directory).

Leasing

1. In leasing, just as in purchasing, contracts are signed and terms are negotiable. Don't pay a price just because you see it in print, and don't sign anything without reading it first. Almost every detail can be bargained, from capitalized cost at the beginning to mileage limits at the end.

2. Pay attention. Read the fine print. Ask a knowledgeable party for insight. (In one survey of drivers who leased a car for the first time, a full 5 percent actually thought they'd signed a contract to buy a car.)

3. When debating whether to buy or lease, compare *all* costs. In making the comparison, add

the comprehensive costs of both. For the purchase, deduct the resale value of the car from your final figure (projected Blue Book value should be given in the leasing contract). For a leasing arrangement, add any nonrefundable charges. Also consider the relative merits and demerits of tying up money in a car purchase. (If it costs $100 more per month to buy than to lease and if you'll make up the difference by charging sofas and vacations on a credit card, remember that you'll be paying 12–19 percent and up on those credit card purchases.)

4. What will your periodic payments be? According to federal law, you must be advised of the amounts, how many, when they are due, and how any late payments will be calculated and assessed.

5. But if you decide to lease, don't just compare periodic payments. Examine and weigh the details of the lease with arrangements offered by other dealers and independent leasing companies.

6. What price is given as the "capitalized cost" of the car you're proposing to lease? Compare it against the purchase price of the same make and model. If it isn't almost identical, put up a fight, because you're going to pay your leasing charges ("money rate") based on this initial figure.

7. If you lease, check the contract for a mileage limit above which you'll be charged extra. What's the extra, and what are the chances that you'll drive enough to have to pay it?

8. If you lease, you're expected to return the car in fit condition for somebody else. If you wreck the car or lose it, you're responsible for the balance of the lease.

9. Gap insurance is an option offered at the time of leasing to cover the remainder on the contract in such instances. But some consumer sources have found gap insurance to be overpriced, and therefore not worthwhile.

10. As a rule, cars can be leased on "walk-away" ("net" or "closed-end") terms, or with an "open-end" lease. With a walk-away arrangement, you walk away at the end of the leasing period

without additional payment unless you've been unusually hard on the vehicle (as specified in the leasing agreement).

11. With an open-end lease, you'll have to pay the difference (or some portion of the difference) between the "residual value" stated in the lease and the actual appraisal value (or sale price if the car is resold) of the vehicle when you turn it in. This means the driver takes some responsibility for the condition of the car.

12. If you sign an open-end lease, try to negotiate that you'll receive a refund if the appraisal value of the car exceeds its residual value—and make every effort to pin down the maximum amount you'll be charged if the appraisal value is less.

13. Both varieties of lease have their merits. Just make sure you understand the kind you're signing and what your liabilities are. If your agreement allows for "reasonable wear and tear," demand specifics and definitions, in writing, in the contract. If they don't seem particularly reasonable to you, negotiate.

14. Federal law requires that you be told all up-front costs before you sign the lease. These may include a security deposit, first and last lease payments, taxes, title and licensing fees, insurance, and a capitalized cost reduction (the equivalent of a down payment).

15. Sometimes, lessors will accept a trade-in in the place of a capitalized cost reduction.

16. The disposition charge (the cost of preparing the vehicle for sale after you turn it in) isn't an up-front cost, but you'll want to know it anyway. Ask to have it included in the signed agreement.

17. If the lessor doesn't provide insurance, federal law says you must be told the type and amount of insurance necessary to fulfill any requirements of the lease.

18. What are the warranties, and what must you do for preventive maintenance to keep the warranty coverage in effect?

19. What are the cancellation penalties if you don't want to keep the car for the duration of the lease? The federal Consumer Leasing Act (CLA) requires the lessor to tell you under what circumstances you can end the lease early, and at what cost.

20. If you don't owe any money at the end of the leasing agreement, federal law says that you should get the security deposit back.

21. When the lease includes the option to purchase at the end of the leasing term, it may be for "fair market value," but according to the CLA, you must be told the purchase price before the lease is signed.

22. Don't assume that you have an automatic purchase option. If it's not in the contract and you choose to buy, the purchase will have to be an entirely separate negotiation.

23. If you get the car for business, leasing may provide certain tax benefits. Discuss them with your accountant or tax adviser.

24. If you have complaints, contact your local Better Business Bureau, your state or city department of consumer affairs, your state department of motor vehicles, or the National Vehicle Leasing Association, P.O. Box 34579, Los Angeles, CA 90034-0579, 310-838-3170, FAX 310-838-3160, for guidance, procedures, and referrals.

25. If you have evidence of a pattern of unfair or deceptive practices relating to car leasing, report it to the Federal Trade Commission, Credit Practices Division, Washington, DC 20580 (202-326-3758), or contact your nearest FTC regional office.

When You Buy a Lemon

1. Read your owner's manual and/or warranty book. Check for procedures and addresses and phone numbers of the offices to contact with complaints.

2. When you buy a car, you must research, research, research. From the moment you own the car, you must document, document, document. Write down any promises that are given orally.

Who gave them, and under what circumstances? Keep a record of repairs: what they cost, what was repaired. Was it the same thing over and over?

3. What expenses were generated by the vehicle's defect—injuries, towing, leasing another car? And for how long did you have to make alternate transportation arrangements as a result?

4. Some repairs are covered by "secret warranties," but you never know it because you're never told. Manufacturers' secret warranties or "goodwill adjustments" authorize dealers to make free repairs when customers bring in a car complaining about a defect that the manufacturer and dealer know to be common in that particular model.

5. Several states are considering legislation that would require direct disclosure of goodwill adjustments *to car owners,* and reimbursement if the car owner has already been charged for repairs.

6. To find out if your state has such a law, contact the state attorney general (see the government listings for your state in your phone directory). You can also ask the dealer, "Is this covered by a goodwill adjustment?" Or you can contact the Center for Auto Safety (CAS) for information on current goodwill adjustments.

7. The Center for Auto Safety, 2001 S Street, N.W., Washington, DC 20009 (202-328-7700), is a national nonprofit consumer organization that works to reduce the deaths and injuries from automobile accidents through safer design of vehicles and highways.

8. The Center for Auto Safety publishes numerous worthwhile periodicals, including *Lemon Times,* as well as reports and information on vehicle safety and quality, auto defects, highway safety, and consumer action.

9. Inquire from the CAS whether you can get a copy of *The Lemon Book* with a contribution of $30 or more to its ongoing efforts on behalf of consumers.

10. *The Lemon Book,* by Ralph Nader and Clarence Ditlow, explains legal remedies for lemon owners and lists state-by-state lemon laws. It should also be available through libraries and bookstores.

11. If you have a problem, first try to work it out with the service manager at the dealership, then with the dealer. If your attempts fail, contact a regional or national office of the manufacturer. The list below is adopted from one provided courtesy of the United States Office of Consumer Affairs.

Acura

Customer Relations Department
1919 Torrance Boulevard
Torrance, CA 90501-2746
1-800-382-2238

Alfa-Romeo Distributors of North America, Inc.

Customer Service Manager
8259 Exchange Drive
P.O. Box 598026
Orlando, FL 32859-8026
407-856-5000

American Honda Motor Company, Inc.

California:
Western Zone
Customer Relations Department
700 Van Ness Boulevard
Torrance, CA 90509-2260
213-781-4565

Utah, Arizona, Colorado, New Mexico, Nebraska, Kansas, Oklahoma, Nevada, Texas (El Paso):
West Central Zone
Customer Relations Department
1600 South Abilene Street, Suite D
Aurora, CO 80012-5815
303-696-3935

Maine, Vermont, New Hampshire, New York State (excluding NY City—its five boroughs—Long Island, Westchester County), Connecticut (excluding Fairfield County), Massachusetts, Rhode Island:
New England Zone
Customer Relations Department
555 Old County Road
Windsor Locks, CT 06096-0465
203-623-3310

Tennessee, Alabama, Georgia, Florida:
Southeastern Zone
Customer Relations Department
1500 Morrison Parkway
Alpharetta, GA 30201-2199

404-442-2045 (collect calls
accepted)

*Minnesota, Iowa, Missouri, Wis-
consin, Illinois, Michigan (Upper
Peninsula):*
North Central Zone
Customer Relations Department
601 Campus Drive, Suite A-9
Arlington Heights, IL 60004-1407
708-870-5600

*West Virginia, Maryland, Virginia,
North Carolina, South Carolina,
District of Columbia:*
Mid-Atlantic Zone Office
Customer Relations Department
902 Wind River Lane, Suite 200
Gaithersburg, MD 20878-1974
301-990-2020

*Ohio (Steubenville), West Virginia
(Wheeling), Pennsylvania, New
Jersey, Delaware, New York (NY
City—its five boroughs—Long
Island, Westchester County), Con-
necticut (Fairfield County):*
Northeast Zone
Customer Relations Department
115 Gaither Drive
Moorestown, NJ 08057-0337
609-235-5533

*Michigan (except for Upper Penin-
sula), Indiana, Ohio, Kentucky:*
Central Zone
Customer Relations Department
101 South Stanfield Road
Troy, OH 45373-8010
513-332-6250

*Washington, Oregon, Idaho, Mon-
tana, Wyoming, North Dakota,
South Dakota, Hawaii, Alaska:*
Northwest Zone
Customer Relations Department
12439 N.E. Airport Way
Portland, OR 97220-0186
503-256-0943

*Texas (excluding El Paso),
Arkansas (excluding Fayetteville,
Bentonville, Fort Smith, Jones-*

*boro), Oklahoma (Lawton, Ard-
more), Louisiana, Mississippi:*
South Central Zone
Customer Relations Department
4529 Royal Lane
Irving, TX 75063-2583
214-929-5481

Corporate office:
Consumer Affairs Department
1919 Torrance Boulevard
Torrance, CA 90501-2746
213-783-3260

American Isuzu Motors, Inc.

California:
Regional Customer Relations
  Manager
One Autry Street
Irvine, CA 92718-2785
714-770-2626

*Alabama, Florida, Georgia,
Mississippi, North Carolina,
South Carolina:*
Southeast Region
Regional Customer Relations
  Manager
205 Hembree Park Drive
P.O. Box 6250
Roswell, GA 30076
404-475-1995

*Illinois, Indiana, Iowa, Michigan,
Minnesota, Missouri, North
Dakota, Ohio, Wisconsin:*
Central Region
Regional Customer Relations
  Manager
1830 Jarvis Avenue
Elk Grove Village, IL 60007
708-952-8111

*Connecticut, Maine, Massachusetts,
New Hampshire, New Jersey (north
of Toms River), New York, Rhode
Island, Vermont:*
Northeast Region
Regional Customer Relations
  Manager
156 Ludlow Avenue

P.O. Box 965
Northvale, NJ 07647-0965
201-784-1414

*Arizona, Arkansas, Kansas,
Louisiana, Nevada (southern),
New Mexico, Oklahoma, Texas:*
Southwest Region
Regional Customer Relations
  Manager
1150 Isuzu Parkway
Grand Prairie, TX 75050
214-647-2911

*Alaska, Hawaii, Idaho, Montana,
Nevada (northern), Oregon, Utah,
Washington, Wyoming, Colorado,
Nebraska, South Dakota:*
Northwest Region
Regional Customer Relations
  Manager
8727 148th Avenue, N.E.
Redmond, WA 98052
206-881-0203

*New Jersey (south of Toms River),
Pennsylvania, Maryland, Delaware,
Kentucky, Tennessee, Virginia,
West Virginia:*
Regional Customer Relations
  Manager
1 Isuzu Way
Glen Burnie, MD 21061
301-761-2121

Headquarters:
13181 Crossroads Parkway North
P.O. Box 2480
City of Industry, CA 91746-0480
213-699-0500
1-800-255-6727

American Motors Corporation: see Chrysler Motors Corporation

American Suzuki Motor Corporation

Attn: Customer Relations
  Department

3251 E. Imperial Highway
Brea, CA 92621-6722
Automobiles:
1-800-877-6900, ext. 445
Motorcycles:
714-996-7040, ext. 380

Audi of America, Inc.

Connecticut, New Jersey,
New York:
World-Wide Volkswagen Corp.
Director, Corporate Service
Greenbush Road
Orangeburg, NY 10962
914-578-5000

Corporate office (and all other
states):
Audi of America, Inc.
Consumer Relations Manager
888 West Big Beaver Road
Troy, MI 48007-3951
1-800-822-AUDI

BMW of North America, Inc.

Arizona, California, Nevada, Ore-
gon, Washington, Montana, Idaho,
Alaska, Hawaii, Colorado, Utah,
New Mexico, Wyoming, Texas
(El Paso):
Western Region
Customer Relations Manager
12541 Beatrice Street
P.O. Box 66916
Los Angeles, CA 90066
213-574-7300

Tennessee, North Carolina, Virginia
(except northern), Mississippi,
Alabama, Georgia, Florida, South
Carolina, Louisiana, Oklahoma,
Arkansas, Texas (except El Paso):
Southern Region
Customer Relations Manager
1280 Hightower Trail
Atlanta, GA 30350-2977
404-552-3800

North Dakota, South Dakota, Min-
nesota, Wisconsin, Iowa, Illinois,
Michigan, Indiana, Ohio, Kentucky,

Kansas, Missouri, Nebraska:
Central Region
Customer Relations Manager
498 East Commerce Drive
Schaumburg, IL 60173
708-310-2700

Connecticut, Maine, Massachusetts,
New Hampshire, New Jersey, New
York, Rhode Island, Vermont,
Washington, D.C., Virginia (north-
ern), West Virginia, Delaware,
Maryland, Pennsylvania:
Eastern Region
Customer Relations Manager
BMW Plaza
Montvale, NJ 07645
201-573-2100

Corporate office:
National Customer Relations
   Manager
P.O. Box 1227
Westwood, NJ 07675-1227
201-307-4000

Chrysler Motors Corporation

Phoenix Zone office:
Customer Relations Manager
11811 N. Tatum Boulevard,
   Suite 4025
Phoenix, AZ 85028
602-953-6899

Los Angeles Zone office:
Customer Relations Manager
P.O. Box 14112
Orange, CA 92668-4600
714-565-5111

San Francisco Zone office:
Customer Relations Manager
P.O. Box 5009
Pleasanton, CA 94566-0509
415-463-1770

Denver Zone office:
Customer Relations Manager
P.O. Box 39006
Denver, CO 80239
303-373-8888

Orlando Zone office:
Customer Relations Manager
8000 South Orange Blossom Trail
Orlando, FL 32809
407-352-7402

Atlanta Zone office:
Customer Relations Manager
900 Circle 75 Parkway, Suite 1600
Atlanta, GA 30339
404-953-8880

Chicago Zone office:
Customer Relations Manager
650 Warrenville Road, Suite 502
Lisle, IL 60532
708-515-2450

Kansas City Zone office:
Customer Relations Manager
P.O. Box 25668
Overland Park, KS 66225-5668
913-469-3090

New Orleans Zone office:
Customer Relations Manager
P.O. Box 157
Metairie, LA 70004
504-838-8788

Washington, DC Zone office:
Customer Relations Manager
P.O. Box 1900
Bowie, MD 20716
301-464-4040

Boston Zone office:
Customer Relations Manager
550 Forbes Boulevard
Mansfield, MA 02048-2038
508-261-2299

Detroit Zone office:
Customer Relations Manager
P.O. Box 3000
Troy, MI 48007-3000
313-952-1300

Minneapolis Zone office:
Customer Relations Manager
P.O. Box 1231
Minneapolis, MN 55440
612-553-2546

St. Louis Zone office:
Customer Relations Manager
P.O. Box 278
Hazelwood, MO 63042
314-895-0731

Syracuse Zone office:
Customer Relations Manager
P.O. Box 603
Dewitt, NY 13214-0603
315-445-6941

New York Zone office:
Customer Relations Manager
500 Route 303
Tappan, NY 10983-1592
914-359-0110

Charlotte Zone office:
Customer Relations Manager
4944 Parkway Plaza Boulevard,
  Suite 470
Charlotte, NC 28217
704-357-7065

Cincinnati Zone office:
Customer Relations Manager
P.O. Box 41902
Cincinnati, OH 45241
513-530-1500

Portland Zone office:
Customer Relations Manager
P.O. Box 744
Beaverton, OR 97075
503-526-5555

Philadelphia Zone office:
Customer Relations Manager
Valley Brook Corporate Center
101 Linden Wood Drive, Suite 320
Malvern, PA 19355
215-251-2990

Pittsburgh Zone office:
Customer Relations Manager
Penn Center West 3, Suite 420
Pittsburgh, PA 15276
412-788-6622

Memphis Zone office:
Customer Relations Manager
P.O. Box 18008
Memphis, TN 38181-0008
901-797-3870

Dallas Zone office:
Customer Relations Manager
P.O. Box 110162
Carrollton, TX 75011-0162
214-242-8462

Houston Zone office:
Customer Relations Manager
363 North Sam Houston Parkway
East, Suite 590
Houston, TX 77060-2405
713-820-7062

Milwaukee Zone office:
Customer Relations Manager
445 South Moorland Road,
  Suite 470
Brookfield, WI 53005
414-797-3750

Corporate office:
National Owner Relations Manager
P.O. Box 1086
Detroit, MI 48288-1086
1-800-992-1997 (toll free)

Ferrari North America, Inc.

Corporate office:
Director of Service and Parts
250 Sylvan Avenue
Englewood Cliffs, NJ 07632
201-816-2650

Ford Motor Company

Customer Relations Manager
300 Renaissance Center
P.O. Box 43360
Detroit, MI 48243
1-800-392-3673 (all makes)
1-800-521-4140 (Lincoln and
  Merkur only)
1-800-241-3673 (towing and dealer
  location service)
1-800-232-5952 (TDD)

General Motors Corporation

Chevrolet/Geo Motor Division
General Motors Corporation
Customer Assistance Center
P.O. Box 7047
Troy, MI 48007-7047
1-800-222-1020
1-800-TDD-CHEV (TDD)

Pontiac Division
General Motors Corporation
Customer Assistance Center
One Pontiac Plaza
Pontiac, MI 48340-2952
1-800-762-2737
1-800-TDD-PONT (TDD)

Oldsmobile Division
General Motors Corporation
Customer Assistance Network
P.O. Box 30095
Lansing, MI 48909-7595
1-800-442-6537
1-800-TDD-OLDS (TDD)

Buick Motor Division
General Motors Corporation
Customer Assistance Center
902 East Hamilton Avenue
Flint, MI 48550
1-800-521-7300
1-800-TD-BUICK (TDD)

Cadillac Motor Car Division
General Motors Corporation
Consumer Relations Center
2860 Clark Street
Detroit, MI 48232
1-800-458-8006
1-800-TDD-CMCC (TDD)

GMC Truck Division
General Motors Corporation
Customer Service Department
Mail Code 1607-07
31 Judson Street
Pontiac, MI 48342
313-456-4547
1-800-TDD-TKTD (TDD)

Saturn Corporation
General Motors Corporation
Saturn Assistance Center
100 Saturn Parkway
Spring Hill, TN 37174
1-800-553-6000
1-800-TDD-6000 (TDD)

GM Service Parts Operations
Director, Public Relations
6060 West Bristol Road
Flint, MI 48554-2110
313-635-5412

Honda: see American Honda Motor Company, Inc.

Hyundai Motor America

Customer Service
10550 Talbert Avenue
P.O. Box 20850
Fountain Valley, CA 92728-0850
1-800-633-5151

Isuzu: see American Isuzu

Jaguar Cars, Inc.

Alaska, Arizona, California, Colorado, Hawaii, Idaho, Montana, Nevada, New Mexico, Oregon, Utah, Washington, Wyoming, Texas (El Paso):
Western Zone
Customer Relations Manager
422 Valley Drive
Brisbane, CA 94005
415-467-9402

All other states: **Eastern Zone**
Customer Relations Manager
555 MacArthur Boulevard
Mahwah, NJ 07430-2327
201-818-8500

Jeep/Eagle: see Chrysler Motors Corporation

Mazda Motor of America, Inc.

Corporate headquarters:
Customer Relations Manager
P.O. Box 19734
Irvine, CA 92718
1-800-222-5500

Mercedes-Benz of North America, Inc.

National headquarters:
1 Mercedes Drive
Montvale, NJ 07645-0350
201-573-0600 (owner service)

North Central Region office:
3333 Charles Street
Franklin Park, IL 60131-1469

Northeast Region office:
Baltimore Commons Business Park
1300 Mercedes Drive (2nd Floor)
Hanover, MD 21076-0348

Southern Region office:
8813 Western Way
Jacksonville, FL 32245-7604

Western Region office:
6357 Sunset Boulevard
Hollywood, CA 90093-0637

Mitsubishi Motor Sales of America, Inc.

Corporate office:
National Consumer Relations
  Manager
6400 West Katella Avenue
Cypress, CA 90630-0064
1-800-222-0037

Nissan Motor Corporation in USA

P.O. Box 191
Gardena, CA 90248-0191
1-800-647-7261 (all consumer
  inquiries)

Peugeot Motors of America, Inc.

National Customer Relations
  Manager
P.O. Box 607
One Peugeot Plaza
Lyndhurst, NJ 07071-3498
201-935-8400
1-800-345-5549

Porsche Cars North America, Inc.

Customer Relations Manager
100 West Liberty Street
P.O. Box 30911
Reno, NV 89520-3911
702-348-3154

Saab Cars USA, Inc.

National Consumer Relations
P.O. Box 697
Orange, CT 06477
203-795-5671
1-800-955-9007

Subaru of America

Arizona, California, Nevada:
Owner Service Manager
Western Region
12 Whatney Drive
Irvine, CA 92718-2895
714-951-6592

Alabama, Georgia, North Carolina, South Carolina, Florida, Tennessee, West Virginia, Virginia, Maryland, Washington, D.C.:
Owner Service Manager
Southeast Region
220 The Bluffs
Austell, GA 30001
404-732-3200

Illinois, Indiana, Iowa, Kentucky, Michigan, Minnesota, Missouri, Ohio, Wisconsin:
Owner Service Manager
Mid-America Region
301 Mitchell Court

Addison, IL 60101
312-953-1188

Maine, Vermont, New Hampshire,
Massachusetts, Rhode Island,
Connecticut:
Subaru of New England, Inc.
Customer Relations Manager
95 Morse Street
Norwood, MA 02062
617-769-5100

Southern New Jersey, Pennsylvania,
Delaware:
Customer Relations Manager
Penn Jersey Region
1504 Glen Avenue
Moorestown, NJ 08057
609-234-7600

New York, northern New Jersey:
Customer Relations Manager
Subaru Distributors Corporation
6 Ramland Road
Orangeburg, NY 10962
914-359-2500

Hawaii:
Schuman-Carriage Co. Inc.
1234 South Beretania Street
P.O. Box 2420
Honolulu, HI 96804
808-533-6211

Alaska, Idaho, Montana, Nebraska,
Oregon, Utah, Washington, North
Dakota, South Dakota, Wyoming:

Owner Service Manager
Northwest Region
8040 East 33rd Drive
Portland, OR 97211
1-800-878-6677

Arkansas, Colorado, Kansas, New
Mexico, Mississippi, Oklahoma,
Texas:
Owner Service Manager
Southwest Region
1500 East 39th Avenue
Aurora, CO 80011
303-373-8895

Corporate office:
Owner Service Department
P.O. Box 6000
Cherry Hill, NJ 08034-6000
609-488-3278

Toyota Motor Sales USA, Inc.

Customer Assistance Center
Department A404
19001 South Western Avenue
Torrance, CA 90509
1-800-331-4331

Volkswagen United States, Inc.

Connecticut, New Jersey,
New York:
World-Wide Volkswagen, Inc.
Director of Corporation Service

Greenbush Road
Orangeburg, NY 10962
914-578-5000
1-800-822-8987

For all other locations:
Volkswagen United States, Inc.
Consumer Relations
888 West Big Beaver
Troy, MI 48007
General assistance and customer
relations:
1-800-822-8987
Replacement and repurchase
assistance:
1-800-955-5100

Volvo Cars of North America

Corporate office:
Operations Manager
15 Volvo Drive, Building D
P.O. Box 914
Rockleigh, NJ 07647-0914
201-767-4737

Yugo America, Inc.

Director, Customer Services
120 Pleasant Avenue
P.O. Box 730
Upper Saddle River, NJ 07458-0730
201-825-4600
1-800-872-9846

12. If the regional and national offices don't meet your needs, consider a third-party dispute resolution program such as those in the following list.

For Hyundai, Lexus, Porsche,
Subaru, Toyota:
American Automobile
    Association's Autosolve
1000 AAA Drive
Heathrow, FL 32746
1-800-477-6583

For Acura, Audi, General Motors
and its divisions, Honda, Infiniti,
Isuzu, Nissan, Saab, Sterling,
Volkswagen:
Better Business Bureau AutoLine
4200 Wilson Blvd.
Arlington, VA 22203-1804
1-800-955-5100

For BMW, Honda, Isuzu, Jaguar,
Mazda, Mitsubishi, Nissan, Rolls-
Royce, Saab, Volvo:
National Automobile Dealers
    Association Autocap
8400 Westpark Drive
MacLean, VA 22102
1-800-544-6232

13. Some manufacturers offer noncertified arbitration programs. Check with your state or city department of consumer protection or state attorney general's office to determine whether the program you've been offered is certified, and what rights of recourse you may forfeit if you opt for this form of arbitration.

14. The Better Business Bureau may help, possibly by referring you to arbitration that is binding on the manufacturer but not on you, giving you the option to accept or try elsewhere.

15. Many states have "lemon laws" to protect consumers against manufacturing defects in automobiles. Basically, these provide that if repairs aren't made in a stipulated amount of time, or if the car is out of commission for thirty days because of a combination of defects, the manufacturer must replace the car or refund your money. Contact your state attorney general's office to determine what laws apply in your case.

16. Lemon laws may also apply to leased vehicles, commercial vehicles, and even motorcycles.

17. If your complaint involves a warranty that's being ignored, you can consult the Federal Trade Commission, 6th Street and Pennsylvania Avenue, N.W., Washington, DC 20580.

18. Report any defect you discover to Auto Safety Hotline, 1-800-424-9393, or 1-800-424-9153 for people who are hearing-impaired, or 202-366-0123 in Washington, DC. This is precisely the sort of complaint that can lead to free authorized repair or recall.

19. If your complaint still hasn't been resolved, contact your state or city department of consumer affairs and state attorney general. CC your senators and congressman, as well as the manufacturer (customer service department, president, chairman of the board) and the dealership.

20. If you believe the defect is significant and endangers a large number of people who bought the same make and model, report it to your state department of motor vehicles, which may have the power to suspend or revoke the manufacturer's license to sell in your state. CC the Center for Auto Safety (2001 S Street, N.W., Washington, DC 20009), your state's department of consumer affairs, the dealership, and the president and chairman of the board of the manufacturing company.

21. You may want to organize fellow car owners who share your complaint. In one instance, motorists who were dissatisfied with peeling paint jobs formed weekend motorcades past area dealerships.

22. The person who organized these motorcades also pulled together some 300 letters and forwarded them all at once to the manufacturer, to make certain they were noticed.

23. For a helpful booklet about establishing local auto complaint groups, contact the Center for Auto Safety.

24. Meanwhile, consider going to court. If you go to small-claims court, be prepared to substantiate the defect with evidence such as repair bills, letters, witnesses, photos, a sworn statement from a qualified mechanic stating that the defect was in manufacture and not because you drove the car improperly, etc.

25. If a dealership or manufacturer is behaving unethically, unfairly, or illegally and a large number of buyers are involved, speak to an attorney about the possibility of a class-action suit. (For more information about class-action suits, see page 15.) Whether or not the case goes to trial, the suit is unlikely to be ignored.

Used Cars

1. The quality of the used car you buy depends to a large degree on the reputation and reliability of the used car dealer. Talk to people who have purchased from the lot. Contact the Better Business Bureau, the Chamber of Commerce, or your state or city department of consumer affairs for the dealer's history of complaints and how they were resolved. Sometimes your state department of motor vehicles can provide this information.

2. Ask how long the company has been in business under its present name, and whether it subscribes to binding arbitration.

3. Some states have used car lemon laws. For instance, dealers may have to certify that a car is in safe condition, is able to render adequate service, and has passed a state inspection. Contact your city or state department of consumer affairs to learn what laws apply where you live.

4. To decide on a make and model, you can consult the publications and services mentioned at the beginning of this chapter under the head "Whether You Buy or Lease."

5. *Edmund's Used Car Guide* and *The Consumer's Guide to Used Cars* list going prices, and are generally available at newsstands.

6. The Buyer's Guide, displayed in the window of a used car sold by a dealer, explains who must pay for repairs after purchase, as well as whether the car has a warranty, what the warranty covers, and whether a service contract is offered.

7. Mobile diagnostic services inspect and appraise used cars. One such service, Car Checkers, runs approximately 3,000 tests with equipment from a computerized van. Consult your telephone directory or phone the 800 numbers information to find out if this company operates in your area.

8. Many lending institutions that finance loans for used cars will reimburse the cost of an inspection. If you're taking out a loan to buy the car, ask.

9. If you get a no, try to negotiate a yes.

10. Some rudimentary inspections are obvious, such as whether the interior of the car seems worn, whether all the instruments and accessories work, and whether the odometer has logged too many miles. But also consider that if the odometer is very low, it may mean the car didn't go far for a reason. Or it may mean the odometer was reset.

11. Under federal law, an odometer can't be reset for the purpose of misrepresenting the car's mileage. If the numbers are changed because the odometer is a replacement, they must be adjusted to reflect true mileage. If they can't be adjusted, the dealer must advise you in writing, with a prominently posted sticker, of the correct mileage.

12. In any written statement concerning the odometer, the dealer must confirm that he or she

knows the law and his or her own liability under the law if the information you were given isn't true.

13. Some state or city departments of consumer affairs can give you the names of the car's previous owners, and you can ask them about the history of the car, including its mileage.

14. Test-drive the car yourself. If you notice small problems that require repair, either get the dealer's written promise that the repairs will be made or negotiate a new price based on deduction of the cost of repairs.

15. Even if you have to pay for the service, ask a trusted mechanic to inspect the car before you buy it.

16. Some used cars are vehicles that were recalled. Your state or city department of consumer affairs or state attorney general's office can tell you what used car dealers must do before selling recalled automobiles in your state. Find out if they have to post notice that the car has been recalled. Must they repair it before reselling it?

17. You may also phone the National Highway Traffic Safety Administration (NHTSA), 1-800-424-9393, or ask the dealer for a copy of the booklet *Motor Vehicle Safety Defect Campaigns,* a listing of recalled makes and models.

18. If you request it, the NHTSA can send you a postcard to complete and send to the manufacturer. The manufacturer can then tell you whether the actual car you have in mind has been repaired and, if it hasn't, what you can do to have the work done.

19. In the event of a dispute, your state or city department of consumer affairs may mediate between you and the dealer, hold a license hearing, impose fines on the dealer, or suspend or revoke the dealer's license, depending on the severity of your grievance.

20. You may be able to sue in small-claims court.

21. Be sure you get the car's title, registration, and bill of sale and copies of all other financial transaction papers needed to register the car in your name.

22. To confirm that the car isn't stolen, compare the VIN (Vehicle Identification Number) on the title with the VIN on the car's dashboard. If you have reason to be suspicious, have the local police department run a check on the VIN.

Repairs

1. People who drive are drivers most of their lives, so any time spent in learning about their cars is time well spent. Your best defense against unethical repair shops is to read your owner's manual, take an adult education course in basic automotive mechanics, and know your automobile.

2. Organizations such as the Car Care Council, One Grande Lake Drive, Port Clinton, OH 43452, 419-734-5343, provide instructive material on performance, preventive maintenance, safety, fuel conservation, and air quality. Although the CCC doesn't handle service problems, what you learn might easily prolong the life of your car.

3. To select a repair shop, ask friends and associates for recommendations.

4. Phone the Chamber of Commerce, Better Business Bureau, or your state or city department of consumer affairs to determine whether any complaints have been lodged against the shop and how they were settled.

5. Know what your state laws, licenses, and registrations require from repair shops. (Find out with a phone call to your state department of motor vehicles.) Depending on the jurisdiction, repair shops may have to provide estimates, limit themselves to needed repairs unless otherwise requested, and itemize bills.

6. In some states, shops don't have to comply unless they're specifically asked by a customer in advance. For instance, they won't be bound by an estimate, or won't have to return replaced parts, unless you raise the issue before agreeing to terms.

7. When you're up against argumentative or incompetent personnel, it's definitely in your favor to be able to cite the law. This may be enough to sway mechanics and service managers. If it isn't, you can report violations.

8. You might consider testing the shop on a minor repair job before going in with a big one. Do all the things you'll want to do in the future: ask questions, keep asking until inquiries can be answered in language you understand, request an estimate, examine replaced parts, etc., and decide whether you're happy with the results or whether you'll want to go elsewhere next time. This is not a fail-safe assessment of attitude and honesty, but if the shop does fail the test, you'll know better next time.

9. Ask if the shop often services your make and model, and whether the technicians are familiar with the type of repair you need. If possible, get it in writing.

10. Check to see whether company policies are posted.

11. Any certification and training is better than none at all, and in this spirit, look at the walls to see what diplomas, community awards, certificates, AAA-Approved Auto Repair status, ASE (National Institute for Automotive Service Excellence) certifications, and membership documents are posted.

12. Realize that such documents may not prove much. For instance, certificates may be posted for employees who won't be around to work on your car, so note and compare the names of the recipients as well as the issuers.

13. Additionally, certificates mean that particular mechanics have passed particular courses, but not necessarily that they consistently and ethically apply the skills they learned, or that those skills relate to your repair job.

14. If a mechanic or garage acts unethically, you might try reporting it to the issuer of a diploma or certificate, but the response may be one of total unconcern.

15. A better course of action might to be report abuses to your state department of motor vehicles, which regulates repair shops.

16. As noted above, your best defense is to be informed. And document, document, document. If you're beginning to notice a problem with your car, journal it. Keep records of when the problem seems to occur, whether it's constant or periodic, and what conditions appear to induce it.

17. Be prepared to detail these to the shop or, better yet, write them down and present them when you take your car in for servicing. This way, you can be sure the mechanic remembers everything you want to convey, and you can prove later that you did indeed convey everything you claim you did.

18. If the needed repair is visual, take a photograph. It may be very handy to have later on—particularly if there's a disagreement at the time of billing as to what needed to be done.

19. Don't expect an immediate estimate. On the other hand, insist that you be contacted when an estimate is ready, and that work not begin at any price until you've authorized it. Leave a phone number where you can be reached.

20. You're entitled to ask for detailed descriptions of what the estimate entails and for a breakdown of the costs involved, as well as how much time is needed and at what rate. Have the garage confirm that the estimate is the price, and not simply a "guesstimate" that may be exceeded.

21. Ask for a guarantee of the work in writing. What does the guarantee mean? If the problem recurs, who will be responsible for correcting it? For how long, and under what circumstances?

22. The Automotive Service Association (ASA) promotes a written Code of Ethics to which members are pledged to adhere. ASA members should, for instance, furnish an itemized invoice for fairly priced parts and services, clearly identify any used or remanufactured parts, and permit the consumer (upon request) to examine replaced parts.

23. Some ASA member shops belong to a nationwide collision limited warranty program, which enables customers dissatisfied with body repairs performed at one ASA shop to take the vehicle to another participating shop anywhere in the United States. According to the ASA, "The warranty will be honored and vehicle repairs will be made to the customer's satisfaction at no additional charge."

24. Member shops post signs with an ASA logo. For more information, call the ASA at 1-800-ASA-SHOP.

25. Before you take a long trip, you may want to have a trusted local garage go over the car. Otherwise, you may find yourself at the mercy of a mechanic in a strange town who takes advantage of your desperation and distant address.

26. If you do have to depend on an unknown garage far from home, try to be selective. If you have an option, look for the diplomas, the certificates, the indications of association membership.

27. If possible, stay by the car while the work is done. If you're away from home, you can offer the excuse that without your car, you have no place else to go. Watch to see what is in fact done, and be sure that further damage isn't deliberately inflicted so that you can be charged for more extensive repairs.

28. Are you on vacation? Is your camera or camcorder handy? Be prepared to photograph behavior that you consider suspicious, and to forward the pictures later to the Better Business Bureau, the Chamber of Commerce, the appropriate state or city department of consumer affairs, and the state department of motor vehicles and attorney general's office.

29. Before you leave, be sure to get a detailed invoice, with the name and address of the garage and the mechanic. If a part was allegedly replaced, ask to take the part with you.

30. If you have any doubts about the mechanic's reliability, take your car to your local trusted garage when you get home. Show the "damaged" parts. Ask for your own mechanic's observations.

31. If you have a complaint against a local or out-of-town shop, first try to settle it with the service manager or owner. Explain your problem and why you feel cheated.

32. If possible, provide documentation—bills, your record of conversations, and so on. These will substantiate your complaint and also will indicate that you can be a tough adversary if forced to pursue the matter with outside agencies.

33. If the person you complain to doesn't please you—or promises to please you at a later time—follow up with a letter. CC the Better Business Bureau, the Chamber of Commerce, the appropriate state or city department of consumer affairs, and the state department of motor vehicles.

34. Any evidence of a padded bill should be reported right away to the same parties, with the same CCs.

35. Ask the Better Business Bureau, the Chamber of Commerce, and the state or city department of consumer affairs about the avenues open to you—such as investigation, mediation, and arbitration—and explore any recourse available through the department of motor vehicles.

36. Complaints against repair shops generally have to be reported within a certain time frame, or before the car is driven a stated distance.

37. Complaints may be mediated by the department, investigated by an on-site inspection, or resolved by a formal hearing.

38. The state department of motor vehicles may order restitution to you, fine the shop, or suspend or revoke the shop's registration or license. If you paid for the repair by credit card, send a letter and photocopies of documentation to your card carrier and request a credit or chargeback.

▲ *See also* CAR RENTAL; CREDIT CARDS.

Bad Debts

(HOW TO COLLECT)

Consumerism is a two-way street. When you are the one doing the selling, in the course of your business or professional life, or when you run an ad in the paper to sell a boat or a sofa, you expect to be treated fairly.

If as a seller you deliberately abuse a deal, it'll serve you right if your victim has read this book. But nothing says you have to consent to being victimized if the tables are turned. You do have defenses when buyers won't pay.

For a Simple Transaction

1. Be cautious about accepting a personal check unless you know the individual.

2. If you don't know the person, asking for a name and address can be helpful. But the name and address could be faked, or you might simply be ignored when you follow up after the check has bounced.

3. If the person doesn't have enough cash, you might offer to wait until the next day for the person to return with cash (or a certified check or money order).

4. If you part with merchandise on any understanding whatsoever of a balance due, make absolutely certain to have it in writing and signed by the other person. This way, if the person defaults, you can prove your right to full payment.

5. It's better if you specify a due date.

If You're in Business

1. Be up on federal, state, and municipal commercial and consumer law. Guessing can cost you a bundle.

2. If you join the Chamber of Commerce, you and fellow members can compare notes on laws, rulings, and the reliability of other members of the business community.

3. If you're part of a chain, be informed of headquarters' policies, promotions, and current advertising gimmicks.

4. If you've got a store, post your policies.

5. Specific contracts and agreements are valuable in any instance when your customer can refuse to pay after the fact. This goes for a toaster that's returned, or work you may have done as a painter, as a home typist, or in some other form of self-employment.

6. Look into credit insurance. If another company owes you money and the company goes bankrupt, your very best collection efforts may not be able to wring blood out of a stone. But insurance might cover you, and banks may be inclined to negotiate better loans with you if you can show you have some guarantee on your receivables.

7. Offer discounts for timely payments.

8. If much of your business involves credit management, subscribe to any of several industry-wide credit and collection publications, or borrow them from the library.

9. If you plan to extend credit and if you deal in volume, you may want to use a credit reporting bureau. Such bureaus maintain data banks that essentially do your research for you. Equifax, Trans Union, and TRW provide credit histories for a fee, as do regional offices of bureaus (look in the business listings under "Credit Reporting Bureaus" or "Agencies," or a similar heading).

If You Have to Collect

1. Check with customer service personnel first. If the customer is disputing a bill, be aware of the history of the dispute before you call or write.

2. Don't delay too long, and don't run a tab. The larger the amount gets, the more unwilling your client or customer will be to pay it.

3. If you speak to the client or customer, be prepared for the usual responses and realize that they may very well be true. The check *may* be in the mail, or the bill *may* never have been received.

4. Respond in kind. If the check was sent, ask when it went out, what was its number and date, and what address it was mailed to. If no bill was received, confirm the customer's name and address and other relevant data.

5. If the check is "in the works," when will it be cut, and when will it be sent? What's the usual payment procedure and cycle? Inventive bookkeepers sometimes cite a different cycle each time you call. If you detect inconsistencies, say so.

6. If you're dealing with a company whose representative assures you that the check will go out on a specific day, you may want to add, with extreme delicacy and courtesy, "I realize that your boss may require you to say this, but do you realize that you've now given me your personal word that it's true? If all I'm getting is a false sense of security, I'd appreciate your leveling with me. You'll actually be compounding the damage if you're not telling me the truth."

7. Make notes of any conversations you have: date, time, name of the person you spoke to, and any promises that were made.

8. Be fair. If the person or company can't pay, try to come to an arrangement.

9. If the person is uncooperative, explain thoughtfully and *within the law* what the person is up against. *Don't* make vicious threats. But you may suggest that you're investigating your options, such as turning the account over to a collection agency and reporting the individual to various national credit reporting bureaus.

10. Before enlisting a collection agency, check its reputation with the Better Business Bureau, the Chamber of Commerce, and your state or city department of consumer affairs. If your state licenses agencies, is this one licensed? If not, why not? Unsavory tactics committed in your name can hurt your professional reputation. If the agency does collect, it may charge 25–50 percent of the recovered debt.

11. If the individual or firm that owes you must be licensed by the state, find out (from the BBB, Chamber of Commerce, or state or city department of consumer affairs) whether your complaint is grounds for investigation or for having the license revoked.

12. If a business has stiffed you, report it to the Better Business Bureau, the Chamber of Commerce, and the state or city department of consumer affairs. If your quarrel is with a professional person, also contact the individual's professional association.

13. Any of these may be able to direct you to avenues of arbitration or mediation. The Legal Aid Society (listed in many phone directories) can offer assistance or, at the very least, advice.

14. If you take the matter to small-claims court, you may win, but then it's generally up to you to see to collection.

15. An attorney may be able to sue on your behalf, or suggest persuasive approaches short of a suit (such as a strongly worded letter on the attorney's stationery).

16. Find out what coverage, if any, your insurance might provide.

17. If you can't collect on the debt, ask your accountant whether you can obtain tax relief by listing it as a bad debt.

18. If you're considering deducting a bad debt from your taxable income, realize that you should be able to substantiate your claim with proof that the debt is worthless, and with documentation of the steps you've taken to collect.

19. A sometimes successful ploy when small businesses owe you money is to phone or write in the early part of the year, using words such as these: "I have established with repeated calls and letters to your offices that you do not intend to make good on your debt to me in the amount of [sum owed], for [goods sold, service performed, etc.] This letter is to advise you that if I do not receive the full amount by [date], my accountant will report it as a bad debt on my upcoming tax returns. I bring this to your attention because you may be investigated by tax authorities in their efforts to confirm the accuracy of my deduction." If the company's finances are at all shaky, its books may not be in the best of shape. For instance, it may have reported your bill as paid for tax purposes. Such companies would rather write a few small checks than be slugged hard for back taxes, interest, and penalties by the tax man.

▲ *See also* BANKING; CREDIT CARDS; CREDIT RATINGS; DEBT COLLECTORS.

Banking

Banks are businesses, the same way that automobile dealerships and dry cleaners are businesses. The business of banks is to provide you with certain services in exchange for access to your money until you want it back. Sometimes they also levy a service charge. In other words, you pay them in the belief that you'll get what you pay for.

The single best strategy for getting what you pay for is to shop around. Although banks operate under the federal Uniform Commercial Code, the Federal Reserve if the bank is a member of the Federal Reserve, and other federal and state bodies, many of their policies differ. You can reconnoiter the market by checking local newspapers for articles and ads and watching bank windows for promotional posters. You can go into the bank and help yourself to flyers explaining the pitches in greater detail. You can contact your city's and state's department of consumer affairs or look in the local library for a copy of the annual bank comparison put out by the consumer affairs departments of most states. The report doesn't rate banks or evaluate their financial health, but it sets forth interest schedules, service charges, costs and types of accounts, and other items for each bank to assist consumers in making their own choices.

Additionally, the National Association of Bank Women, 7910 Woodmont Avenue, Suite 1430, Bethesda, MD 20814-3015, 301-657-8288, offers general advice on looking for a bank, approaching a loan officer, and the like.

Some Considerations

1. Banks compete by offering choices intended to look appealing to customers. Compare them *according to how you spend your money* before committing your funds.

2. One bank might offer a higher interest rate, but charge more for checks and services.

3. In comparing banks, find out how much each charges for check printing, check processing, deposits, monthly maintenance, ATM (automated teller machine) use, processing bounced checks, stopping payments, and other services you may need.

4. If interest is paid—and/or maintenance is assessed—find out if it's computed from an average monthly balance or a lowest minimum balance. If lowest minimum, you tend to lose money if your balance drops below the established limit for even a day.

5. As an alternative to paying the bank's check-printing charges, consider having checks printed by one of the outside stationery companies that advertise bargain prices for imprinted checks.

6. *But first,* find out if your bank will honor them. Speak to a bank service representative or platform officer, and if you get a yes, note the person's name for future reference.

7. Even if the person says yes, submit one unimportant check for bank processing before using a stack to pay your rent, phone bill, and taxes. This is the safest way to send up a trial balloon.

8. If the person says you can only order checks through the bank, ask why. Perhaps the bank uses a special magnetized ink, or a trademarked logo that outside printers aren't allowed to reproduce.

9. If you get a no, find out whether the objections are legitimate by phoning the state banking commission (look under the government listings for your state in your telephone directory) before giving up. Or speak to the stationery company to see if someone will argue on your behalf.

10. Find out if your bank returns your checks to you after processing them. It's cheaper for banks not to, but most often it's in your best interest to get them back.

11. If you're a senior citizen or qualify as low-income, ask whether the bank offers "lifeline" checking, which waives certain fees while assuring you basic service.

12. There are arrangements that look like checking accounts but according to law can't be called checking accounts because they're offered through other types of accounts, such as savings accounts or credit unions. They're well worth studying, but you should apply the same standards to them that you would to any other deal.

13. Banks like to offer relationship banking, which means you have several types of financial arrangement—checking, savings, CDs, mortgage—in one place. A relationship might entitle you to free checking, but study it carefully. If the checking is free but your CD draws 1 percent less than it would elsewhere, you may be losing hundreds of dollars annually.

14. You can bargain: "You mean I've got three hefty accounts with you and you're charging me a bigger maintenance charge than any other bank in town? Is there someone you can consult to try doing better on that?"

15. Get your bank's schedule for allowing you access to funds from deposited checks. (The federal Competitive Banking Equality Act of 1987 sets deadlines, but some institutions compete by trying to beat them.)

Once You Decide

1. Study the entire agreement that the bank gives you when you open the account. It will be more explicit and probably more restricting than what was spelled out by the ads and flyers. Don't sign it unless you understand and accept the terms.

2. Read all updates that arrive in the mail with your statements. They may inform you that the bank is merging, or terms have changed, or something else has occurred to modify the original agreement.

3. Review and reconcile your statements when you get them. If you spot a discrepancy, advise your bank immediately.

4. Don't stop comparing your bank with other banks. An institution can offer the best deal in town just long enough to attract new customers, then systematically hike its profits at your expense, year after year after year.

5. People occasionally start an account to be set aside for a special event—for instance, Grandma's $1,000 gift when Junior was born, stashed away to earn interest until he's ready for college. Bad idea. States have laws that entitle them to take over inactive bank accounts after a specified number of years.

6. You can keep the account active by doing something to it every so often—making a small deposit, a small withdrawal, whatever. But it may be wiser to add the money to an account where it increases your average balance, earning you higher interest in several accounts across the board.

7. If the state seizes your inactive account, you can often get it back by proving ownership. Your bank or state banking commission can tell you how to proceed.

If You Have a Complaint

1. Have your facts straight and arranged in a presentable order. Have your fully reconciled

statement, photocopies and/or letters that support your position, and the original check if a check is involved.

2. If you're confused, don't be embarrassed to say so. Don't pretend you understand terminology if you don't.

3. If you're speaking to someone who seems intent on taking advantage of your uncertainty, it's perfectly reasonable for you to say calmly, "What may seem obvious to you is brand-new to me. If I understood what you already know, perhaps I wouldn't be here today. You may deal with this a hundred times a week, but it's my money, my credit rating, and my financial well-being that we're discussing. Please put yourself in my shoes, and bear with me. If you came into my place of work, I'd realize that I had a better grasp of the intricacies of my job than you do, and I'd be patient in my efforts to help you understand them."

4. Even if a great deal of money is involved, avoid hysteria, and avoid going into a litany of past wrongs inflicted on you by the bank. Either approach will in all likelihood cause the service representative to back away (visibly or in spirit) until you can name the present problem and say what is needed to resolve it.

5. Suppose you've written a rent check and it bounces. Your bank will debit your account for a service fee, and the bank of the landlord who received your check will debit the landlord's account as well. But further suppose that your check was good, and your bank was absolutely at fault. What's your recourse?

6. Go to your bank armed with proof that the check was good, and that you've been billed to repay the service fee debited by your landlord's bank. Assuming you convince your service representative that the check had been covered, request (a) a written apology to that effect, from the bank to your landlord, with a CC to you to keep for your records; (b) a credit to your account for the full amount of service charges debited by your bank; (c) a credit to your account, or another form of payment, to reimburse you for the debit the landlord has passed on to you.

7. Most banks will agree to (a) and (b) if they've been in error, but (c) may require a little persuasion. Stick to your guns, and work your way up the pecking order.

8. The pecking order is essentially as follows:

- *Tellers.* **They're a source of information, but generally can do next to nothing in matters requiring a departure from standard policy.**

- *The tellers' supervisors.* **They can clarify policy, or back you up if you find the teller has processed your transaction inadequately, but they usually aren't equipped to override standard policy.**

- *Service representatives.* **Often referred to as "the bank executives" or "platform officers," they sit at desks or stand behind open counters, sometimes side by side with sales representatives. They approve transactions when tellers are in doubt and handle customers' problems. Depending on the authority of the representatives you speak to, they might be able to adjust your account to include a credit for—for instance—a reimbursement covering the landlord's debit.**

- *Service manager and sales manager.* **Not all banks have them, but in banks that have service and sales representatives, the managers are the officers directly over them, and are second in command.**

- *Branch manager.* **This is the boss of the branch. Most legitimate complaints can be resolved at this level if not before.**

- *Director of marketing services and product management.* **Employed by your bank's head office, this person succeeds or fails according to the bank's ability to win over new customers. If newspaper ads proclaim a particular policy but nobody at your bank seems to care, the director of marketing services and product management ought to be informed.**

• *Director of consumer banking.* **Also employed by the head office, this person would be appropriately CC'd if your bank is operating against advertised policy, or in any way tending to scare away customers.**

9. Banks occasionally distribute complaint forms and handouts describing their "personal touch" and their belief that "your opinion counts." When you see these, take a handful home with you and file them with your banking papers. One day they may come in very handy.

10. The same techniques and pecking order apply whenever the bank is at fault—for example, if the bank has cashed a forged check bearing a signature not remotely resembling yours. (In the new age of electronic banking, your financial institution could easily clear a check drawn on your account and signed "Cheese Sandwich," which is all the more reason to review your statements as soon as you receive them.)

11. In the present mixed-blessing era of automated banking, a common explanation is "But we don't really look at checks the way we used to. It's all done electronically now." This may be an explanation, but it's no excuse. If the bank made the mistake, the bank ought to correct it. Banks require you to play by the rules. They owe it to you to place the same demands on themselves.

12. Large utility companies don't present your checks to your bank for payment. They conduct transactions electronically. As a result, your payment on a utility bill might be incorrectly encoded, with the result that your bank pays out (for example) $54 instead of $45 from your account. You'd be completely within your rights to insist that your bank redo the transaction correctly, or you could leave the $9 as a credit on your utility bill to be applied to next month's charges. The choice is yours, but the latter course requires less paperwork and is the one your bank hopes you'll accept. Fine. But if the error has cost you any incidental money along the way—for instance, by reducing your balance to the point where you're paying a service charge you'd otherwise avoid—

offer to compromise: You won't request a refund provided the bank drops the incidental charges and your utility account is credited.

13. If you feel your bank hasn't handled a complaint fairly, or isn't acting in a timely manner, consider going to a higher authority.

14. It's helpful to have your bank's annual report to shareholders. It will provide names and titles of officers, and will indicate the bank's credentials, such as whether it was chartered by the state. Ask for a copy at your branch bank or, if there aren't any available, phone or write the customer service department of the headquarters office.

15. Bring your complaint in writing to the attention of appropriate officers named in the annual report. CC your branch manager, and the director of marketing services and product management, and/or the director of consumer banking, if appropriate. (Realize that a bank vice president won't get very worked up about a $9 mistake, though. This tactic is most effective when you're dealing with a serious inequity, or one that you suspect is part of a larger pattern.)

16. If the bank is state-chartered, complain to the state banking commission. This agency can also answer questions on other banking matters and refer you to other appropriate agencies.

17. If your bank is a member of the Federal Reserve, contact the Federal Reserve Bank of your state (look in the government listings for the state in your directory).

18. If it's a national bank (with "National" or "N.A." in the title), contact the United States Comptroller of the Currency (look in the U.S. Government listings).

19. The Federal Deposit Insurance Corporation (FDIC) will hear complaints about mutual savings and commercial banks and any that are FDIC-insured (look in the U.S. Government listings). The FDIC has an Office of Consumer Affairs, 550 17th Street, N.W., Washington, DC 20429; 1-800-424-5488.

20. Credit unions aren't banks and operate under different rulings. The Credit Union National

Association (CUNA), P.O. Box 431, Madison, WI 53701, 1-800-358-5710 or 608-231-4000, is the national trade association for credit unions and can refer you to appropriate federal and state regulatory agencies. The CUNA also publishes a series of consumer booklets and a quarterly magazine.

21. To varying degrees, these agencies will intervene, attempt informal settlement, make an inquiry on your behalf, or at the very least refer you to the governmental arm that can.

22. Once you've complained, your comments will be on file. If enough similar allegations are lodged, the bank may be investigated. If the bank has been acting illegally or in extremely poor faith, its charter may be revoked.

To Complain on a Broader Scale

1. "Washington Wire" (American Bankers Association, 1120 Connecticut Ave, N.W., Washington, DC 20036; 1-800-424-2871, or 202-663-5477 in Washington) is a prerecorded update about the world of banking and its response to pending regulations. Phone for an idea of prevailing moods and weigh your feelings about them.

2. If you have a reaction, pro or con, write your elected officials to voice it. Perhaps the lobbyists are in Washington, but your opinion is yours alone, and only you can express it.

3. You can also write to—or CC your correspondence to—strong consumer-oriented organizations such as the American Association of Retired Persons (AARP), Department of Consumer Affairs, 601 E Street, N.W., Washington, DC 20049-0002, 202-434-2277; and Consumers Union, 101 Truman Avenue, Yonkers, NY 10703-1057, 914-378-2000.

If Your Bank Fails

1. Banks are in trouble when they look substantially better "on paper" than they in fact are, as when their portfolios carry huge volumes of real estate loans that aren't being paid on a regu-

lar basis. On paper they're collecting a bundle. In reality, they're thinking foreclosure.

2. If you fear for your bank's stability, call the FDIC regarding its coverage, and follow local newspaper financial sections and money-oriented magazines for insights.

3. If your bank is covered by state deposit insurance, be aware that state insurance funds have failed in several states. Inquire whether the bank in question is also federally insured.

4. Weiss Research, Inc., 2200 N. Florida Mango Road, West Palm Beach, FL 33409, 1-800-289-9222, provides ratings for a fee, by phone and in printed form.

5. Veribanc, Inc., Box 461, Wakefield, MA 01880, 1-800-442-2657, rates banks and credit unions.

6. In 1989, the Financial Institutions Reform, Recovery, and Enforcement Act (FIRREA) transferred the responsibilities of the former Federal Savings and Loan Insurance Corporation (FSLIC) to the FDIC. As a result, the FDIC insures deposits in banks (through the Bank Insurance Fund) and savings associations (through the Savings Association Insurance Fund).

7. If a bank fails, the FDIC first tries to sell the business to a healthy institution. If this succeeds, the customers' service and accounts should be uninterrupted.

8. "Healthy institution" is a relative term. If your account is transferred to another bank, examine the policies and overall financial picture of your money's new home, and decide whether you wish to remain there.

9. Don't assume that the new institution will honor specific details of agreements you had with your previous bank. If you have to assume anything, assume that it won't. Your CD might be taken over without interruption but at a lower rate.

10. If the FDIC can't find a buyer for your original bank, it will pay depositors *up to the insurance limit of $100,000.*

11. FDIC-insured deposits are backed by the full faith and credit of the United States.

12. The $100,000 limit treats multiple accounts of a single depositor as a single account. If you have three separate $100,000 accounts in the same bank, you *are not* covered for $300,000.

13. However, individual (single-ownership) accounts, IRAs, Keoghs, joint accounts, and trusts are viewed separately. You can hold up to $100,000 in each category and be fully insured.

14. Accounts in different branches of the same institution are considered to be in the same bank.

15. The $100,000 limit includes principal plus interest.

16. When you bank in different institutions (not branches of the same institution), those accounts are separately insured by the FDIC. However, if the two institutions merge and your two accounts become one, the new combined account is insured only up to $100,000.

17. For further information or to see if any of the above rulings have changed, contact your bank or savings association, or write the FDIC.

18. Credit unions aren't insured by the FDIC but instead by the National Credit Union Share Insurance Fund, operated by their independent federal agency, the National Credit Union Administration, 1775 Duke Street, Alexandria, VA 22314-3428, 703-518-6300.

▲ *See also* AUTOMATED TELLER MACHINES; CREDIT CARDS; CREDIT RATINGS; INSURANCE.

Banquets and Parties

If your vision of the ideal scenario is you saying, "I want hors d'oeuvres and dinner for fifty people, followed by dancing to band music," and the banquet manager replying, "Excellent. I'll get back to you with a price. Leave the details to us," then this chapter isn't for you. Get out your checkbook, write a blank check, and work a second job to pay for what this wingding will cost. But for the record, even planners of elegant charity balls personally worry about details. They've learned from experience that only they can set the tone and standards for their own events.

And if you're arranging a special catered celebration at a hall, the one right person to set the level of expectation is you. This doesn't mean you can't trust professionals to do their jobs. But you do have to lay the foundation, monitor its progress, and build in certain assurances that you won't be shortchanged on the day of the event. You also have to fight the urge to "give them a free hand, because after all, they do this all the time"—because, far from being free, free hands are usually expensive.

The single biggest warning to imbed in your brain is that you can negotiate a brilliantly comprehensive contract with the sales manager, then get to the party to find your terms haven't been met. What do you do? Send your guests home? You can't. So you're stuck—or that's what the staff want you to believe.

Intentionally or otherwise, banquet halls and catering establishments tend to operate on this principle. Sales managers are expected to make promises. But these promises sometimes have little to do with what these places will actually deliver. When the day comes and promises are forgotten, you're told, "The sales manager didn't have the authority to agree to that," or "Okay, we said you'd have a piano. We made a mistake. We can't get a piano to magically appear in the middle of the room. But relax—the kazoo and cymbals will work well enough," or "Maybe it's not perfect, but they're eating the food and using our room, which is pretty much what you paid for. It's not like we're going to give you your money back."

At this point you've got a gun to your head. Don't make it worse by sheepishly pulling the trigger. What you should be pulling instead—out of your pocket—is the contract you cleverly negotiated to cover such contingencies.

Here's how you arrived at it:

Choosing the Hall

1. Don't go by ads and brochures alone. If location and ambiance are very important, fine. Give them plenty of weight in making your decision. But don't permit them to be the only considerations.

2. Solicit advice from friends and associates. What places have worked for them? Were the staff cooperative and professional? What were the names of the staff they dealt with? (If an event was successful primarily because Mrs. X arranged it,

ascertain that Mrs. X hasn't left for a new position at the hall across the street.)

3. Sometimes, caterers will recommend halls and even arrange for them (*see* CATERERS). They can be enormously helpful, but never give them unsupervised authority over your event.

4. Check with the local Chamber of Commerce and Better Business Bureau. Have any complaints been filed? Does the facility participate in any program for binding arbitration?

5. Find out from your state or city department of consumer affairs whether licensing is necessary. If it is, is the hall licensed?

6. What about state liquor laws? Who's responsible if someone has an accident after drinking at your party? Is the responsible person or group licensed and insured to serve liquor?

7. Is the banquet hall insured? What's its coverage? Don't settle for a verbal yes. Get a copy of the actual certificate of insurance, and be sure the coverage is realistic.

8. Are *you* covered? Ask what's involved in having your name or group added as an additional insured. If your group is part of a large organization, find out from your group's headquarters if a certificate of insurance can be forwarded to you.

9. If the event will be held in your home, don't assume it's covered by your homeowner's policy. Confer with your insurance agent before making any potentially catastrophic commitments.

10. Comparison shopping never hurt anyone. Even if you've got your heart set on one venue, speak to several. See what the competition offers. This will improve your negotiating position as well as your grasp of the options, and will give you a fallback if your first choice simply won't meet your terms.

11. The more organized you are, the more professional the sales manager and other staff members will be with you.

12. Ask when you can stop by to see an event in progress, and if you'll be able to sample the food the staff plan to serve you.

13. Ask very specifically if there will be hidden expenses. Are all taxes included? Are gratuities additional? Are there add-ons? Are union employees involved? If so, what is your responsibility toward them? For instance, will you be expected to pay an electrician for six weekend hours simply to turn lights on at noon and off at five o'clock (and otherwise, to sit around scowling and eating your food)?

14. What will you have to rent for extra money? Sound equipment? Special lighting? Decorations? Think about—and ask about—everything you need, or you'll pay dearly when you finally remember to request it.

15. Will special equipment and decorations be set up by the staff? Operated by the staff? Taken down by the staff?

16. What staff will be provided?

17. If you don't want to pay for extra equipment or staff, are you permitted to supplement basic equipment and staff with your own belongings and friends?

18. What will it cost you if more people show up than expected, or fewer? (If this is a factor, determine who will make the count and who will confirm it.)

19. Are you paying by the hour or a flat fee? Either way, have you allowed for set-up and clean-up time? How much more will it cost you if you run over?

20. Will everything be operational throughout the event? If not, what won't be? The bar? Coat check? Valet parking?

21. Will there be dancing? Is the floor suitable for it?

22. If you need a disk jockey, when will the disk jockey work and what will the fees be?

23. If there might be smoking, does the hall have a smoking policy?

24. Some halls may be better suited to these arrangements than others—for instance, a nightclub would have the dance floor, sound equipment, bar, and similar items already.

25. In such situations, determine whether the nightclub will be closed to outsiders, or whether uninvited walk-ins will be allowed.

26. What's the cancellation policy?

27. What's the payment schedule?

28. Remember that any initial arrangements are a negotiation. No aspect of the deal is carved in stone. It stands to reason that any standard contract prepared by the establishment will be more focused on protecting the establishment than on covering you. If you don't request what you want up front, don't expect it to fall into your lap later. This doesn't mean that the establishment's negotiators have to cave in to your every desire, but it certainly increases your chance of satisfaction, and it prepares you for what you can and can't expect.

29. It's good if you can be flexible but bad if you have to give up anything that really matters to you. Think hard about what you can revise easily. For instance, can you select another date? Another time of day, such as brunch instead of dinner?

30. Whatever answers you get, get them in writing.

31. Watch out for disclaimer language stating that the hall will deliver what you request or "its best effort." If you don't get what you negotiated for, "best effort" usually won't do.

32. It isn't easy to negotiate "teeth" in the contract, but it's well worth the effort. The idea is to have a final payment due after the event, or to place it in an escrow account, or in any other way to arrange that the facility won't have all your money pocketed before your banquet. The hall will have greater incentive to deliver according to contract if payment can be withheld if all terms aren't met.

33. If possible, negotiate the contract with a cost associated with each item. Have it spelled out in the contract that if any item is not delivered as promised, its default value will be rebated to you. This should apply not only to pianos and other tangible objects, but also to such promises as "Yes, we are fully accessible for people with disabilities."

34. Ask if the establishment will agree in advance to arbitration. If so, who is designated to arbitrate? If the choices appeal to you, get this in writing.

35. If you're thwarted at every attempt to negotiate teeth, put the sales manager or facility representative on the spot: "Let's face it. If all I want is music and food, I can take my friends and a battery-operated cassette player to Dairy Queen. What I want is what I've described to you. If I don't get what I want on this special occasion that will only come once in my lifetime, I'm going to be very disappointed. And I shouldn't have to pay for a whole event if you only deliver three-fourths of one.

"You can't put a price on my happiness, and I know a court of law would be hard pressed to put a price on my pain and suffering if you let me down, so let's devise a table that even a court of law could administer without difficulty. You tell me. How can I put teeth into this?"

36. If this doesn't bring you any closer to accord, consider carefully whether you want to do business with the facility.

37. Don't be surprised if someone accuses you of expecting the worst: "Why are you so sure we'll let you down? Lighten up. Why make such an issue?" You can respond by explaining that if your terms can be met, you'll be especially sure that nobody will let you down; and if the establishment has confidence in its promises, it should be willing to put them in writing.

38. The establishment can say, "Take it or leave it," and you may not want to leave it. Make your choice, but make it the most informed choice possible. Maybe nothing will go wrong. Or maybe the establishment is just negotiating, and if you leave it, the sales manager or someone else of authority will reconsider and get back to you.

39. If you're planning the event for a public occasion rather than a private one, make it clear that the eyes of the community will be watching. If other groups see the party is a dud, they'll probably want to take their future business elsewhere.

40. If you're not working for a club, community organization, or union but belong to one, inject your memberships into the conversation. Hint that your satisfaction can pay off with bigger

deals down the road, and your dissatisfaction could sabotage future business.

41. If you're dealing with a few hundred dollars, or if the last payment can be for a few hundred dollars, consider using your credit card. It will give you the option to challenge the last payment, and to request a credit or chargeback on your account, if arrangements weren't up to standards (*see* CREDIT CARDS). Of course, you can put everything on your card up to its full limit, but remember that if you don't pay your statement on time, you'll run up hefty interest fees.

42. You'll need checklists—at least three, set up in chart form, with all information accessible at a glance. One list will indicate guests' names and table assignments, whether you've received RSVPs, and where guests will be staying if they're coming from out of town. Another list will schedule the things you have to do before the event (such as contacting the band or arranging flowers), phone numbers and dates of conversations, prices, and a column for needed follow-ups. Most people arranging banquets, even for the first time, are intuitively aware of the need for these two resources.

43. The third list may be the most crucial, but it's the one most often overlooked. It's the one representing the day of the event. It lists what has to be done and reviewed, *the name and phone number or extension of the staff member who will be responsible for executing each task,* and (if you're a terrific negotiator) the home number of the sales manager or other responsible person who can be contacted if those present can't help. Make absolutely sure that you have the names of employees who will be there that day; perhaps you've only dealt with the sales manager, and the sales manager may not be around.

44. Be realistic about the demands on your time on the day of the event. If you'll be too busy to tend to details yourself, delegate a general. If you're twirling in the middle of the floor being torn in six different directions, you'll be undercutting all the hard work you've done and wasting the energy you've already expended.

If You Have to Complain

1. On the day of the event, refer to your list of people to contact. The more complete your list, the more worthwhile it will be if a real problem arises.

2. Be prepared to exhibit your contract: "It says here that the facility will return $200 to me if dinner is more than a half hour late. Are you sure you want to explain to your boss that this delay has cost him $200?"

3. Make your threats specific: "I understood that you would have an access ramp at the front entrance. It's not there. Do you understand that I will report this to local newspapers and TV stations and to the mayor's Office for People with Disabilities? Do you have any idea of the harm this will do to your image and the fines it may entail? Are you sure you don't want to phone around to see if a nearby building might be able to lend you one?"

4. At most social events, someone has brought a videocamera. Use the camera to record your misfortunes. If the rest rooms are filthy, or waiters have dropped food on the floor, or some tables are situated so close together that guests can't move their elbows, get it on videotape. Use the tape subsequently to embarrass the sales manager or establishment owner, or, failing that, send it to your area newspapers and TV stations.

5. But remember that if your guests aren't ready to sit down to eat on time, or if you're otherwise unprepared, you may make it impossible for the staff to satisfy you—and you relinquish quite a few of your contractual rights.

It's Your Turn to Put Teeth into It

1. If you're ignored on the day of the event, don't permit yourself to be so distracted by other matters that you don't pursue your grievances the next morning.

2. Complain to the sales manager and the owner. Specify the terms of the contract that were

violated. If you paid by credit card or into an escrow account, or have not made the last payment, renegotiate the balance owing. Repeat that you cannot be expected to pay for a whole event when you only received three-quarters of one.

3. Report your objections to the Better Business Bureau, the Chamber of Commerce, and the state or city department of consumer affairs, in writing. CC the sales manager of the hall, as well as the president and/or owner of the company.

4. If your contract allows for arbitration, press for it. Also, see if arbitration is available through the BBB, Chamber of Commerce, or state or city consumer affairs department.

5. If your complaint concerns food or food service, report it to the state or city department of health.

6. If the fault might be covered by the facility's insurance, ask how to contact the insurer and see what you can recover by this approach.

7. If the difficulties concerned accessibility, it's entirely possible that the federal Americans with Disabilities Act has been violated. Find out if your city or state has an office for people with disabilities (telephone information may be helpful). File your complaints with that office. CC the sales manager, owner, and insurer of the banquet hall.

8. You might want to send copies of the same letter to various organizations concerned with specific disabilities, such as a local chapter of the Multiple Sclerosis Society, or Eastern Paralyzed Veterans, and perhaps to the AARP (American Association of Retired Persons). These groups may choose to exert pressure and may encourage their members to do so.

9. Banquet halls depend on positive word of mouth. Widespread negative word of mouth can ruin their business. If you feel you've had a raw deal, spread the word—through friends and associates, and—provided you are careful to avoid slander or libel—via local newspapers and TV stations.

10. If you have a friend who's well placed with a large civic group or other sizable organization that's planning a big banquet, perhaps that friend can call the sales manager and say something like "We wanted to give you a chance to bid, but I understand that your service is slow and sloppy. Can you assure me that we won't get the same bad service?" When the sales manager promises superb service, your friend can respond, "But what happens if you don't keep your promise on the day of the event? You'll have our money, and we'll look like frauds to the people we're trying to please." When the sales manager extends further assurances, your friend can say, "That sounds fine, but I know for a fact you made the same promises to so-and-so and didn't honor them, and now you don't care. I won't believe you until I hear that you've made good." If the stakes are high enough, the sales manager may settle with you in hopes of winning over your friend.

11. You'd really make your point if another individual or group cancels a booking after having heard of your difficulties. If this happens, warn the one canceling to be sure this won't incur penalties, and make sure you don't come off as having slandered or libeled anybody. By no means should you misrepresent or exaggerate the inconvenience or harm you suffered.

12. If you threw the event for a civic group or other organization, not only should you do your correspondence on official stationery, but you should consider asking your headquarters to write a letter of complaint as well, on *its* official stationery. No banquet facility wants to hear from potential clients that it has a bad reputation.

13. Contact your lawyer, who may be able to resolve difficulties with a phone call or two.

If the Banquet Is Part of a Convention

1. If it is, be alert to signs of a take-it-or-leave-it attitude from the sales manager and staff. If you're treated like a captive audience as early as the negotiating stage, don't expect any better during the actual event.

2. Ask for a copy of the convention planner's kit, with price scales, meeting-room diagrams and capacities, and related information.

3. When you've bargained and bargained for the best banquet deal but still feel you could have gotten more, push for discounts related to other aspects of the convention. For instance, how about 10 percent discounts for your group in the gift shop?

▲ *See also* CATERERS; CREDIT CARDS; DISABILITIES; HOTELS; INSURANCE.

Cable Television

In its early days of popularity, cable television was deregulated. Prices were susceptible to whatever increases the market would bear, occasionally rising at three times the rate of inflation. But by the beginning of the 1990s, federal regulators stepped in—and the federal cable law came to comprise fiber optics, telecomputing, satellite transmission, and cellular and personal communication systems as well as cable TV itself.

So consumer protections that weren't available ten years ago are currently aimed at regulating prices and eroding franchise monopolies. The laws are sure to be modified, particularly as new means of communication spring up to rival those already in use. But as laws change, some companies may try to take advantage of the confusion to maintain their profit margins, or they may change terminology in an effort to get around the laws.

In other words, follow developments in the newspapers and—

Before You Sign

1. Do your research. Ask friends for recommendations. Comparison shop. Phone the Better Business Bureau and your state or city department of consumer affairs to determine whether any complaints have been lodged against the company and how they were resolved.

2. Read and compare the agreements provided by the various companies if there is a choice in your area. Even if there isn't, other options than those originally offered may be just over the horizon.

3. Don't sign anything that will commit you for an unduly long period of time. What may be a good price today by comparison with other offerings may not be too attractive six months from now if the other prices drop or when new services become available to you.

4. Although your TV may be "Cable-Ready," don't be fooled into thinking you don't need additional equipment. You do.

5. In all probability you will be renting the additional equipment from the cable company. What's your liability if you damage it? If it malfunctions through no fault of yours, do you pay for the service call anyway?

6. Does the cable company accept liability for items that may be broken in your home in the course of installation? If it does, get the specifics in writing.

7. Are you required to prepare your home in any way—by, for instance, moving furnishings—prior to installation?

8. If you live in a rental dwelling, does the landlord have to be informed? If the landlord expects any sort of compensation, ask the cable company if this is legal. You may also wish to ask your state consumer affairs department, state commis-

sion on cable TV, or state department of telecom-munications and energy if such offices exist where you live.

9. Does the cable company need access to some part of the building other than your home? Ask in advance, and be sure it can be arranged before the service call is made.

10. What will you be charged for installation?

11. Understand exactly what you're getting. What is "basic cable" and what options do you have for "premium channels" such as HBO and ESPN?

12. Realize that a premium channel may tout three blockbuster movies that it will run next month to entice you to subscribe, but another pre-mium channel may feature the same films a month or so later. And the original channel may keep repeating them ad infinitum throughout the year.

13. Feel free to pick and choose, to drop and add premium channels depending on the sched-ules. You may want to wait for specials. For instance, the Disney Channel and Showtime often promote discounts on their service if you buy a selected grocery product.

14. Don't be caught off guard. Read the flyers and rates, policy, and rights notices that come with your bills. They'll tell you about new promo-tions, and sometimes also about new pricing and rate hikes, as well as what you will be charged for late payments, bad checks, and the like.

15. Check the contract for reference to service calls and making inquiries about your account. How and when will you be billed? What is your account number? When is the business office open? What commitments does the company make concerning service?

16. If the contract is vague, phone the business office. Ask your questions, and ask to have the answers in writing.

17. If you receive a call or a notice that new equipment is required, confirm not only whether it's true, but also if it's legal. Contact your state consumer affairs department, a cable commission if there is one, and any other agency named in the statement of subscriber rights that your cable fly-ers should provide.

If You Have a Complaint

1. Organize your records. Keep notes of the dates you call, the names of the people you speak to, what they say, what rates they confirm, and so on.

2. If you make an appointment for a service call, ask what recourse you have if nobody shows up. Whom can you phone? How much can you deduct from your bill if you are without service for several days because nobody comes?

3. If you speak to somebody about service or a bill and receive an unsatisfactory answer, ask to speak to the supervisor. You may also try to work it out with the cable company's customer service department.

4. If you complain in writing, write to the address on your bill. Cite the names and dates of conversations, and what you were told. Include copies of documentation, if appropriate.

5. If you have no luck writing to the company, contact the state public service agency (look in the government listings for your state). You can write or call.

6. Other agencies that may assist you include the Federal Communications Commission (FCC), 202-416-0903, and the Federal Trade Commission (FTC), 202-326-2222, the city and state department of consumer affairs, the offices of the state attor-ney general, and your local and state politicians.

7. If the infraction is severe, ask whether steps can be taken to have the company's license revoked.

8. Register your complaint with the Better Business Bureau.

9. Any time you complain to any of these agen-cies, send CCs to the cable company—one to the customer service department, and another to the company president.

10. If your complaint would be of interest to a large number of neighbors, write a letter to the editor of your newspaper.

11. If the problem inconveniences or defrauds a large number of citizens, speak to an attorney about initiating a class-action suit (*See* RUNG ELEVEN: CLASS-ACTION SUIT in Part I) and to your local politicians about the possibility of a public hearing.

▲ *See also* PUBLIC UTILITIES.

Car Rental

There are four primary snags in the area of car rentals:

1. Rental companies that don't fully disclose all charges until the last possible moment, when you're over a barrel and unlikely to change your mind.
2. Companies that disclose incorrect charges to you and never bother to inform you. They simply submit a higher billing to your credit card company and allow the monthly statement to break the news.
3. The collision-damage waiver and related charges, which may cost you more than you need to pay, and/or provide less coverage than you think you're buying.
4. The degree to which renters are vulnerable to thieves.

These are the ways to approach them.

Full Disclosure

1. Do your homework, or you may not discover the restrictions and extras (such as geographic limits, age-related and fuel charges, and airport surcharges) until you go to pick up the car . . . or worse, when you drop it off.
2. Really careful homework would include writing to the Public Reference Branch, Room 130, Federal Trade Commission, 6th Street and Pennsylvania Avenue, N.W., Washington, DC 20580, for a copy of the FTC's free *Car Rental Guide.*

3. When you make your reservation, ask about restrictions. If the computerized reservation system or 800-number operator seems unwilling to provide specifics, repeat your questions. Write down what you are told. This still may not help you when you go to get your car, but it will stand you in very good stead if you have to take up the matter later with a manager, a customer service person, and your credit card company when you write to challenge the charge.

4. Ask what documents or information you may need to bring. Don't make yourself vulnerable by being underprepared when you reach the counter.

5. By agreement with the Federal Trade Commission, some rental companies must disclose their mandatory charges.

6. If you feel you have been denied full and fair disclosure, complain to the FTC. You may request copies of complaints, consent agreements, and various analyses from the Office of the Secretary, FTC, same address as above. The FTC won't enter into one-on-one negotiation to get your money back, but it does pursue sufficient evidence of misconduct to the point of legally binding consumer protection settlements.

7. Complaints can also be directed to the department of consumer affairs of your city or state.

8. For long-range solutions, you may want to bring your grievances to the attention of your

U.S. senators and congressmen, who pass laws the industry is obliged to obey.

9. As always, if an unauthorized charge appears on your credit card statement, ask your card company to remove it. Provide your reasons and photocopies of documentation. The card company ought to drop the charge pending investigation, and if the rental agency fails to prove validity, the charge shouldn't reappear.

10. Occasionally, charges will appear on a credit card statement long after the rental agreement has receded into memory—for instance, for traffic tickets presumably generated during a trip abroad. European officers who don't stop you may still have written tickets which were forwarded to the rental agency. You may request your card company to remove these items and ask how to go about contesting them, but you may never have to take on the foreign government as the charges may never reappear.

Charges After the Fact

Sometimes a driver wants a trip to end in a city other than the one originally planned. This hapless, trusting soul phones the rental agency, explains the situation with flawless accuracy, asks what the difference in charges will be, and, if the answer seems reasonable, modifies plans accordingly. When the trip is over, the driver returns the vehicle to its new destination and signs a charge slip which reflects the figures given over the phone. A month later the credit card statement arrives. Zowie! The fee is five times what was quoted. The driver phones the rental agency to find out what has happened and is told, "The person who quoted the figures made a mistake." What does the driver do?

1. Let's first consider what the driver should have done. The driver should have made a record of the name, phone number, and mailing address of the person who quoted the charge, preferably someone in authority such as the manager. The driver could also have attempted to confirm the charge by phoning an 800 number, or by phoning parties in both rental offices (original and new destination) and getting each name.

2. If one person quoted a price and another furnished the price on the charge slip, that too constitutes a confirmation, because two employees corroborated the same fee.

3. If this is you and you've done your homework, as soon as the credit card statement arrives, phone and write your credit card company. CC the manager of the rental agency. State the information you were given and who gave it to you. Indicate that you had the figures confirmed. Point out that you signed a charge slip, not a blank check. If the credit card company will accept amounts unilaterally increased by the rental agency, where does your liability end? If the agency can alter the figure once after the fact, what's to prevent it from discovering a dozen "mistakes"?

4. Simultaneously, take it up with the customer service 800 number for the rental agency. Speak to a supervisor.

5. If the supervisor won't help, get the phone number and address of the head office. From the head office, get the name of the house counsel, and attempt to speak to that office. Explain that you agreed to the terms as stated, and if the true terms had been honestly declared to you, you would not have agreed to the deal, because when you first inquired, you still had options.

6. Presumably, the agent to whom you return the car should advise you that the billing office can alter the charge if a mistake is later discovered. If you aren't given this warning, remember to say so when you're in touch with your credit card company and the rental office customer service people.

7. If you are warned, try to control your justified stupefaction. Instead, ask the agent to write out the nature of the "mistakes" that may later be discovered or, better, ask whom you can speak to in order to avoid signing the equivalent of a blank check.

Damage Waivers

1. The Collision Damage Waiver (CDW) or its relative the Loss Damage Waiver (LDW) is included in most car rental contracts. It releases the renter from financial liability arising from the use of the vehicle. Needless to say, this coverage doesn't come free.

2. Some states have banned the sale of CDWs, and federal legislation is in the works. In many states, rental agencies must inform renters that CDWs are optional, that the same protection may be included in the renter's personal policy, and the like. Strictly speaking, protection isn't optional because drivers should be covered. However, the coverage doesn't necessarily have to be provided by the rental company.

3. *Before* going to get the car, determine from your insurance broker whether your own automobile policy covers rentals. Don't simply accept a yes or no. Find out what portion of your policy applies to rental mishaps, precisely which mishaps are covered, the limitations and restrictions on coverage, and whether this protection extends to all rentals or only those occurring because your car is being repaired.

4. Much of this is state-regulated. Depending on your state, your insurance may automatically cover rental cars, or certain aspects of rentals. Ask your insurance broker how you fit into the picture.

5. Your credit card may cover you in full or part. Consult your credit card agreement for specifics, but remember that your card won't cover any rental that wasn't charged to it originally. If you have more than one card, read each agreement and use the card that gives you the best coverage.

6. Clarify in advance whether the rental agency will deal directly with your insurer. You don't want the agency coming after you directly, expecting you to settle with it first and then work things out with your insurer yourself.

7. Whatever you are told, read the rental agreement and confirm that it doesn't contradict the verbal assurances. Whether you accept or refuse the CDW, the contract should spell out the coverage you've opted to use.

8. Both with insurance and credit card coverage, check that it matches your itinerary. Excellent protection good only in the United States will be no help if you're motoring around Europe.

9. Intimidation at the counter isn't unknown. You may be harried to take and pay for the CDW, told that the agency doesn't honor your particular type of credit card, or threatened with horror stories of what it will cost if you're underinsured. Your best defense is to be armed with the facts. Know in advance what cards are accepted and what coverage you have.

Thefts

1. Decals and special license plates call attention to rental cars. Thieves deduce that valuable luggage, large amounts of money, and expensive cameras are inside.

2. They further project that drivers are from out of state and won't be available to pursue a case, press charges, or testify in court.

3. Thieves make the fairly safe guess that rental cars aren't equipped with alarms.

4. Your defenses are to avoid rental cars with large stickers, limit the valuables you carry, and be sure that theft and vandalism are protected by your CDW, insurance, or credit card coverage.

5. Drivers have reported leaving an agency in a rental car that soon after broke down on the highway. Strangers offered assistance, but instead robbed the renters. Apparently these wolves in good Samaritan's clothing had disabled the cars and then followed them. Your defense in this instance is to be extremely wary of offers of help, and to report incidents to local law enforcement personnel or, if abroad, to the U.S. embassy or consulate.

6. One study revealed that in some cities, damage losses via CDWs were unusually high, and concluded that a disproportionate number of clients were renting the cars preparatory to rob-

bing a bank or committing some other crime and engaging in high-speed flight from the police. The result was that agencies passed their extra costs on to renters in those cities with a surcharge (which many jurisdictions are contesting).

Advice and Mediation

In the event of a problem or complaint you can't solve via the usual channels, try writing a travel columnist. For example, the Ombudsman, *Condé Nast Traveler,* 360 Madison Avenue, New York, NY 10017, accepts letters considered to be of interest, responds in the column, and attempts to work out a solution with the company in question. If you wish to fax your letter, use 212-880-2190. Whether you write or fax, include your daytime number.

▲ *See also* CREDIT CARDS.

Caterers

Talented students and homemakers have discovered that they can make money by doing something they've done for free all their lives—cooking. What they tend to have in common is their extraordinary culinary skill.

What they may also have in common is a lack of business experience in this particular line of work. They may feel they're too small to worry about insurance. If your state licenses caterers, they may not be licensed. They may not know the first thing about contracts, or may agree to anything without the slightest ability to deliver. They may have no contacts or resources beyond themselves. In short, they're novices at a time when you need expert guidance.

Naturally, many small caterers are thoroughly professional and impeccably informed, while many large caterers are slapdash clods. Your goal is to get the best and tastiest deal possible, while assuring yourself of the broadest possible protection.

The Search

1. There's nothing wrong with consulting the business listings in your telephone directory (probably under "Caterers"), but remember that anyone can advertise.

2. Your best bet is to ask around for recommendations from people who've done events similar to what you have in mind.

3. Once you've gotten recommendations, confirm with the Better Business Bureau and Chamber of Commerce that the caterer has a complaint-free record, or at least has resolved complaints to the satisfaction of clients.

4. Ask your state department of commerce whether your state licenses caterers. Small caterers may not bother to be licensed. If you deal with them, remember that you relinquish a degree of protection—because a substandard licensed caterer risks having a license revoked. Unlicensed caterers have less to lose.

5. If your state licenses caterers, if you plan to work with a large caterer, and if the caterer is not licensed, ask whether you can have the records checked. For example, is it possible that the caterer has had a license revoked because food preparation was in violation of state law?

6. When you first sit down with your caterer, bear in mind that you're doing the interviewing. You'll want to see a portfolio with letters of reference and recommendations.

7. You may want to note the names on the letters so that you can follow up by speaking firsthand to former clients.

8. Ask the caterer for success stories. Biggest party? Fanciest? These will serve as an index to what the caterer has done and is able to handle.

9. Request a tasting. If you're going to be paying for food for friends, family, and/or associates, you're entitled to make an informed choice.

The Deal

1. Don't just ask prices and agree to everything you're told. Negotiate. If something is too high, be prepared to say so. If the caterer won't come down in price, ask for alternatives: "I *cannot* go higher than $15 a head. If you can't serve a warm dish, what cold dishes do you do for the money?"

2. Be specific about your choices and how they'll be served. How many courses? How big are the portions? Sit-down or buffet?

3. How many guests will be served?

4. How will you be charged if more attend? If fewer?

5. Request and study a rate sheet. Comparison-shop among several caterers. If the prices differ dramatically, find out why.

6. Ask about variables. Would a brunch be cheaper than dinner? Would one cuisine be cheaper than another?

7. What are the beverages? Discuss cost and who provides them.

8. Will you pay by the head, by the hour, or by the amount of beverage consumed?

9. If you bring the liquor yourself, arrange with the store that you'll be able to return any unopened bottles for a full refund. If you're making a volume purchase, most stores will agree.

10. If liquor is served, is the caterer licensed to serve liquor? Is the site licensed to serve liquor? Are you in any way liable as organizer of the event?

11. Whose insurance will cover the event, and is it fully covered? Ask for copies of certificates of insurance. Talk to your insurance agent. If it's a small event, or if it's held in your home, it might easily be added as a rider to your group's policy (if this is a group function) or your homeowner's policy (if it's yours).

12. Does the caterer deliver the food to a specified location? Agree to terms. Name a time. Otherwise, food might arrive at the last minute or entirely too soon.

13. What equipment does the caterer need at the serving site? Will the food have to be heated? Refrigerated? Confirm that the equipment will be available, and whether there's a rental fee.

14. If you're holding the event in a rented facility, make sure the caterer is allowed to serve there. Management may insist that you can't hire outside services or staff.

15. What will be needed for food service—in terms of staff and setup—and who provides it? What exactly will the catering staff's involvement be?

16. A full-service caterer can do more than food. Some even recommend and scout sites and entertainment. Expect to be charged for these extras.

17. Are there any hidden costs? Taxes? Gratuities? Overtime? Explain that you won't pay for anything not spelled out in the agreement, and then be sure everything you want is included.

18. What's the cancellation policy?

19. What's the payment schedule?

20. Your hand is strongest during negotiation and weakest when the event is in full swing. You have the fewest options when they hand you the wrong order and you can either accept it or starve—unless you've designed your contract to cover such situations.

21. Once you've reached the deal you want, get it *all* in writing. Try to put teeth into it. For example, arrange to make your last payment after the event, or have dollar amounts attached to specifics so that you won't have to pay for individual items you never got (*see* BANQUETS AND PARTIES).

22. Will the caterer agree to arbitration in the event of a dispute? If yes, by whom? If you accept the arrangement, include it in the contract.

23. If your deal is with a small shoestring operation, be aware that you may have no backup if your caterer lets you down. And if you have to go to litigation and you win, what will you have to do to collect? Seize somebody's personal property? It's in everyone's best interest if you raise the question before you sign on any dotted lines.

The Backup

1. If you have your contract in hand on the day of the event, you can point to it when terms aren't being met.

2. Be sure you have a home number to call in case nobody shows up, and confirm that someone will be at the number.

3. If you've agreed to a count, arrange to confirm the count with a member of the catering staff during the event.

4. If quality is falling short of the mark, word of mouth is a powerful weapon. Inform the caterer that you know a great many people who throw parties socially, professionally, and for community groups (if indeed you do), and that you'll feel obliged to recount your fiasco to each of them.

5. If someone at the event has a camera or camcorder, make a photographic record of items you intend to dispute later. The very fact that your caterer knows pictures are being taken may instantly improve service.

6. If matters weren't resolved during the event, follow up with calls and letters afterward. Refer to specific terms of your agreement that were violated.

7. If matters weren't resolved because you failed to live up to your end of the deal, don't expect to have much of a case.

8. Assuming you met your part of the bargain, your letter might say: "You agreed to one set of terms and, when you had us over a barrel, forced us to accept awkward substitutes. You responded with such disdain when I asked for the order to be corrected that I wonder whether you really don't care, or whether this is some sort of business strategy on your part to get the most money for the least effort. Because you've violated a written agreement, I'm filing complaints with the parties and agencies named below. Because you've embarrassed me among my friends [or business associates, clients, etc.], I'm taking my account elsewhere and advising others to do the same. Perhaps you'll develop more respect for your clients and your reputation when you no longer have any to lose." But never stoop to slander or libel.

9. At the bottom of the letter, CC the caterer's boss, the Chamber of Commerce, and the Better Business Bureau.

10. If the caterer considers his business too small to be concerned about complaints to these agencies, the caterer is no doubt small enough to worry about bad word of mouth. Remind the caterer that there's only one way to prevent it.

11. Deduct everything from the bill that you didn't receive.

12. If your final payment wasn't made yet, don't pay it until your grievances have been settled.

13. If the caterer is licensed, complain to the licensing agency. CC the caterer.

14. If you feel the food was prepared or served in an unsanitary manner, complain to the state department of health. CC the caterer.

15. If the caterer insists on being paid in full, and if you refuse to pay because you didn't receive full value, consider agreeing to a large discount off your next party by way of apology—or see what the caterer is willing to suggest.

16. If your contract included an avenue of arbitration, go for it.

17. Speak to a lawyer. A few formal-sounding letters from attorney to caterer may be enough to do the trick.

▲ *See also* BANQUETS AND PARTIES; CREDIT CARDS; HOTELS; INSURANCE.

Credit Cards

Credit cards have revolutionized the way we live—from the way we clothe ourselves to the way we celebrate and travel. Besides the obvious advantage of any system that provides an instant loan, they offer added control over any transaction by enabling the consumer to challenge a bad deal after the fact. Additionally, some credit cards include extra warranties, coverage, insurance—even the equivalent of frequent flyer programs.

The only way to know what your card offers is to read not only the glossy, colorful solicitation brochure but also the boring, smaller-print agreement. Like any contract, it binds both parties; but unlike other contracts, you don't necessarily have to sign the document itself to signify your acceptance of the terms. The understanding is frequently that the cardholder isn't bound until the card is used once.

By extension, if you later receive bitty-print revised agreements from the same company, read them to learn if any terms have changed, and realize that you will probably not be bound to the new terms if you pay off your balance and quickly advise the issuer that you've closed the account—but if you continue your relationship or use the card again, you will in all probability be considered to have consented to the new terms.

Incidentally, if you get an unsolicited card in the mail and have no intention of joining the program, don't just throw it away. Particularly with new environmental recycling codes that discourage the incineration of garbage, the card will exist forever with your name on it unless you take the precaution of cutting it to pieces. If it's used by an unauthorized party who forges your name, you'll have the opportunity to contest subsequent bills— but it's easier to spare yourself the inconvenience by simply destroying the card when you have the chance. Besides chopping up the card, demolish any papers that have the number and your name on them. If you have the choice, don't discard everything in the same wastebasket.

When You Select a Credit Card

1. Consider the interest rate if you don't usually pay in full every month. But if you're one of the 30 percent of cardholders who don't leave statements unpaid long enough to run up interest charges, look for a low-annual-fee or no-annual-fee card.

2. If interest rates will be an issue, don't let yourself be blinded by them. You'll still want to review other features:

- **Are the annual fees disproportionately high?**
- **Are interest rates constant, or are they pegged to a number of points above the prime rate? Some cards charge a lower fee until two payments are missed, then raise the rate.**
- **Is the credit limit unrealistically low?**
- **What customer service is available to cardholders in terms of 800 numbers, twenty-four-hour access to information, and numbers to contact in the event of theft?**

- **Is there a grace period that gives you, for example, twenty-five days in which to pay before interest begins to accrue?**
- **If you haven't paid in full one month, do all new charges incur interest immediately, or do you still have a grace period with respect to them?**
- **Are finance charges calculated on your average daily balance (ADB) in the previous month or, as some companies do, on your ADB over the past two months? Needless to say, if you pay on two-month accumulations, you stand to be billed a higher figure.**
- **On some low-interest cards, interest charges begin at the moment of purchase. It's hard to believe that this would ever be a favorable arrangement.**
- **Will you be entitled to amenities such as extended warranty coverage, purchase protection, and travel-accident insurance?**
- **If you're swayed by these enhancements, read the terms carefully to be sure of what you're getting. For example, insurance may be secondary insurance that kicks in only for the amount your regular insurer won't pay.**
- **Read the material that comes with each statement to be certain that the enhancements haven't been phased out while you weren't looking.**

3. Under many states' usury laws (laws governing the lending of money for interest), credit card companies are forbidden to charge late fees. (That's why so many card issuers are headquartered in Delaware and South Dakota, where usury ceilings and late fee restrictions are relaxed.) If you live in a state that bars the fees but you use a card issued from a state that allows them, you may have a legal case against paying the fee. Some attorneys have filed class-action suits (*see* RUNG ELEVEN: CLASS-ACTION SUIT in Part I). Some have won on certain levels. To find out where you stand, phone your state banking commission (look in the government listings for your state).

4. The above details, including the method of computation, should be spelled out in the contract and on monthly statements.

5. If you belong to a credit union, it might offer advantageous terms on a credit card. Ask what's available.

6. Certain universities, associations, and charitable organizations offer cards that remit a donation to the group for each use of the card. This is very clever and perfectly respectable, but don't get carried away with the idea that you're doing a good deed. If the group only gets 20 cents per transaction and you pay another $300 per year in interest and annual fees, you'd do better all around to send your group a $200 check possibly deductible on your taxes. Feel free to contact the organization chapter or headquarters to ask exactly what it gets when you use the card.

7. If your bank offers a credit card and if you have a substantial or long history there, try negotiating for a better rate on your card. Banks have been known to tailor arrangements to retain valuable accounts.

8. A good general resource for questions about credit card rates and benefits is Bankcard Holders of America, 524 Branch Drive, Salem, VA 24153, 703-389-5445.

9. Make a list of your credit cards, with numbers, expiration dates, and the emergency number for users. Keep it in a safe place. You'll need it for making reports if your cards are ever lost or stolen.

10. Sign new cards as soon as they arrive. Cut up and throw away expired cards.

11. Some card companies offer credit card insurance that allows you to report all your card numbers to one central agency. If the cards are lost or stolen, one call to the agency will alert all your card issuers. If you enlist such a service, remember to update it when you acquire new cards.

When Shopping with Your Card

1. If a stranger phones you with any business deal that involves your disclosing a card number, don't. If the deal sounds really terrific, find out

where the company is located and how you can call back. Then check with the Better Business Bureau and Chamber of Commerce in that jurisdiction before proceeding. (*See* SCAMS.)

2. It would be appropriate to provide your number over the phone if, for instance, you phone an airline or hotel to book a reservation. But make sure you're comfortable with the reputation of the hotel or airline, and check your next few statements very carefully to be certain the deal was charged correctly.

3. Stores may require personal information from you before they'll accept your card. They may ask for photo I.D.s, or your driver's license, or your phone number and address on the charge slip. This may very well be store policy, but it could nonetheless be in violation of state law or the card issuer's policies (not to mention your privacy). Once you've connected your name and address with your card number, you've made it that much easier for anyone with access to the trash pail to use your number without authorization.

4. You can determine state law by contacting the state banking commission, or the local Better Business Bureau, Chamber of Commerce, or state or city consumer affairs department. If your inquiry establishes that the merchant is ignoring the law, report the merchant.

5. Also, ask how you can obtain a printed statement of the ruling, and carry it with you when you shop to prove to other merchants that you *don't* have to disclose personal information just because they demand it.

6. A call to the card issuer's 800 number will tell you if its policy is being abused by the demanding merchant. If it is, write to the card issuer. State the merchant's name and address. The issuer might in turn revoke the store's credit card acceptance privileges.

7. Minimum purchases are not allowed under many standard contracts between merchants and credit card issuers. If your boutique or appliance store has a minimum-purchase-for-credit-cards policy, phone the issuer's 800 number. Ask if this is permissible. If it isn't, write to the credit card

company with a CC to the retailer. You may also wish to advise the Better Business Bureau and the Chamber of Commerce.

8. Watch your card after giving it to a salesperson. Promptly take it back. Confirm that it's yours. Take tissue carbons with you to destroy when you get home.

9. Never sign a blank receipt. Draw a line or scribble through any blank spaces when you put your signature on a receipt.

Once You've Made the Purchase

1. Your card affords you added clout, because if you have a legitimate complaint and the retailer won't budge an inch, you can pursue any dispute with the card company.

2. You might mention this to the retailer by giving him or her one last chance to make amends before you go to the card company, pointing out that it's much easier for the store to resolve matters with you than to incur possible service fees and unavoidable bookkeeping hassles once you demand a chargeback through the card company.

3. If the storekeeper relents at any level— whether the salesperson, the manager, or a customer service supervisor—get a letter confirming that your card company will be notified. Make sure the credit subsequently appears on your statement.

4. If it doesn't, send a photocopy of the letter to the credit card company, using the "for correspondence" address appearing on the statement. Request a full credit, including any penalties or finance charges the item may have created. Don't forget to identify yourself with name *and* account number.

5. Always check your credit card statements carefully and promptly. Report any billing errors and unauthorized charges immediately, in writing. Include all identifying data from the statement, such as posting date, amount, transaction description, and your name and card number.

6. If any amount is incorrect, report it in the same manner, but attach a photocopy of the cor-

rect charge slip (which you've undoubtedly kept on file in your home for your protection and peace of mind).

7. If you're being charged for an item now in dispute—for instance, if the appliance store won't take back your toaster and it was defective from the moment of sale—inform the card issuer in writing. Include the names of those you have dealt with at the store.

8. When telemarketers are denied authorization from banks to accept credit card charges, they've been known to turn to legitimate merchants who "lend" authorization in exchange for a percentage of the profit. When card issuers find out, they tend to respond by revoking the merchant's card acceptance privileges. If you see a charge from a mysterious source, it could be a billing error, an illegal use of your card, or a telemarketer billing through a third party. In each case, report the matter in writing immediately for your own protection, and perhaps to catch a thief.

9. If you suspect you've been scammed, or if you suddenly have the uncomfortable feeling that an item you've been billed for will be unreasonably delayed, write your card company to delete the amount from your statement if you haven't paid, or to initiate a chargeback if you have. The Fair Credit Billing Act provides that you can request a credit or chargeback within sixty days of receiving the bill. For this reason, some scam artists require sixty-plus-day advance payment. Don't agree to these advance-payment conditions unless you're happy about making yourself vulnerable.

10. The concept of "keeping files" has changed in the credit card business. For the most part, the days of cabinets with slide-out drawers are long gone. Letters you write may eventually be stored in a warehouse, with their salient points surviving as no more than a brief summary on the computer. This means that if you phone to follow up on a matter, you can't assume that the person you speak to has access to the letter or the photocopies your letter may have contained.

11. If your discussion would be improved by the person having the letter in hand, suggest that he or she order it from the warehouse and get back to you. If this isn't possible, speak to a supervisor. If the letter no longer exists, point out that you already sent documentation and that if it was discarded, the company accepted responsibility for its nonexistence when the choice was made to destroy it.

12. Similarly, the contents of telephone conversations are recorded on computers in key words, not details. When you speak to customer service people over the phone, they may have only an inch of space on which to summarize the entire conversation. Therefore, when somebody later pulls up your account, don't assume it will be the whole story.

13. Feel free to begin your call with "Let me briefly fill you in on the history." Then both of you will be dealing with the same facts—instead of the other party having half the facts, or a wrong idea based on incomplete information logged in the computer.

14. If you are charged a finance fee for late payment but feel the missed deadline was not your fault—for instance, the check was delayed by the U.S. Postal Service—phone the card company, explain your situation, and ask to have the charge dropped. The representative may be willing, and easily able, to comply.

Under the Fair Credit Billing Act (FCBA)

1. You have to write (not just phone) your objections to protect your rights under the act.

2. Your letter must be received within sixty days following the date on which the issuer mailed the first bill or statement referring to the charge.

3. Use the "correspondence" or "billing inquiries" address appearing on the statement—not the "send checks to" address.

4. Include your name and account number; the date, amount, and nature of the charge; why you

believe you shouldn't pay; and a request for the document or proof on which the credit card company based its payment.

5. Mail this letter separately from any check you may be sending. Not only should checks and correspondence often be sent to different addresses, but also you want to be sure that the envelope isn't discarded as soon as the stub and payment are removed.

6. To substantiate your having responded in time, you may consider sending the letter via certified or registered mail.

7. When you've followed these steps, the card issuer must acknowledge your letter in writing within thirty days of receipt unless the matter has already been settled.

8. The issuer must investigate the dispute and notify you within ninety days, either reporting correction of the error or explaining why the charge was valid.

9. If the issuer upholds the charge and if you asked for proof, the explanation must include adequate documentation.

10. According to the Federal Trade Commission, "Under the FCBA, the card issuer cannot close your account just because you disputed a bill under the law."

11. By the way, you may find the proof insufficient. For instance, you might receive a response that "we enclose a facsimile sales draft. The merchant involved submits all sales electronically and therefore this copy is the only information available to us." This doesn't eliminate the possibility that the merchant invented a figure. If you have a photocopy of the correct charge slip, or if you have a reason why the charge couldn't possibly apply, repeat your objection. For example, if you're being billed for a hotel stay in Nevada when you have airline tickets and restaurant receipts proving you spent the week in Tibet, send photocopies.

12. You may receive a statement of dispute. Read it and fill it out carefully. Observe the strict time limits for your reply. Keep clear photocopies

of everything you send, as well as evidence (such as a certified or registered mail stub) of your having acted within the limit.

13. Your card number can be stolen even when your card has never left your sight. Thieves comb garbage cans for car rental and ticket stubs that have your number on them, then use them to run up unauthorized charges.

14. When you report these, be sure to identify them as *unauthorized charges* rather than billing errors. (You remember that billing errors must be reported within sixty days.)

15. If your cards are lost or stolen and someone phones you with great news—"Don't worry. I have them. I'll put them in the mail"—*worry*. The call may have come from a thief hoping that now you won't put a stop on your cards.

If You Still Get Nowhere

1. Contact your local consumer protection agencies for advice.

2. If you need legal advice but aren't ready for the expense of a lawyer, try the nearest Legal Aid Society, if one is listed in your phone book.

3. Contact your regional FTC office, or FTC headquarters in Washington, D.C.: 202-326-2222, or 202-326-2502 (TDD).

4. Write to "Fair Credit Billing," Public Reference Branch, Federal Trade Commission, 6th and Pennsylvania Avenue, N.W., Washington, DC 20580.

To Play It Safe

If you ever, ever, ever receive an inaccurate dunning notice from your credit card company (claiming that you're in severe default of payment, or you've let matters go too long, or words to similar effect), it won't be enough to clear things up by phone. It won't even be enough to see the correction on your next statement. *Write* to the card company, and require that it in turn write to the national credit-tracking bureaus to which it reports, to remove any history of the matter from their files. Ask for copies of the correspondence, and keep it in the event your credit rating is subsequently in question. (*See* CREDIT RATINGS.)

If Your Card Is Stolen

1. Report the theft immediately. Your statement tells you how to call, and whom. Under the law, you may be responsible for only a limited amount of charges run up after the theft—currently $50 per card—if you phone within the specified time.

2. Report the theft to your local law enforcement agency.

3. Your credit card company will arrange a replacement card. To do so, it will cancel your present card number, and you'll have to wait until the new one—with a new number—arrives. For this reason, it's handy to have a no-fee card from another issuer which you keep at home only for emergencies. As long as it doesn't cost you anything to keep, it provides a free backup for the period when your regular card is out of commission.

4. Contact any company you've recently paid by card, or which may have delayed submitting its request for payment. Explain that your card was stolen and if the charges for your transaction are rejected, you'll be happy to redo the billing with your new card when you receive it.

5. Remember that even after the old number is withdrawn, you'll still be liable for debits incurred while the card was being used by you.

▲ *See also* APPLIANCES; AUTOMATED TELLER MACHINES; BANKING; ELECTRONIC FUND TRANSFERS; SCAMS; TELEMARKETING.

Credit Ratings

In general practice, three main credit reporting bureaus (TRW, Equifax, and Trans Union) compile the information that businesses use to decide whether or not to extend credit to you.

This is legal, and as concepts go, it's fair enough. If you were in business, you'd rather offer credit to someone with a good track record than to someone with a history of delinquent payments, repossessions, and bankruptcy.

The problems arise when the concept is applied to real life, because, as we all know, any system with people involved is susceptible to human error—and when computers are put in people's hands, watch out. It's entirely possible that your credit record contains at least one error, and this error could cost you a new appliance, a new car, or even a new job.

Determining Your Credit History

1. If you haven't seen your credit history before, prepare yourself for a shock.

2. Request a copy of your credit history from TRW. The report won't be identical to those from Equifax and Trans Union files, which charge a small fee, but you'll get it without cost. (It might be a good idea to check, as such rules do change.)

3. Write to TRW, Consumer Assistance, Box 2350, Chatsworth, CA 91313. Request the free report by sending your full name, addresses for the last five years with ZIP codes, year of birth,

name of spouse (if you're married), your Social Security number, and a copy of a document such as a utility bill or driver's license that links your name with your current address (to prove that you're you).

4. TRW will provide a free copy annually of his or her own report to anyone sending the above information.

5. If you're denied credit or a job because of a bad rating, the Fair Credit Reporting Act requires that you be told the name and address of the credit bureau that furnished the information.

6. The credit bureau must send you a free copy of the report upon written request received within thirty days of the denial.

7. The Federal Trade Commission has ruled that under the same circumstances you can also receive your "risk score" (a system of assigning point values to several indicators of your ability to pay).

8. All three major bureaus not long ago agreed to send a free report to anyone denied credit, even if another bureau was named in the letter of denial.

9. A credit bureau can reveal what your report contains, but only the creditor can tell you why you were turned down.

10. Many major creditors devise their own scoring systems. So far, federal law doesn't require them to explain or even reveal your score to you. However, under the Equal Credit Opportunity Act (ECOA), they must tell you why you were rejected.

11. Don't wait until you're turned down for something before correcting an error, and don't

assume that the basic soundness of the system is on your side.

12. It's a good idea to review your credit report for inaccuracies before making any major purchase.

Common Sources of Error

1. Credit delinquencies of people with names and addresses similar to yours may appear on your report.

2. Merchants may make faulty reports to credit bureaus.

3. Even if you've successfully disputed a return or credit with a merchant, the merchant may have reported the transaction to the credit bureau as a failure to pay.

4. Make certain that fraudulent uses of your credit card number don't appear on the report.

5. If a dispute with you is handed over to a debt collection agency (however irrationally), don't be surprised to see it on your credit report.

6. If you've done business with a store that's gone bankrupt, a collection firm may come after you for alleged unpaid bills—not because you didn't pay, but because it's hard to prove you did, and because the collection firm is itching to turn a profit. Needless to say, the firm may report you.

7. "Too many inquiries" can look bad on a credit report. Maybe they indicate that you're on your way to becoming overextended. But they could just as easily mean several credit card companies are simultaneously weighing whether to raise your line of credit.

If You Find an Error

1. Now that you realize any number of inaccuracies can go on your report without anyone giving you the chance to defend yourself, you'll want to know about self-defense.

2. You're entitled by law to correct any inaccurate information that appears in your file.

3. If you find an error, write to the credit bureau stating why you think the item is incorrect. Provide appropriate photocopies of paid bills or credit card statements if possible. Unless the request is frivolous, the bureau has to reinvestigate.

4. The credit bureau is required to remove any items it finds to be in error, and to delete any that can't be verified.

5. If you disagree with the findings of the reinvestigation, you can file a statement of up to one hundred words defending your point of view. At your request, the bureau must note your statement on future reports.

6. You can also take it up with the creditor who reported the information, by sending documentation and suggesting as persuasively as you're able that the creditor must advise the bureau to delete the item.

7. If information is unflattering but correct, you can't remove it but time can. Bankruptcies are purged from your report after ten years, and other negative information after seven.

8. If you find something sufficiently damaging on the report of one major bureau, find out whether it appears on the reports of the other two, and if it does, correct it on all three.

9. Be persistent. Statistics show that it takes people an average of six months to see errors corrected, and sometimes multiple attempts before getting any response at all.

10. Two of the three major bureaus have 800 numbers: TRW's is 1-800-392-1122, and Trans Union's is 1-800-851-2674. But *never* rely on a phone call to straighten out a credit dilemma. Confirm and have everything confirmed in writing.

11. Local offices of national bureaus, along with local agencies, are in most telephone directory business sections under "Credit Reporting Agencies" or similar designations.

12. To date, credit bureaus are required by law to correct errors speedily but creditors such as banks and department stores aren't. For complaints against them, contact your state or city

department of consumer affairs, as well as their own executives on local, regional, and national levels.

13. The good news is that tougher fair-credit-reporting bills are in the works.

14. If you're contemplating a major purchase, if time is a factor, and if a single item on your credit report appears to stand in your way, arm yourself with photocopies and paperwork to substantiate your claim. Be prepared to present this evidence if your credit history becomes an issue.

If You're Denied Credit

1. Get the reason. If a credit bureau's error is responsible, follow the above steps.

2. It may be something easily remedied. For example, if you haven't been at the same job long enough, try reapplying in another six months or a year.

3. Creditors use different scoring systems. If one creditor turns you down, you may be accepted somewhere else.

4. But don't make the mistake of asking for credit everywhere you go. Each new creditor you visit is likely to request a report from a credit bureau, and one of the items bureaus list on your report is excessive inquiries (interpreted as a warning signal that you're routinely being turned down for credit!).

5. You can ask to have unfamiliar inquiries deleted from your credit report the same way you'd protest an error, though the bureau isn't required to investigate. Even if you do nothing, inquiries are generally purged after two years.

6. You may have no credit history because you're too young, or because you've always made purchases jointly with your spouse and now you're divorced or widowed. But you can build one. Try opening an account at a department store, or borrowing money from a bank or credit union. Then be sure to make your payments on schedule.

7. A better strategy is not to wait until you're without credit. While you're still married, maintain some accounts in your own name, or ask credit bureaus to list accounts under your name as well as your spouse's.

8. If your objective is to start a credit history, confirm that the creditor you've gone to reports to a credit bureau. (Most do, some don't.)

9. You may have had credit under another name (such as a maiden name), or in a different location, but it hasn't caught up with your file. Contact the bureau with proof that you're who you claim to be, and ask to have earlier records included.

10. If you are in fact a poor credit risk, there are steps you can take to improve your standing.

If Your Credit Is Bad

1. The truth is that a whole lot of people whose credit reports are bleak are people who consistently don't pay their bills.

2. If you're one of them, don't wait until your debts are turned over to a debt collector (*see* DEBT COLLECTORS).

3. If there are bills you won't be able to pay, don't ignore them. Contact the creditors and explain your situation. Attempt to work out something, if only a schedule of minimal payments.

4. If you're very ill, disabled, or out of work, government and social service agencies may offer relief. (*See* DISABILITIES; MEDICARE, MEDICAID, AND MEDIGAP; SOCIAL SECURITY; WORKPLACE. Consult your phone directory and call your local congressman for the phone numbers of agencies to contact.)

5. Utilities frequently arrange reduced payment schedules, and sometimes have subsidy programs, for people who legitimately can't pay.

6. Be fair and be honest. If you say you're doing your very best to meet your payments and then you go on an expensive cruise, don't expect sympathy. And yes, such information can turn up on your credit report.

7. Whether or not it's your fault, face reality and make sacrifices. For example, consider giving up your credit cards.

8. Be suspicious of credit repair companies that promise to remove unflattering items from your credit report. Many charge a big fee and do nothing. Many do what you could do yourself. None can permanently erase true items from your report (unless the credit bureau was about to purge them anyway).

9. You may want to contact a Consumer Credit Counseling Service (CCCS), a nonprofit organization with more than 200 offices located in forty-four states. Their services are available free or at minimal charge. You can find the office nearest you by checking the white pages of your directory for Consumer Credit Counseling Service, or contacting the National Foundation for Consumer Credit, Inc., 8611 Second Avenue, Suite 100, Silver Spring, MD 20910; 1-800-388-2227.

10. Nonprofit counseling programs are sometimes operated by the Legal Aid Society, universities, military bases, credit unions, and housing authorities.

To Protest the Practice

1. Credit practice is controlled and enforced by laws. If you object to the rules themselves, your elected officials want to know. Write your senators and congressmen (state and federal).

2. Advise your state attorney general. (Many improvements in current practice were brought about when state attorneys general sued credit bureaus for inaccurate reporting and inadequate investigation of complaints.)

3. If you were misled about a credit arrangement that was promoted by mail, tell your local postmaster and also contact Chief Postal Inspector, United States Postal Service (Room 3021), Washington, DC 20260-2100; 202-268-4267.

4. The Federal Trade Commission (FTC) will file complaints and investigate them if enough accumulate, though it won't take action on the strength of one individual's grievance. Contact Division of Credit Practices, Federal Trade Commission, 6th and Pennsylvania Avenue, N.W., Washington, DC 20580.

5. For further information, write the Public Reference Branch, Room 130, Federal Trade Commission, 6th and Pennsylvania Avenue, N.W., Washington, DC 20580. Publications include *Equal Credit Opportunity, Fair Credit Reporting, Women and Credit Histories,* and *Solving Credit Problems.*

▲ *See also* BAD DEBTS; BANKING; CREDIT CARDS; DEBT COLLECTORS.

Debt Collectors

It isn't fair to let bills go unpaid indefinitely while you dine at expensive restaurants every night. On the other hand, it sometimes happens that you land in debt through no fault of your own—for instance, when you become very ill, or when you lose your job. It's also entirely possible for you to receive dunning letters about debts you never owed in the first place, or purchases that were settled long ago.

Fortunately, there are laws and agencies on your side. If you keep your wits about you, there's common sense too.

If You Think You'll Owe Money You Can't Pay

1. If someone provides services to you on an ongoing basis, for example an attorney or accountant, have a written agreement up front, and ask to be billed at regular intervals. Then you can question any misunderstandings before they get out of hand.

2. If disputes arise, confront them immediately. If you come to an oral agreement, ask to have it confirmed in writing.

3. If written confirmation doesn't follow, *you* follow up with a letter, stating the terms of the understanding you reached.

4. If the matter still isn't resolved in writing, write to the head of the firm or company president.

5. Call your local Better Business Bureau, Chamber of Commerce, and state or city department of consumer affairs to learn what else you can do.

6. Keep copies of your correspondence, and make a written record of any phone calls concerning payment.

7. If the person responds by stopping work or threatening to, call the same agencies or the individual's professional association to determine whether this is legal. For instance, lawyers may need approval of a court before dropping a case.

8. If stoppage isn't legal, ask the above organizations how to file and follow through on a complaint.

9. If your creditor's response is to threaten to turn the account over to a debt collection agency, point out that if the bill isn't legitimate, nobody's going to collect, and even if the collection agency succeeds, it's going to rake off 25–50 percent for services rendered. It is therefore in the best interest of your creditor to work something out *with you.*

10. If you don't dispute a bill and don't pay it either, creditors often hand the matter over to a collection agency. If they warn you first, approach them with the above reasoning.

11. Under no circumstance should you ignore your bills hoping they'll go away. Contact your creditors. If you have a past history of prompt payments and explain your cash squeeze, they ought to be willing to work something out.

12. Some creditors have insurance that will cover your debt for you if you've been disabled.

Ask them to check their policies, because they may be unaware until you mention it.

13. There's something known as being "judgment-proof," which means that you're so broke, there's nothing for creditors to collect. If you have no personal belongings beyond basic necessities, no savings, no real estate, and no income except government benefits or disability checks, you may be safe from lawsuits. But don't assume. Ask your local Legal Aid Society or state or city department of consumer affairs.

14. If you're embarrassed and tempted to play ostrich, discuss your situation with someone you trust, such as a clergyperson. Don't be immobilized by shame. It's dangerous to do nothing.

15. If you have assets and can't reach a settlement, creditors that take you to court can have your wages garnisheed and/or win liens against your personal property.

16. If you seek the services of credit repair specialists, be sure you understand what they can and can't do. Get it in a written contract, with all costs spelled out. Then check the company's reputation through your Better Business Bureau.

17. Free or low-cost credit counseling is available in most states through the nonprofit Consumer Credit Counseling Service (CCCS). Look it up in the business listings of your directory, or ask the National Foundation for Consumer Credit, Inc., 8611 Second Avenue, Suite 100, Silver Spring, MD 20910; 1-800-388-2227.

18. Nonprofit counseling programs may be operated by the Legal Aid Society, military bases, universities, credit unions, and housing authorities in your area.

If a Debt Collector Contacts You

1. The Federal Fair Debt Collection Practices Act of 1977 makes strong-arm and abusive tactics illegal, as do quite a few state and city laws.

2. The federal law doesn't apply to attorneys, creditors collecting for themselves, federal or state employees performing official duties, and individuals performing actions required by law.

3. The federal law only protects consumer debtors. Commercial debtors (companies or factories, for example) aren't included.

4. Contact your state or city department of consumer affairs for a printed statement of the laws that cover you. They may give you greater protection than the federal law alone.

5. In many municipalities, debt collectors are licensed and can have their licenses revoked if they abuse their power.

6. In general, the laws describe the ways you can and cannot be approached. For example:

- **A collector may be forbidden to contact you at an unreasonable hour, or at your place of business, or too frequently, without first getting court approval.**

- **If a lawyer represents you on the debt, the debt collector may be required to talk to the lawyer and leave you alone.**

- **If you've informed the collector in writing to stop bothering you, the laws may demand that he or she obey.**

- **If collectors try to locate you through other people, they may not be allowed to say that you owe money.**

- **If you are legally separated from a debtor and living apart, the collector may not be permitted to annoy you.**

- **The collector is generally allowed to contact the following to discuss your debt without your consent: a credit reporting agency, the creditor, the creditor's attorney, and your attorney.**

- **The collector cannot misrepresent something as a legal document when it isn't and cannot threaten to take an action against you that it isn't legal to take.**

- **The collection letter cannot threaten and misrepresent in bold letters on the front, then get off the hook by stating your rights under the law in tiny print on the back. Information must be clearly presented in a way that tells consumers about their rights and how to protect them.**

- **The collector cannot threaten violence, or commit violence, against you or your property.**

7. The laws also enumerate the recourse you have:

- **The debt collector usually has to identify the amount and source of the debt, including the name and address of the creditor and an address you can use if you dispute the charge.**
- **There should be a time limit for you to reply and an indication that if you dispute the bill in time, the collector must either correct it or send an explanation clarifying the debt.**

If the Debt Collector Breaks the Law

1. Report it to the police, the Better Business Bureau, the Chamber of Commerce, and the state or city department of consumer affairs.

2. Report it to the creditor who originally hired the debt collector. Suggest that the creditor break off its relations with the debt collector.

3. If the creditor refuses, ask the police, Better Business Bureau, and department of consumer affairs whether refusal makes the creditor party to a crime.

4. If you file a complaint, consider filing against the creditor as well as the collection agency, and consider filing with the Chamber of Commerce as well as the department of consumer affairs.

5. Your state or city department of consumer affairs may be authorized to investigate complaints, intervene on your behalf, seek court-imposed fines against repeat offenders, and revoke their licenses.

6. If your basic rights as a consumer are being violated in a way that leads you to believe the debt collector routinely abuses alleged debtors, you might want to alert such consumer and advocacy groups as:

American Civil Liberties Union (ACLU)
132 West 43rd Street
New York, NY 10036
212-944-9800
FAX 212-869-9065

National Consumers League
815 15th Street, N.W., Suite 928
Washington, DC 20005
202-639-8140

National Legal Aid and Defender Association
1625 K Street, N.W., 8th Floor
Washington, DC 20006
202-452-0620
FAX 202-872-1031

At Whatever Point Settlement Is Reached

1. Get the resolution stated formally, and fully, in writing.

2. Be sure that the matter is removed from, or at the very least accurately revised in, reports from credit reporting agencies.

If You Lie That You Are Unable to Pay

You haven't been paying attention. Computerized services—not just limited to credit reporting bureaus—can prove otherwise.

▲ *See also* BAD DEBTS; BANKING; CREDIT CARDS; CREDIT RATINGS.

Diet and Weight Loss Centers

There's nothing wrong with wanting to drop pounds if you're overweight. It's an important step toward better health. Neither is there anything wrong with the centers and doctors that can help you safely and honestly, as many do.

The danger is that safety and honesty aren't always included when you strike a diet deal. Because your health and hard-earned money—not to mention your life—may be at stake, consider the following before you sign on the dotted line.

Safety

1. Make the distinction between quick weight loss centers and diet centers. Rapid weight loss can be dangerous.

2. Never, ever undertake a dramatic diet regimen without consulting your doctor. Ideally, get the specifics of the center's plan and let your doctor see them. If your doctor has any reservations, you should too.

3. Some centers have fact sheets about possible side effects, which can range from hair loss to gallbladder damage. Ask if your center has such a sheet. Show it to your doctor.

4. Read the contract. If it contains any warnings that may apply to you, don't brush them off. They're there for a reason.

5. Find out what sort of supervision the center has. Doctors? Trained staff? Find out what sort of preparation the staff had, and how long it lasted.

6. Before signing up, contact your local Better Business Bureau, Chamber of Commerce, and/or state or city department of consumer affairs, and ask whether any complaints have been filed against the center.

7. Must diet centers in your area be licensed? Ask the department of consumer affairs, and if yours isn't licensed, find out why not. (Perhaps the owners did not apply for a license because they previously lost one while operating under another name.)

8. Has the diet center posted a bond? If it has, and if the center later goes under, this gives you a better chance of getting your money back.

Smart Spending

1. Even when your health is protected, your money may not be. First and foremost, read the contract. If the terms seem too confining for your life-style, be realistic about the true value of signing up.

2. Can you get out of the contract at will? If you pay an annual fee, will it be prorated if you choose to leave after a few months? You can probably walk away at any time if you're willing to forfeit the sign-up fee, but prorating is a long shot. See if you can have a trial period before committing yourself.

3. Bear in mind that the eighties were boom years for diet centers, but the recession was a bust.

If your local center closes its doors, will the parent company claim that you're not entitled to a refund because you're expected to travel sixty miles to another center in another town?

4. If the center is a franchise, find out how much control is exercised by the head office. Whatever you're told, ask to have it in writing. In some cases, the franchisees sincerely want to run a great operation, but they're locked into a difficult contract themselves. Franchisees have been known to sue franchisers for questionable practices, but until the cases are settled, their hands may be tied with regard to satisfying local customers. On the other hand, sometimes the franchisers are terrific and the local center is a waste. In this case, you'll want the franchiser to accept responsibility.

5. A call to your Better Business Bureau, Chamber of Commerce, or state or city department of consumer affairs can guide you in this. Have there been any complaints against the center? How long has it been in business? If it's a new operation, what were the owners doing before, and were there any complaints against their previous business?

6. What are the center's hours? What are your hours? If the center doesn't give you plenty of flexibility in relation to your available time, the only weight you lose may be your wallet's.

7. Forget what the TV or newspaper ad said. What does the contract say about extra fees? For instance, maybe the annual registration is minimal, but are you required to eat prepackaged foods only available from the center? What do they cost?

8. Ask what happens if the parent company has a shipment problem, leaving your local center without decently stocked shelves. Are you still required to make your weekly purchase? Or suppose there's a shortage of most entree items. Will you be forced to eat (or at least pay for) the same meal every day for four weeks?

9. Some centers advertise that you must shed a predetermined number of pounds or they'll rebate a portion of your fee. Read this agreement particularly carefully, because they can always argue later that you would have lost weight if you'd followed the rules. Also, if you lose the weight and then regain it, they've complied with their end of the deal, but you're back to being overweight.

If You've Been Cheated

1. Complain to the manager of the center.

2. If you believe the center absolutely violated its contract and if you paid by credit card, contact your credit card company and see if it will process a chargeback.

3. If it's a branch and you can't obtain satisfaction, complain to the head office.

4. Many diet chains are subsidiaries of multimillion-dollar corporations. If the head office isn't interested in your complaint, write to the corporate president and, if you're angry enough, the board of directors. (This information should be available in *Standard & Poor's,* in the reference section of your library.)

5. Register a complaint with the Better Business Bureau, Chamber of Commerce, and state or city department of consumer affairs. Find out from them if they offer arbitration and how you can initiate proceedings against the diet center.

6. The Federal Trade Commission (FTC) has investigated numerous diet companies with a view toward tightened regulations. Report any misdoings, or misleading advertising, to the FTC, Correspondence Branch, Room 692, 6th Street and Pennsylvania Avenue, N.W., Washington, DC 20580.

7. If you feel that your health has suffered as a result of the diet, speak to your doctor. If the doctor draws the same conclusions, it may be appropriate to speak to a lawyer.

▲ *See also* CREDIT CARDS; SCAMS.

Disabilities

The biggest problem confronting consumers with disabilities is often merchants who do not understand what disabilities mean. Whenever a seller, salesperson, or company representative makes an assumption based on a stereotype, soluble challenges can become discouraging barriers.

This works two ways. The first is when you call ahead to ask, "Is your place accessible to someone in a wheelchair?" and are told, "By all means," based on the assumption that you need a ramp but not a bathroom, and don't mind wedging your wheelchair into a revolving door. The other is when you make the same inquiry and get a no, based on the speaker's unwillingness to be bothered or face a possible lawsuit if an accident happens.

These contradictory responses invite three basic observations:

1. Just as sellers can't assume what your needs might be, you can't assume that the seller is a mind reader. A well-intentioned doorman may be thinking of the time Aunt Maudie got down the stairs on a cane, ostensibly "proving" accessibility. Educate the person when you call. Specify the features you expect. If they're not there, explain why they should be. Then decide if you want to sue or go anyway or go someplace else. At least you give yourself flexibility in deciding.

2. People who put you off for fear of accidents and subsequent lawsuits ought to be aware of the Americans with Disabilities Act of 1990. Now they can also be sued for failure to comply with federal law, which assures significant access rights in employment, public accommodations, transportation, and telecommunications to our nation's 43 million people with disabilities.

3. Businesses that exclude the access of 43 million possible consumers are doing themselves a disservice. Better they should follow the lead of Nordstrom and Target Stores, which have used models with disabilities in their catalogs to attract, and show their support of, a highly desirable market.

The Law

1. Because the Americans with Disabilities Act of 1990 (ADA) is still quite new, even "the law" doesn't know what the law is yet. Some requirements remain imprecise and are yet to be nailed down by the outcomes of court cases.

2. But the ADA, combined with other federal, state, and municipal laws, gives added clout to your legitimate consumer complaints.

3. Under Title V, section 504, of the Rehabilitation Act of 1973 (Public Law 93-112), a physically or mentally disabled person has the same rights as anyone else to:

- **Education.**
- **Employment.**
- **Health care.**
- **Senior citizen activities.**
- **Welfare.**

- **Any other public or private sector service that U.S. tax dollars help support.**

If you are otherwise qualified, your disability doesn't count.

4. Section 504 says an employer receiving federal assistance may not discriminate in recruitment, advertising, processing of applications for employment, hiring, promotion, leaves of absence, fringe benefits, and numerous other areas.

5. Section 504, with the Education for All Handicapped Children Act (Public Law 94-142), assures your disabled child's right to a free appropriate education in a school district that benefits from the use of federal funds, services, or properties.

6. Your public school district must provide an education for your child regardless of the type or severity of his or her disability.

7. A college or training program can't ask you to take a preadmission test that can't properly measure abilities because it makes no special provisions to accommodate the fact that you're blind, deaf, or have another disability.

8. The Americans with Disabilities Act of 1990 mandated the removal of barriers that block access to and through privately owned places open to the public if the changes are "readily achievable": restaurants, offices, hotels, airports, theaters, and so on.

9. "Readily achievable" turned out not to be readily interpreted. Legal cases ensued, most of them unresolved at this writing. Yet you don't have to sue to remind restaurants and theaters that the law exists.

10. Accessibility goes beyond what may be obvious to the most oblivious souls: there must be not only elevators and wide doors, but also such modifications as visual alarms for the deaf in the event of fire.

11. Property owners and their tenants are liable under the law—in other words, both the woman who owns the travel agency and the landlord of the building where she operates are liable.

12. Provisions include rail and rapid-transit lines, long-haul buses, cruise ships, and ferries, as well as stationary places. It's best to call first to confirm what's in place and what you must do to arrange for it.

13. The ADA amplifies section 504 in making it harder for employers to discriminate on the basis of physical or mental conditions.

14. Employers must define jobs according to their actual functions and make sure job descriptions reflect those duties.

15. Employers must provide equal access for all workers to all benefits and privileges of employment, including cafeterias, lounges, and recreational areas.

16. If an advertisement for a job doesn't meet the requirements of the law, both the employer and agency may be liable—for instance, if a phone number is given without an address, excluding a deaf person from responding.

17. Along with federal laws are state and municipal laws that may be even more stringent. Your state and local advocacy offices for people with disabilities can tell you what applies.

Social Security

1. Don't overlook the possibility of financial assistance from the government if you're disabled. (*See* SOCIAL SECURITY.)

2. You may be entitled to receive Supplemental Security Income (SSI).

3. You may be eligible for Old Age and Survivors Disability Insurance (OASDI)—the basic Social Security retirement program.

4. If you file with the Social Security office, you'll be interviewed by a claims representative. Be sure to provide facts and documentation. A state examiner will then review your case.

5. If denied, you can file with the Social Security office to reconsider your request.

6. If you're denied again, you can appeal to an administrative law judge (Social Security Office of Hearing and Appeals).

7. From there, you can take it up to the Appeals Council.

8. Depending on your affiliations, financial assistance might also be available through your insurance, worker's compensation, and association memberships.

How to Make It Work

1. This book doesn't pretend to be a law course, and besides, you probably don't want to go to litigation every time you try to buy a fitted sheet or socket wrench.

2. Discussion is more than possible. Begin by doing your research. If you're in a wheelchair and planning to check into a hotel, ask in advance to be on a suitable floor. Confirm that your room has a roll-in shower and special parking spaces. If you're going to an airport or railroad terminal, you may have to call ahead to be met by a courtesy vehicle. Note the times and dates of calls, and the names of the people who give the information.

3. If you arrive and encounter a problem, particularly if you've made advance arrangements that have been ignored, cite the conversations you had and name your sources.

4. You may have to ask for a manager or supervisor.

5. State the problem. Ask how it can be resolved. If the misinformation creates an added financial consequence, ask how the company intends to reimburse you.

6. Whether or not the matter is resolved, report it to higher management, with a CC to the manager or supervisor. Higher management can be a customer service department for a chain (of theaters, hotels, restaurants, etc.), or a regional manager, or the company president.

7. Mention that what the establishment you're patronizing may perceive as mere inconvenience goes deeper. For instance, the offer to carry a wheelchair up two flights of stairs to an observa-

tion deck may seem considerate, but actually, it's demeaning, and it poses a safety threat.

8. If employees treat you improperly, your letter to higher management might urge that the individuals or the whole staff be offered a class in sensitivity training. Such courses are becoming increasingly important to service industries, and most informed executives are aware of them.

9. Read articles about compliance with the ADA. If the CEO of a theater chain is quoted as saying, "We want to be recognized for our excellence in sensitivity," write to him or her about your experience. Refer to the article. CC the supervisor or manager.

10. Write a letter to the editor of the area's leading newspaper. You express an opinion. Others see the letter. Your unfortunate incident, if not corrected, may have a negative impact on business.

11. Write to the Chamber of Commerce, indicating that inhospitable service from an airport or hotel (or whatever) could eventually be expensive to the whole town. After all, if a conference center isn't accessible, organizations would have to take their meetings and members elsewhere.

12. If you feel you've been discriminated against, contact your state division of human rights or equivalent office to find out how to file a complaint.

13. State advocates for the disabled (or offices for protection and advocacy for people with disabilities, or similar designations) are valuable resources of information and referrals.

14. The Office for Civil Rights enforces federal laws prohibiting discrimination against persons on the basis of race, color, national origin, religion, sex, age, or mental or physical disability. Call to find out how you can initiate an investigation. Look in your phone directory under "Civil Rights" in the government listings or such designations as "Law, Department of"; or phone the Civil Rights Hotline, 1-800-368-1019, (202-376-8312 in Washington, DC). FAX 212-264-3039.

15. Your area Equal Employment Opportunity Commission (EEOC) handles employment com-

plaints filed under the Americans with Disabilities Act. Look in the U.S. Government listings in your directory or contact the Equal Employment Opportunity Commission, 1801 L Street, N.W., Washington, DC 20507, 1-800-669-4000 (800-800-3302 TDD). For publications, call 1-800-669-3362.

16. There are also lawsuits. As with any aspect of consumerism, it's easier to use the law and other resources through discussion or negotiation than to go through the courts.

17. Companies may try to use this reluctance to their advantage, believing most consumers who threaten "I'll take you to court" never do. It's too costly. It eats up time. But *you* may be in the position to consider a test case. If your complaint relates to provisions of the law in general, you may be able to secure the backing of a well-funded advocacy group.

18. *Or* you may simply want to suggest as much to your adversary.

19. If you opt for legal remedy, there are specialists in disability law.

Other Resources

1. Contact area Centers for Independent Living, Social Service agencies, and organizations that focus on a single disability (such as the Lighthouse or American Cancer Society), and ask your elected officials for their suggestions.

2. Hearing- or speech-impaired individuals who use a Telecommunications Device for the Deaf (TDD or TTY) can get assistance with calls made to and from a telecommunications device by calling TDD/TTY Operator Services, 1-800-855-1155 or 202-708-9300 (Washington, DC, metropolitan area). Following is a federal TDD directory, courtesy of the United States Office of Consumer Affairs.

Federal TDD Directory

This section lists Federal government offices that have Telecommunications Devices for the Deaf (TDDs). These offices can respond to questions and complaints from persons with speech and hearing impairments. If you are a voice user, the Federal Information Relay Service (FIRS) will relay the call for you. Call FIRS on **1 (800) 877-8339** (toll free) or (202) 708-9300 in Washington, DC, and a relay operator will come on the line. Additional TDD numbers are published in the *U.S. Government TDD Directory,* available free by writing the Consumer Information Center, Item 573X, Pueblo, CO 81009.

Architectural and Transportation Barriers Compliance Board

1111 18th Street, N.W., Room 501
Washington, DC 20036-3894
202-653-7834 (voice/TDD)
202-653-7848 (voice/TDD)
202-653-7951 (voice/TDD)

Central Intelligence Agency

Handicapped Program Office
Washington, DC 20505
202-874-4449 (voice/TDD)

Commission on Civil Rights

1121 Vermont Avenue, N.W.
Washington, DC 20425
202-376-8116 (voice/TDD)

Congressional TDD Numbers

United States House of Representatives
Congressional Telecommunications for the Deaf (TDD message relay service—to leave messages for representatives)
202-225-1904 (TDD)

Subcommittee on Select Education
Majority Office
202-226-7532 (voice/TDD)

United States Senate
Senate Special Services
202-224-4049 (TDD)

Senate Human Resources
202-224-7806 (TDD)

Committee on Labor and Human Resources
202-224-1975 (voice/TDD)

Subcommittee on the Handicapped Majority Office
202-224-3457 (TDD)

Minority Office
202-224-9522 (voice/TDD)

United States Capitol Switchboard
202-224-3091 (TDD)

U.S. Consumer Product Safety Commission

5401 Westbard Avenue
Bethesda, MD 20207
1-800-638-8270 (TDD)

Department of Agriculture

14th Street and Independence
Avenue, S.W.
Washington, DC 20250

Central Employment and Selective Placement Office
202-447-2436 (voice/TDD)

Meat and Poultry Hotline
202-447-3333 (voice/TDD)
1-800-535-4555 (voice/TDD)

Department of the Army

Civilian Personnel Office
Arlington, VA 22212
703-697-3887 (voice/TDD)

Department of Commerce

14th Street and Constitution
Avenue, N.W.
Washington, DC 20230

Bureau of the Census
Population Division
Statistical Information Staff
Suitland and Silver Hill Roads
Federal Building #3, Room 2375
Suitland, MD 20233
301-763-5020 (voice/TDD)

International Trade Administration
Office of Commercial Information
   Management
Herbert C. Hoover Building,
   Room 1848
Washington, DC 20230
202-377-1669 (TDD)

National Institute of Standards and Technology (NIST)
Office of Information Services,
   Room E106
Gaithersburg, MD 20899
301-975-2812 (TDD)

NIST Personnel Office
Administration Building
Room A123
Gaithersburg, MD 20899
301-975-3007 (voice/TDD)

National Weather Service
National Meteorological Center
World Weather Building,
   Room 307
Washington, DC 20233
301-427-4409 (voice/TDD; official
   business—no forecasts)

Office of the Secretary
Office of Civil Rights Programs,
Planning and Systems Division
Herbert C. Hoover Building,
   Room 6010
Washington, DC 20230
202-377-5691 (voice/TDD)

Department of Education

330 C Street, S.W.
Washington, DC 20202

Captioning and Media Services
330 C Street, S.W.
Washington, DC 20202

202-732-1177 (voice)
202-732-1169 (TDD)

National Institute on Disability and Rehabilitation Research
330 C Street, S.W.
Washington, DC 20202
202-732-1198 (TDD)

Office of Civil Rights
330 C Street, S.W.
Washington, DC 20202
202-732-1663 (TDD)

Office of Deafness and Communicative Disorders
330 C Street, S.W.
Washington, DC 20202
202-732-1398 (voice/TDD)

Rehabilitation Services Administration
330 C Street, S.W.
Washington, DC 20202
202-732-1298, 2848 (TDD)

Department of Health and Human Services

Handicapped Employment Program
200 Independence Ave., S.W.
Washington, DC 20201
202-475-0073 (TDD)

Food and Drug Administration
5600 Fishers Lane
Parklawn Building
Rockville, MD 20857
301-443-1970 (voice/TDD)

Equal Employment Opportunity Office
301-443-1818 (TDD)

Office of the Secretary
Personnel Office
202-619-3540 (voice/TDD)

Office for Civil Rights
200 Independence Ave., S.W.
Washington, DC 20201
202-472-2916 (TDD)

Social Security Administration
6401 Security Boulevard
Baltimore, MD 21235
301-965-4404 (TDD)

Department of Housing and Urban Development

451 Seventh Street, S.W.
Washington, DC 20410
202-755-5965 (TDD)
1-800-424-8590 (TDD)

Department of the Interior

18th and C Streets, N.W.
Washington, DC 20240

Personnel Office
202-208-4817 (TDD)

Department of Justice

10th Street and Constitution
Avenue, N.W.
Washington, DC 20530

Immigration and Naturalization
202-514-4012 (voice/TDD)

Civil Rights Division
202-307-2678 (voice/TDD)

FBI Tours
202-324-3553 (TDD)

FBI Identification Division
202-324-2334 (voice/TDD)

Department of Labor

200 Constitution Avenue, N.W.
Washington, DC 20210

Office of Civil Rights
202-523-7090 (voice/TDD)

Department of the Navy

Civilian Personnel Office
Washington, DC 20376
202-692-2658 (TDD)

Department of State

2201 C Street, N.W.
Washington, DC 20520

Personnel Office
202-647-7256 (voice/TDD)

Department of Transportation

National Highway Traffic Safety Administration
400 7th Street, S.W.
Washington, DC 20590
202-366-2602 (voice/TDD)

Department of the Treasury

Bureau of the Public Debt
13th and C Streets, S.W.
Washington, DC 20590
202-287-4097 (TDD)

Internal Revenue Service
1111 Constitution Avenue, N.W.
Washington, DC 20224
202-708-9300 (TDD)

Department of Veterans Affairs

810 Vermont Avenue, N.W.
Washington, DC 20420

Personnel Office
202-233-3225 (voice/TDD)

Environmental Protection Agency

401 M Street, S.W.
Washington, DC 20460
202-260-2090 (voice/TDD)

Equal Employment Opportunity Commission

2401 E Street, N.W.
Washington, DC 20507
202-663-4494 (TDD)
1-800-800-3302 (TDD)

Executive Office of the President

The White House
1600 Pennsylvania Ave., N.W.
Washington, DC 20500
202-456-6213 (TDD)

Federal Communications Commission

1919 M Street, N.W.
Washington, DC 20554
202-632-6999 (voice/TDD)

Federal Deposit Insurance Corporation

1776 F Street, N.W.
Washington, DC 20429
202-898-3537 (voice/TDD)
1-800-442-5488 (voice/TDD)

Federal Reserve Board

20th and C Streets, N.W.
Washington, DC 20551
202-452-3544 (voice/TDD)

General Services Administration

18th & F Streets, N.W.
Washington, DC 20405

Clearinghouse on Computer Accommodation
202-501-4906 (voice/TDD)

Council on Accessible Technology (COAT)
202-501-2296 (TDD)

Federal Information Relay Service
202-708-9300 (TDD)
1-800-877-8339 (voice/TDD outside DC)

Interstate Commerce Commission

Constitution Avenue and 12th
Street, N.W.

Washington, DC 20011
202-275-1721 (TDD)

Library of Congress

1291 Taylor St., N.W.
Washington, DC 20542
202-707-6200 (TDD)

Merit Systems Protection Board

1120 Vermont Avenue, N.W.
Washington, DC 20419
202-653-8896 (voice/TDD)

National Aeronautics and Space Administration

400 Maryland Avenue, S.W.
Washington, DC 20546

Personnel Office
202-426-1436 (voice/TDD)

Greenbelt Personnel Office
301-286-3729 (voice/TDD)

National Archives and Records Service

8th and Pennsylvania Ave., N.W.
Washington, DC 20408
202-501-5404 (voice/TDD)

National Council on Disability

800 Independence Ave., S.W.,
   Suite 814
Washington, DC 20591
202-267-3232 (voice/TDD)

National Endowment for the Arts

1100 Pennsylvania Ave., N.W.
Washington, DC 20506
202-682-5496 (voice/TDD)

National Science Foundation

1800 G Street, N.W., Room 212
Washington, DC 20550
202-357-7492 (voice/TDD)

Nuclear Regulatory Commission

Washington, DC 20555
301-492-4626 (voice/TDD)

Office of Personnel Management

1900 E Street, N.W.
Washington, DC 20415

Equal Employment Opportunity Division
202-606-2460 (voice/TDD)

Job Information Center
202-606-0591 (TDD)

President's Committee on Employment of People with Disabilities

1111 20th Street, N.W.
Washington, DC 20036
202-653-5050 (TDD)

Securities and Exchange Commission

450 Fifth Street, N.W.
Washington, DC 20549
202-272-2552 (voice/TDD)

Small Business Administration

409 Third Street, S.W.
Washington, DC 20416
202-205-7333 (TDD)

Smithsonian Institution

Special Education Program
Washington, DC 20560
202-357-1696 (TDD)

Tennessee Valley Authority

400 West Summit Hill Drive
Knoxville, TN 37902
615-751-8500 (TDD)

United States House of Representatives

Washington, DC 20215
202-225-1904 (TDD)

United States Information Agency

301 4th Street, S.W.
Washington, DC 20547
202-485-7157 (voice/TDD)

United States Postal Service

475 L'Enfant Plaza West, S.W.
Washington, DC 20260
202-268-2310 (voice/TDD)

United States Senate

Washington, DC 20510
202-224-4049, 4075 (TDD)

▲ *See also* INSURANCE; SOCIAL SECURITY; WORKPLACE.

Doctors

When you go to your doctor, you're absolutely within your rights to have two concerns: your health, and your bank account. This isn't to say you ought to seek cut-rate service, or that you should nickel-and-dime your chances of recovery, but it does mean that nobody should pressure you into settling for only one of the two concerns. You hire a doctor just as you hire anybody else to work for you, and in that spirit, you shouldn't be overcharged, and you shouldn't pay for services, care, or tests you don't get.

The same applies to doctors in institutional settings such as hospitals. See HOSPITALS for those specifics, and see below for office visits.

Note: This information may be affected by the adoption of a National Health Care Plan.

Where You Stand

1. It's in your best interest to understand the plight of private practitioners today, for the same reason you'd want to know if your bank were in danger or if your contractor were bankrupt. It's simple self-defense.

2. Many doctors continue to be rich people. Many others collect great gobs of money from patients, then pay it out for malpractice insurance, new equipment, and additional staff to do paperwork. They've invested ten or fifteen years in learning to care for the sick, then have to master the subtleties of diagnostic codes ("ICD-9CM") and procedural codes ("CPT/HCPCS") in order to

fill out patients' claim forms, then devote a fifth of each day to completing insurance forms, using time they'd prefer to spend with patients.

3. The average visit generates ten pieces of paper. That's ten different documents on which mistakes can be made. If an error occurs, the patient must become a medical investigator to set things straight; the doctor's office has to devote more time to the additional paperwork; the doctor feels further hassled; and the patient is furious.

4. To maximize time available for patients, doctors often instruct their receptionists/nurses/billing clerks to "handle the hassle factor." Some doctors either don't realize or prefer not to notice that their staffers interpret this as an instruction to make decisions the doctor should be making and, in general, to "protect" the doctor from patients.

5. Doctors have been "stiffed" by insurance companies and patients who find ways not to pay. Once cheated, doctors can be just as furious, just as wary, as any patient arguing a doctor's bill.

6. *If* you fully appreciate this situation, you may find yourself showing your doctor more sympathy than your doctor has ever displayed to you. It may not seem terribly fair, but your power as a medical consumer is definitely enhanced by your knowledge of the terrain.

Before You Go

1. If there are items you want to be particularly certain the doctor hears and appreciates, don't

hesitate to put them in a letter in advance. Hand it to the doctor at the beginning of the visit and ask that it be added to your file after the doctor has read it.

2. Some medical advice is available through nurse-call lines operated by trained nurses who may suggest approaches to your symptoms, or even what to ask the doctor during your office visit.

3. Nurse-call lines may be available through your employer, your insurer, or your local hospital. The Cleveland Clinic's line (216-444-1234) operates daily from 7:00 A.M. to 11:00 P.M. EST.

4. The Center for Medical Consumers, located in New York City, is open to the general public (212-674-7105).

5. The Health Information Center of the U.S. Public Health Service (1-800-336-4797) provides printed guidelines on specific conditions, as well as referrals to other resources.

6. The National Institutes of Health (301-496-4000) will direct you to useful health consumer organizations and information about your condition.

7. Written reports on specific conditions are also available from the Agency for Health Care Policy and Research (Division of the U.S. Department of Health and Human Services). Known as practice guidelines, they're free from the AHCPR, P.O. Box 8547, Silver Spring, MD 20907; 1-800-358-9295.

8. The National Women's Health Network (202-347-1140) concentrates on advice for women with medical queries.

9. For a fee ranging from $85 to $225, Health Resource, Conway, AR 72032 (501-329-5272), sends extensive reports, including choices and options and names of specialists and consumer awareness organizations concerned with your illness.

10. For just under $100, you can order a bound index of current information on your condition from Medical Information Service, 3000 Sand Hill Road, Bldg. 2, Suite 260, Menlo Park, CA 94025 (1-800-999-1999 or 415-233-6940).

11. Read over your insurance before your visit. Familiarize yourself with your carrier's procedure, and with the extent of your coverage.

What to Do

1. You'll have to dawdle in the waiting room anyhow, so ask if the doctor has a service book. The request shows you to be a savvy medical consumer, and if the doctor has one, it means the doctor harbors some desire to keep you happy.

2. The service book ought to focus on the doctor's background and services and enumerate office policies on billing and insurance, laboratory tests, emergencies, and patient's responsibilities. The first page will probably be signed by the doctor.

3. Make notes of statements that might pertain to you if problems later arise. Remember, it's a signed document placed in public view to solicit your business.

4. The doctor will probably leave you waiting again in the examining room before the visit begins. Use this time to read the diplomas and certificates on the wall, and write down the names of the review boards, universities, etc.

5. You may want the doctor to be fully cognizant of you as a whole person and to be aware of all your considerations, including any financial ones, and you may expect the doctor to put aside any sense of his or her time or financial pressure in order to devote every ounce of attention to your problem. But this isn't realistic.

6. If you try to see things from your doctor's perspective, you'll come to the point when you describe your symptoms.

7. There's evidence that a majority of doctors interrupt their patients within the first minute of any visit. If you've saved up symptoms to discuss, state them all at the outset and don't leave without a response to each.

8. If you were previously in the care of another physician, give the name and address to your new doctor, who can request that the records be forwarded and added to your current files.

9. With exceptions, you yourself ought to be entitled to review all information relating to your examination and treatment. If access is denied, contact your state department of health (look in the government listings for your state in your tele-

phone directory). You usually have to start by filling out a form.

10. Whatever you ask your doctor, you have a right to understand the response and to ask for clarification.

11. If drugs are prescribed, be sure you're warned of possible side effects. Never neglect to mention any other medication you might be taking and any other conditions you have.

12. Books such as the *Physicians' Desk Reference* and *Graedon's Best Medicine* discuss drugs and their side effects and can be found in libraries, doctors' offices, and bookstores. See what they say about the drug prescribed for you. If you have questions about what you read, ask your doctor.

13. You're always entitled to ask, "What are you going to do and why are you doing it?" You'll be most appreciated if you do it politely.

14. Tell your doctor that you want to approve any tests before they're performed, and before you approve anything, ask why it's indicated, what the potential risks may be, and what alternatives are available.

15. As you grill your doctor, have the courtesy and good sense to write down anything you may forget, and even the tidbits you believe you'll "probably remember."

16. The wise consumer asks, "What will this cost?" even if insurance covers the visit. The assumption that coverage is a free ride is largely responsible for the skyrocketing cost of coverage today.

17. Along with asking the cost of what the doctor wants to do, inquire about the cost of alternatives. You're not in the market for a bargain, but you deserve to be informed.

18. Request and insist on receiving an itemized bill for your insurance company. If you're not insured, get it anyway—for tax purposes, for your home records, and for comparison if the procedures are ever repeated.

19. If you're self-insured or if there are limits on your insurance, make the doctor aware. Doctors will sometimes run optional tests believing "the insurance picks them up anyway," leaving you stuck with a whopping bill if it turns out you lack sufficient coverage.

20. If the doctor recommends tests, determine whether the laboratory is accredited and the technicians certified, and if the doctor has a financial interest in the lab. (According to one survey, patients sent to physician-owned labs tend to pay more and have more tests done.)

21. If the doctor does have a financial interest in the lab, does the doctor profit in any way from the number of patients referred, and are you free to use a different lab?

22. New regulations are in the works to discourage doctors from making these arrangements. Contact your state or city department of health to determine what rulings apply in your area.

If You're Referred to a Specialist

1. Ask your doctor what risks you face with and without treatment, and what alternative treatments are possible.

2. Determine from your insurer if you're covered for a second opinion, even if you feel comfortable with the first.

3. If you go for a second opinion, realize that if a doctor refers you to a close friend, you may not get an entirely impartial evaluation (even when the basis of the friendship is the doctors' mutual respect for each other's professional skill).

4. Your insurer or a local medical society may suggest sources of a second opinion.

5. Even if you don't want a second opinion, your insurer may require one before agreeing to pay for further treatment.

6. Confirm that the specialist is board-certified, which means he or she has met certain standards of education and expertise.

7. You may want to look up your specialist in the *Directory of Medical Specialists* and the *American Board of Medical Specialties' Compendium of Certified Medical Specialists,* both found in libraries.

8. General and specific questions about specialists can be put to the American Board of Medical Specialties (1-800-776-CERT). If someone there can't tell you exactly what you want to know, he or she can at least suggest ways to go about getting answers.

9. Ask how often the specialist has performed the procedure in question, then find out from your doctor, insurer, a medical school, or an organization such as the People's Medical Society (462 Walnut Street, Lower Level, Allentown, PA 18102; 1-800-624-8773) how this compares with others in the field.

10. Find out if the specialist will perform the entire procedure, or whether a resident will do it under the specialist's supervision.

Billing Errors

1. Be nice. If you discover an error in your bill, assume it's an oversight rather than careless neglect. Phone the office and explain.

2. Ask what needs to be done to correct it.

3. If the person you speak to agrees to correct it, ask for the person's name and title and a CC of any correspondence that will be written.

4. If the person disagrees or tries to stonewall you, ask to speak to the doctor or one of the doctor's associates, and ask this individual to explain it to the person who took the call.

5. Most offices require you to sign a release before each visit. By signing, you agree to be responsible for all charges not covered by insurance. But you may still insist at the outset of your visit that the doctor advise you of each test and procedure for which you'll be charged, and you have the option to refuse. If you say, for example, "My insurance will not pay for a blood test and I will not pay either," and the doctor swears there won't be a charge, the doctor can't simply ignore your wishes, send the blood off to a lab, have the lab bill you, and expect you to pay without a fuss.

6. If this happens and you receive a bill, phone the doctor's office and immediately report the unauthorized charge. If told, "You have to pay because you signed the release," explain that through whatever oversight or good intention, the doctor misrepresented the test to you and you do not feel obligated to pay.

7. If the receptionist, nurse, or billing clerk stonewalls you, and you can't get through to the doctor or one of the doctor's associates, send your objections in writing. Request that the doctor cancel the charge and ask for a copy of any resulting correspondence. CC the local Chamber of Commerce and the state or city department of consumer affairs.

8. If you don't get a reply in a reasonable amount of time, write to the doctor again and repeat the CCs—to avoid giving the impression that you're simply ducking the bill.

9. Your doctor's billing office may decide to ignore you and pass the matter along to a collection agency. (*see* DEBT COLLECTORS.)

10. Depending on the particular circumstances, your Chamber of Commerce, state or city consumer affairs department, or state health department or the People's Medical Society (1-800-624-8773) may be able to suggest your next move.

11. Report all billing complaints to your insurer or Medicare or whoever pays the costs in part or in full. If you suspect deliberate overcharging, or negligence that results in overcharging, find out how to report it to the company investigative or frauds division if there is one. CC your doctor, along with copies of any related correspondence.

12. If a doctor "accepts Medicare assignment," it means that the doctor will bill the fee approved by Medicare. After your deductible, Medicare will pay 80 percent and you'll pay the remaining 20 percent. (*See* MEDICARE, MEDICAID, AND MEDIGAP.)

13. The Physician Payment Reform Law limits the amount above Medicare's approved fee that a nonparticipating physician (one who doesn't accept assignment) can charge if Medicare is paying.

14. See your Medicare Benefits form for the phone number of your Medicare carrier. Ask what the current limit is and how the carrier enforces it.

15. If the carrier won't enforce it, contact the AARP Medicare/Medicaid Assistance Program (601 E Street, N.W., Washington, DC 20049) for advice.

16. More information on Medicare overcharge is available for $1 from Medicare Beneficiaries Defense Fund, P.O. Box 523, Merrifield, VA 22116-0523.

17. If an insurer refuses to pay a claim, check with your doctor's office to confirm that the procedure was properly described and coded.

18. If a mistake was made or if rephrasing will result in coverage, request that the doctor's office process a correction and send you copies of the correspondence.

19. If the receptionist, nurse, or billing clerk won't send you copies of correspondence, ask for a letter on the doctor's stationery, stating when and how the revision was or will be made.

20. A doctor who refuses to complete insurance forms that entitle you to reimbursement may be guilty of professional misconduct, in which case, see below.

Professional Misconduct

1. Your state department of health wants to hear your complaints in any instance of professional misconduct by physicians or physicians' assistants. Depending on your state, these might include:
- **Guaranteeing a cure.**
- **Refusing to complete insurance forms.**
- **Refusing to provide medical records to another doctor.**
- **Ordering excessive tests or treatment.**
- **Sexual harassment.**
- **Filing a false report.**
- **Abandoning or neglecting a patient in need of immediate care.**
- **Performing services not authorized by the patient.**
- **Intimidating a patient.**
- **Keeping inadequate patient records.**

2. Written complaints to the state department of health should include the doctor's full name and address and the nature of the complaint. If you wish your observations to be kept confidential, say so in the letter.

3. Complaints will be reviewed and may lead to an investigation and/or a full hearing. If evidence warrants, the doctor's license could be suspended or revoked.

4. Ask if final misconduct actions will be reported to the National Practitioner Data Bank, which is consulted in connection with the credentialing of doctors.

5. Complaints about dentists, optometrists, psychologists, and other practitioners may be referred to a separate state office. A call to your state department of health will tell you how to direct your queries.

6. Complaints may also be directed to the following organizations, located with the help of your phone directory, telephone information, or your local librarian:
- **State licensing agencies.**
- **Medical society.**
- **Specialty boards.**
- **The physician's malpractice insurance company underwriting panel.**
- **State peer review organizations.**

7. Does your health insurer have an office care review program? If so, find out how it can assist with your complaint.

8. If you suspect your physician of drug or alcohol abuse impairment, contact the state health department or a local medical society for advice.

9. If you feel you were a victim of malpractice, you might want to consult one or more of the above-named agencies and organizations for comments on the legitimacy of your claim *before* you spend money on a lawyer.

10. If you're considering a malpractice suit, remember that it can be instituted long after care is provided, although some statute of limitations is likely to apply.

▲ *See also* DEBT COLLECTORS; HOSPITALS; INSURANCE; MEDICARE, MEDICAID, AND MEDIGAP; NURSING HOMES; SOCIAL SECURITY.

Dry Cleaners

The value of a good dry cleaner is emphasized every time consumers go half an hour out of their way to patronize a superior shop instead of simply the nearest one. This is no rare occurrence. It's only a shame that more harried shoppers with too few hours in the day don't force themselves to take a stand on quality despite the inconvenience. If fewer consumers would settle for inferior service, eventually fewer bad shops would be able to stay in business, and more would learn there's an actual dollars-and-sense reason to do things properly.

In some of the best shops, signs are posted on the counter warning of the types of fabrics that can't be dry-cleaned. With or without the signs, service personnel will at least warn you verbally about beads, sequins, and different materials, and they'll examine each garment for obvious problems. They'll occasionally refuse to take an item because they don't want to risk ruining it. When they return your dry-cleaned clothing to you and results are less than perfect, they'll point out the spot that wouldn't quite come out, and they'll tell you why.

In the worst shops, there are no warnings, and your clothing may be returned shrunk to miniature or with holes the size of planets—but don't expect anyone to mention it. If *you* mention it, prepare to hear a truly infantile explanation, such as "It was this size when you brought it in" or "The hole was there all along." In other words, there's no reasoning with these people.

The Single Most Important Thing

The single most important thing you can do is *never bring that shop another stitch of business.* Why reward incompetence? Why allow the staff to believe that incompetence is tolerated? Perhaps the most amazing phenomenon in the dry cleaning industry is the number of customers who wail, "It's a terrible shop. Each time I go, they ruin something else." Why let them? No wonder they think their job is supposed to be your gamble.

The good news is that there are other steps you can take. The bad news is that consumer agencies do not, as a rule, consider these disputes easy to resolve. This is all the more reason to go to a shop you can trust.

Other Things You Can Do

1. Show that you're an aware consumer. When you take the garment in, don't just ask what it will cost and how soon you'll get it back. If you have a particular stain, bring it to the dry cleaner's attention. State what it was—coffee, ink, or whatever—or if you just noticed it and have no idea where it came from, say so. Ask if there's anything unusual about the fabric or stain that you should know.

2. Remove everything from pockets before leaving your clothes to be cleaned.

3. Ask the dry cleaner whether he or she intends to remove and replace buttons, zippers, or

anything else. If the answer is yes and it makes you uncomfortable, reconsider. Maybe you'd rather take the garment somewhere else.

4. Examine each garment when it's returned to you.

5. Some dry cleaners, having handed you damaged goods, will glower at you as if you should be ashamed of yourself for having brought something so shoddy into the shop. This is supposed to dissuade you from asking why the zipper is fused shut. Don't be browbeaten. Glower back. Inquire, "Why have you welded my zipper shut forever?"

6. You may get one of the classic stupid replies, such as "Those zippers shouldn't be dry-cleaned." This is supposed to mean you were the architect of your own misfortune. Nonsense. It's not as though you broke into the shop at night and replaced the original zipper with another one. The zipper was there from the outset. The dry cleaner claims to be the professional. If a professional dry cleaner didn't know about "those zippers" you were surely under no obligation to know. Part of what you paid for was presumably the professional's expertise.

7. Questions raised after the fact could have been raised before the fact, so why weren't they? If the dry cleaner didn't recognize the fabric or stain, he or she should have asked you. If the dry cleaner didn't know and knew he or she didn't know, he or she shouldn't have acted in ignorance. Dry cleaning isn't a chemistry experiment. Professionals should be familiar with fabrics and treatments prior to using them. If you are told that the cleaner "didn't know" a particular result would occur, then explain that a person who knowingly acts in ignorance has accepted full responsibility. For example, it's not very convincing to shoot a person and then offer as the defense "I didn't know the gun was loaded." Cooler heads will wonder why anyone would aim a gun at someone else and pull the trigger without first establishing the status of the weapon.

8. This logic may or may not prove effective with the shopkeeper or manager, who may abso-

lutely believe that chemistry experiments and incredible shrinking wardrobes are part of the job. If it fails, try again when the shop is full. Be logical. Be audible. Deal in facts. Restate, for all the world to hear, the incompetence in which the shopkeepers apparently take pride. You might want to chide yourself out loud: "That's what I get for settling for someone cheap and fast, when Jack Sprat's down the block across from the butcher's has always done much better work."

9. Dry cleaners generally depend on neighborhood business. Consequently, they need favorable word of mouth. Eventually, even the worst dry cleaners will figure this out.

10. If the dry cleaner belongs to a chain, you can try working through the main office, or the customer service department.

11. If the owner is never on the premises, find out (perhaps from the Chamber of Commerce) how to contact this person. Write a letter explaining the nature of the damage, and your concern that the owner may not realize the extent of negligence being cheerfully defended in his or her absence. Indicate that you feel you must report your complaints to the Chamber of Commerce, the Better Business Bureau, and the state or city department of consumer affairs.

12. When you report it to the protection agencies, ask if there have been complaints before. Ask how many must accrue before action is taken.

13. If your BBB or department of consumer affairs has a binding arbitration program for dry cleaners and if your dry cleaner is a registered participant, you can request intervention. In some cases, the BBB will attempt to mediate with non-members as well.

14. In many states, dry cleaners' associations have arbitration programs. Ask your BBB or department of consumer affairs if one is available to you.

15. Check the walls of the establishment. If a membership certificate is posted (or diploma from some professional course or school), note the name of the issuing institution. Contact the institution

and ask for its advice. Explain that the activities of its member (or graduate) reflect badly on the institution, and you feel it would be in its interest to correct the poor impression being given.

16. You can take the matter to small-claims court (*see* RUNG TEN: SMALL-CLAIMS COURT, in Part I).

17. Check your phone book (try under "Cleaners") to see if there is an area trade association for them. For a fee, many of these associations will arrange lab analysis, and if the cleaner was at fault, they may be able to mediate the dispute.

18. If the dry cleaner destroyed your clothing, it isn't enough for you to refuse to pay. Negotiate for restitution. If other resources aren't available, contact the International Fabricare Institute, 12251 Tech Road, Silver Spring, MD 20904. For a fee the I.F.I. will evaluate the damage and what caused it. If the fabric was at fault, present the report to the store that sold you the clothing and request a refund. If the cleaner is responsible, show the report to the cleaner and ask for compensation.

19. You'll do yourself a huge favor if you keep store receipts when you buy clothes, at least as long as the garments are new. If you have a receipt, you can prove that the garment was new and what you paid for it. Receipts are excellent bargaining tools when you go up against your dry cleaner.

20. If you don't have the receipt and the dry cleaner loses your garment, you'll never forgive yourself. If you have the receipt, the dry cleaner may try to wheedle and shame you anyway. Don't be a sap. Stand your ground. (If standing your ground quietly in the middle of the morning doesn't help, refer to item 8 in this list.)

21. If you're using a dry cleaner for the first time, it wouldn't hurt to ask whether there's a policy for lost garments. If there isn't, suggest that one be developed.

22. If the garment has been lost and you're arguing for compensation in the presence of a crowd, press the dry cleaner for a return policy: "What about these people? What happens if you lose their garments? Perhaps we should tell them now about the miserable settlement you're prepared to make with me."

23. If you store clothing with your dry cleaner, make sure the dry cleaner is insured. Find out what the insurance covers. Try to get it in writing.

800 Numbers

An 800-number call is toll-free, set up to enable you to phone a company or agency without charge to you. Some are set up by corporations and businesses, some by the government, some by citizens' groups. Occasionally, they're employed by scam artists. (It's possible for you to phone an 800 number for information and be billed for the service. *See* SCAMS.)

To find out if the organization you're calling has an 800 number, phone 800 Information (1-800-555-1212). If 800 Information has no free listings, call the toll number and ask, first, "Is there a toll-free number I can use?" You may be given one at that time. Some 800 numbers operate everywhere in the nation except in their home states, where residents can make intrastate calls; others only function for residents of a particular state, and won't work if dialed from across state lines.

Many useful 800 numbers are listed throughout this book. Or, for a quick source of 800 hotlines, read below.

1. The Auto Safety Hotline/National Highway Traffic Safety Administration (1-800-424-9393, or in Washington, DC, 202-366-0123) provides information on safety recalls and defects in automobiles. Leave message on the machine between 8:00 A.M. and 5:30 P.M. EST, Monday through Friday. Someone will get back to you.

2. The Civil Rights Hotline (1-800-368-1019, or in Washington, DC, 202-376-8312) accepts calls about discrimination on the basis of race, color, national origin, handicap, or age occurring in Health and Human Services programs such as hospitals and nursing homes.

3. The U.S. Consumer Product Safety Commission Safety Hotline (1-800-638-2772, or in Maryland 1-800-492-8104) will tell you about products that have been recalled for safety reasons, and will take complaints about unsafe products.

4. The U.S. Federal Crime Insurance Hotline (1-800-638-8780, or in Washington, DC, and Maryland 202-652-2637) will help you secure "affordable" homeowner's insurance.

5. The Federal Deposit Insurance Corporation Bank Complaint Hotline (1-800-424-5488, or in Washington, DC, 202-389-4767) will help you with complaints and questions about state-chartered banks, including lost deposits and disputed bank procedures.

6. The Funeral Services Consumer Arbitration Program (1-800-662-7666) helps to resolve disputes between funeral directors and those who have paid for their services.

7. Magazine Action Line (1-800-645-9242, or in New York 516-883-5432) is the means by which Publishers Clearing House helps subscribers with subscription complaints.

8. The Major Appliance Consumer Action Panel (1-800-621-0477, or in Illinois 312-984-5858) works on behalf of consumers with complaints about kitchen, laundry, and other major appliances.

9. The Medicare/Medicaid Complaint Line (1-800-368-5779, or in Washington DC, Maryland, and Virginia 202-472-4222) can be of help if you

have been refused medical aid because of your income, or because you are a recipient of Medicare or Medicaid. When you call, you'll have to leave a message, after which the call will be returned.

10. The National Council on the Aging (1-800-424-9046, or in Washington, DC, 202-497-1200) is an information and consulting hotline for senior citizens.

11. The National Organization of Social Security Claimants Representatives (1-800-431-2804)

provides addresses of regional attorneys who specialize in claims against the Social Security Administration.

12. The Right-to-Know Hotline (1-800-535-0202, or in Washington, DC, 202-479-2449) provides assistance when you want to inquire or complain about chemical storage and spills.

▲ *See also* **900** NUMBERS; SCAMS; TELEMARKETING.

Electronic Fund Transfers (EFTs)

When a purchase is made by credit card or check, there's always the possibility of stopping payment if you aren't satisfied with what you receive for your money. But when you pay for retail purchases with an EFT (Electronic Fund Transfer) card or other device, it's the same as paying cash. If the merchandise is defective or not delivered, you've got to resolve the problem directly with the seller, or with higher consumer authorities. But your card issuer has no obligation to intervene.

There's one exception to this.

1. If you've arranged for your institution to automatically transfer regular payments from your account to a third party such as a utility or life insurance company, the federal EFT (Electronic Fund Transfer) Act says you can stop payment if you notify your issuing institution at least three business days before the scheduled transfer.

2. Confirm your institution's policies regarding notification. Can your instructions be oral or written? If oral, are you required to follow up with a written statement of your instructions?

3. If written notice isn't received, is your instruction automatically voided?

4. Under federal law, financial institutions can't require you to agree to electronic fund transfer as the means to repay a loan, but if you agree to the arrangement, your right to stop payment doesn't apply to mortgage or loan payments owed to the institution that issued your EFT card or device.

5. State laws or individual bank policies may extend your rights as an EFT user. Your state banking commission (look in the government listings for your state in your telephone directory) can provide further details about the law.

6. Ask your bank representative what rights and coverage you have. Ask if this is competitive with other banks. Then do your own research before committing yourself.

▲ *See also* AUTOMATED TELLER MACHINES; BANKING; CREDIT CARDS; CREDIT RATING.

Funeral Homes

At such stressful periods in our lives as the death of a loved one, it seems unnatural to place ourselves in the consumer mode. Even when we feel we could have done better elsewhere, even when we sense that we've been overcharged for services badly rendered, we lack the energy to complain, and we don't want to appear petty in the face of great loss. We would rather not ask, "What does this cost?"—particularly when we know full well that the profit-driven reply might be "How can you pinch pennies at a time like this?"

As a result, whether wishing to be consumers or not, we make ourselves vulnerable to a business with which, for the most part, none of us is likely to have had extensive dealings.

Recognizing this, the Federal Trade Commission (FTC) passed a series of rules requiring certain professional responses by funeral directors. Among them:

1. You must be given an itemization of services offered and what they cost, in writing.

2. You're entitled to a price list for caskets.

3. If you phone for this information, it must be provided over the phone.

4. You may request and receive just selected services if you don't want to purchase an inclusive package.

5. You should get an itemized bill.

6. If you ask any of the above and are refused, the funeral director is acting unethically and you ought to wonder what would cause this refusal to comply. While you're wondering, point out to the funeral director that the FTC can impose penalties up to $10,000. (The FTC, not you, would get the money; but if you make an impression with the threat, you may get the satisfaction you're seeking.)

Furthermore

1. You have the right to shop around. There are options. There are "streamlined" services.

2. It is totally appropriate and highly advisable to ask friends and associates for recommendations.

3. Does your state health department license funeral directors and register funeral homes? If so, malpractice—such as billing for services not rendered, misrepresentation, or failure to meet established standards—can result in fines and revocation of licenses. If you have a complaint, complain. The health department will investigate on your behalf and attempt some form of mediation.

4. If you have a complaint, register it with the Better Business Bureau, Chamber of Commerce, and state or city department of consumer affairs.

5. The Funeral Service Assistance Program will provide information as well as mediation assistance in the event of disputes. The address is 2250 E. Devon Avenue, Suite 250, Des Plaines, IL 60018.

6. If you need certain paperwork, or need to have it redone because of some error or ambiguity, and if you meet with resistance, see if your insurance agent can make a call for you. After all, misstatements of fact may have insurance implications.

7. If you feel you've been cheated but you're too distraught to pursue the matter, ask a friend or clergyperson to act for you. Even if you don't regularly attend a house of worship, the clergy are there for you in time of need.

8. If the nature of the disservice is tasteless, heartless, or unjust, write a letter to the editor of your local newspaper. Because the funeral director depends on good word of mouth in the neighborhood, this may provide him or her with new incentive to address your concerns. If you feel too shaken to write, ask a friend, relative, or clergyperson.

9. Arbitration may be available through the Funeral Services Consumer Assistance Program, 1-800-662-7666.

Guarantees

The Federal Trade Commission's *Guides for Advertising Warranties and Guarantees* takes a firm position on what a guarantee entails.

1. Whatever the price of the consumer product, "satisfaction guaranteed" and "money-back guarantee" mean that if the customer returns the merchandise for any reason, the advertiser has to make a full refund.

2. If there are any strings attached, such as a time limit, they have to be disclosed in the same ad.

3. A "lifetime" guarantee can have three meanings. If you buy a bicycle seat, it may mean that the seat is guaranteed for the life of the bicycle, or for the life of the biker, or for as long as the original owner owns the bike. The FTC advises advertisers to clarify their lifetime guarantees. If you're given a lifetime guarantee and the meaning is conveyed orally, don't spend any money until you can have it in writing too.

4. If a guarantee is misrepresented in a newspaper or magazine, write to the president of the offending company. Send a CC of your letter to the Chamber of Commerce, the Better Business Bureau, the closest FTC branch, and your state's attorney general.

5. You may also wish to write to the advertising office of the publication that carried the ad. It's true that publications derive most of their income from advertisers, but they don't want to jeopardize their integrity by running lies. Suggest in the letter that if one ad in an otherwise reputable publication cannot be trusted, readers may begin to wonder about the other ads. Other advertisers who hear about this may respond by taking their business elsewhere. Obviously, you'd be overreacting to take this course of action every time you're miffed. But in the case of a flagrant violation of truth in advertising, you'd be doing the publication a favor by taking the time to write.

▲ *See also* **WARRANTIES.**

Hairdressers

Beauty is a matter of personal taste. What looks great to you may not appeal to anyone else. If you instruct your stylist to whack your hair down to one-inch ringlets and you emerge looking like a Chia Pet, remember it was your idea. On the other hand, never allow yourself to be intimidated into giving free rein if you've got specific instructions. If the hairdresser is obviously not listening to your directions (or talking to somebody else), insist on waiting until he or she can pay attention before any service is begun.

If he or she responds, "I'm not sure I can do that," or "I'll do my best but I can't guarantee it will look like the picture," be fair. You've been warned. You decide.

But if you say, "I want to use that coloring, but because my hair has been bleached, I'm afraid of a chemical reaction," and the stylist answers, "Don't worry," you've got a significant complaint if your hair turns pea green.

In general, your approach with a hairdresser (or barber) isn't much different from your approach at a dry cleaner. In other words:

1. Solicit the opinions of your friends and associates before selecting a hairdresser. Have they used this shop? Are they satisfied? Do they recommend one stylist over the others? What are the stylist's strengths and weaknesses?

2. Contact the local Better Business Bureau and Chamber of Commerce and/or the state or city department of consumer affairs. Find out whether complaints have been lodged, and if so, how they were resolved.

3. Does your state license hairdressers? Is this hairdresser licensed?

4. Note whether diplomas and professional certificates are posted on the wall. Note the names of the issuing institutions.

5. Explain what you want. Ask if the stylist can do it. Listen carefully to the answer.

6. If chemicals are to be used, you're within your rights to ask to read the label on the product before proceeding.

7. If you aren't satisfied with service and you feel the stylist has acted improperly, ask what steps the stylist intends to take to correct the problem. This wouldn't apply if you don't come out looking beautiful enough, but it would if your hair is damaged, or if the hairdresser deliberately ignored your specific instructions and expects to be paid for doing the opposite of what you requested.

8. If the stylist won't help and is an employee of the shop, speak to the owner or manager.

9. If the owner is an absentee owner, or if the shop belongs to a chain, find out how you can contact the owner or business office (or customer service department of the business office) of the chain. Send your written complaint to this address. CC the shop manager and the stylist.

10. If your hair is damaged in any way as a result of the treatment, get the name, address, and

phone number of the manufacturer of the product used and the exact name of the product. If there's a series number or other identifying number on the bottle, note that too.

11. Contact the customer service department of the manufacturer. State how the product was used and what damage followed. Ask for recommendations on how to repair the damage, and how to proceed with your complaint. However, if you're advised to do something additional to your hair, think twice. You may jeopardize your complaint against the stylist if you take it upon yourself to compound the error.

12. Also, ask whether the manufacturer would know from your description if the product was used incorrectly, and ask for written instructions on how the product should have been used.

13. You'll score subtle points by telling the customer service representative that you'll cooperate with any efforts on his or her part to investigate the product or its misuse. Provide the series or batch or identifying number of the bottle. Add that if the product continues to be used improperly by this stylist and others, it will give the product itself a bad name.

14. Ask if the customer service representative is aware of arbitration programs that might be available to you in your state or locality.

15. File written complaints with the Better Business Bureau, Chamber of Commerce, and state or city department of consumer affairs. Ask about possible arbitration that might be open to you. CC the shop, owner, and business office of the chain (if applicable).

16. Contact the issuing institutions of diplomas and the stylist's professional organizations for their suggestions or recommendations. Explain that their graduate's or member's lack of professionalism is a reflection on them, and ask that they keep a record of your grievance. Maybe they will. Maybe they won't. If they don't, you've only lost the cost of a call. But if they can say something worthwhile, you're ahead of the game.

17. If the hairdresser is licensed by the state, contact the state department of consumer affairs to find out what government branch issues licenses and how you can file a complaint. A large number of complaints about the same shop can result in investigation, fines, and even suspension of license.

18. Talk to your state's department of state (look in the government listings for your state). Can it conduct an informal hearing that would lead to the suspension or revocation of a license or a fine if your allegations are found to be justified?

19. Armed with copies of the above correspondence and replies to it, return to the manager or owner of the shop. Restate your request for satisfaction, and be prepared to specify what it would take to satisfy you.

20. If you go during a quiet time of day and get no satisfaction, return at a much busier hour. Without creating a public nuisance, and without resorting to physical threat, raise a fuss that other customers will hear. Bring your correspondence and refer to it in clear view of the crowd.

21. Small-claims court is a possibility, though usually it will not be helpful in these instances. (*See* RUNG TEN: SMALL-CLAIMS COURT, in Part I.)

22. If you've sustained physical injury, see your doctor and see a lawyer.

Home Building

If you build a home, it's likely to be the biggest financial step you ever take, not to mention a maddening proposition. Considering the magnitude of the project, don't fall into the trap of thinking that the builder seems like a nice guy so you'll trust him with your business. Also, don't kid yourself that reading these few pages in a book about complaining will tell you everything you need to know about hiring a builder. (Variations in state laws alone would fill several volumes, and any statement of coverage below is subject to change.)

When preparing for home building, bone up, snoop around, and do thorough research. Some high schools offer adult education courses on the subject. They're well worth your time.

Until—by no means as a substitute for—real preparation, here are a few hints to point you in the right direction.

Getting Ready

1. Ask friends and associates to recommend builders.
2. If you have someone in mind, ask for the names of satisfied customers. Speak to them and ask if it would be all right for you to see the work. Are they pleased with the job and the treatment they received? If they're satisfied, they probably won't mind cooperating to some degree. If they're not, they'll welcome the opportunity to vent their frustrations and warn you of the builder's weaknesses.
3. Builders with any sense will avoid naming clients they've infuriated, but you can still inquire around the neighborhood and at work.
4. The builder ought to be willing to name a few of his or her suppliers and subcontractors. Contact them. How long have they been dealing with the contractor? Are the contractor's bills from them paid up?
5. Contact your local Chamber of Commerce, Better Business Bureau, and/or state or city department of consumer protection. How long has the contractor been in business? Always under the same name? (A name change may betray a bad reputation under another name.) Are there complaints on file? How were they resolved?
6. Find out from one of the above organizations whether there's a home builders' association in your area. Call it for suggestions and guidance.
7. Is your contract complete and concise? For a step this big, don't just rely on your judgment. Consult someone with experience.
8. Nonetheless, you'll want to give the contract at least a once-over yourself. When you do, look for a clause describing how changes in the agreement will be made. For instance, will they be put in writing?
9. Does the agreement make the contractor responsible for meeting obligations under building codes? Obtaining permits? If the contractor applies for the permit under his or her name and

the work doesn't pass inspection, you shouldn't be financially responsible for any corrections that must be made.

10. Does it state that final payment won't be due until the construction passes inspection by municipal inspectors?

11. Is there a penalty clause to compensate you for an unduly long delay—or, in fact, for any delay—in completion? Remember that you'll have the expense of living someplace else until you can move in.

12. How will debris be removed? Don't accept a verbal explanation. Get it in writing.

13. What insurance do you need to protect yourself in the event the contractor fails? Bear in mind that if he or she can't pay, unpaid subcontractors may go after you.

14. Builders who say "my insurance covers that" aren't necessarily covered, or even insured. See it in documentation from the builder's insurance company. Does it include a provision for workers' compensation if someone is injured while working on your house?

15. Don't sign a contract that has blank spaces. Fill in or draw a line through any blanks.

16. What does your attorney have to say? Does the contract meet your needs? Can you recover your deposit if something goes wrong?

17. Arrange for regular inspections by your own impartial inspector while work is in progress.

The Warranty

In much the same way that you get a warranty on a toaster or VCR, it's possible to get various sorts for houses. The Home Owners Warranty Corporation, National Housing Center, 15th and M Streets, N.W., Washington, DC 20005, offers a program in which builders participate voluntarily. It covers shortcomings in workmanship and materials (for several years) and financial failure of the builder (for two). It can be a definite plus if your builder is one of them, for obvious reasons, and because lending institutions have been known to

lower mortgage payments on houses constructed under the warranty. (However, one school of thought maintains that HOWs are designed to protect the builder by limiting liabilities. If you incline toward this thinking, investigate home-buying options with the FHA or Veterans Administration.)

If your house is built under a HOW warranty:

1. Get the agreement, signed by you and the builder.

2. Get the certificate of participation, confirming that the builder is covered by the master policy.

3. Read and study the Home Owners Warranty Corporation's consumer information booklet.

If Problems Covered by Home Owners Warranty Occur

1. A walk-through is mandatory before you move in. List repairs that need to be made.

2. If you move in and the repairs haven't been made, or if you don't notice shortcomings until later, inform the builder. Allow a realistic amount of time for the work to be done.

3. Keep records and copies of correspondence. Document the dates that problems were discovered and reported and what steps were taken by you and the builder. Take photos. Date the photos.

4. Report the problems to the warranty company, with complete documentation.

5. Within the first two years, the builder is responsible for the quality of workmanship, materials, plumbing, electricity, etc.

6. If the builder doesn't comply, write to the local Home Owners Warranty Council. (Check the phone book for the address, or contact the National Housing Center to request it.) Enclose copies of previous correspondence, photos, etc.

7. The council will advise the builder to make necessary repairs.

8. If you're still not satisfied with the results, request that the council initiate conciliation proceedings.

9. If proceedings fail, arbitration is an option.

10. For the next eight years, a national insurance plan provides protection against major structural defects. In practice, major structural defects are considered to be the kind that make a home unsafe or unlivable; items such as a leaky basement aren't included.

11. Consequently, insist that nonmajor defects be repaired promptly. Don't let the builder run out the clock and then inform you, "Your warranty will take over now," because maybe it won't.

If Not Covered by the Warranty

1. If something goes wrong, or the job goes way over budget or time schedule, ask the local Better Business Bureau and state or city department of consumer affairs about filing a complaint.

2. If the builder behaved unethically and if he or she has to be licensed in your area, you can inquire as to having the license revoked. Municipal officials can also refuse to issue the permits the builder needs for future projects.

3. Check your insurance. It may include provisions for these eventualities.

4. Tell the bank or institution that handles your mortgage. If your arguments are persuasive, the bank might direct the builder to either do the job right or find another patsy to finance his next job.

5. Contact local, state, and federal housing administrations (see the various government listings in your telephone directory).

6. Talk to your attorney.

If the Builder Goes Bust

1. It may not be the builder's fault. For instance, suppose the bank financing him or her fails. But you're still stuck. Or are you?

2. If you're covered by the Home Owners Warranty Corporation, you're protected for the first two years.

3. Find out if the builder posted a bond or put your down payment in an escrow account. If he or she did, find out if any of the funds are available to complete your work.

4. If your builder was not simply a builder but was a developer, or your house was part of a subdivision or condo project, the operation didn't evaporate into thin air when the builder ran out of money. Did the bank that provided financing take over? Did the government?

5. Somebody's got to pick up the reins. Find out who. If the answer isn't immediately apparent, your land records office, which keeps real estate records, might be of help. Consult the government listings in your phone book or ask Information, or get a referral from your city, town, or county clerk.

6. Remind the new owners, as eloquently as you're able, that the development isn't much of an investment when its units are unfinished and its roads are unpaved mud.

7. The larger the development, the greater the number of neighbors who can join with you to apply pressure.

8. The greater the number of neighbors, the greater the number of voters. So if the new owners are uncooperative, approach members of your local government and, as a group, ask for intervention on behalf of your appreciable segment of the community.

▲ *See also* HOME IMPROVEMENTS.

Home Improvements

Adding a room or a deck isn't nearly as costly as building a whole house, but like home building, it's no picnic. Remodeling requires much the same research that goes into finding a contractor to build your house.

One by-product of the recession is that unemployed workers went after much-needed cash by becoming free-lance handymen. But just because someone can run an ad in a local newspaper doesn't make this person an accomplished contractor. Even a skilled professional can be miserable at keeping books.

The National Association of the Remodeling Industry would like to see all contractors not only licensed but also certified. Unlicensed contractors can undercut the prices of licensed professionals who pay for workers' compensation and liability insurance. With fewer expenses, they pass on the savings to attract clients. But when they can't or don't finish the job, the client has far less opportunity for compensation.

Unless you enjoy taking chances with the floor you walk on and the roof over your head:

1. Take bids based on precise specifications, materials, and completion schedule.

2. Speak to other people who hired these contractors. Was the work done in a timely and workmanlike manner?

3. Speak to the Better Business Bureau and the local home builders' association. Do the contractors in question have a clean record?

4. Speak to their subcontractors and suppliers. Do they speak well of past dealings? Do they plan to do business with the contractors again?

5. Some municipalities require licensing, and in some instances, part of the license fee goes into a fund to recompense consumers with significant complaints against their contractors.

6. In some situations, licensed contractors contribute toward a single municipal fund. In others, they pay into separate escrow accounts.

7. Ask your local home builders' or contractors' association or state or city department of consumer affairs what arrangements exist in your area, and what steps you'd take to seek a judgment against a contractor.

8. If the contractor doesn't belong to a local trade association, why not? It's possible that a negative track record made your contractor ineligible. Ask—the contractor, *and* the trade association.

9. Whether or not licensing is the law where you live, you have the option to request it. A licensed contractor will have the license number on his or her business card, stationery, invoices, and contract.

10. Look into the possibility of a rider or other insurance you may need to protect yourself in the event the contractor fails. Bear in mind that if he or she can't pay, unpaid subcontractors may go after you. Also, whose insurance pays if someone is injured while working on your property?

11. Never accept a contractor's assurance that "I'm fully insured." See it in documentation from the insurance company, and confirm that it's indeed complete.

12. Plan your payment schedule to correspond to the progress of the work and include this in the contract.

13. If the contractor demands all the money up front, or even a very large advance payment, be suspicious. If nothing else, you'll have more to lose if the job is never finished.

14. Research the permits you need to undertake your project. Even if the contractor says they've been taken care of, they are legally the homeowner's responsibility.

15. Remember that if any digging, drilling, or blasting will take place, local utility companies should be contacted to ensure that cables and pipes won't be damaged. If necessary, and usually without charge, a representative can come to your yard and mark the locations of underground equipment.

16. Don't sign any contract with blank spaces. Draw a line through blanks, or fill them in.

17. Even if you feel absolutely sure the contract meets your needs, it's not a bad idea to see what your attorney has to say.

18. At least one good point to raise: If the contractor fails and a subcontractor sues you for payment, you'll have to defend yourself in court. This might be prevented if you have each and every subcontractor sign a waiver of lien rights in advance. Your attorney can advise you on the approach and appropriate wording.

19. Alternatively, if state law permits, you can add a release-of-lien clause to the contract, or arrange to make payments into an escrow account until the work has been completed and passes inspection.

20. A few "before" photographs never hurt if remodeling is planned. This way, if your property is ruined instead of improved, you have hard evidence of the starting appearance.

21. Don't sign a certificate of completion or make your final payment until you feel everything has been done as agreed, that subcontractors have been paid, and, if necessary, that work has been approved by local building officials.

22. Don't forget to check the written warranties on construction materials (for example, windows), and keep them in a safe place.

Home Improvement Law

Some states have a home improvement law stipulating terms that must all be met in order for a contract to be enforceable against a contractor. Some specify amounts or limits of deposits and scheduled payments. Depending on the state, the terms will be similar but not necessarily identical to the following:

1. The contractor and salesperson must be registered.

2. The contract and all contract modifications must be in writing.

3. The contract is to be signed by both the homeowner and contractor/salesperson.

4. The contract states a start and completion date.

5. The contract includes notice of the homeowner's right to cancel within a specified number of business days.

6. If more than a specified number of days go by from the start date and the contractor hasn't provided a substantial amount of the work you contracted for, you may request a refund of your money.

7. If the contractor doesn't refund your money within a specified number of days after your request, the contractor is subject to criminal action.

8. Whether or not your state law so stipulates, these are worthwhile items to include in any home improvement contract.

9. Another is a penalty clause. If the contractor doesn't finish on time, it may create unexpected expenses for you. Include wording that will cover or defray your added costs.

Complaints

Take all the above precautions and something may still go wrong. If it does:

1. Reread your warranties and contracts. Locate the specific promises that weren't fulfilled and make these the basis of your complaint.

2. Persist in your complaints to the contractor. If it's in his or her power to make reparation and it's clear you won't let up, he or she is more likely to come through.

3. Contact your Chamber of Commerce, Better Business Bureau, and city or state department of consumer affairs.

4. Does your contractor belong to a trade association? Contact it.

5. If a bond was posted or an escrow payment made, or if your state has a guaranty fund established to assist in these situations, determine what you need to do to collect.

6. Talk to your lawyer.

7. A picture is worth 1,000 words. Take "after" snapshots to go with your "before" photos. Better yet, pull out the camcorder. One frustrated North Carolina homeowner won a case by using a videotape of a bowling ball rolling around on his floor. The tape showed him placing the ball at his feet without applying pressure in any direction. The ball rolled up. The ball rolled down. It rolled right. It rolled left. It all but executed dance steps. The court drew the conclusion that the contractor hadn't constructed a level floor.

▲ *See also* HOME BUILDING.

Hospitals

Except for the fact that people still go to them to get better, hospitals have changed amazingly in the past half-century. As employers (through company benefits, health maintenance organizations, preferred provider organizations, and the like) and the federal government (through Medicare and Medicaid) picked up more and more of the tab, new approaches to payment were introduced—and with them, new pressures were exerted to make certain these big-time bankrollers got their money's worth. On the one hand, the treatment you receive and the length of your stay may be determined primarily by what your insurer is willing to pay. Yet on the other, a major insurer wields more clout on your behalf than you could possibly hope to muster by yourself.

Are you overcharged for care? Sent for unnecessary tests? Prescribed drugs you don't need? You can object and you can complain and your hospital may not care—but if Medicare, Medicaid, and/or other insurers find out that somebody padded a bill, they'll apply pressure till it hurts.

In addition, state and joint regulatory agencies and professional peer groups inspect every facet of hospital care, from food and housekeeping to surgical techniques. If a hospital doesn't measure up, the state can refuse to certify or license the institution.

A new trend in hospital management has been to adopt business techniques such as QA (Quality Assurance) and CQI (Continuous Quality Improvement), to maintain data banks, and to consider patients as "health care consumers." The "era of the patient as customer has arrived," according to one nursing management journal, and "the opportunity to provide service excellence" is its motto. This, coupled with the proposed sweeping moves toward a national health care plan, means that bigger changes than ever are on the way.

You may benefit from this as a health care consumer—or be on the receiving end of staffers' resentment when they feel there are too many agencies looking over their shoulders and not enough time to meet their prime objective of curing patients. Either way, you have the satisfaction of knowing that agencies everywhere are eager to hear and investigate your gripes.

Note: This information may be affected by the adoption of a National Health Care Plan.

Before You Go

1. Check your insurance. Be sure you aren't overlooking an important step that will protect your benefits.

2. If you aren't covered by insurance, find out from the business office how you'll be billed.

3. If you have time and aren't rushing to emergency treatment, ask for an advance look at the papers you'll be given to sign. It's easier to review

them when you're clearheaded and don't feel over-whelmed. It's certainly better than pacing in the lobby with papers you don't want to sign, and knowing your admission hinges on signing them anyway.

4. Some state laws and Medicare/Medicaid rulings require the hospital to give you various papers about "advance directives." These might include a health care proxy (so a person of your choice can make decisions about your care if you aren't able to make them) and a living will (generally used to provide your instructions for life-sustaining measures to be taken or withheld if you're unable to make decisions—for instance, if you lapse into a permanent vegetative condition).

5. If you appoint a representative or assign a proxy, don't just do it on paper. Advise the person you've designated and make your wishes clear.

6. If the hospital has a patient representative or ombudsman, you may want to introduce yourself—and raise your questions—while you still feel completely in control. Ask if the hospital has a mission statement, and if the state recognizes a Patients' Bill of Rights.

7. Ask for a statement of the hospital's policy of informed consent (your right to understand treatment, know the alternatives, and refuse).

8. The law often holds that once you've signed a release, you've consented, whether or not you understood. So find out what to do if you have second thoughts, and never pretend to understand if you don't.

9. Find out when new residents come on. If it's July 1 and if you have a choice, you may be more comfortable scheduling yourself for a later month, after they've learned their way around the hospital.

10. Not that you'll get a straight answer if you ask, but inquire whether any contracts or union negotiations are coming due. As a rule, you'd rather not be in a hospital during a strike. Service and care will continue, but not necessarily by the

personnel who usually provide it, and often not by staffers in the best of moods.

11. An extremely useful item you'll never get if you don't ask for it, and may not get anyhow, is the hospital's internal directory. It lists hospital departments with the names of supervisors and responsible parties. If you can lay your hands on one, it can prove invaluable during your stay and long after.

12. Understand that preparation won't be the same in emergency situations. You may not have the chance to read and sign forms; and if you're in an accident and a health care professional responds to the scene, most states (under the "Good Samaritan Law") are very lenient about mistakes made by these people acting with reasonable judgment and in good faith.

13. If you go to the emergency room, try to determine what expenses will and won't be covered by your insurance. It isn't unusual for someone to swallow a chicken bone, rush to emergency, wait for a doctor—and then to be billed $800 which the insurance company won't pay because the hospital phoned for a specialist who wasn't on duty that night.

Once You're Admitted

1. You may be convinced that the entire team of medical professionals has gathered to study your sick organ, but nobody in the building has taken any notice of you.

2. This is natural. Realize that your desire for personal attention is different from your need for medical attention.

3. If you make a sincere effort to recognize the difference, the staff owe it to you to appreciate the attempt and to respond to your real needs.

4. Encourage staff members to address you by name (first name or last, your choice). They'll have a better sense of you as a person, and be less

prone to the errors that occur when one patient is mistaken for another.

5. To play it safe, insist that your physician write prescriptions legibly and explain them to you. When anyone brings you medication, ask what it is, and compare the information with what your doctor said.

6. Selected hospitals are experimenting with a questionnaire known as SF-36, which reflects a patient's physical well-being and quality of life. In the days of family doctors, your physician already knew about the whole you. Today, it may take SF-36 or a similar key to open the doorway to genuine communication.

7. Your state law may contain a Patients' Bill of Rights and may require it to be posted prominently throughout hospitals.

8. If you don't see one, ask your patient representative or call your state health department.

9. This document may include such rights as your right to an interpreter (or someone to explain papers and procedures you don't understand), your right to treatment free of discrimination, your right to respectful care, your right to emergency care, your right to complete information about your condition and prognosis, your right to refuse treatment and to be informed of alternatives, your right not to be deceived, and your right to an itemized bill.

10. It provides information for contacting a state office that hears and investigates complaints when your rights have been violated.

11. During your stay, keep track of the tests, treatments, and medications you receive. If a lab test is canceled and nobody has advised the billing office, don't be surprised if it appears on your bill. How many times was blood taken? How often did you go for X-rays?

12. Don't request an item such as facial tissue without asking what it will cost, because in your wildest dreams you might not imagine that the going rate is $12 for one box. If such items are moved by a staff member, make sure they come back.

If You Have a Complaint

1. If applicable, consult the Patients' Bill of Rights.

2. Ask to see the hospital's policy manual. A section should be devoted to the established complaint procedure, the time frame within which the hospital has to respond, and what you can do if you don't agree with the hospital's resolution.

3. The response to your complaint should be in writing. Whatever it says, keep one for your records and forward a copy to your insurer.

4. If you believe you've been subjected to rude personnel, unpalatable food, or exceptionally long waits, report it to the nurse, head nurse, hospital administrator, patient representative, or ombudsman.

5. Depending on the nature of more severe complaints, you may want to contact the
- **Hospital administrator.**
- **Patient representative or ombudsman.**
- **Social services department.**
- **Discharge planners.**
- **Risk manager (if a hospital policy or standard has placed you at risk).**
- **Safety manager (if a physically unsafe condition exists).**
- **Nurse and head nurse.**
- **Nursing office (for complaints about nurses).**
- **Office of medicine (for complaints about doctors).**
- **The executive offices. (A real attention-getter—though not to be attempted without just cause—is for a patient to march into a VP's office in a hospital gown. But don't be surprised if a well-intentioned secretary calls for security personnel to escort you back to your bed.)**

6. If possible, quote mission statements and pledges of "service excellence"—particularly when speaking to VPs and hospital presidents.

7. The average turnover for hospital CEOs is 25–30 percent per year. Odds are that this enables yours to make amends without accepting blame

and to explain away distressing policy with "My predecessor was an idiot." Don't count on this being infallible, but it has been known to work.

When Things Go Wrong

1. If you have a complaint at all, chances are it will be the food or the television reception. But it's a hospital, and your health is at stake. So—

2. Be alert for yourself or for a hospitalized friend. For example, imagine the disaster you might avert by noticing that another patient's chart is hanging from your or your friend's bed in error.

3. Malpractice suits have been filed against doctors and nurses for:
   - **Negligence.**
   - **Incorrect medication or dosage.**
   - **Misdiagnosis.**
   - **Charting errors—incorrect or unrecorded information.**
   - **Illegible or incomplete records.**
   - **Patient falls.**
   - **Foreign objects left in patients.**
   - **Inadequate care involving intravenous tubes and catheters.**
   - **Injuries from delays in notifying doctors.**
   - **Injuries from delays in any treatment.**
   - **Breach of confidentiality (including elevator conversations that abuse a patient's right to privacy).**

4. From a monetary point of view: If you believe any of the above mistakes have been made, advise your insurer. Your insurer prefers not to pay for botched work and may wish to investigate and insist on corrective action.

5. From the perspective of your wellness: Advise your nurse, doctor, the patient representative, ombudsman, or hospital administrator, and a close friend or family member.

6. If it worries you, document it. Write down incidents, dates, times, and names of individuals. If one person makes a mistake and somebody else very obviously refuses to correct it, get both names.

7. If negligence is apparent to the eye, call it to the attention of others who can later serve as witnesses. If possible, take pictures (but not in a way that will upset other patients, or the hospital might have a valid complaint against you).

8. If equipment was used improperly, you can ask for documentation that the doctor, nurse, or technician was trained in its use. If it can't be documented, ask your state health department how you can forward this discovery to the authorities who issue credentials for the individual and the hospital.

9. If a staff member becomes aware that a mistake occurred (for instance, a sponge was left in a patient), the hospital may be required to report it to the state department of health. If you're the one with the internal sponge, find out from the department of health whether a report was made. If it wasn't, ask how you can follow up, and what recourse you have against the hospital.

10. If a hospital is understaffed and a nurse feels that he or she will be stretched in too many directions to function safely, an Unsafe Assignment report generally should be filed by that nurse.

11. If you feel you've been harmed as the result of short staffing, try to find out whether an Unsafe Assignment report was submitted. If it wasn't, you may have a legitimate complaint against the nurse. If it was, you may have one against the hospital.

12. If you feel a staff member has exhibited professional misconduct (intoxication, substance abuse, sexual harassment), speak to your patient representative, ombudsman, or hospital administrator, your insurer, and the state health department.

13. If you feel the hospital is aware but chooses to ignore the individual's behavior, your insurer and the state health department should definitely investigate. When you speak to the health department, ask whether you should convey your obser-

vations to state credentialing and peer groups. Get names and addresses.

14. If an individual was at fault in any of the above instances, you (or you and your insurer, or you and your insurer and your lawyer) may want to go after the individual. Most doctors and many nurses carry malpractice insurance.

15. If hospital policy created or covered up the problem, or increased the likelihood of its happening, you may be able to nail the hospital for corporate negligence. This doesn't mean you have to take anyone to court (although you have the option). It simply means you'll have considerable leverage with the hospital, particularly if you state your case in an eloquent letter written to the hospital's executive director, with a CC to the chairman of the board.

16. If you're seriously considering a court case, remember that one contributing factor to the high cost of medical care today is the malpractice insurance premiums health professionals have to pay. Don't sue frivolously. It isn't fair, and it runs up everybody's bills.

17. If you go to court, remember that juries evaluate the standard of care more than the quality of care. This means that if you received a reasonable and customary level of care, you probably don't have a strong case.

When You Leave

1. Insurers such as Medicare and Medicaid used to reimburse hospitals for each day of a patient's stay. Now they pay a flat fee based on your DRG.

2. DRGs, or Diagnosis Related Groups, are classifications of about 500 conditions (by diagnosis, age, sex, and so on) for which people go to hospitals. The insurer pays on the basis of how long people with your DRG are expected to be hospitalized.

3. Because payment is a flat fee, hospitals paid by these insurers lose money if they keep you beyond your DRG. They come out ahead if you leave before.

4. No matter what your DRG, hospitals aren't supposed to discharge you if you aren't well enough to leave.

5. State laws vary, but in general, you'll receive a written discharge notice prior to your scheduled discharge. It will inform you of what to do if you disagree.

6. Discuss your concerns with your doctor, discharge planner, and possibly the patient representative, ombudsman, or social worker in deciding whether you want to appeal.

7. If you appointed a personal representative to act for you, that person may appeal the discharge decision.

8. Consult the discharge notice for a time limit or deadline. Your failure to respond promptly may mean that you, rather than your insurer, will pay for the extra days.

9. A vital part of discharge planning is to provide you with instructions to follow after you leave. If you're going to need equipment or special assistance, or if you're being referred to another type of facility (nursing home, hospice, etc.), a discharge planner, social worker, patient representative, or ombudsman should be on hand to answer all your questions.

When You Get Your Bill

1. Prepare to get sick all over again. The figures are staggering.

2. Even if you don't pay a cent, consider that some audits show 95 percent of hospital bills to have errors. Not long ago, a man had two heart valves replaced and—thanks to a typographical error—was charged for 200. His insurer paid the enormous bill without question.

3. In other words, proofread yours carefully. Look for:

- **Your correct name, address, insurance carrier, and I.D. numbers.**
- **Language you can understand. If you don't understand what something means, request an explanation, preferably written.**
- **An itemized bill. "Laboratory $700" can refer to one test or twenty. Demand that each be listed and priced separately.**
- **Procedures that took place. Don't pay for procedures that didn't.**
- **Code and clerical errors. A typo—as in the example of the heart valves—can cost a fortune. Check numbers. Check dates. Confirm that codes stand for what they're supposed to.**
- **Duplicate billing. A charge for two X-rays may mean you had two, or that one charge is a clerical error. It may also mean you had a second after the first was done wrong. If this happened, the hospital shouldn't be paid for two.**
- **Consistent pricing. All other factors being equal, the same procedure shouldn't cost two different amounts on two different occasions. (When possible, compare your bill with that of a friend who had similar procedures at the same hospital.)**
- **Unrequested or unauthorized items. If you accepted an elective item (such as $12 facial tissue), you have to pay for it. If you refused it and didn't use it, you don't.**
- **Extravagantly priced merchandise. Hospitals are famous for their overpricing. But you're entitled to be disgusted with paying $7 for a roll of toilet paper, whether you requested it or not.**
- **Exorbitant rates for copies of medical records. Most states give you the legal right to see them. Many cap the cost of copies to you. (If you're refused access to them, contact your state health department about procedures for appeal.)**
- **Language that the hospital doesn't understand. For example, one major metropolitan hospital**

charges for "room and board" and then levies a second figure for meals. But "board" *is* meals.

4. If you find errors, inform the hospital promptly and in writing.

5. The hospital may retain the error on its computers for a very long time, and periodically send you the same bill until you pay it. Stand your ground. Send the hospital a copy of your previous correspondence. Call its business office to discuss your complaint, but never rely exclusively on the telephone. You must document your complaint and the date(s) on which you made it.

6. Some insurers and employers offer incentives to patients who spot overcharges. Find out if yours does. If not, suggest the idea—and don't wait until you're hospitalized.

7. You can be certain that your insurer, employer, Medicare, and Medicaid don't want to pay an erroneous bill. Their auditing and fraud divisions would be delighted to know of any discrepancies you find. They may even offer lawyers to help you fight the hospital.

The Outside Agencies

Your insurer may be your strongest ally. Additionally, contact your local library, telephone directory, or telephone information for the addresses and phone numbers of the following organizations that offer assistance if you have to wage war:

- **Your state health department.**
- **Your state office of professional misconduct.**
- **Medicare, Medicaid.**
- **Accreditation agencies such as the Joint Commission on the Accreditation of Healthcare Organizations (JCAHO).**
- **The American Medical Association.**
- **The American Nurses Association.**
- **The National Practitioner Data Bank.**
- **Local TV news and newspapers (the media often love a juicy story about incompetence in a hospital).**

Other Watchdogs

American Association of Retired
Persons
1909 K Street, N.W.
Washington, DC 20049

American Health Care Association
1202 L Street, N.W.
Washington, DC 20005

Committee on Patient's Rights
Box 1900
New York, NY 10001

People's Medical Society
462 Walnut Street, Lower Level
Allentown, PA 18102

United Hospital Fund
55 Fifth Avenue
New York, NY 10003

▲ *See also* DOCTORS; INSURANCE; MEDICARE, MEDICAID, AND MEDIGAP; NURSING HOMES; SENIORS AND ELDERLAW.

Hotels

Working behind a U.S. hotel desk used to be a terrific job for a youngster because hotels used to be associated with the glamour of travel and because employees who applied themselves could earn advancement to management positions. Today, in many hotels, the mood is bleak, the desk personnel are despondent, and advancement seems as distant as the moon. Consequently, the first people you meet upon checking in may regard their jobs as variations of working behind a fast-food counter. When asked questions, they provide information based not on an understanding of the query or a knowledge of the facts, but on a desire to deal as quickly as possible with the patron asking the question in order to shut the patron up. Ironically, when their wild guesses backfire and the inconvenienced patron asks, "Why did you tell me something that wasn't true? Why didn't you just tell me that you didn't know?" the service person will often respond, "I was trying to help," and will honestly believe that misleading a guest is at least being agreeable, and therefore about as helpful as any guest has reason to expect.

Understandably, the world behind the desk isn't what it used to be either. Employees are frustrated by infinitely more details, which are kept in computers that tend to "go down" at the worst possible moments. Furthermore, the hotel industry as a whole is in trouble. It overbuilt during the recession, while travel in general and business travel in particular was being cut back. Many hotels that failed were repossessed by the banks and insurance companies that financed them. These institutions, unwilling to bankroll new buyers, have had no choice but to run the hotels. It isn't a task they relish. Neither do they enjoy pumping more money into investments that may backfire spectacularly.

Where does this put you, the weary traveler? It gives you certain leverage because the hotels need your patronage, especially when yours promises to become repeat business. When you hit a snag, your chief assignment will be to locate the employee who realizes as much.

There Are Ways to Snag-Proof Your Visit

1. When you make an advance reservation (which you can often do using a toll-free 800 number), be sure to get a confirmation number if applicable. Make yourself a note of the name of the person you spoke to, the room rate and terms, and the date on which you booked the reservation.

2. Feel free to shop via the phone. Ask if there are any special promotions or packages. If you're quoted a special rate, make sure you know all the terms and that they apply to you. If you're quoted a price for a Friday arrival, ask if the rates are cheaper for Thursday or Saturday check-ins or under other circumstances. You may be pleasantly surprised by the options you hear.

3. If you're quoted a special rate (or any rate), it's a good idea to phone again the next day. *Confirm* that the computer shows the rate you were given and that the terms apply to you. Record the name of the person you speak to and the date of the conversation. (The value of this follow-up will become clear should you check into the hotel and be told the rate you're expecting never existed. If you cite two different reservationists who confirmed that rate, the hotel should be willing to honor it.)

4. When you book the room at whatever rate, find out how late they'll hold the reservation—because some hotels let the room go if you haven't checked in by a certain hour. You can usually guarantee they'll hold accommodations for a late check-in by providing your credit card number.

5. Once you've guaranteed any arrangement with your credit card number, find out what you have to do in the event you need to cancel. If you simply let it slip your mind and don't show up, the hotel may charge you. After all, the room was not available to other guests because it was being held for you.

6. If you arrive to check in and are told there's no record of your reservation, produce the names, confirmation numbers, and dates you so carefully jotted down. If told "You must have booked it through the 800 number and they never entered it to our computer," explain that you were extremely careful to confirm and reconfirm the arrangements, and evidently the problem is poor communication between the hotel and the 800 number, for which you cannot be held accountable. If this doesn't work, ask to speak to the manager. If the manager seems reluctant, call the 800 number. Ask for a supervisor. Confirm with the supervisor that the information regarding your original reservation is on the computer, and ask the supervisor to phone the manager immediately, providing for him or her the manager's name and number. This ought to do it.

7. If you didn't book in advance, try negotiating the rate at check-in. Most hotels need 65 per-

cent occupancy to break even. If a room is about to go unoccupied for the night, a bargain isn't impossible. But negotiate with the manager, not the desk clerk. The desk clerk probably lacks the authority to make the deal.

8. When you check in, read the reservation card. Confirm dates, rate, and terms. The clerk may ask for your credit card to make "an imprint"—a precaution taken to protect the hotel against people who leave without paying. It's standard procedure, *but* when you check out, ask to have the imprint returned. The chances are at check-out the hotel will prepare a new charge slip, with totals on it, for your signature, and has no need for the previous slip. The best way for you to certify that the original slip will be destroyed is to get it back and destroy it yourself.

9. If you belong to a hotel club, frequent flyer club, or have any affiliation that gives you credits for the stay, make certain that the information (such as membership numbers) is on the computer.

10. If you're not too tired when you check in, ask to see two or three rooms at the specified rate. It's better than settling into a room, beginning to unpack, and discovering that the TV or blinds don't work.

11. If you're too tired to check out several rooms, try to find the energy to ask for a room upgrade at the same rate. If you're refused, flop onto whatever bed you're given. But you may get the upgrade. It doesn't hurt to ask.

If the Room You Booked Is Gone

If you have legitimately made the reservation and have the confirmation number, but the hotel staff won't accommodate you because they've double-booked or overbooked, and they say, however apologetically, you'll have to stay elsewhere, try the following:

1. Ask whether every room is occupied or whether some vacant rooms are still being held for late arrivals. If empty rooms are being held, point

out that you're already there and are on time, you have the confirmation number, and you don't understand the basis of the hotel's decision to treat the late arrivals better than you.

2. If you're told the late arrivals guaranteed their rooms by credit card, point out that they guaranteed *for late arrival,* but as you are not a late arrival and never expected to be you had no reason to guarantee by card, but your confirmation is as good as anybody else's.

3. At this point, you may wish to be agreeable, and you can without being a patsy. If the hotel agrees to accommodate you elsewhere—if all other terms are equal (for instance, if you don't relinquish frequent flyer or hotel club points that you would have earned by staying at your first-choice location), if they will negotiate with the neighboring hotel to get you upgraded accommodations at the same price, and if the hotel will transport you either in a courtesy vehicle or taxi at their expense—you may be ready to concede to the move.

4. If you selected the hotel because it's particularly convenient, perhaps across the street from the factory you've come to do business with, whereas the other hotel is ten blocks away, see what sort of arrangements the manager will make for your visits to the factory during the length of your stay. If the hotel won't provide you with transportation, suggest that it's out of line to expect you to pay for several cabs.

5. If you do have to relinquish something— club points, proximity to your client, etc.—negotiate for a courtesy or two in exchange. A hotel manager has more than enough power to authorize a free meal in the hotel restaurant. Caution: Once you have the verbal agreement, get it in writing too.

If You Have Valuables

1. Protect them. Don't carry large amounts of cash when you can use traveler's checks. If you

know you'll be packing a certain valuable item, phone the hotel in advance to ascertain whether the hotel will store the item in the hotel safe and accept full responsibility for it. If the hotel refuses, call other hotels in the area, and see if you can do better.

2. Innkeeper-liability laws are an outdated conglomeration of state-set limits that are remarkably pro-hotel. When a theft occurs—even when negligence is undeniable—you may be able to recover only a modest fraction of the value of your loss.

3. Your coverage is greatly enhanced when items are stored in the hotel safe. Liability limits are still low, but not as low as in a case where the valuable is stolen from your room.

4. Security information is usually posted in your room, often in a notice on the door. The notice may state the hotel's disavowal of all responsibility for items not left in the safe.

5. If you do leave anything in the hotel safe, get a receipt describing the article.

6. Try bolstering your protection by adding a floater to your homeowner's or home-renter's policy before you travel. In fact, the rider may already be part of your policy. Read it and see.

7. If a loss occurs, you may be covered by the sort of free traveler's insurance frequently thrown in by credit card companies to attract and retain subscribers. Bear in mind that the credit card company will expect you to use its card to pay for your stay. If you've used another card, it will most likely deny liability.

8. If the lost or stolen items were recently purchased by credit card, they may be covered by the credit card company through another of those subscriber incentives. Read the membership brochure or call the card company to find out.

During Your Stay

1. Speak to the desk clerk if you have questions. Speak to the concierge about matters other than hotel service, such as where the post office is

or how to take a bus to the zoo. Speak to the manager if you have a complaint that the desk clerk can't address. Understand that in some instances, the desk clerk has no authority to resolve complaints—and may be afraid to pass them on for fear of appearing incompetent.

2. Many people who answer the phone when you request the manager may be only assistant managers or night managers. If they can't help, insist on speaking to the general manager, even if it means your calling back the next day during business hours.

3. If the general manager is unhelpful or unavailable, call the 800 number. Get a number for customer service, and find someone there who will speak to the manager of the hotel on your behalf.

When You Use the Television

1. Make sure you know how to use it. An instruction card should be provided, although it might have been knocked under a table so that you have to search for it. Don't just push buttons willy-nilly unless you're ready to pay the price for damaging the set.

2. Most channels will be free, but in some cases there may be other pay channels as well. Hotels have different policies. With some, if you watch a pay movie for more than ten minutes, you'll be billed for it.

3. If you've made an honest error—for instance, if you discover that Junior has been playing with the remote control for short periods all week—call the desk immediately and explain the error. Apologize for the inconvenience and offer to pay for one full viewing of the movie.

When You Use the Telephone

1. TVs are a snap compared to phones. Look for an instruction card. If you don't see any instructions, call and ask the desk if there's anything you should know—for instance, what local calls cost and whether there are any unusual arrangements for toll calls. Get the name of the person you speak to.

2. In some hotels, you will be charged for a long distance call any time you dial and let the phone ring more than three times, even if nobody picks up at the other end.

3. Don't assume that the hotel's carrier is *your* carrier. If, for instance, you want to use your AT&T card, be aware that other carriers can take your AT&T number and bill your AT&T account for the call at their own rates. If you have any doubt, ask how to dial 102880 (1-0-ATT-0) or request the hotel operator to put you through to an AT&T operator. When you get what you think is an AT&T operator, be sure the person answers "AT&T."

4. Both here and abroad, hotels can block phone access lines, forcing guests to place calls through more expensive systems. One way to guard against this is to inquire when making the reservation whether the hotel affords access. (You may also wish to ask for the name of their long-distance carrier.)

5. Don't think you can go down to the lobby to circumvent big charges. In many hotels, *all* phones—pay phones included—are serviced by the same expensive access system.

When You Check Out

1. Don't wait until you're rushing for a cab to see your bill. Ask to have it prepared in time for you to be able to review it. (In some hotels, you can do this from your room by accessing a special code on the TV and reading it from the screen.)

2. Check the bill. If it's wrong, explain what's wrong. Don't be surprised if the clerk assumes you're at fault and tries to justify the charges, even illogically. (A friend of mine once questioned an overcharge of $75 and was told, "That's because you stayed seven nights." His first reaction was to believe that he'd miscalculated the length of his

stay. Then he counted—up to six. He said, "Six nights. How do you get seven?" The clerk answered, "It has to be seven. That's the only way to explain the charge.")

3. If you don't reach accord with the clerk, get the manager. If the manager is no help, pay the bill and approach the matter later through your credit card company (see page 91). It's no good to walk out without paying because they have your imprint and can charge your credit card without your final signature.

4. Even if the bill is flawless, keep a copy, at least until you receive the credit card statement covering the transaction.

5. Ask to have your imprint back.

6. Even when you sign a charge slip for the correct amount and even when you destroy the initial imprint yourself, hotels will occasionally submit a higher figure to your credit card company. If you ask the credit card company for a copy of the signed charge slip that reflected this transaction, you'll probably be told "Oh, the information was submitted electronically. We do that with large operations such as hotels." Fine. But even if it was an honest mistake, such as someone else's dinner ending up on your bill, you don't have to pay. Write to the credit card company. Send a photocopy of the correct invoice and the correct slip you signed. The card company will generally remove the charge and contact the hotel. The hotel may protest. Stick to your guns. You have the bill and the signed invoice. They have nothing. You're under no obligation to treat a stranger to a feast.

7. Many hotels offer "express check out," a system that lets you leave without having to stand in line at the counter. Generally, you sign a credit card imprint when you check in, and you drop your key in a slot when you depart. It's faster, but not foolproof. If you plan to take advantage of this time-saver and if you can review your bill on your TV screen, at least glance at it on the final morning of your stay. If you spot errors, you can correct them more easily while you're still on the premises.

8. If you receive an erroneous express check-out billing after you've left, contact your credit card company, explain the error, and ask that the incorrect charge be deleted. Send a CC to the manager of the hotel, requesting acknowledgment of receipt of your letter and confirmation that the error will be corrected by the hotel's accounting department.

After You Leave

1. If you received poor service, write to the general manager. When the manager doesn't hear about it, he or she can't take steps to improve it. You may have informed the desk clerk of your displeasure, but you only indirectly pay the desk clerk's wages. By writing to the general manager, you stand to achieve two desirable goals: The clerk will be instructed about good service by the person who authorizes the paychecks, and the manager may write you a thoughtful letter of apology, which might include an invitation to return as the hotel's guest (or receive a free meal when you return, or some other amenity).

2. Again, if the general manager doesn't care to respond, write to the customer service department of the hotel chain. Find out if a bank or insurance company owns the hotel, and write to the president of that proprietor institution. Don't expect the hotel itself to give you the information, but the 800 service number or your travel agent may be of assistance.

▲ *See also* CREDIT CARDS; TOURS.

Insurance

How smart it would be if consumers shopped for insurance as carefully as they weigh the advantages and disadvantages of their next purchase of breakfast cereal! Insurance bought from a stranger who rings you at random while you're eating dinner—or from your brother-in-law because your sister will never speak to you again if you don't, or through your employer because it's easier than having to compare alternatives—may be very limited when you need it most.

Cheap rates can't be your only consideration, either. If money is a problem now, think what a problem you'd have with a catastrophic illness and not enough insurance to cover most of your bills.

While you're at it, think what a wreck you'd be if your insurance company turned out to be in worse health than you. So before signing the policy, do a little research in your library. Consult reference books by Standard & Poor's and Moody's. Also look at Weiss's Insurance Safety and the A. M. Best Company annual ratings guide. Or you can phone Standard & Poor's at 212-208-1527 (for a free verbal report on up to five insurers, or $25 per insurer for a written report), A. M. Best (1-900-420-0400 at $2.50 per minute or $20 per insurer for a detailed report), and Weiss Research (1-800-289-9222, at $15 for each telephone rating, which can be applied against subsequent fees if you request written reports). Additionally, the National Association of Insurance Commissioners (NAIC) tracks companies on its "watch list" of troubled operations (available for $5 from The Insurance Forum, P.O. Box 245, Ellettsville, IN 47429). Benefits consultants such as Wilkinson Benefit Consultants, Inc., 1-800-296-3030, will research their databases for a fee. Their report will narrow down the field to a few plans best suited to your requirements, and analyze each.

Your state insurance department might also be able to alert you to companies in unstable shape, or not licensed in your state. Look in the government listings for your state for an office or agency with "Insurance" in the name.

A solid source of brochures, as well as information on state laws and regulations, is the National Insurance Help Line, 1-800-942-4242.

Note: This information may be affected by the adoption of a National Health Care Plan.

When Buying a Policy, Ask Questions

1. What are the deductibles and coinsurance provisions?

2. Is there a lifetime maximum benefit?

3. How can you contact the insurer? What's the address? The phone number? Is it a local number, an 800 number, or a toll call?

4. What does the claim form look like? Can you understand it? Will you be the one who submits it?

5. How long do claims take to be processed?

6. Is the insurance company licensed in your state?

7. Get a summary of benefits or an outline of coverage. If you ask and are refused, start wondering whether you wouldn't prefer to entrust your well-being to another agent or insurer.

8. Ask whether you're entitled to discounts. A person who doesn't smoke may pay less for individual health insurance. A house with smoke detectors and burglar alarms may earn a reduction on the homeowner's coverage. A family may get a break for insuring all its cars under one policy. You might also qualify for a discount by having the same company meet multiple insurance needs (health, home, and car).

9. What are your options for arbitration, mediation, or peer review if you and your insurer don't see eye to eye on a claim?

10. If you have a very specific insurance need not named in the policy, ask your insurance agent or broker if you can have a rider added to your agreement. For instance, if you're going to build a swimming pool, you'll want extra wording to cover not only the finished pool, but possibly the mishaps that can occur during construction. Don't be put off the trail by fears that your rates will go up. Riders don't have to affect premiums.

11. Your insurance agent or broker can and should be more than willing to help you with these concerns. Anyone reluctant to cooperate at this stage of the proceedings is likely to retain the same character traits when you're trying to file a claim later on.

12. If you don't have a completely executed policy in hand within thirty days, write to your agent and insurer for a written explanation of the delay.

13. After sixty days, contact the insurer again, and if you are not entirely comfortable with the response, report the incident to your state insurance department.

14. As a rule, you have a "free look" period after you've signed. This means that if you reread the policy and decide it's not for you, you can return the policy within the specified period for a full refund.

15. If your insurance comes to you through your employer, ask the same questions about deductibles, coinsurance, forms, and processing. The personnel department, benefits manager, or union office should have the details.

16. An insurer will occasionally sell your policy to another company. This may be to your advantage if the new company is stronger than the first. But it may not be. Depending on the laws of your state, the insurer may not be required to inform you (even though the new company may not be licensed in your state).

17. Indications that your policy may have been sold might (but don't always) include an instruction to send your premiums to a new business address. Also, "assumption reinsurance" means "transfer" in the language of insurance.

18. Some states require written consent from the insured party before a transfer can go through. But whether or not your state demands it, you can—*before* you sign the policy.

19. If an insurer informs you that a transfer will take place and you don't want it to, you may only have to notify your insurer that you intend to sue. There have been instances when this was enough to make an insurer agree to continue coverage.

20. Never drop coverage through one source until you're certain you've got it through another.

21. Whatever your various policies on health, home, and belongings, review them from time to time to be sure they still meet your needs. If you'd like to have them enhanced, talk it over with your agent or broker and say that you've heard that upgrades can be arranged without commission.

Health Insurance

1. If you work for a company having twenty-five employees or more, and if the company offers health insurance, federal law may require that a health maintenance organization (HMO) be one

of your health insurance options. The larger the group, the more the options that may be available to you. If the group is small or if you're entirely on your own, you may be financing your health insurance on your own.

2. If you and your spouse are both offered coverage through your employers, compare policies carefully, including what options you have to sign up later. Realize that there are circumstances under which one policy could cancel out the other. For example, one plan might say that a husband's plan is always the primary plan (the one that pays first) while the other could say the older spouse has the primary plan. (In such situations, call your state insurance department to determine whether this is permissible in your state, or whether there is a law in place that compels the insurers to pay.)

3. If you're self-employed and find yourself flinching at the cost of even the most basic individual policies, look into group policies offered through professional and alumni organizations. If you're not a member of any such organization, consider joining one to gain access to group benefits. Also, contact Families USA, 202-628-3030, for referrals to area programs that might be available to you. If finances make it impossible for you to afford health insurance, consider Medicaid (*see* MEDICARE, MEDICAID, AND MEDIGAP; and phone your state or local department of human resources or social services agency).

4. If you aren't truthful about your health in order to obtain insurance, that's called misrepresentation. Misrepresentation can be grounds for an insurer's refusing to pay your claim. The company may cancel the claim and return your premiums. If you deposit the check, you're agreeing with its decision. If this happens to you, don't do anything with the check until you've spoken to a lawyer, insurance agent, or other adviser.

5. Some of the following suggestions will apply across the board to all health insurance complaints. Others will apply only to those having to do with company insurance. If your complaint has

to do with Medicare, see MEDICARE, MEDICAID, AND MEDIGAP.

Managed Care Plans

1. With managed care plans such as health maintenance organizations (HMOs) and preferred provider organizations (PPOs), your company or you (or you and your company combined) pay a flat fee for you to belong to the plan. Once a member, you are entitled to service in exchange for no further fee, or for a small copayment, or sometimes after a deductible. Your choice is limited to specified groups of health care providers at one or more specified facilities. (With a PPO, your benefits cover preferred providers from a specific list. If you choose to see a physician not on the list, you pay more, though the plan may still pick up much of the cost.)

2. With an open-ended HMO, you enjoy the advantages of a regular HMO but have the option of seeing doctors outside the system if you're willing to pay some of the cost of those visits.

Other Group or Individual Insurance

If health insurance isn't managed care, it's considered "fee for service." In other words, you receive a service and get billed for it. You then either pay the bill and request reimbursement from your insurance company, or the provider bills your insurance company directly. There may be deductibles and coinsurance provisions.

Risk Pools

If you have no group coverage and can't obtain individual coverage because your health is considered a poor risk, contact your state insurance department and ask whether your state has a risk pool. Like assigned risk pools for automobiles, these represent a possible source of coverage for people who otherwise might have none.

If You Lose Your Job

1. The Consolidated Omnibus Budget Reconciliation Act of 1985 (COBRA) says that if you leave

a company that has a group health plan and twenty employees or more, you have the right to continued coverage at your own expense (which expense can run up to 102 percent of the original premium). Coverage would extend no longer than eighteen months, or thirty-six months for dependents of covered employees who pass away, or who divorce the remaining spouse. If COBRA coverage interests you, notify your employer within sixty days. COBRA extends to dependents no longer considered to be dependent children under a parent's health insurance policy. (*See* WORKPLACE.)

2. If the COBRA option isn't open to you, ask your employer what you have to do to convert from group to individual coverage.

3. If COBRA and conversion are out of the question and if you're not ready for Medicare, interim policies are available from commercial insurance companies, and are certainly better than no protection at all.

If You're Hurt at Work

1. You may be fully or partly covered by worker's or state disability compensation (*see* WORKPLACE).

2. If you're hurt at home, or traveling, or driving, see what protection you have under your homeowner's and automobile insurance.

Before You Submit a Claim

1. Understand what your insurance covers.

2. If you have doubts—or if the procedure promises to be very costly—ask the doctor, hospital, or insurer for written verification of what will be covered.

3. Some tests and treatments represent refinements over traditional approaches. They may be less painful for the patient. They may be faster. But because they're far more expensive, insurers often balk at covering them. Also, because they're new, insurers argue that there isn't sufficient evidence to prove that they're any better. If your doctor suggests one of these for you, and if you discover you wouldn't be covered, ask if there's a

large medical center pioneering the technique; such institutions may be willing to absorb the cost under a research grant.

When You Submit a Claim

1. Follow the claim procedures carefully.

2. Don't expect to make a profit if you submit to two companies for the same treatment. Under "coordination of benefits," your combined coverage would not exceed 100 percent, and less if neither of the plans provides 100 percent coverage.

3. Photocopy everything you submit. Don't settle for poor-quality reproductions because if you have to protest later, you'll want to make legible copies of the copies you kept on file.

If Your Claim Is Rejected

1. Ask why. Phone numbers and addresses to contact should be on the written notice itself. If not, find them in your policy.

2. If you don't understand the explanation, keep asking until you do. If you in fact did something wrong, you want to know before you do it again on your next claim.

3. If you spoke by phone and the discussion itself was unsatisfactory, don't be afraid to call again and speak to another representative. Be polite. Say something along the lines of "I phoned earlier today and thought I'd asked all my questions, but I'm still not clear on . . ." Then recap your earlier conversation and see what sort of reply you get.

4. If you omitted something when presenting the claim, find out what procedure you have to follow to add it to your claim and how much time you have to submit.

5. Check the math. If coinsurance is involved, was it correctly calculated? If there is a deductible, do you agree with the way it was applied?

6. If you're told your policy doesn't cover the service in question, reread the policy. If you believe you're covered, ask your doctor or hospital to double-check the procedure code and the diagnosis given on the claim form.

7. Keep written records of conversations.

8. Follow up any significant conversation with a letter recapping what was said. If appropriate, CC the individual's manager, and your insurance agent.

9. Speak to your insurance agent.

10. When you think everything needed is in front of the insurer, ask for a review of the claim. If you ask in writing, you'll have the satisfaction of knowing that you stated your case exactly as you wanted to. (You can use identical words over the phone, but the person listening to you may not remember them, or may not even be listening.) A letter also gives you a permanent record that a review was requested.

11. If a deadline is involved, consider sending your letter via registered mail to prove that you've honored the deadline.

12. If the dispute is over "reasonable and customary fee," find out if the matter can be submitted to a peer review board (made up of the medical provider's peers, who compare notes on what would be reasonable and customary in your case).

13. You can conduct your own peer review by surveying the fees charged for the procedure by other doctors in your area. Try to get the answers in writing. Submit them to your insurer.

14. If the response seems less than fair—or if you have any questions or doubts at any point—contact the health insurance consumer complaints division of your state insurance department. Request an investigation and ask for suggestions about arbitration or conciliation.

15. Check the policy. What does it say about arbitration?

16. Contact state senators and congressmen. Complain, suggest an investigation, and ask for their guidance with respect to your own claim.

17. Talk to a lawyer. Find out if you can, or would be well advised to, sue.

18. If you feel you were denied in a discriminatory way because of the nature of your illness (such as AIDS), contact an advocacy group allied to the condition (such as Gay Men's Health Crisis,

Legal Services Department, 212-807-6655; 212-645-7470 TDD for hearing-impaired consumers).

If You're Rejected Under a Group Plan

Do the above, and also contact your employer, personnel or human resources office, union, or professional organization.

Homeowner's Insurance

1. Don't shortchange yourself when you buy coverage. Consider very carefully what you want protected, and if it's not in the policy, ask your agent or broker to add it to the wording.

2. Don't overlook the power of inflation. The agreement you sign as a young married may not reimburse you for the value of two sofas and a lamp twenty years down the road. Ask your agent about updating your papers to maintain adequate protection of your home and belongings.

3. Ask about the difference in premiums between current cash value compensation and replacement value. Replacement value actually covers the cost of replacing what was lost. Current cash value reimburses you for the market worth of your used furniture.

4. Notice whether the policy covers personal items lost away from home (for instance, when you're on vacation) and personal liability (if someone is hurt on your property).

5. What must you do to protect your house when you're gone? Some policies require a certain level of attention (such as a neighbor checking daily, or you turning off the water pipes) if you're away for an extended period; otherwise insurers will refuse to pay.

6. Make a complete inventory of your home and belongings. Four photos of each room, taken from different angles, and a videotape of home and property could save you a bundle if you ever need to put in a claim.

7. Keep receipts of major purchases if possible. If you don't have receipts, canceled checks

or credit card statements may help substantiate later claims.

8. All things being equal, you'd do well to sign with an agent who has "draft authority"—in other words, one who can authorize the settlement of small claims without the intervention of an adjuster.

9. The Insurance Information Institute, 110 William Street, New York, NY 10038, 1-800-942-4242, can offer general guidelines about property and casualty insurance policies, as well as referrals to other resources.

When Submitting a Claim

Follow the steps given above, and furthermore:

1. Don't dawdle. Failure to advise your agent in a timely fashion can jeopardize your claim.

2. If you're making a claim for fire damage or theft, extensive paperwork could be involved. Organize it neatly and completely. The easier it is to read, the faster it can be processed.

If You're Rejected

The steps outlined above for health insurance generally apply. Essentially, only the terminology is different.

1. Coding errors aren't limited to health insurance. Computer and human failure can result in mistakes. So check and double-check codes.

2. Understand that if an agent or claims investigator denies your claim, it may be because the person isn't sufficiently familiar with your policy. Reread it, and if you feel you have a legitimate argument, speak to the person's manager.

Automobile Insurance

1. Some state insurance commissioners offer price guides reflecting the going rates of selected insurance companies. To find out if yours does, contact the automotive division of your state insurance department.

2. Some cars are notoriously expensive to repair. Ask your agent for help in identifying cars that aren't.

3. Before buying anything, ask your insurer to list in writing the claims that will raise your rates. It would be a shame not to submit a claim in order to keep your rates down if the request wouldn't have cost you a cent.

4. Keep your insurer informed of any changes that could lower your rates, for instance if you move from city traffic to a placid retirement community or if your teenagers no longer use your cars because they've left for college.

If Your Claim Is Rejected

Again, the terms are different but the procedure is much the same. If you have any suspicions of hidden charges, or any doubt that your insurer isn't playing fair, contact the automotive division of your state insurance department.

1. Check coding. Compare figures. Keep receipts.

2. Don't settle for verbal assurances. Document your conversations and follow them up with letters stating the agreements that were reached.

3. If the company delays in settling, see if your policy covers rental of another vehicle while your insured auto is indisposed. If it does, and if you rent one, your insurer will have an added incentive to hurry up.

4. If your state has no-fault insurance, find out what procedures are available to you—from the insurers involved, from your lawyer, and from the state. Speak to more than one state agency because you may hear different answers. Ask what avenues of arbitration, conciliation, and mediation apply, and whether you have to act within a certain time limit. (If you wait for someone to volunteer the information, you may not be told until after the deadline has passed.)

Life Insurance

Life insurance is phenomenally important for those you leave behind. But unlike health, homeowner's, and automobile insurance, life insurance rarely involves shades of difference in proving a claim or in determining the amount to be paid. There is, nonetheless, homework to be done in order to secure the best arrangement:

1. Don't believe that Social Security will be enough.

2. If you have life insurance through your place of business, can you transfer it when you leave? If so, find out how, and how long you have to be employed there before you qualify.

3. If you don't have life insurance, note that bereaved dependents may be entitled to COBRA benefits (see above, under the heading "If You Lose Your Job" in the discussion of health insurance).

4. Term policies are generally less expensive when you're young. They're renewed each year. They build no cash value.

5. Notice the "re-entry" or "revertible" terms, which mean the rates stay down if you stay healthy. Get sick, and the rates start to climb. When considering a re-entry policy, review good-health *and* bad-health payment schedules and be sure you're comfortable with both.

6. Permanent insurance tends to start higher, but it doesn't increase for the life of the policy. It builds cash value against which you can borrow. In a pinch, you can surrender the policy for cash.

7. Premiums for term insurance go up as you get older. So if you start with term, see if the policy has a favorable conversion option, free of medical restrictions. In a worst-case scenario—if you're in poor health—it's much easier to convert a current policy than to pass a physical exam for a new one.

8. If you purchase life insurance, by all means research the company's stability as explained at the beginning of this section. A company can't cover you for fifty years if it goes out of business after ten.

9. The American Council of Life Insurance, Information Service, 1001 Pennsylvania Avenue, N.W., Washington, DC 20004 (202-624-2000), provides general answers about life insurance, as well as referrals to other helpful agencies.

If Your Insurer Isn't Healthy

1. Relax. Most insurers are perfectly safe.

2. Speak to your insurance agent, accountant, lawyer, financial planner, and others who may have answers.

3. Don't stop paying premiums because you have doubts. If you fail to keep up, your policy could lapse.

4. If you have group coverage, the group will have answers. In fact, it may very likely be the group that breaks the news to you—in a written notice explaining your options.

5. If it's group coverage and you get word through some other channel, contact by phone (for speed) and in writing (to prove that you acted promptly) your employer's personnel or human resources office, union office, or professional organization.

6. If it's individual coverage, you may hear of the failure via news media, or through the state regulators who take over the business.

7. If you receive a communication from state insurance regulators, it will explain your position.

8. When state regulators take over an insurer, expect them to freeze the assets to prevent a run on remaining funds. This is encouraging in the sense that the company doesn't go totally broke, but you may not like it because what's being frozen is, for instance, your ability to borrow on or cash in a life insurance policy.

9. The state will attempt to restructure or sell the insurer in a way that protects assets and policyholders as much as possible.

10. If the insurer is liquidated, an industry-funded state guaranty fund may be prepared to make good on your policy, but not all states have guaranty associations. Property/casualty funds exist in most states; health and life insurance funds are available in many.

11. If your insurer has an out-of-state headquarters, take heart that some states recognize and pay out-of-state claims. Therefore, contact the headquarters office (if it hasn't contacted you) as well as the insurance department of that state.

12. You can try to sue your insurance agent, but unless he or she acted recklessly, or the company was insolvent or unlicensed in your state when the policy was initiated, victory won't be easy.

13. If your agent carries errors-and-omissions insurance, an out-of-court settlement may be workable.

14. Contact your state senators and congressman. Ask what assistance groups are available to you, and what programs, panels, or hearings you can attend.

15. Perhaps a class-action suit is advisable. (*See* RUNG ELEVEN: CLASS-ACTION SUIT, in Part I.) Suggest to your state attorney general, senators and congressman that the state should institute one against the negligent insurer.

16. Don't accept a settlement without consulting a trusted adviser. For example, if you accept partial cash on a life insurance policy, you may be forfeiting your rights to the balance of its value.

17. You may qualify for a hardship withdrawal that would entitle you to 100 cents on the dollar. Call the company. Ask for written information on how to apply.

If Your Insurer Does a Really Fancy Dance

Suppose you're preparing to enter a hospital for an organ transplant. To be absolutely certain of your group coverage, you request and receive written verification from your hospital. Not until the anesthesia wears off does a friend tell you that coverage was denied retroactively because the insurer now feels your employer allegedly falsified records to qualify for a policy. What can you do?

1. You can—and may have to—sue. But don't lose all hope, because such stories are enormously newsworthy.

2. Take your story to the press and television.

3. Contact your area's consumer advocate reporters who do "Shame on You"–type programs.

4. Phone—and try to make an appointment with—your state attorney general, congressman and senators. Convince them that what happened to you could happen to many other people, and some arrangement must be made to protect them. A politician rescuing victimized sick constituents stands to sway lots of votes.

5. Don't rule out the obvious: union office, state insurance department and department of consumer affairs, etc. Each is responsible for whole populations potentially threatened by the same fiasco.

A Final Word: Insurance Cheats Cheat You

Insurance fraud runs up everyone's premiums. Now there's a hotline—the National Insurance Crime Bureau, 800-TEL-NICB—poised and ready to accept callers' tips.

▲ *See also* AUTOMOBILES; CREDIT CARDS; DOCTORS; HOME BUILDING; HOME IMPROVEMENTS; HOSPITALS; MEDICARE, MEDICAID, AND MEDIGAP; PENSIONS; SOCIAL SECURITY; WORKPLACE.

Investment Brokers

Don't stop investing. Investments are the backbone of capitalism. Just remember two rules:

1. Don't be a schnook. Realize that any investment involves a gamble. Avoid taking any risk that you're not financially prepared to take.

2. Don't trust a schnook. There are plenty of honest men and women whose business it is to manage other people's investments. There are also scads of unscrupulous souls who prey on the unwary. There are even, occasionally, honest brokers who commit foolish blunders for which *they, not you,* are obliged to accept the consequences.

Before You Invest

To apply these rules in a practical way, do your homework both before and during the life of an investment.

1. If anything is pitched to you over the phone, demand details and demand them in writing.

2. If you invest on the basis of a printed advertisement or mail solicitation, keep the document, because its words should be legally binding.

3. If a claim to be insured or backed by a bond is false, the wording may be used to prove fraud but you've still got no insurance or bond. So research, research, research before signing or investing.

4. Federal and state laws require most investment offerings to be registered, and most brokers to be licensed and to meet certain criteria.

5. Don't take the broker's or salesperson's word for it. ("Registered? Me? You bet!") Contact the investment and securities division of your state department of banking (look in the government listings for your state in your telephone directory).

6. If the only number in the phone book is a toll exchange (not an 800 number), phone 800 Information (1-800-555-1212) to determine whether there's a free number. If you're told there isn't, call the number in the book, and when someone picks up, ask immediately if there is a toll-free number. If yes, hang up and call back free—you may be on the phone for a while.

7. The information you receive should also be free, but it's always a good idea to confirm your understanding before proceeding.

8. Ask for a complete background check on the investment and the individual or firm representing it, including:
   - **If the investment is registered.**
   - **If the broker is licensed.**
   - **If the broker (or firm) has been charged with crimes, fraud, or breaking securities laws.**
   - **If the charges were dropped, or if disciplinary action was taken.**
   - **If a bond has been posted.**

9. A bond is not necessarily required, but it could help protect you if the investment goes sour. If there is a bond, ask its amount and the extent to which you'd be protected by it.

10. Note that some investments, such as government securities, are exempt from registration. Your state agency can tell you more about this.

11. Find out if there are other agencies you should consult, such as the federal Securities and Exchange Commission (SEC) and the Central Registration Depository (CRD), a national computerized registry.

12. The Public Reference Office of the Securities and Exchange Commission can be reached at 202-272-7450 and can tell you if an offering is registered and whether it has to be.

13. Unless you're a lawyer, you can find out about "concluded actions" against a broker by phoning the National Association of Securities Dealers, Inc., 1-800-289-9999. If you're a lawyer calling on behalf of an investor, the call will cost (at this writing) $30.

14. Commodities brokers can be checked through the Commodity Futures Trading Commission, Office of Proceedings, 2033 K Street, N.W., Washington, DC 20581; 202-254-3067.

15. Realize that none of these agencies can or would endorse an investment. The most you can reasonably expect to learn is whether an offering, broker, or firm has complied with state laws and has a track record of honest dealings.

16. If you don't understand the answers you receive, feel free to ask for a supervisor, or to call back at another time.

17. It never hurts to get the name of the person you speak to, in case you need to follow up or refer to the conversation at a later time.

18. If you feel you'd like to have the information in writing, ask how that can be arranged.

19. Visit your local library. See what recent articles have been written about the area of investment or the company that interests you.

An Investor Has the Right to Know

1. Has the investment or firm been in legal trouble?

2. What is the broker's background? Where did he or she study? How long has this person been with the firm?

3. How many clients does your broker have? The larger the number, the longer it may take for your call to be returned. Ask for references.

4. How do the broker and firm get investment recommendations? Do they have researchers on staff? Would you be free to talk to analysts and researchers directly?

5. How healthy is the firm? Ask for the latest financial statement, as well as for the last annual statement.

6. For a given investment, how is the rate of return calculated? On what assumptions does it depend?

7. Who pays the person who sells the investment to you? Is there a commission?

8. What other costs will you be responsible for? Are there service charges?

9. Would you ever have to come up with additional money to protect your investment? Are you creating any obligation that could cost you more than your original investment?

10. Are there any time limits that apply?

11. Could you ever be required to make decisions, or pay out money, on short notice?

12. Under what circumstances would you be denied access to your funds? What penalties would you have to pay to get them?

13. How often is the status of your investment reported, and what form does the report take? Whom do you contact if you don't receive the report, and how would you question entries on it?

14. Ask for literature, including a prospectus, written disclosure statement, or annual report if applicable. The securities and investments division of your state department of banking can tell you when these are required by law.

15. Though none of these may be required, you still have every right to ask for a written explanation of the risks.

16. Ask what protection you have if the brokerage firm goes bankrupt. Nearly all accounts are insured up to $500,000 per investor by the Securities Investor Protection Corporation, but

confirm that you'd be covered, and that you're covered for the full value of your portfolio.

17. You have the right to set ground rules and to have them confirmed in writing. For instance, you can require the broker to contact you before each trade. Or you can state a point at which to sell without your authorization should a stock plummet.

18. Even under the best of circumstances, you might not agree with your broker. Ask in advance what means of arbitration, mediation, and reparation proceedings would be open to you in the event of an unresolved dispute. Ask for this in writing.

19. Some agreements specify the agency that will be used in the event of arbitration. Make sure you're comfortable about it before signing. For instance, you may prefer to work through the American Arbitration Association (which is neutral and nonprofit and is located at 140 West 51st Street, New York, NY 10020; 212-484-4000) rather than through a panel sponsored by the brokerage industry.

20. Read the agreement before you sign it. Read any material you receive after you've signed it.

21. If the new-account form overstates your income level, have the figure corrected. A broker is required to invest suitably with respect to the income of a client and can be disciplined severely for investing irresponsibly.

If an Investment Goes Bust

1. It may have been a good idea that simply didn't pan out, in which case it's generally nobody's fault.

2. It may have been a great idea that paid handsomely for people who actually invested, but your salesman or broker lied to you about your investment. If this happened:
- **Alert the company you thought you had shares in. Be assured, its president wants to know when the company's name or image has been used to defraud.**

- **Report the salesperson or broker to the head *and* the compliance department of his or her firm and to professional associations, and to the agencies listed below. If you believe the entire firm is guilty, report the firm.**

3. It may have been a deliberate fraud, in which case, report it to the agencies below and read the section SCAMS.

4. If you're a shareholder, read shareholders' reports, and if you're interested, attend shareholders' meetings. Bring your concerns to the attention of fellow shareholders and to the attention of the board. If you feel the company is illegally diverting shareholders' funds, report the company.

5. If you propose to make a charge that could destroy a broker's career, consult with an attorney or regulatory agency to make sure you can't be sued for your allegations.

If a Broker Is Unethical

1. Brokers are expected to apply legal and ethical standards to their business relationships, to exercise their best efforts, and to behave responsibly with clients' money.

2. Any broker or investment salesperson who assaults you with high-pressure tactics is probably not acting with your best interests at heart.

3. Be very cautious about assigning custody of your assets to an investment adviser, or giving a broker discretionary power over your account.

4. It's considered questionable practice for a broker or salesperson to rave about the virtues of any investment without first knowing your financial status and goals.

5. If you've set ground rules and they've been ignored, the broker has behaved unethically.

6. Keep copies of all correspondence and a careful journal of any conversations you have with your broker. Note the time and date that orders are placed and any other stipulations you may have made.

7. If you place an order and lose money because the broker didn't act promptly on your behalf, the firm is responsible. But don't expect satisfaction unless you can prove that it was the broker who delayed.

8. Brokers aren't supposed to make unauthorized investments for you (ones outside of the perameters of an already authorized investment program). Check confirmation slips and monthly statements to see what your money's been doing without you. Compare them against the records you've kept.

9. Brokers shouldn't manipulate your money excessively (it's called "churning") simply to generate commissions for themselves.

10. If you feel you've been the victim of any form of unethical behavior or misappropriation of your funds, or if the broker acted in direct contradiction of your instructions, demand a full and immediate explanation.

11. If it's less than satisfactory, go to the broker's boss or branch manager. Be prepared to prove your charges—and at this point, be very grateful that you've kept a detailed journal and supporting documents.

12. If you can demonstrate that the broker acted in a manner contrary to your instructions, the branch manager may be able to revoke the transaction and refund commissions to you.

13. If that doesn't work, you can write a complaint letter to the Securities and Exchange Commission (SEC).

14. You can go to arbitration. Check your agreement to see whether an agency is specified.

15. Some studies have shown that investors do better in arbitration in a face-to-face situation than when it's conducted purely on the basis of written submissions, and that they improve their chances of success if accompanied by a lawyer.

16. If the security dealer is a member of the National Association of Security Dealers, Inc. (approximately 5,700 are), provide the NASD with a written statement setting forth the circumstances of the dispute. Be specific about the name and business address of the account executive, and furnish any statements, confirmations, correspondence, or other documentation supporting your position.

17. The NASD may investigate and, if appropriate, take disciplinary action.

18. If the initial response doesn't please you, you can refer your grievance to the Arbitration Department of the NASD district office.

19. The securities division of your state banking department can provide guidance and referrals and accept complaints. Additionally, it might investigate, take administrative action, issue a cease and desist order, revoke or suspend a license, or send a case to the state attorney general if evidence seems to warrant these actions.

20. Any of the following agencies may assist in suggesting further steps for you to take. Check your telephone directory for regional divisions or contact the head offices as noted. If your complaint relates to mail fraud, contact the Consumer Advocate, United States Postal Service, Room 5910, Washington, DC 20260-6720; 202-268-2284; TDD 202-268-2310.

American Association of
 Individual Investors
625 North Michigan Avenue
Chicago, IL 60611
312-280-0170

American Stock Exchange
Rulings and Inquiries Department
86 Trinity Place
New York, NY 10006
212-306-1450

Commodity Futures Trading
 Commission
2033 K Street, N.W.
Washington, DC 20581
202-254-6387

Council of Better Business Bureaus
4200 Wilson Boulevard, Suite 800
Arlington, VA 22203
703-276-0100

National Association of Securities
 Dealers, Inc.
1750 K Street, N.W.
Washington, DC 20006
202-728-8000

National Consumers League
815 15th Street, N.W., Suite 516
Washington, DC 20005
202-639-8140

National Futures Association
200 West Madison Street,
    Suite 1600
Chicago, IL 60606
1-800-621-3570
1-800-572-9400 (in Illinois)

North American Securities
    Administrators Association
1 Massachusetts Avenue, N.W.
Washington, DC 20001
202-737-0900

▲ *See also* SCAMS; TELEMARKETING.

Mail Orders

Most mail order firms are fair, reliable, and save you hours upon hours of valuable time. Occasionally, reputable companies make mistakes, but they are reasonable about correcting them. Sometimes, however, otherwise excellent companies have unmotivated employees, or unmotivated companies get your money, and then mail order becomes a fiasco. Though mail ordering deprives you of face-to-face contact, you've got the clout to bring them around to your point of view.

Just remember to go into it the same way you enter into any other arena of smart shopping. Do your homework, keep records, and insist on your rights if things go wrong.

When You Order by Mail

1. If you order by credit card and the merchandise is defective or doesn't arrive, you'll have the option of instructing your credit card company to cancel the charge or issue a chargeback.

2. If you use your credit card, exercise caution. It's one thing to give your card number when you call or fill out an order form and deal with a reputable mail order operation, but quite another if somebody phones to sell you something and asks for your card number.

3. If you place an order by phone with a company you call, be absolutely certain you know all the charges. Taxes? Shipping and handling? Small-order charge? Minimum charge? Get a specific total. Confirm it with the person who speaks to you. Get the name of that person. The last thing you ever want to do is authorize an order with open-ended charges while charging the total to your credit card.

4. Ask when you can expect to receive the order.

5. In general, don't give your card number to anybody who phones you. It could be a scam to learn your card number. No merchandise will ever arrive.

6. Even if you're shopping with a reputable firm, don't write your number on a postcard. Place the card inside an envelope before mailing it.

7. If you order based on a TV promotion, note the name, address, and phone number of the company. (It may be different from the number you use for ordering.) Phone the Better Business Bureau or the department of consumer affairs for the state or city in which the company is located. Inquire whether there have been complaints and how they were resolved.

8. You might also ask how long the company has been in business and operating under its present name. (Perhaps it had violations a mile long under another name, in another state.)

9. If you order by credit card and the charge appears on your monthly statement but the merchandise hasn't arrived, write your card company to request a chargeback. If the merchandise shows up later, don't worry. The amount will be reinstated. But if you don't challenge the figure and

the bill goes too long, you may forfeit your chance for reimbursement even if you never see your merchandise.

10. When you order by mail, read all the terms. Keep a copy of everything related to the transaction—the "how to order" page, the product description, and a photocopy of the form you send. If you pay by check, write the check number and date on your copy of the order.

11. Read the catalog or advertisement for a guarantee or return policy, and note the phone number and address to be used in case problems arise.

12. Some mail order companies will state that they substitute "a comparable or better item" if the merchandise you order isn't in stock. But if you want a particular style of shoe that isn't available, the odds are that you won't love the company's choice of an appropriate substitute.

13. Read over the form. Is there any box you can check to indicate that you don't want a substitute? If not, write it very visibly across the face of the order form.

14. If you order an expensive item and an inexpensive one, and additionally pay corresponding shipping, handling, and taxes, it's possible that the expensive one will be out of stock. You'll receive a refund for the expensive item, meaning that the inexpensive piece will end up costing you three times its price because you've still paid shipping, handling, and taxes.

15. Legally, you can't be taxed on the transaction if it wasn't completed. Check the math. If you're owed for taxes, write to the customer service department of the company, and CC the president, as well as the tax department of the state for which the taxes are allegedly collected.

16. Perhaps you'll be refunded the proper proportion of taxes, shipping, and handling, but the net result is that you've paid $5 handling for a $4 item—which you'd never have done by choice. To avoid this happening, write plainly on the order, "Please cancel *entire order* and refund full amount if [specify the item] is not in stock."

17. The Federal Trade Commission (FTC) requires mail order companies to advertise honestly and ship in a reasonable period of time.

18. Under the FTC's "Mail Order Rule," companies have thirty days to ship an order unless their advertisement or catalog states different terms.

19. If there's a delay, the company has to inform you, and you must be provided with a postpaid card to use if you decide to cancel your order for a full refund.

20. If you don't reply, the company is allowed to proceed with the order.

21. Before you return the card, make a photocopy. You may need the information if you have to follow up later.

22. You have the right to cancel at any time before the order is shipped. Once a company has been informed of your intention, it has seven days to send a refund, or one billing period to have your credit card account adjusted.

23. If the merchandise comes and it's junk, or priced entirely too high considering its quality, complain. Ask how you can return it for credit or a refund. If you return it, must you insure it? If yes, who pays? If no, do they accept responsibility if it doesn't arrive?

24. Some companies will simplify refunds by sending you a postage-paid, preaddressed label. Ask if your company will do the same.

25. If you return merchandise, do you have to pack it in a particular way? The return policy may or may not spell out requirements. Ask if you're uncertain.

26. Don't return anything without complete identification, such as an order number, packing slip, or whatever may be required. You want to be sure the company knows it came back *from you.*

27. Whether or not you insure the parcel, send it in some way that proves it was received (such as return-receipt mail). Otherwise, the company can simply keep your money and claim you never returned anything.

28. If you have a question or problem with an order, phone or write the company. Give the date

the order was sent and a description and the catalog number(s) of the merchandise.

29. Unless the company is blatantly dishonest, you should get satisfaction, but it may take several calls and letters. If you have to write more than once, enclose copies of previous correspondence, copies of supporting documents, copies of canceled checks, and whatever substantiates your complaint.

30. If the company seems extremely negligent and if the advertisement appeared in a magazine or newspaper, CC the advertising manager of the publication. No matter how much the publication wants advertising dollars, its executives don't want to be party to intentional fraud.

31. If you heard about the offer by means of direct mail (an advertisement or promotion mailed to you), write the Direct Marketing Association, Mail Order Action Line, 6 East 43rd Street, New York, NY 10017-4646. The DMA will usually investigate consumer complaints and apply pressure as appropriate. Enclose copies of previous correspondence with the company.

32. On your request, the DMA will also try to remove your name from mailing lists.

33. The Federal Trade Commission (FTC) tracks complaints against mail order companies. If enough pile up, the FTC will investigate. If complaints are valid, companies can be fined. To complain, write to the Federal Trade Commission, Correspondence Branch, Room 692, 6th and Pennsylvania Avenue, N.W., Washington, DC 20580. Enclose copies of previous correspondence with the company, the DMA, etc.

34. The U.S. Postal Inspector investigates complaints and has the power to put companies out of business if fraud has occurred. Write to the Chief Postal Inspector, U.S. Postal Service, Washington, DC 20260-6720. Enclose copies of relevant previous correspondence.

35. CC the director or manager of customer service on any letters to outside agencies. Your cover letter might indicate that you've spent whatever sum for postage and photocopying in an attempt to get what you paid for, and you'd really appreciate a satisfactory resolution without further delay *plus* reimbursement for photocopies and postage.

36. If your dispute is with policy rather than employee error, you might ask to speak to the company's house counsel or legal department. If you get through, explain that an agreement was entered into, and your money was accepted on the basis of the agreement. Ask what steps can be taken to bring the company's actions into accordance with the agreement.

37. If the house counsel doesn't seem to care, you might suggest that you want to speak to your attorney about a class-action suit (*see* RUNG ELEVEN: CLASS ACTION SUITS in Part I). Say that you realize consumers don't come out much ahead on these, but if your case is as legitimate as you believe it to be and if the class of wronged consumers is established to be very large, your attorney stands to turn a handsome profit at the expense of the mail order company, and the mail order company can expect a bad and costly year.

38. If a company suddenly goes out of business, and if the FTC receives enough complaints, it may take action to force the company to reimburse complainants from its assets.

39. If not, there's always a class-action suit.

40. If you place several mail orders a month, keep a running record of each, and check off the items when you get them. This will be very helpful if, for instance, you one day realize the substitute mailman on your route has your address confused with somebody else's, or has been methodically marking your packages "Moved, Return to Sender."

Unordered Merchandise

1. If you receive something you didn't order, federal law says it's yours, free.

2. According to the Office of Consumer/Business Education, Federal Trade Commission, "If

you are sent clothing, cookware, linens, office supplies, or any other merchandise that you did not order, you have a legal right to keep the shipment as a free gift."

3. Before you embrace it as a freebie, be sure you didn't do anything to authorize it. For example, if you agreed to accept a sample or merchandise on approval, it's not unordered.

4. For your protection when you receive unordered merchandise, write the company to advise that you didn't order it and have no obligation to pay for it. Keep a copy of the letter, because you'll need it if you start getting dunning notices.

5. If it's an expensive item, consider sending your letter by certified mail, return receipt requested, in order to have proof that you wrote.

6. If you get a dunning letter, answer it with a brief explanation. Attach a copy of your previous letter along with a copy of the signed return receipt.

7. If you feel that an honest error was made and that it wouldn't be fair for you to keep the item, write the sender. Explain what happened, and offer to hold the merchandise for a period of time within which *the company* can arrange to get it back.

8. Suggest that the company pick it up, or provide you with some means to return it. But insist that the arrangements involve no cost or inconvenience to you.

9. If a company persists in billing you for unordered merchandise, speak to someone in the office of the local U.S. Postal Inspector, the state or city consumer affairs department, the Better Business Bureau, or the DMA (see above).

10. Report the incident to the Correspondence Branch, Federal Trade Commission, Room 692, 6th and Pennsylvania Avenue, N.W., Washington, DC 20580. The FTC won't fight a battle exclusively for you, but it can discipline a company if it finds evidence of deliberate deception, unfair practices, or statutory violations. This comes under the "Unordered Merchandise Statute"—write to the Washington address, phone the Washington number (202-326-2222), or contact your regional FTC office.

▲ *See also* CREDIT CARDS; GUARANTEES; SCAMS; TELEMARKETING; WARRANTIES.

Medicare, Medicaid, and Medigap

Medicare is an excellent example of a perfect idea embedded in an imperfect system. Worse, it's a *big* system. So be prepared to become frustrated. Program yourself to follow through on every claim. Stay informed about changes through newspapers and magazines, the American Association of Retired Persons (AARP), and the Social Security Administration (SSA). And unfailingly, keep careful records.

The Social Security office will be your main contact for general questions and answers. The Social Security Administration has local offices, or can be reached by phone at 1-800-772-1213 between 7:00 A.M. and 7:00 P.M. on any business day. The Medicare carrier designated for your area can respond to specific concerns about bills and coverage (the SSA will give you the number).

If you're vigilant, you ought to come out on top. You may even develop a marked agility in wielding the Medicare hammer: Health care providers that accept Medicare *must* observe many pro-consumer rules. If they don't, you almost won't have to go after them. Just advise Medicare, and Medicare will investigate.

Note: This information may be affected by the adoption of a National Health Care Plan.

Medicare, Medicaid, and Medigap

1. Medicare is our country's basic (but *not* comprehensive) health insurance program for eligible people sixty-five or older, certain disabled people under sixty-five, and people of any age who have permanent kidney failure. The Social Security Administration and Medicare carrier can answer your questions about Medicare.

2. Medicaid (MediCal in California) is a state-run program designed essentially for low-income individuals. Each state sets its own terms for eligibility and benefits. For further information, contact your area offices of social services and welfare, or phone 1-800-638-6833.

3. Some people qualify for both Medicare and Medicaid. Your state offices will have details.

4. Many private insurance companies sell insurance to fill the gaps in Medicare coverage. This sort of protection has been nicknamed Medigap (also MedSup). Medigap is *not* a government program, although federal and state rulings regulate aspects of it.

Medicare's Two Parts

1. Part A, or Hospital Insurance, is financed by payroll withholdings regularly deducted from your paycheck along with Social Security.

2. Part B, or Medical Insurance, is an option for additional coverage available to you when you agree to pay monthly premiums.

• • •

Medicare Part A

1. Most people sixty-five or older are eligible for Medicare *hospital insurance* based on their own or their spouse's past employment; for instance:

- **If you're getting Social Security or railroad retirement benefits.**
- **If you're not getting them but have worked long enough to qualify for them.**
- **If you'd be entitled to Social Security benefits based on your spouse's work record and if your spouse is at least sixty-two (even if your spouse hasn't actually applied).**
- **If you've worked long enough for federal, state, or local government to be insured for Medicare.**

2. Most people under sixty-five are eligible for *Part A:*

- **If they've been getting Social Security disability benefits for twenty-four months.**
- **If they've worked long enough in federal, state, or local government, and meet the requirements of the Social Security disability program.**
- **If—after a waiting period—they receive a disability annuity from the Railroad Retirement Board. If this applies to you, your Railroad Retirement Office will have more information.**

3. Based on your work record, your spouse, divorced spouse, widow, widower, and dependent parent may qualify upon reaching sixty-five.

4. Disabled widows and widowers under sixty-five, disabled divorced widows and widowers under sixty-five, and disabled children may also be eligible through your employment history.

5. People with permanent kidney failure, who are on maintenance dialysis or have had a kidney transplant, may qualify for Medicare at any age if certain conditions are met. A spouse or dependent child with kidney failure may qualify based on your employment history.

6. If you aren't eligible for Medicare by virtue of your or somebody else's employment record, you may qualify to pay a monthly premium to enroll. When you select this option, you agree to take and pay for Medicare Part B Medical Insurance too.

7. If you're disabled and under sixty-five and used to get disability insurance benefits and Medicare but lost the benefits only because you were working, you may pay the monthly premium to enroll in Medicare Part A coverage without having to take or pay for Part B.

8. Part A doesn't pay all your hospital costs, but it covers most of such inpatient expenses as semiprivate room and meals, regular nursing service, operating and recovery room, intensive care and coronary care, drugs, lab tests, X-rays, medical supplies and appliances, rehabilitation services, and preparatory services related to kidney transplant surgery.

9. Coverage is tied to benefit periods. A benefit period starts the day you enter the hospital and ends when you've been out (of the hospital or other facility primarily providing skilled care) for sixty consecutive days. If you stay on in the nonhospital facility ("SNF"—Skilled Nursing Facility), the period ends when you haven't received skilled care for sixty consecutive days.

10. Part A hospital insurance contributes toward the cost of up to ninety days of inpatient care in a Medicare-participating hospital during each benefit period. However:

- **Hospital insurance pays for all covered services for the first sixty days *less a deductible*. A deductible is the amount a beneficiary must pay before the insurer kicks in.**
- **It pays for all covered services for days sixty-one through ninety *less a daily coinsurance amount*. Coinsurance (or copayment) is the dollar amount or percentage of expenses you must pay for covered services (or have covered by a secondary insurer such as a Medigap policy).**
- **No limit is imposed on the number of benefit periods allowed for hospital and skilled nursing facility care, though there are conditions to be met for hospice care.**
- **You have a sixty-day reserve for your lifetime. You can dip into it if your inpatient stay extends beyond ninety days, but once you exhaust the reserve, it can't be replaced. You**

will be responsible for a copayment for reserve days.

11. Hospital insurance pays for necessary inpatient skilled care in a Medicare-participating nursing facility for up to one hundred days if several conditions are met. All services are paid for the first twenty days; the next eighty days are covered *less a coinsurance amount.*

12. Medicare will pay the full approved cost of home health visits from a Medicare-participating home health agency if various conditions are met (such as that you're confined to your home). A copayment applies to covered "durable medical equipment"—wheelchairs, hospital beds, etc.

13. Hospice care (for terminally ill patients) may be covered in part in a Medicare-certified hospice if certain conditions are met. Specific benefit periods apply.

Medicare Part B

1. Almost anyone sixty-five or older, or under sixty-five but entitled to Part B, can pay the monthly premiums to obtain this form of *medical insurance.*

2. It covers most of the cost of doctors' and related services, such as medical and surgical services, diagnostic tests appropriate to treatment, X-rays, limited treatment of mental illness, blood transfusions, drugs that can't be self-administered, care in an emergency room or outpatient clinic, ambulance transportation, radiation treatments, and various therapy services.

3. An annual deductible applies. After you've exceeded and paid the deductible, Medicare will (at present) pay 80 percent of approved charges for covered services during the remainder of the year.

4. If you're covered under an employer group health plan and you work past sixty-five, or you're older than sixty-five and the spouse of a worker of any age, you can wait to enroll in Medicare Part B during a seven-month "special enroll-

ment period" which starts the month your group coverage ends (or the month the employment ends if the job ends first). You may not have to wait for the general enrollment period, and you won't have to pay the usual late-enrollment surcharge (see #1–3 under *Signing Up,* below).

Signing Up for Medicare

1. If you're already getting Social Security checks at age sixty-five (*see* SOCIAL SECURITY), your hospital insurance should come automatically. A package will arrive two or three months before your sixty-fifth birthday, advising you of your coverage and offering the option of Part B enrollment.

2. You have seven months to sign up for Part B (from three months before the month you first become eligible to three months after that month).

3. If you waive Part B the first year, you can sign up in later years during the *general enrollment period* (January 1 to March 31), but at a higher (with some exceptions) monthly premium. Coverage would begin in July.

4. If you're still working but plan to retire at age sixty-five, give the Social Security Administration about three months advance notice. You can sign up for Social Security retirement benefits and Medicare at the same time.

5. If you don't want to retire at sixty-five, call anyway. You have the option to sign up for Medicare immediately but defer your Social Security benefits.

6. If you're eligible and a government employee, a government retiree, a government employee disabled before sixty-five, disabled and under sixty-five, or a disabled widow or widower between fifty and sixty-five, or if you're not certain whether you qualify with respect to your plans for ongoing employment, contact the Social Security Administration for specifics on how to proceed.

7. When given specifics, make a note of the date, time, and person's name. In an experimental

program, some SSA offices send receipts of conversations, briefly summarizing what was discussed, confirming and identifying the source of the information.

Filling the Gaps

1. Insurance through your employer, association, or private carrier may already fill in the gaps not covered by Medicare. Or you can shop around for additional protection that would cover Medicare copayments and deductibles and other expenses.

2. Don't expect any policy to cover every possible medical situation.

3. For simplification and to allow you to compare plans from different companies, effective in 1992 all Medigap insurance policies were required to conform to a selection of standardized benefit plans.

4. Because insurance issues are largely regulated by states, there will be variations. For example, state insurance departments might limit the number of plans that can be sold within their jurisdiction, or permit additional standardized plans.

5. Be sure that you're buying extended protection—not simply paying twice for what one policy already gives you.

6. It's illegal for any insurance company or agent to knowingly sell you a policy that duplicates Medicare coverage or your private health insurance coverage. Advise your state insurance department and the U.S. Department of Health and Human Services (1-800-638-6833) if you believe anyone has done or tried to do this.

7. When you retire from your company, ask for assistance in understanding the coverage you have, the changes you can expect, and the forms you'll have to complete.

8. If you feel you'll be duplicating benefits or for some other reason want to drop other insurance, be sure not to terminate anything until you're positive your Medicare coverage is in effect.

9. Medicare has prepayment contracts with various health maintenance organizations (HMOs) and competitive medical plans (CMPs) through which enrollees receive Medicare-approved services. A listing of programs in your area should be available for review in your local Social Security office.

What Can Go Wrong?

Anything and everything. It's a big system. But you can reduce your frustration quotient by taking some precautions.

1. Inquire about costs and procedures before going for health care. Keep careful records of conversations, noting date, time, and names of the people you spoke to.

2. Be sure the physician or facility participates in Medicare. The "Medicare-Participating Physician/Supplier Directory" is available free from your area Medicare carrier, and on file for review in Social Security offices, area agencies for the aging, and most hospitals.

3. Don't assume anything will be covered. Confirm beforehand that yours will be an approved charge. Custodial care—such as assistance with eating and dressing not needed in conjunction with medically skilled care—is an example of something that *wouldn't* be covered. Also, most prescription drugs, foot care, dental care, and nursing-home and long-term care wouldn't be covered by Medicare.

4. As noted above, charges not covered by Medicare may be paid by other insurance you have. If you need the care and have no other means to pay, call the Social Service Administration or area social services and welfare agencies to find out if you qualify for other types of financial aid.

5. If your resources are limited, the Qualified Medicare Beneficiary (QMB) program may be able to pay your monthly Part B premiums, deductibles, and coinsurance plus some supplemental coverage. Alternatively, the Special Low

Income Medicare Beneficiary (SLIMB) program might be able to pick up your Part B premiums only. Rules vary depending on your state. Contact your state or local medical assistance agency or social services or welfare office and ask for a copy of *You Should Know About QMB* (Publication #05-10079) from the Social Security Administration. Or phone 1-800-638-6833.

6. Insist on itemized bills.

7. Do your health care providers accept assignment? To accept assignment is to agree to accept the Medicare-approved amount as the total charge for covered services and supplies. However, the patient is still responsible for deductibles and copayments either out-of-pocket or through a supplemental insurer.

8. If they accept Medicare payments but not Medicare assignment, they're not to charge more than a fixed percentage over the Medicare fee schedule. Your local Medicare carrier can give you more information on this.

9. If a physician overcharges you in this respect, report it to your Medicare carrier. You aren't responsible for charges that go over the limit.

10. A doctor may ask you to sign a waiver in cases covered by Medicare, in which you agree to absorb whatever cost Medicare won't pay. Unless the procedure isn't covered by Medicare (such as cosmetic surgery), the request may be illegal. When in doubt, phone your Medicare carrier or the state insurance department.

11. In advance, ask the doctor or facility *and* Medicare carrier, "What will you need from me? What numbers? What proof? What papers? Who will file what? Whom can I call if I get the bill and discover a problem?"

12. If you have Medicare *and* accept an employer's health insurance plan from an employer with more than twenty employees and you're sixty-five or older and continuing to work, or are sixty-five or older and the spouse of a working person, Medicare will be the *secondary payer* of hospital and medical bills. In other words, bills are initially presented to the primary payer, with Medicare considering only the unpaid balance.

13. If your employer has fewer than twenty employees, Medicare is your primary payer. Your employer's health plan is the secondary payer.

14. Once you retire, Medicare becomes the primary insurer.

15. Confusion over primary and secondary payers isn't unusual, so be very clear in instructing your health care provider. If you don't, it's entirely possible the bill will go to the wrong payer first, drag through a long delay, and bounce back rejected.

16. When this happens, the doctor or hospital might forward the bill to you for full payment. At this juncture, repeat, "If you will please submit the bill to my primary payer, I believe it will resolve the problem." Provide the necessary address, I.D. number, and other details.

17. Follow up in writing. CC your Medicare carrier and other insurer.

18. If the hospital or doctor ignores your request, advise your Medicare carrier and other insurer in writing. CC your doctor's or hospital's billing office.

You've Got Clout

1. Percentages and dollar amounts can't remain the same forever. Keep informed about changes.

2. Medicare rules seem destined for modification as the new move toward national health care gathers steam.

3. Because lawmakers and insurers are keenly interested in what you think about these plans, don't hesitate to express your opinion. Write to your U.S. senators and congressman concerning federal programs, and your state senators and congressman on state insurance issues.

4. To wield the Medicare hammer locally: If your doctor attempts to overcharge you, tell Medicare. A provider who has overcharged, has performed unnecessary or inappropriate services, or is billing Medicare for services not delivered can be hit with thousands of dollars in fines per incident, and excluded from Medicare for years.

5. With your Explanation of Benefits (EOB, sometimes called EOMB) in hand, call your area Medicare carrier to determine whether a doctor has overcharged for a procedure. Give the procedure code. Ask what would constitute an overcharge and how you should respond to it.

6. You may not have to phone if your EOB shows the approved amount.

7. If you report the abuse to your Medicare carrier but the carrier doesn't respond suitably, call or write the U.S. Department of Health and Human Services, Office of Inspector General, 1-800-368-5779 (hotline). The address is OIG Hotline, P.O. Box 17303, Baltimore, MD 21203-7303.

8. If overcharge isn't the problem but your claim is rejected by Medicare once, try, try again.

9. Ask your health care provider if Medicare has covered identical treatment in the past. Confirm that the identifying codes are correct.

10. To request a review by Medicare, send Medicare a copy of the EOB with a signed note stating, "Please review." You have approximately six weeks from the date on the EOB to do this.

11. If you're rejected again, send the EOB with a signed note and make a "request for a fair hearing." You can ask for an in-person hearing, or indicate that you wish to be informed by mail.

12. If you're a Medicare hospital patient, you have quite a few rights, among them the right to be fully informed about decisions affecting your Medicare coverage and payment for your hospital stay and for any post-hospital services; and your discharge date must be determined solely by your medical needs, not by DRGs (*see* HOSPITALS) or the status of Medicare payments.

13. If you receive a notice of noncoverage from your hospital (stating that Medicare will no longer pay for your care), you have the right to request a peer review.

14. Peer review organizations (PROs) are groups of doctors whom the federal government pays to assess medical necessity and the quality and appropriateness of hospital treatment furnished to Medicare patients.

15. Contact your area peer review organization to report any violations of those rights.

16. Your hospital's patient representative or social worker should be able to help you with this. The admitting office ought to have such information as well, and, in fact, is generally required to give it to you when you arrive for treatment.

Other Resources

1. Most states have a senior health insurance counseling program. To locate the one in your area, call your local area agency on aging or your state insurance department.

2. The American Association of Retired Persons Medicare/Medicaid Volunteer Assistance Program is a valuable resource for members. Consult your directory to see if there is an office in your area.

3. *The Medicare Handbook* is available free from the Health Care Financing Administration of Health and Human Services. Phone the SSA toll-free number, 1-800-772-1213.

4. *Guide to Health Insurance for People with Medicare* (published by the National Association of Insurance Commissioners and the Health Care Financing Administration) is free with a phone call to the Health Care Financing Administration, your state insurance department, or your Medicare carrier.

▲ *See also* DOCTORS; HOSPITALS; INSURANCE; NURSING HOMES; SOCIAL SECURITY.

900 Numbers

Depending on your opinion of politics in general, 900 numbers began either legitimately or under a cloud. First used by ABC Television in 1980 for viewers wanting to cast their votes for the winner of the Reagan-Carter debate (at 50 cents per response), 900 numbers grew into a lucrative and often deceptive business. Not all 900 operations are shady; often, as in the case of many Better Business Bureaus, they constitute an efficient and totally respectable means of billing consumers for valuable services. But others aren't so trustworthy.

The big growth didn't begin until 1988, when several major long-distance carriers agreed to lease service to private companies. The long-distance carriers would charge callers on callers' regular monthly phone bills (but billed by the local phone company), making payment virtually automatic. The companies that leased from the carriers were largely free to set their own rates. Soon horoscope and sex lines advertised that they would give advice to people calling their 900 numbers. They didn't always make it clear that the calls would be expensive.

Unfortunately, laws and consumer protection regulations have yet to catch up entirely with this still-young industry. Nonetheless, you do have recourse and protection when wrongly charged for a 900-number call.

Pay Attention Before You Call

1. Some advertisements offer advice or information via an 800 number, which is toll-free. But when you phone this number, you're referred to a 900 number. The problem is that although you hear the new number clearly, the message is fuzzy or inaudible when the cost of the second call is explained.

2. Not all high-priced toll calls are 900 numbers. Calls with 976 exchanges function the same way and can be just as costly.

3. If you place a call with a 900 area code or a 976 exchange, note the per-minute cost and the length of time you remain on the line. When your phone bill comes, compare your computations with the stated charges to make sure they match.

4. There are certain toll-free 800 numbers dialed by people believing they've won a prize. Smothered in the instructions for claiming the booty is an unclear announcement that further instructions won't be free. If you don't hang up immediately, expect a bill for the call, for an amount much higher than what you would have paid for the same dubious treasure in any store.

When the Bill Comes

If you find a 900 (or 976 or sometimes 700

number) charge which you believe was billed unfairly:

1. Write to your telephone company immediately. You can ask the phone company to delete the charge, although it is not legally obligated to do so.

2. If this attempt is unsuccessful, ask how you can contact the company that leases the number and the long-distance carrier from which it's leased. Write to both, instructing them to delete the charge.

3. These long-distance carriers have toll-free numbers to handle complaints about 900 numbers:

AT&T   1-800-222-0300 (If AT&T gives you a different 800 number on the long-distance page of your phone bill that lists the 900-number charges, call that 800 number instead.)
MCI   1-800-444-3333
US Sprint   1-800-366-0707

4. If the information provider or service bureau that leased the number refuses to credit you and has a debt collector contact you, write the collection agency telling it not to contact you again.

5. Under the law, once the collection agency receives your letter, it cannot contact you again except to say there will be no further contact or that some specific action will be taken if such is the intention. (*See* DEBT COLLECTORS.)

6. Because the debt, if not resolved, can remain on your credit record, you are legally entitled to have your explanation of the incident included in your credit report (*see* CREDIT RATINGS).

7. AT&T cannot disconnect your phone for failure to pay. For other carriers, call the carrier or the Federal Communications Commission (FCC), 1919 M Street, N.W., Washington, DC 20554; 202-632-7000.

8. In addition, you may wish to contact the Federal Trade Commission, Correspondence Branch, Room 692, 6th and Pennsylvania Avenue, N.W., Washington, DC 20580. Complaints about 900-number scams help the FTC in its law enforcement efforts.

9. If you received the solicitation for the 900 number in the mail, contact the Chief Postal Inspector, U.S. Postal Service, Washington, DC 20260-2100; 202-268-4267.

10. Under FCC rulings, phone companies must provide blocking of 900 calls on request, unless the company has older equipment that cannot block calls.

Help Is at Hand

1. Long-distance carriers have accepted more responsibility for the sorts of businesses they'll accept for a leasing arrangement. Some carriers now lease but won't include the charges on your monthly phone bill. Some set a price cap on calls. Some investigate contents before agreeing to a leasing arrangement.

2. When you feel you've been cheated, contact the long-distance carrier to determine what rules have been set. If the charge on your bill violates any of them, ask the carrier to arrange a credit for you.

3. Effective December 1991, the FCC has required 900 numbers to (a) declare the per-minute cost in the message itself, (b) give callers time to hang up before charges begin, and (c) on programs aimed at children, announce in a message that parental permission is required.

▲ *See also* 800 NUMBERS; SCAMS; TELEMARKETING.

Nursing Homes

Most middle-aged couples today have more living parents than living children, and the over-eighty-five group is the fastest-growing segment of our country's population. In other words, the need for good nursing homes will be of vital concern to an increasing number of people in the coming years. Consumers can take heart in this, because greater pressure will doubtless be brought to bear as the army of concerned citizens expands and the average age of voters climbs.

But waving angry fists should never be the first-line defense. First, do your homework for yourself and those you love. Second, bring your complaints to the attention of nursing homes, state licensing authorities, and the area politicians whose job it is to protect the quality of life of every constituent. If pressure is to have real meaning, this is how to apply it.

Preparing for Long-Term Care

1. Long-term care doesn't have to be provided in a nursing home if appropriate care can be given elsewhere, such as in the individual's own home. Contact your local area agency on aging, county or state office on aging, or state department of social services for options and services. Look for appropriately named agencies and offices in the state, county, and city government listings in your phone directory.

2. Friends and relatives, doctors, lawyers, and clergy are good sources of referrals and recommendations.

3. The National Council of Senior Citizens, 1331 F Street, N.W., Washington, DC 20004, 202-347-8800, offers guidance on nursing home standards and regulations and can provide you with material on patients' rights and a list of services to consider.

4. *Adult day-care centers* provide fellowship, recreation, and supervision during daytime hours. Often these facilities, when combined with other available evening and night care, are sufficient to meet the individual's needs, and they allow the at-home caregiver(s) to work and engage in other activities.

5. *Congregate homes* for seniors are buildings or apartments clustered together with a view toward assuring essential services and day-to-day assistance. They feature group dining and light housekeeping but generally not medical care. The applicable area office of U.S. Department of Housing and Urban Development should be able to tell you what's available to meet your particular needs.

6. *Assisted living* is like congregate housing, but additionally offers personal attention such as assistance with bathing and grooming.

7. *Continuing care communities* provide housing, meals, social activities, private living units, and personal and nursing care as needed.

8. Don't assume that Medicare will pick up the cost. Medicare may cover short-term skilled nurs-

ing home or at-home care following hospitalization but not, for instance, for active employees still covered by their employer's plans. And Medicare's definition of "skilled nursing home" might not fit the residence at all, in which case the claim would be disallowed.

9. Medicaid can step in to take over nursing home payments, but only after the individual's resources are essentially gone (all but roughly a few thousand dollars beyond burial costs). It used to be that the spouse who remained at home would also have to become impoverished, but recent revisions in the law enable the spouse to keep a certain level of income and savings, as well as the family home, a car, some personal possessions, and a monthly income derived from Social Security, pensions, and investments (under a ceiling set by each state).

10. Medicaid pays for at-home care on a very limited basis.

11. Medicaid is not available in every state, and not every nursing home accepts Medicaid.

12. Plan to protect personal assets in advance. Find out what Medicare/Medicaid/Medigap might cover, and then get advice from a financial consultant (or a clergyperson who knows you, or an area agency on aging) to determine whether the individual's money should be maintained in a different account, or in a different way.

13. Don't wait too long to do this. Most states won't recognize a transfer of assets that occurs too close to (a year or two before) nursing home admission.

14. See what help is available from employee's insurance and benefits, veteran's benefits, and state disability.

15. Some life insurance policies pay long-term care benefits to the policyholder while alive instead of to the beneficiary after death. Check whether yours has these "accelerated" or "living" benefits.

16. If your prospects for future coverage seem inadequate, bear in mind that "long-term care" insurance is available, offering different options as

to deductible periods, preexisting conditions, and renewability. Most policies can't be canceled if you pay premiums on time and haven't falsified answers on your application.

17. A "waiver of premium" in such a policy means you don't have to pay premiums while receiving benefits. The policy will spell out any waiting period or other restrictions that apply.

18. As with any insurance, don't buy until you've done your homework (*see* INSURANCE). Obtain the company's A. M. Best Company rating and a summary or outline of benefits and coverage. Read the policy—perhaps with a trusted friend or adviser—to be sure it says what you want it to say.

19. For a list of insurers that offer long-term care insurance, write to Health Insurance Association of America, P.O. Box 41455, Washington, DC 20018.

Selecting a Nursing Home

1. Ask around. Ask clergypersons, area social service agencies and agencies on aging, and friends.

2. Attend free community programs about options for long-term care. These events may take place in libraries, houses of worship, and senior centers; watch your local paper for notice of them.

3. Inspect the sites personally—at least once unannounced.

4. Chat with residents. Have a meal there.

5. Ask to see the most recent fire inspection report. Does it seem recent enough?

6. Make sure you understand the billing schedule. What are the fees? For which extras do you have to pay more, and how much?

7. It may or may not be legal for the home to require a deposit. It's a violation of federal law for skilled nursing facilities to demand deposits from Medicare or Medicaid recipients, unless they know for a fact that the stay won't be covered.

8. If a facility illegally demands a deposit, file a complaint with local and state licensing agencies.

9. Violations of Medicare procedure should be reported to the U.S. Department of Health and Human Services, Office of Inspector General. Use the toll-free hotline, 1-800-368-5779, or the address OIG Hotline, P.O. Box 17303, Baltimore, MD 21203-7303.

10. It's generally illegal for a home to require a large donation as a condition of admission, but it's also hard to prove. Report it to the state or city department of consumer affairs or a local elected official if this happens to you.

11. What can you expect other insurance to cover?

12. How is the home covered if it experiences financial difficulties? Is it insured? Bonded? Ask for copies of the documents that prove coverage.

13. How many doctors are on staff or visit regularly (including geriatric specialists, dentists, psychiatrists, and licensed therapists)? How many nurses?

14. Find out what, if any, restrictions apply to residents. Is there any reason they can't put pictures on the walls or bric-a-brac on their dressers?

15. What are the social activities? Are residents taken on outings? How can they attend religious services? What arrangements are made if they want to vote?

16. Ask what happens when a resident must be sent to a hospital. How long will the nursing home hold the person's bed?

If You Have Problems

1. It's important for people in nursing homes to have visitors. Visitors can observe conditions first-hand, they can complain more convincingly than when friends and family seem for the most part to have neglected the individual, and they will be taken more seriously if they have to bring their grievances to higher authorities. Unfortunately, nursing homes will occasionally dismiss valid objections coming from residents, but they find it much more difficult to argue with a half-dozen frequent visitors who confirm that every word is true.

2. If the individual is physically ill but otherwise mentally alert, visitors *remain* extremely important. Friends and families are great reasons for living, and shouldn't fade out of an elderly person's life simply because he or she changes residence.

3. Some visitors make small marks on bandages and dressings to confirm that they're changed regularly.

4. If there's a complaint and the individual has a favorite nurse or staff member, the individual or a friend should speak to that person.

5. If that doesn't work, ask for the head nurse or charge nurse at the nursing station or the equivalent.

6. Keep a record of complaints, immediate and long-term. Note whether and when they're resolved. Remember that complaints will be more meaningful if someone visits often and monitors progress or negligence.

7. Speak to the patient representative, ombudsman, or social worker if one is available. Skilled nursing facilities should conspicuously post a local ombudsman's number. If you don't see one, ask for it, and contact your local area agency on aging.

8. Speak to the nursing home director.

9. If the list of grievances grows without improvement, go to the manager or owner of the facility.

10. If the home belongs to an organization that runs several, contact the head office—the consumer relations department if there is one—and/or the president of the organization.

11. If the home belongs to a charitable institution, write to board members and leaders of the charity itself.

12. Always remember that there are area agencies for the aging and other social services. Seek assistance from them, and register your complaints.

13. If you aren't paying every cent out of your own pocket, there is another party that will share your concern: the insurer who *is* paying. Medicaid certainly wants to know about inadequate service, as does your personal insurer. Write, stating your dispute and requesting that an investiga-

tion be made before further payment is authorized. CC the owner, manager, and nursing director of the home. Include copies of any relevant correspondence.

14. If you are unhappy with the way your personal insurance agent is handling matters, contact someone in the insurance company itself. Failing that, talk to your state insurance department, or try the area agency on aging, a state or county office on aging, the Better Business Bureau, the Chamber of Commerce, and the state or city department of consumer protection.

15. Your state department of health licenses nursing homes, investigates complaints, can impose penalties for violations, may revoke licenses, and usually will refer serious cases to the state district attorney. Many have twenty-four-hour numbers and/or can be called collect about allegations of mistreatment and neglect.

16. You may wish to write directly to the state district attorney, as well as the state attorney general. There may be a twenty-four-hour number for use in reporting Medicaid fraud.

17. Increasingly, a nursing home will live or die by its image and by its ability to attract well-paying residents. Even if Medicaid and the health department don't find fault with the facility, a history of reported abuses and lawsuits will discourage higher-income patients. Consequently, a well-worded letter to the local newspaper may prove very effective, as would any visit you can encourage from the local TV action newsperson.

18. Tell your story to local senior leagues and centers. Mobilize their letter-writing support.

Additional Resources

AARP (American Association of Retired Persons)
601 E Street, N.W.
Washington, DC 20049-0002
202-434-2277

American Health Care Association
1201 L Street, N.W.
Washington, DC 20005
202-842-4444

Council of Better Business Bureaus
4200 Wilson Boulevard, Suite 800

Arlington, VA 22203
703-276-0100

Friends and Relatives of Institutionalized Aged
11 John Street
New York, NY 10038
212-732-4455

National Citizen's Coalition for Nursing Home Reform
1224 M Street, N.W.

Washington, DC 20005
202-393-2018

National Consumer's League
815 15th Street, N.W., Suite 516
Washington, DC 20005
202-639-8140

United Hospital Fund
55 Fifth Avenue
New York, NY 10003
212-645-2500

▲ *See also* **DOCTORS; HOSPITALS; INSURANCE; MEDICARE, MEDICAID, AND MEDIGAP; PENSIONS; SENIORS AND ELDERLAW; SOCIAL SECURITY.**

Pensions

Even when you go to work, you're a consumer. Perhaps you're a consumer of the products your supplier sells. At the same time, you're a consumer of the services and goods offered by other departments in your place of business. And if your company provides a pension plan for you, money is invested in it on your behalf. Your years of diligent labor earn that money, so never doubt that you're paying for it.

It used to be that a young person starting out in a job expected it to be a job for life. If a pension came with the position, the assumption was made that the company "knew what it was doing"— that the funds would be sufficient, and the promises kept.

We've seen changes since those days. People often don't stay with one firm. Pensions aren't necessarily designed to keep up with inflation. Employers don't or can't always abide by the promises they made.

But you've put years into honoring your end of the deal. Those years give you rights.

When You're Offered a Pension

1. You probably have no choice of plans. The company has picked a plan to cover its employees and it offers to include you. Period. But ask if you have any options, and if any supplemental plans are available.

2. Ask what statements and reports you'll get as a member of the plan.

3. If you decide you want the complete annual report (Form 5500), will you have to pay a copying fee? Can you get the Summary Annual Report, an abbreviated version?

4. Find out how you'd contact the person responsible for the plan if you have questions down the line. What is the person's title, and will that person be readily accessible to you?

5. If you don't stay long enough to collect a pension, will you be vested after a certain number of years on the job? In other words, will you accrue some sort of investment that you can take with you if you don't retire from the firm? How long will it take before you become vested? Get full details of the arrangement.

6. If you leave the job with retirement benefits being owed to you, when will you see the money? Must you wait until you retire? Would there be some way to roll it over into another plan? If there's a waiting period, how long is the wait?

7. What are the provisions for early retirement? At what age can you do it, and what would it entitle you to collect?

8. Most larger companies have a personnel policy manual that spells out your entitlements. Ask for a copy when you're hired, or find out how you can consult one if you need to.

9. If specific terms of a pension are part of your employment negotiation, get every point in writing and signed. Whether or not you've haggled over the plan, get it in writing anyway.

10. Make sure the signature belongs to someone in sufficient authority that the document is

beyond question. For instance, a large company might not want to recognize the signature of an interviewer or clerk.

11. If you have a financial adviser—your banker, your accountant, or a friend in the field—get a "second opinion" on the plan and on its report. Do the investments seem sound? Does your adviser agree with projections on how the money will grow?

12. Some plan literature identifies investments by type rather than name. But the Employee Retirement Income Security Act (ERISA) says that you have the right to know where your money has gone. "Assets Held for Investment," a section of the annual report, should name the investments and ought to be available to you for free.

13. Ask how the funds are insured. Get this in writing too.

14. Retiree medical benefits aren't pensions but are related to them. Find out what yours are, how they're protected, and whether you are asked or might later be asked to share the cost.

15. If you're not comfortable about the deal you're offered but you really need the job, you may have little choice. But remember that if you agree to a plan you don't trust, you're gambling with your future.

16. If you can't bring yourself to discuss the pension plan in detail before you take the job, then arrange for an appointment with the pension plan administrator, benefits manager, or whoever is appropriate in your company as soon as possible after you're hired.

17. Employers don't have to offer any pension plan. Don't assume you have one unless you're told, and have it in writing.

When You Collect

1. In a best-case scenario, you get the money you expected and it's enough to last through your retirement.

2. There's no assurance that your pension program was realistically structured to beat the rate of inflation in the year 2022 or 2044, and there's every likelihood that you'll live longer than the planners originally estimated. You may get the money you were promised, but it may be worth less than you'd hoped.

3. Plans for government employees may be tied into cost-of-living adjustments (COLAs). Corporate and private plans may not be.

4. However, public employees aren't protected by the Employee Retirement Insurance Security Act (ERISA) and the Pension Benefit Guaranty Corporation (PBGC). Their employers—their governments—can use money from pension funds to balance other areas of their budgets without much opposition.

5. A defined-benefit plan is the sort that spells out what you'll get in exchange for the time you put in and the level of salary you attained.

6. A defined-contribution plan—profit sharing, money-purchase, 401(K), and the like—indicates how much will be invested, but doesn't commit to how it will grow. As a rule, these aren't protected by the PBGC.

7. If your employer intends to supply your retirement checks by buying you an annuity, the insurance company becomes liable. If the insurance company later fails, your best hope for restitution will be the state insurance guaranty association.

8. You may be given options, such as a lump-sum payout rather than regular stipends. Don't be pressured into a decision. Ask fellow employees, your banker, your accountant, and your insurance agent for their thoughts.

9. You may be given the option of choosing a single-life plan for yourself, or a joint-and-survivor variation that would pay your surviving spouse after your death. If you select the survivor plan, you usually reduce your own benefits—a decision that's irreversible if your spouse then predeceases you.

10. Some advisers suggest the single-life plan, and that you make yourself spend some of it on additional insurance to cover your spouse. If your spouse predeceases you, you can drop the policy

while retaining your higher single-life stipends. But if premiums rise faster than your ability to pay, you may be forced to drop the policy with nothing to show for it, leaving your spouse with no protection.

11. Don't make any decisions until you've done your homework. Read about retirement options in magazines and books, and speak to a trusted adviser.

Why Companies Break Pension Promises

1. A company may have made impractical investments.

2. It may have invested pension funds in its own stock. If the company is foundering or goes out of business, the value of the stock is shot.

3. It may have projected wildly high returns on its investments.

4. The economy is unpredictable. The company may have acted with the best of intentions, but nonetheless fallen short.

5. A bank may have defaulted on the company's pension funds. Funds kept in unstable banks no longer enjoy full FDIC coverage of up to $100,000 per individual. Unless the bank totally satisfies federal requirements, present coverage is $100,000 per plan, no matter how many individuals are included.

How to Protect Yourself

1. Federal, state, and municipal law is on your side. Enforcement may not be 100 percent, but lawmakers are aware of the weaknesses and are trying hard to eliminate them.

2. The Pension Benefit Guaranty Corporation (PBGC) is a U.S. agency that insures pension plans for approximately one out of every three working people. If your company can't honor its pension commitments and if it operates under PBGC protection, the PBGC will cover the difference up to a certain amount (currently $28,227, with a possible reduction for higher figures).

3. The Employee Retirement Income Security Act (ERISA) requires companies to invest pension funds responsibly in diversified investments, and usually not in their own stocks and bonds.

4. The last thing Washington wants to see is another S&L disaster. If too many underfunded employers run to the PBGC for a bailout, beneficiaries will be compensated, but taxpayers will foot the bill.

5. As a citizen, you can write to your elected officials, urging them to put teeth in legislation that will compel underfunded companies to shore up their investments.

6. Ask these officials how you can become more active. For instance, if a public hearing is scheduled on a pension issue that interests you, find out how you can attend.

7. Often, the size of the audience at a hearing is interpreted as an index of public concern. It may be that just a "show of force" is vital, and that your presence will have an effect even if you don't say a word.

8. If you have a problem or merely a doubt about what you'll get from your pension plan, start phoning your pension plan administrator, benefits office, or the equivalent department or person in your company. If you need clarifications or updates, ask to have them in writing.

9. Keep copies of correspondence, and log any conversations noting date, name and title of the person you spoke to, and what assurances were made.

10. Remember that if the clarifications, updates, and assurances matter, you'll want to have them from someone authorized to speak for the company—not simply a well-intentioned clerk who guesses but isn't sure.

11. You ought to have a case anyway if some seemingly designated but unauthorized person gives you wrong information—but do you want a formal proceeding that won't be settled for years,

or do you want to get correct answers the first time you ask?

12. If the company's designated personnel can't give the help you need and if you belong to a union, bring your concerns to the union's attention.

13. If the plan is administered by a bank, insurance company, brokerage house, or similar operation, find out if anyone there can assist you.

14. Find out what access you have to the members of the pension plan's board of trustees. Alert them to your concerns.

15. Find out what it takes to *be* a member of the board. It's a long shot, but if you can get a seat, you'll be directly involved in policy-setting.

16. The U.S. Department of Labor can tell you what laws protect you. If you suspect your company isn't meeting its legal obligations—for instance, not contributing regularly to the fund, borrowing from pension funds, or making ridiculous investments—contact the Pension and Welfare Benefits Administration, Office of Program Services, Department of Labor, 200 Constitution Avenue, N.W., Washington, DC 20210; 202-219-8921.

17. By the same token, if you've lost money in a badly managed plan, the Labor Department can investigate for you, and if the evidence is compelling, it can sue on your behalf.

18. If your company fires you just before you become eligible for retirement benefits, notify the Labor Department, because your employer may have broken the law. If you're a union member, alert the union.

19. The assets of your pension plan are supposed to be kept separate from other money, safe from creditors if your company is in deep financial trouble or goes bankrupt.

20. If the company is in serious trouble, your plan may be considered a creditor of the company and legally entitled to other company assets.

21. Fiduciaries and trustees who have responsibility for the plan are required by law to exercise prudent judgment, diversify assets, and manage the plan for the sole benefit of its members. They're allowed to make honest mistakes. But if they break the law, you can sue.

22. If they've broken the law, chances are you're not alone in your grievance. Find out what other employees are doing. You may want to hire a lawyer jointly for a class-action suit, or you may want to speak to the Legal Aid Society. By all means, contact the Labor Department.

23. If union employees are involved—whether or not you're a union member—find out what the union is doing.

24. If your employer is a large corporation endangering the benefits of hundreds of workers, it's also a community issue. Call your local elected officials and encourage them to become involved. (Protecting the rights of disgruntled voters is always a big plus for politicians when elections roll around.)

▲ *See also* BANKING; INSURANCE; MEDICARE, MEDICAID, AND MEDIGAP; SOCIAL SECURITY.

Product Liability and Recalls

American consumers have extensive recourse against faulty products that have the potential to hurt them. Moreover, they have access to a solid warning system to protect them from merchandise that already harmed somebody else.

That's the good news. Better still, a reformed federal product liability law is on the way, via the Federal Product Liability Fairness Act introduced on the floor of the Senate in September 1992. It will have several effects:

- **Rulings will be more uniform. Traditionally, most liability law came under state jurisdiction. But today, most goods are marketed nationally, or cross interstate lines between manufacture and sale. Greater federal intervention seems to be in order.**
- **The statute of limitations will begin with the date of "discovery"—in other words, when the consumer first discovers that a consumer product caused the injury. Under present statutes in certain states, the clock starts running when the injury occurred. This is clearly unfair to an individual who, for example, may have been exposed to asbestos or radium or a hazardous material long before anyone imagined the danger.**
- **Parties will be encouraged to settle, which is likely to result in faster, less expensive resolutions.**
- **The liability of wholesalers and retailers will be reduced. Though they'll continue to be held accountable in many cases, a greater burden for faulty products will rest on the shoulders of the companies that made them.**

Because the law will not have been passed with its full complement of editorial changes before this book goes to press, it's impossible to detail the changes and how they'll affect consumers. For specifics, contact your U.S. senator or congressman, or the Consumer Product Safety Commission, 1111 18th Street, N.W., Washington, DC 20207; 1-800-638-CPSC.

Current Federal Protection

1. The Consumer Product Safety Commission (CPSC) was set up under the Consumer Product Safety Act of 1972. (A valuable bit of information for getting the attention of uncooperative salespeople and manufacturers: "Do you have any *idea* of the penalties and fines you face under the Consumer Product Safety Commission Act of 1972?")

2. The CPSC can enforce mandatory standards on consumer products, with civil and criminal penalties including time in jail.

3. It may require product recall, repair, replacement, or refund.

4. Its National Electronic Injury Surveillance System monitors and records hospital emergency rooms across the nation for incidents of product-related injuries.

5. Consumers can file reports directly with the CPSC, using the address and number given above.

6. Consumers can also petition the CPSC to issue, amend, or revoke a consumer product safety rule. The CPSC must then grant or deny the written request within 120 days. If the petition is denied, the CPSC has to publish its rationale in the *Federal Register*.

7. Consumers have the right to appeal the decision in court.

8. Consumers can sue the CPSC if it fails to act on a petition within the requisite 120 days.

9. If you write to the CPSC to complain about a particular product, be sure to CC the consumer service department and the president of the manufacturing company. No company president wants to learn that his or her failures have become the basis of a petition before the CPSC and therefore may feel a greater urgency than the general staff to reach an accord with the unhappy consumer.

To Further Protect Yourself and Your Family

1. Before you buy a product, contact the Consumer Product Safety Commission (address and number as above) to check its records for recalls, complaints, or warnings.

2. This is particularly important with goods for infants and children, who can't be expected to read labels, and who love to put strange objects into their mouths and other kids' eyes.

3. Consumers Union (Information Services Department, Consumers Union, 101 Truman Avenue, Yonkers, NY 10703-1052; 914-378-2000) does an excellent job of rating merchandise for safety and other considerations. If you phone, you'll be told the issue of *Consumer Reports* that covered your product most recently. Most public libraries carry a complete set of back issues for precisely this sort of research.

4. Watch the business section of your newspaper, *Good Housekeeping,* and similar publications for regular columns about product recalls.

If a Problem Arises

1. If you have a problem or if you hear that a product you bought has been recalled, contact the manufacturer to learn what you should do next. You may be directed to return the product to the store for a refund, or to the manufacturer for a replacement, or to deal with it in another way.

2. If you can't contact the manufacturer or if the manufacturer is no help, phone:

- **The Consumer Product Safety Commission for items ranging from toys and games to appliances (1-800-638-CPSC).**
- **The Federal Drug Administration (FDA) about pharmaceuticals and medical devices (301-443-3170).**
- **The National Highway Traffic Safety Administration (NHTSA) about defects in new cars (1-800-424-9393; 202-366-0123 in Washington, DC).**

3. If you purchased the item under a warranty (*see* WARRANTIES), the coverage may protect you.

4. Speak to the dealer. Explain what's wrong with the merchandise. Ask for a replacement or refund. If the best you can wangle is the offer of repair, ask for a "loaner" until the faulty item is fixed.

5. Contact the consumer service department of the manufacturer (using the information that came with the purchase, either in an insert or on the box), or phone 800 Information to see if the company has an 800 number you can use.

6. Follow up any phone conversation, favorable or unfavorable, with a letter. Include photocopies of sales receipts and other documentation as necessary.

7. If you used a credit card, you may have an extended warranty or other protection through your card carrier. Read the credit agreement and accompanying papers to determine the extent of your coverage.

8. If the dealer and manufacturer are hopeless, or don't act within a reasonable period of time,

and if you used a credit card, write your credit card carrier and request a credit or chargeback (*see* CREDIT CARDS). Don't wait too long.

9. If matters are subsequently resolved, don't doubt for a minute that the charge will rematerialize on your statement. But if they aren't and if you wait more than sixty days after the item first appears on your statement to register your complaint, your carrier is under no obligation to investigate the dispute.

10. Product hazards are always of interest to TV consumer reporters. Though it's no fun for you when you've been injured, local broadcasters may be delighted to use the story.

11. Advise consumer protection and advocacy groups such as Consumers Union and the National Parent-Teacher Association, as well the CPSC.

12. CC the letters to the consumer service department and the president of the manufacturing company.

13. If the injury was job-related, speak to your human resources or personnel office and/or union representative. Be certain to take all the steps required by your employer: to file an accident report if needed, go to the medical office if that's part of the procedure, and so on.

14. In the event of a serious personal injury, you may be doing yourself a disservice if you try to settle without the intervention (or at the very least, guidance) of a lawyer.

▲ *See also* APPLIANCES; CREDIT CARDS; RETAIL SHOPPING; WARRANTIES.

Promotional Items

Promotional items are fun, but they're tricky. Suppose a cereal company offers decorated tins in exchange for proofs of purchase and a few dollars shipping and handling, and suppose that when the tins come, they're smashed flat. Of course, manufacturers don't set out to disappoint you. But when they do, you ought to be entitled to redress even though the items are more or less free.

Manufacturers' ads may contain disclaimers that they're not responsible for lost mail or damaged merchandise or whatever fulfillment mishap they wish to disavow. But even so, they must be aware that:

1. They've used printed media that crossed interstate lines, and they've used it to collect money from you. This brings them under the jurisdiction of the FTC (Federal Trade Commission, Division of Marketing Practices, 6th and Pennsylvania Avenue, N.W., Washington, DC 20580; 202-326-2222).

2. They've asked you to mail money, which puts them under the watchful eye of the U.S. Postal Service. You can report dissatisfactions to your local postmaster, or to the Chief Postal Inspector, U.S. Postal Service, Washington, DC 20260-2100; 202-268-4267.

3. The purpose in launching promotions is to attract customers. If a marketer or manufacturer's response has embittered a customer, surely it's in their best interest to restore a smile to the customer's face.

To Complain

If you have an experience with a promotion that backfires, never arrives, or is of substandard quality:

1. Call 1-800-555-1212 (800 Information) to see if the company has an 800 customer service number. If it does, phoning is free and much less trouble than writing a letter. (Try this too if you can't understand an offer, or if the terms are contradictory.)

2. Sad but true, some customer service department employees don't know the meanings of many simple words. Consequently, you won't get far in your conversations with them. If you sense this might be the difficulty, use shorter words. *Don't* start insulting the representative—because you'll only force this person to stonewall you to protect his or her job. If you still can't get through, ask for a supervisor.

3. If there's no 800 number, or if you still have to write, don't use the address to which you sent the money and proofs of purchase. It's usually the address of a fulfillment house, not the manufacturer. In fact, those post office box numbers can be withdrawn when an offer expires, in which case your letter will come back to you, months later, marked "Undeliverable. Return to sender."

4. Write to the customer service department of the manufacturer, whose address generally appears on the product label. If the address is incomplete, call telephone information to get a

street address, or consult a copy of a *Standard & Poor's* reference book at your local library.

5. Keep your letter brief and polite, and state immediately what went wrong. In your next (short) paragraph, indicate what you want the company to do. Be reasonable and specific in your request—in other words, ask for a new tin, not $1,000. Close with thanks "for your prompt response to this request" or words to this effect. Most companies will respond by sending a nice letter, the tin, and cents-off or free coupons for their products by way of apology.

6. If the company lets you down again, write to the customer service department supervisor. Mention that the company must have poured tremendous expense into creating the promotion for the purpose of attracting customers. You understand that mistakes can be made, but not why a customer service department would willingly compound them. Customers aren't being enticed but alienated. Furthermore, money was accepted on the basis of advertisements that appeared in print and crossed state lines. If the company does not intend to honor the terms of the transaction, it is in violation of the law and the matter will be reported to the FTC, the U.S. Attorney General, and the U.S. Postal Service. Include your phone number. Some supervisors would rather discuss the matter with you than prolong the correspondence.

7. When you write this letter, CC the company president by name. The name can be gotten from the 800 number if you're really lucky, from *Standard & Poor's,* or, if you're mad enough to pay for a toll call, by phoning the executive offices of the company.

Some Companies Can Be Lovely

1. Rank-and-file customer service personnel may be overworked, bored, and/or unduly protective of their company to the extent that they distrust every letter they receive. But supervisors and presidents tend to understand that promotions are indeed designed to build customer loyalty, not seething resentment.

2. Some companies will go out of their way to ensure goodwill, sending cards or letters if shipments are delayed. If you receive a card inquiring whether you still want the item, don't ignore it. Ignoring it may void the order.

If the Product Was Damaged and Therefore Dangerous

1. Take a photo or make a video of the danger or its consequence (cut finger, broken pitcher, hole blown through your bedroom wall . . .).

2. You have an absolute obligation to inform the company. The promotion wasn't created to slice up consumers. The sooner the company is advised, the sooner it can correct the source of the problem—or discontinue the offer if necessary. The company will generally respond *to you* with a particularly solicitous letter, coupons, etc.

3. If you've hurt yourself to the extent that you had to see a doctor, send the doctor's bill with an explanation of why you feel the company should pay. If you anticipate any chance of later complication, or if it's a personal injury case of any magnitude, don't try to resolve it yourself. Talk to a lawyer.

It's Always Easier If You've Done Your Homework

1. Be sure to read the terms of the offer. If you're asked for a dated register slip, make sure there's an appropriate date on the register slip. If the offer is one-to-a-customer, keep a record of the mailing so you don't later forget and exceed the limit. If you repeat yourself, the fulfillment house may answer you with a curt note that you've gone

overboard. You'll get your check back, but nobody is obligated to return your proofs.

2. It never hurts to keep a photocopy of the proofs, check, certificate, and whatever else you initially send.

3. Most promotions include disclaimers that the company is not responsible for lost mail. But because companies want to keep your loyalty, many will send the item if you've waited a reasonable length of time without receiving it and if you then follow up with a photocopy and explanatory letter directed to the company's customer service department.

4. Occasionally you'll receive a letter from the fulfillment house, claiming that you didn't meet the terms of the offer. Consult your photocopy. If you met the terms but some well-intentioned fumbler lost part of your mailing, follow up with an explanation and photocopy to the company's customer service department.

On General Principles

1. If you think you've waited too long for a parcel, if you were disappointed by shabbiness of the product inside, or even if you found the wording of the ad to be misleading or inane, write to the company's customer service department.

2. Most companies genuinely appreciate the input of customers, and many reply with a nice note, the item itself, and perhaps coupons or another small token of appreciation. The example comes to mind of a coupon printed recently on which, in one corner, it read "Buy two get one free" and elsewhere on the same coupon, "Buy two for the price of one." Customers who wrote to the company to explain that the contradictory wording created confusion at the supermarket were rewarded with no-expiration-date coupons redeemable for free products.

Public Transportation (Buses, Taxis, Trains)

As any experienced consumer knows, the bigger the system, the more futile it seems to complain. It's as though it doesn't matter what wrong information you're given, because the next service representative will simply nod apologetically and repeat that you were given wrong information.

You will hear:

- **"I'm sorry you were misinformed about our policy, but our policy hasn't changed, and I can't change it for you."**
- **"The public never agrees to increases when we ask for them, so this is the best service we can provide for the money."**
- **"If we were a private company, we could give you a refund. But we're a public trust. All we can do is apologize."**

And then you're supposed to gamely accept the consequences. But all the talk in the world doesn't make it fair for you to be overcharged or stranded by a subway, railroad, or bus line (airlines are covered in a separate chapter), and you owe it to yourself to follow through on your complaints—first, because satisfaction isn't impossible, and second, because if you don't, the service supplier is going to continue to believe that your inconvenience is acceptable.

When You Plan Your Bus or Train Adventure

1. Make no mistake about it. A simple trip on a village bus can be an adventure these days, particularly if you're not a regular passenger.

2. Don't rely on a printed schedule. If you aren't sure of the times, fare, stops, or route, phone a service representative for specifics.

3. Don't leave it for anyone to assume you mean one thing because you didn't ask something else. Ask if different times, fares, or routes apply for different days of the week, peak or off-peak. Ask for a definition of peak and off-peak.

4. If tickets must be purchased in advance, ask if penalty situations apply—for instance, if you can't use the ticket, or if you can't buy it at the station and have to buy it on board.

5. If you don't use your ticket right away, for how long is it good? Do you have to return within some number of days after your departure?

6. If you'll be buying the ticket in person with your credit card, make certain your card will be accepted for the amount in question. Otherwise, don't be surprised when you can't buy a $14.95 ticket from a counter with a $15 minimum. If minimums are not allowed by your state or by your card carrier, you can protest (*see* CREDIT CARDS), but you may also miss the train or bus.

7. If you're told you can use the card, *repeat* the exact ticket you'll be getting. It sometimes happens that long-distance bus companies share counters with another carrier, and a well-intentioned employee of the other company assumes the companies share the same rules.

8. To be sure you have the employee's full attention, you might want to say, "If you tell me

to get cash, I'll stop for cash and catch a later departure. But if you tell me I can use my card, I won't stop for cash, and if you're wrong, I'll be stuck. If you're at all uncertain, please level with me now."

9. Whatever information you're given, note the name of the person who gave it and the time, date, number, and business location.

10. Why business location? If you've called an 800 number, you may think you've phoned Baltimore but be talking to a rep in Denver (who may think that York, Pennsylvania, is a suburb of New York City). If the person isn't physically situated at the counter you'll be visiting, confirm your information.

11. One of the most frustrating aspects of long-distance rail and bus service is that so many station buildings are closed. The "station" is a platform, with no personnel, no working phone, and no means of communication until the vehicle arrives. If a vehicle whizzes past you at four in the morning, you don't know whether you've missed your ride or if you should keep waiting.

12. When you're phoning for other information, inquire whether there's a real station where you're going. What are its hours? What numbers can you call when it's closed? Do *those* numbers operate twenty-four hours a day, every day of the week?

13. If you'll need a cab on arrival, don't assume one will be waiting. Find out in advance what number you can call.

14. The "station" may be a concession area in a soda shop. If so, the clerk on duty when you get there might be a part-timer who says, "Read the schedule, but don't bother me unless you need a root beer float."

15. Your only hope of dealing with this when it happens is to have brought names and phone numbers with you. Call them. When you've found out what you need to know, ask how you can report the clerk.

16. It's never a bad idea to confirm what you're told. Call back. Ask the same questions of an entirely different person. Note name, date, time, and business location. If you hear discrepancies,

investigate. If not, you've got a better case should things not work out.

Surprise—You've Got Problems

1. If you get to the counter or on board and find out you were misinformed, say so. The first thing you will be asked is "Who told you?" If you can't give a name, expect to be treated as though you made it up.

2. If you whip out a pad with two names, plus times, dates, numbers, and business locations of the people who misled you, expect to be told, "They were both wrong."

3. Next, expect to be told what this person believes to be the correct policy, as though your knowing it after the fact magically makes you responsible for having known it from the outset.

4. Don't lose your temper. If you yell, it's to the other person's advantage more than yours.

5. Explain that you phoned for information because you *didn't* know the answers. You asked careful questions to be sure you understood. You acted on the basis of what you were told. Whether someone now advises you one time or a hundred times that you were misinformed, it doesn't change the information you were originally given.

6. Ask if there's a supervisor or manager you can speak to. If you have the numbers of the people you talked to previously, and if you have access to a telephone, call them. Ask what you can do to square their version of the facts with the new version.

7. It's very possible that your first sources will be right, and will be able to correct matters on the spot.

8. If not, ask to speak to the supervisor of one of your first sources.

9. It may be that you don't have access to a phone, and nobody is available other than the person refusing to honor what you were told. Get this person's name and any relevant identification details. Ask *this person,* "How can I fol-

low up? I don't believe you've handled this fairly."

10. Be prepared at any point for silly or irrelevant replies, ranging from "This is all because Congress didn't raise the cigarette tax" to "If you say another word, I'm putting you off at the next stop."

11. Have the sense to know when you've hit a brick wall. But never accept such nonsense without following up.

12. Read whatever schedules are posted or are in your pocket. Look for a complaint or service number. *Use it* at your earliest opportunity.

13. When you complain, phone first. State your concerns and verify the procedure. If you're told to write, say, "I've already been inconvenienced and overcharged. If I write a letter, what can I expect beyond the apology I've already gotten?"

14. If you're told you'll just get an apology, ask to speak to a supervisor.

15. There's no guarantee that you'll get a refund. But you may. Or you may get a voucher toward your next ticket. In any event, don't expect to get a whole lot you haven't pressed for.

16. If you're told that the letter might result in a refund, get the name and other appropriate identification of the person who tells you. Begin your letter with "On [date and time], [name, I.D.] advised me to write on the understanding that you can authorize a refund. I have been greatly inconvenienced [or overcharged, or whatever] and I said I would not inconvenience myself further by writing a letter unless something more than an apology would definitely be forthcoming. [Name] assured me that I will get more than an apology."

17. Then state your case. Mention the trip you took and the dates you traveled. Include a photocopy of the ticket.

18. Your main concern may be reparation. But don't overlook the importance of educating the representatives who misled you. Mistakes can be made, and overburdened employees shouldn't be persecuted for them. But neither should you be penalized for somebody else's error.

19. Mention their names and I.D.s, and suggest what action you feel should be taken: training session, a word to their union representatives, and so on.

20. Unless the person behaved badly, it should be sufficient to suggest some type of training. But if you were insulted, threatened, or dismissed out of hand, you'll probably want more. Ask that a copy of your letter be included in the individual's personnel file.

21. If you paid for your ticket by credit card and the misinformation deprived you of use of the service, consider advising your card company to credit your account or process a chargeback.

22. If your complaint involves long-distance service to a small town, write to its Chamber of Commerce and office of tourism, if it has one. Point out that when inadequate public transportation keeps large numbers of people out of the town's business district, everybody suffers. Suggest that perhaps the organization can intervene not only on your behalf, but in the interest of the town.

23. Check your telephone directory for "Department of Transportation" or "Transit Authority" headings in the state or local government listings. Find out what offices receive complaints about your problem, and how you can initiate investigation or proceedings.

24. If public funding is involved, contact your local elected officials. Find out what specific committees oversee this aspect of transportion, and how you can write to them. It's mighty unlikely that a U.S. senator will arrange a $6 refund for you, but your communication may inspire the solution of a deeper problem.

25. If the complaint involves Amtrak, contact Amtrak Customer Relations, Union Station, 60 Massachusetts Avenue, N.E., Washington, DC 20002; 202-906-3860.

26. If the complaint involves any other interstate bus or train travel, contact Office of Compliance

and Consumer Assistance, Interstate Commerce Commission, 12th and Constitution Avenue, N.W., Washington, DC 20423; 202-927-5500.

Taxis Are an Adventure Too

1. One convenient difference between buses and trains on the one hand and taxis on the other is that even in a major metropolitan city, your complaint against a taxi driver can be traced to one individual.

2. What is customary in one area may not be in another. For instance, some cabs charge according to a meter, while others charge by districts covered. Some are allowed to charge each passenger full fare for traveling to the same destination on a shared ride; some aren't. Some can require a surcharge for out-of-state, rush-hour, or late-night travel.

3. Fee schedules and restrictions should be posted prominently in the cab. If you're in a strange town, you may want to do your research before calling the cab. Ask a hotel concierge, ask at the airport, or phone the taxi and limousine commission (which may be the same as the transit authority in your area).

4. It's more than reasonable for you to request an estimate of the fare over the phone. If the fare is by district, the dispatcher should be able to tell you the *exact* amount. If the driver later attempts to charge you more, insist that the dispatcher be contacted, and insist on paying the fare that was quoted to you.

5. Whether you're speaking to the dispatcher or the driver, clarify your destination if there might be any confusion—such as when a town has two bus stations.

6. In some cities that charge by district, the station may be in one district and your hotel across the street in another district. The driver will obligingly put all your bags in the trunk, drive you across the street, and charge you a per-item trunk charge plus a two-district charge.

7. Defend yourself against this by asking before you get in, "If you put those in the trunk, do I pay extra?" and "How far is the hotel?"

8. If the driver behaves uncooperatively when you enter the cab, get out. If the driver has been waiting in line at an airport, hotel, or other cab line, indicate that if you leave, the cab will probably lose its position in line. Under those circumstances, the driver may become more considerate. If not, get another cab—and report your complaint to the dispatcher immediately.

9. If the driver is deliberately ignoring your directions en route and if a police officer is on the scene, roll down the window and invite the officer over. Explain your problem. Say that you don't think you should have to pay, and ask what procedure to follow.

10. If you're going to want a receipt, give the driver fair warning. Don't wait until you're getting out in traffic to request one.

11. If you're planning to file a complaint, get the driver's name, license number, and medallion number (if applicable) from the license (which should be plainly in view). Note the name and phone number of the cab company.

12. When you file your complaint, be prepared with this information, the date and time of your trip, and your points of departure and arrival.

13. If a hotel arranged the cab for you, or if you caught it at an airport taxi stand, report your complaints in writing to the hotel or airport. CC the owner of the cab company. As a rule, the owner would rather make amends with one customer than lose future referrals.

14. Complaints can be lodged with the cab company and with the local taxi and limousine commission (or transit authority). A formal procedure exists in most areas and will be explained if you call.

15. Different jurisdictions will have different definitions of what constitutes a serious infraction. But it would be wise to report any of the following when they happen to you:

- **Driver deliberately took the long way to run up the fare.**

- **Driver refused to take you to a low-income neighborhood.**
- **Driver spoke to you abusively.**
- **Driver abandoned you.**
- **Driver lied in an attempt to overcharge you.**
- **Driver refused to give you a receipt.**

16. Complaints may lead to a hearing, fines, and restitution to you. If your town or city licenses taxi drivers, the driver's license can be suspended or revoked.

17. Realize that so-called gypsy cabs may be underinsured and very possibly not licensed.

To Complain About Policy

1. Attend hearings about transportation issues. If you don't show up, the "system" will conclude that the public doesn't care.

2. Write letters to the editors of your area newspapers. Urge readers who feel the way you do to attend the hearings, to contact their elected officials, and so on.

▲ *See also* AIRLINES; CREDIT CARDS.

Public Utilities

There are a few more choices for public utilities than there used to be. For example, consumers now have their pick of different carriers for long-distance calls. But even when there's only one option, you may have more flexibility than you realize in the sense that you can investigate the availability of services that suit your special needs: medical emergency, life support, third-party notification, or simply basic plans for limited incomes.

Whenever you begin to do business with a public utility, such as when you move to a new town—

1. Remember that it isn't free! If you move into an apartment and aren't billed for electricity for four months, don't assume it's included in the rent. It may be, but more likely you'll be socked with a cumulative bill once the electric company pulls your file together.

2. Some prices you can negotiate (such as fuel oil). Others you can't (such as electricity). Find out from neighbors and associates about the choices they've made, and whether they're pleased with the results.

3. Understand the billing system, such as meter readings for the gas company. Read the flyers that come with each bill. They may announce rate or computation changes.

4. Learn what emergency service is available. What are the numbers? Can they be reached twenty-four hours a day, seven days a week? Are there alternate numbers if the main number is tied up?

5. Keep a log of your communications with the utility—names, dates, the content of each conversation. Refer to it if disputes arise later.

6. Also, log your usage. Compare it from year to year. If you notice a dramatic change in usage that seems to be without explanation, notify the business office of the utility company at once.

When You Have a Complaint

1. Refer to your logs. The more complete your records, the more compelling your argument.

2. You should be able to phone the business office at a number appearing on your bill. Have your account number, and all the facts, at hand.

3. If you can't make sufficient headway with your first contact, ask to speak to a supervisor.

4. You can also ask for the name and number of the regional manager of the business office, or an office manager of the business office.

5. If these employees don't come through for you, inquire whether the company has a consumer appeals group or its equivalent, and what procedure you would follow to be able to use it.

6. If you write, send copies of documents as appropriate.

7. If the utility is still less than helpful, contact the public service commission or its equivalent in your area. The number ought to be on every utility bill.

8. If you complain to this organization, the utility company has to respond to its inquiry.

9. Under rulings of many of these commissions, the utility may not turn off your service for non-payment of an amount in question while the dispute is being reviewed. However, you must pay any portion of the amount not being contested.

10. If you aren't happy with a decision of the commission, you may request a review. Or you may have the option of asking for a hearing with a mediator and the utility.

11. The commission can order redress. For instance, if food is spoiled because your electricity failed, and the utility was at fault, you may be reimbursed up to a certain amount for your loss.

12. You can also talk to your local and state politicians, state attorney general, and state or city consumer affairs department.

13. If the issue is of far-reaching implications, speak to local officials about the possibility of a public hearing.

14. If you believe the infraction warrants it, ask what must be done to initiate an investigation.

15. Write a letter to the editor of your newspaper.

16. Consider court action, including a class-action suit. (*See* RUNG ELEVEN: CLASS-ACTION SUIT, in Part I.)

If Services Fail in an Emergency

1. Listen to a portable radio for information about restoration of services, or alternate services available.

2. Report hazardous conditions, such as live wires dragging across the street in a storm.

▲ *See also* CABLE; 800 NUMBERS; 900 NUMBERS; SCAMS; TELEMARKETING.

Restaurants

Three aspects of restaurant-going are of particular interest to any consumer: health considerations, service, and value for money.

Health Considerations

These are obviously the most serious, and most people would want to report them.

1. If you notice (or suspect) unsanitary conditions, vermin, or the like, or if food has made you ill, contact the state or city department of health. Inspectors are generally available and will investigate within days.

2. If you feel strongly that health, environmental, or other issues have been wantonly disregarded by corporate offices and if you can't persuade local personnel to show sufficient concern, check out the United States Sentencing Commission, 1 Columbus Circle, N.E., Suite 2-500, Washington, DC 20002, 202-273-4500. This is heavy-duty complaining. If justified, it can lead to criminal prosecution, jail time, a fortune in penalties, and shareholder suits.

Service

This is the area of restaurant-going that tends to receive the greatest attention in terms of consumer response.

1. People tend to limit their complaints to what they say to the waiter or manager. They can do more.

2. If the waiter is downright difficult or uncooperative, go to the captain or maître d' and ask for a new waiter.

3. If the captain or maître d' is less than helpful, seek out the manager.

4. Realize that the person on the premises who goes by the name of manager may only be an assistant manager. Consequently, if this individual won't resolve your dispute, don't lose heart. But do get a name.

5. Phone the restaurant during daytime hours. Get the business office. Speak to the general manager.

6. If you've come to the restaurant intending to take advantage of a gift certificate, special coupon, or promotion, confirm before ordering that the deal is in effect and that you'll be able to apply it. (You may also want to do this when you book the reservation.) In either case, get the names of the people who confirm the terms to you.

7. Once in a rare while, a restaurant will wait until after you've eaten a meal to disavow the promotion. For instance, "This offer isn't good on weekends."

8. Your first recourse is to explain very calmly that you confirmed the deal with the waiter or with the person who took the reservation, and either one would have had to know the exact date and time you planned to eat.

9. Chances are that your logic won't work on the first person you speak to. Ask for the manager. Repeat your arguments.

10. If the manager says a mistake was made, or that the waiter or reservation desk wasn't authorized to give such information, explain that you have no way of knowing when you receive wrong answers from employees that the employees are speaking out of turn. You're entirely within your rights to act on the details as given. If the restaurant made the mistake, then the restaurant shouldn't attempt to foist the burden onto consumers.

11. Emphasize that you're the one party not responsible, and the one who attempted to verify the promotion. Ask the manager, "Do you believe me when I say this is what I was told? I've given you the names of the people who confirmed it. I clearly identified the offer to them, and I specified when I intended to use it. If you believe that I'm not lying to you, why would you want to penalize me for wanting to take you up on your promotion?"

12. Remind the manager that the promotion was designed to attract new customers, and that it really would be better business for the restaurant to honor it than to use it as a tool for extorting money from you.

13. If the manager is adamant, point out that you can put the bill on your charge card and instruct your credit card company to issue a chargeback when the statement comes. Once the manager realizes you won't back down, he or she may decide to give in rather than become embroiled in lengthy paperwork with the card company.

14. You might add that if this is the way the restaurant does business, you will suggest to the credit card company that it revoke the restaurant's card acceptance privileges (*see* CREDIT CARDS).

15. If this doesn't work with the "manager" who confronts you, try it on the general manager in the business office on the following day.

16. If the promotion was carried in a newspaper, write to the managing editor of the publication. You may also want to express your sentiments in a letter to the editor, hoping that it will be printed to warn off other unsuspecting area residents.

17. Because such incidents relate to how the restaurant does business, consider filing complaints with the Chamber of Commerce, the Better Business Bureau, and the state or city consumer affairs department.

Value for Money

Whether you encounter the problem described above or any other, follow through.

1. Many restaurants have customer comment cards on the tables. If you don't see one, ask. Complete it. Mail it in; don't leave it out to be thrown away by the offending parties.

2. It's perfectly permissible to advise the general manager, owner, or head office (or customer service, office of the president, etc., of the chain if it belongs to a chain) if anything doesn't ring true. If the appearance is substandard, if the bathrooms are cruddy, if an alleged deluxe establishment barely rates half a star—report it.

3. When a disappointed patron takes time to write, good restaurateurs take note (and may invite him or her to return, as their guest, to give them a second chance).

4. Restaurants rely on repeat trade and glowing reviews. Consider sharing your negative observations in letters to area newspaper restaurant reviewers, being careful to CC the restaurant's general manager as well as president. But don't commit libel, and don't exaggerate your tale.

5. If the restaurant is located in a big city or tourist city, it's probably covered in guidebooks available throughout the country (or world). A little research at the bookstore will provide titles, along with publishers' addresses. Write to the authors of the books care of their publishers. CC the restaurant personnel, who by this time will be hating themselves for not having been more agreeable when you gave them the opportunity.

▲ *See also* CREDIT CARDS; TOURS.

Retail Shopping

Retail shopping is your golden tongue's adventure of a lifetime. If you keep your cool and choose your words carefully, you'll have surprising control over the most illogical situations. This is true even when the storekeeper obstinately refuses to acknowledge that his or her operation is answerable to state law, and even when individual clerks seem to invent arbitrary "company policy" out of thin air, applying it differently from consumer to consumer and register to register.

The best argument for doing your homework in this instance is that it's fun. Odds are that you don't have to read a book to be able to stroll into any shop around, read a price sticker, slide your money across the counter, and figure out whether you've gotten the right change. But think of the clout you'll carry when you've boned up on the law. In *certain states,* for example:

1. Comparison price advertising law requires that if a store advertises a sale, it must compare the sale price against the true price at which it retailed before the sale—otherwise the state department of consumer affairs wants to know about it. If your department of consumer affairs has a frauds division, so much the better.

2. You have the legal right to a rain check if stock is exhausted (with a few exceptions), and if the store cannot honor the rain check within sixty days, it must substitute comparable merchandise at the same or lower price.

3. If a price is posted, even in error, the store must honor it.

4. The only way to know your state's retail shopping laws is to call or write your state or city department of consumer affairs and ask for whatever free printed material is published. Once you receive it, read it over.

5. If you expect to be citing it on a particular shopping foray, bring the literature with you. You'll be more convincing if you can hold an appropriate paragraph or two under your adversary's nose. Bear in mind—and expect to remind your opponent—that responding to state agencies after a complaint has been filed can be very time-consuming for merchants . . . that bureaucratic agency computers have a way of fastening onto details for ages, and spewing forms that have to be answered throughout eternity . . . that some agencies impose fines and penalties on merchants who don't answer inquiries promptly . . . and that, really, it would be much easier for the merchant to simply honor your request without further fireworks.

About Store Policy

1. Retailers can be fanciful and their clerks may commute in each morning from one of the rings of Saturn. They can look you in the eye and make the loopiest assertions of store policy that you've

ever heard—yet when you ask for a manager or other worker to add a note of reason, this new person might nod approvingly in confirmation of every loopy syllable.

2. This doesn't put the loopsters in the right. It simply means you have to seek a higher authority. A woman from Kansas City was actually harassed by a clerk, an assistant store manager, and a store manager because she was making comparison notes of various prices. Only after she insisted on phoning the district manager did her antagonists apologize and allow her to keep her list.

3. If you can't find a higher authority on the premises, be sure to get the names of the people to whom you've spoken. Then pursue the matter later, attempting to reach the manager or the owner, the district or regional manager, the customer service office of the chain if it's a chain, and the president's office if necessary. Relay the names of the parties you spoke with at the store.

4. When you find someone willing to state correct policy, get the name of your source and ask to have the information in writing. If you are told it won't be necessary to have it in writing, point out that if you have to waste your time shopping again, and waiting in line again, only to have the same pair of employees misquote store policy to you again, it will indeed be necessary for you to have something in writing.

5. Occasionally, store policy is assembled by personnel who haven't bothered to inform themselves in matters of state law, with the result that their policy is in violation of state law. You'll want to report this to the state or city department of consumer affairs, and perhaps to the state attorney general's office.

6. As long as you're going to report it anyway, tell the manager of your plans and ask for the name of the store's house counsel, whom you wish to CC. At this juncture, somebody's eyes might widen—accompanied by an offer to "bend" store policy for you.

7. Your state law may require that store policy, or at least specified aspects of store policy such as

refunds, be posted in a conspicuous place. If there is no conspicuous notice, state policy will prevail.

8. If the policy concerns refunds on defective merchandise, the store may not be free to set policy. Warranty and implied warranty are involved (*see* WARRANTIES), and the merchant (with some limitations) is responsible under the law for replacing, repairing, or refunding.

9. If policy seems genuinely arbitrary to you— if time after time, you shop and wait in line only to be told at the register that an offer was a typo, or the store no longer accepts manufacturers' coupons—and if changes in policy seem to be dumped on you without warning, and with no effort to post the correction or new policy, consider filing a report with the state office of discrimination, if there is one in your area, or the state attorney general's office. It's probably sloppiness rather than discrimination, but if employees routinely defend their right to look over each consumer individually before deciding on terms, an investigation may in fact be in order.

10. If you do feel an investigation to be warranted, CC the store manager, the store's house counsel, and a local congressman. A sane shopkeeper ought to respond by posting policy more prominently.

11. In the meanwhile, you're not a captive audience. Properly speaking, you're a "business invitee"—invited into a store open to the public to *consider* making a purchase. If the terms of the deal suddenly change only when the clerk rings up your purchase on the register, you have every right to say, "Void the sale." If the store was not prepared to have a succession of transactions voided at the register by a parade of disgusted patrons, the patrons should have been given better warning of the revised terms.

12. At times, you'd swear that store policy is to irritate and disappoint consumers. Ads, specials, and promotions are intended to attract shoppers and win them over. Yet some stores regularly fail to stock advertised merchandise, and the staff is rude if you ask for it. By all means,

report such behavior to the manager, the owner, the chain, etc. If the chain or company has a vice president or director of marketing, also CC him or her.

13. Your primary question should be: "Why did you bother to spend money to get me into the store if you were going to turn me away angry? I'm here. I want to make a purchase. If you weren't planning to treat your patrons any better than this, why did you invest your company's money and your employees' time on the promotion in the first place?" If you ask politely and a fairly sensible person hears you, enlightenment may follow, and maybe an attempt to satisfy your request.

14. See what you can negotiate. For example, if you receive a postcard announcing the grand opening of a retail outlet in your neighborhood and you can get 10 percent off your first purchase "within the next thirty days," it's more than reasonable for you to phone the manager to say you'd love to take advantage of the 10 percent incentive discount and you're eager to check out the facility, but you can't get there within thirty days. If you need an extension, ask for one. There's nothing magical about thirty days. It's just a device to attract your business. A sharp merchant will find a way to accommodate you. (Be sure to get a name and note the date of your conversation.)

15. There are instances of truly wretched corporate policy governing stores within a chain— perhaps there are food and drug offenses, or environmental hazards. Such stores run the risk of heavy criminal penalties, huge fines, and the potential liability of shareholder actions. The United States Sentencing Commission (1 Columbus Circle, N.E., Suite 2-500, Washington, DC 20002; 202-273-4500) can be extremely harsh. If you have a complaint in any of these areas, and if you can't achieve satisfaction through standard channels, advise the manager, house counsel, president, and chairman of the board that you will bring your concerns to the attention of the USSC.

False Advertising

1. Suppose there's a fabric store with a sign in the window reading "Take an additional 20 percent off every marked price in the store." You have the shopkeeper cut a five-yard piece, and only after the cutting are you informed, "This piece wasn't on sale." The bonehead thinks you're over a barrel. You're not, but any businessman who persists in such practices may end up destitute. This isn't clever. It's lying with the intent of cashing in on it. It's a dangerous game that ought to backfire on its creator. With a little help from you, it will.

2. Let's hope you wouldn't be gullible enough to buy the fabric at full price but that instead you'd insist, "Then you've just cut yourself an expensive remnant." The shopkeeper would probably counter by arguing that you have to pay because the piece is already cut. No, you don't. You don't have to be embarrassed into a purchase, and you might want to express wonderment that the shopkeeper isn't embarrassed to be guilty of such a blatant lie.

3. You'd do yourself, your community, and society in general a favor by pursuing the matter. Take the time to write down the exact wording of the sign or, if you have easy access to a camera, photograph it. Report this person to the Chamber of Commerce, the Better Business Bureau, the state or city department of consumer affairs, and the office of the state attorney general. CC the owner and manager of the store.

4. In each case, ask specifically whether the store can be compelled to honor its offer and what fines or penalties can be levied for this deliberate deception.

5. If this ad, or any intentionally deceptive ad, appeared in a newspaper, keep the ad and send photocopies of it to the protection agencies you contact. Inform the editor that the newspaper has accepted money to hoodwink its readers.

6. If the ad appeared in a flyer that went through the mails, report it to your local post-

master and/or the Chief Postal Inspector, U.S. Postal Service, Washington, DC 20260-2100; 202-268-4267.

7. Fraud in advertising is of great interest to the Federal Trade Commission. The FTC won't initiate a special case just for you, but if enough evidence accumulates (in the form of reports from consumers), investigation and enforcement may ensue, and the storekeeper will squirm. Send your written complaint to Correspondence Branch, Room 692, Federal Trade Commission, 6th Street and Pennsylvania Avenue, N.W., Washington, DC 20580.

8. Remember that even if your charges don't lead to specific prosecution, the storekeeper stands to be bombarded with official forms over the next epoch or two.

9. If an ad represents a store to be selling a product that costs a certain amount "after manufacturer's rebate," the purchase had better include each element necessary to satisfy rebate conditions. In other words, the offer can't have expired; it can't require a peel-off wrapper that the actual product lacks; it can't be based on refund after you've purchased the item plus something else (unless the ad clearly states the additional terms).

10. If you get the product home and realize you don't qualify for the rebate, contact the store and explain your dilemma. Ask the store to make up the difference.

11. If the person you speak to is resistant, request that the store either work it out with the manufacturer's representative or salesman (or supplier or jobber who provided it), or put you in touch with that individual.

12. If the store simply won't cooperate, report the incident as described above.

13. If you're disputing defective merchandise, a refund, or any related matter and reach an impasse, the state or city department of consumer affairs or the Better Business Bureau may have an arbitration program. Phone to ask what they have and how you can use it.

Billing Errors

1. Keep your eye on the register. Your best defense against an overcharge is to be attentive to the figures as they're entered. Challenge them if you doubt them.

2. If you believe the figures to be incorrect, you can ask the clerk to give you a second before he or she rings up the total. If the clerk hits the total button to rush you off the line, saying that you can go to customer service if there's a problem, you can counter by refusing to pay.

3. It is unacceptable for a clerk to put you through a half hour of waiting in another line simply to avoid spending another two minutes with your transaction. Your refusal to pay will be an excellent object lesson for the clerk.

4. Perhaps the clerk has been instructed to handle matters this way. Dandy. Then it becomes a practical object lesson in cause-and-effect for the store. It will take more time voiding out the sale than it would have taken to accede to your request, and there will be no profit to show for it.

5. Even if prices are read by a scanner via UPC codes, pay attention. Surveys have shown that scanner errors, whether from programming or malfunction, can occur with one item out of ten (in some cases, more).

6. Clerks and salespeople may not have the authority to settle disputes. If there's a customer service desk but no one in attendance, or the line is enormous, you may prefer to ask for the manager.

7. Some chains are notorious for never having the manager available. According to the clerks or the customer service desk, the manager is always "in a meeting." When being given this information becomes a pattern, get the names of the people who report the absence and ask for the manager's name.

8. Write to the president's office, and CC the district or regional manager and the store manager. Note in your letter that according to so-and-so (state the names), the manager was unavailable on occasions x, y, and z (give dates and times, but

otherwise be brief in your complaints, because all you're complaining about in this letter is the absentee manager). Ask whom you can contact when the manager is unavailable, and what management hopes to achieve by having a manager who is never around. (You may discover that the manager usually is present, but employees feel they can avoid trouble by keeping customers and manager apart.)

9. It isn't your plan to get anybody in trouble. However, if you feel that you had a reasonable request and the employees didn't respond in kind, it's appropriate for you to have the request reevaluated for them by the person who authorizes their paychecks.

10. If you make your purchase by credit card and subsequently discover a billing error on your statement, dispute it in writing as you would any credit card error (*see* CREDIT CARDS). You have certain protection under the Federal Fair Credit Billing Act, but only if you observe proper procedure, such as making your report within sixty days.

11. If you make your case stick, the store must delete not only the charge itself but also any accrued interest on the transaction.

12. If a merchant has openly misused your bank credit card (such as VISA or MASTERCARD) or falsified a purchase price, report it to the card company or the issuing bank. Inquire what would be involved in having the store's credit card acceptance privileges revoked, and decide whether you're angry enough to follow through.

Presidents Can Be Dandy People

I once went to a store that had the coming week's sale flyers posted in the window. Convinced it was a mistake, I reported it to the information desk. The clerk told me that it was no mistake. I doubt her to this day. I suspect she merely assumed it had been done on purpose and then found ways to justify it. I said, "Okay, now I know what will be on sale next week. How do I find out what's on sale today?"

She replied, "If you wanted to know that, you should have been here last week to read the windows."

I wrote to the customer service manager with a CC to the president, pointing out that perhaps this person needed clarification regarding store policy. I added that under the circumstances, I certainly did. I never heard from the customer service manager, but the president wrote me a lovely letter, which he CC'd to several staff members. He didn't explain policy either—but he did send me a gift certificate for $20.

▲ *See also* APPLIANCES; CREDIT CARDS; GUARANTEES; PRODUCT LIABILITY AND RECALLS; WARRANTIES.

Scams

When you're scammed, you don't get what you pay for, you've already paid for it, and nobody waits around to hear that you don't want to pay at all. After the fact, you should report the incident to every conceivable authority—ranging from the police and/or sheriff and/or airport/hotel/stadium security to the FTC and the FBI, depending on the nature of the crime. But if the operation has packed up and left town overnight, or changed names to duck investigation, you may never have any more satisfaction than the thought that with your assistance, the bad guys may be brought to justice.

Before you're bilked, remind yourself that swindlers have the entire scenario mapped out in advance. It's what they do for a living. Months of careful planning may have gone into a maneuver which you have to assess within seconds. They're counting on your trusting soul, and in their ability to force you to act or respond faster than you can think. Most business people don't set out to rook you, and will make some effort to win back your good will. But a deliberate cheat has no such scruples. With these folks, your best and often only defense is to be suspicious and say "no."

Here are twenty-five popular routines to avoid. There are enough others to fill volumes.

1. *Bait and switch.* You pay for something and are asked or pressured to settle for something else, as in: "We apologize for the delays in shipping your back-ordered Victorian sofa. But you can have the Early Age of Reptiles loveseat at the same price. Otherwise, we won't be responsible for the delay." If they won't be responsible, why should you absorb their failure? Ask that a refund be processed immediately.

2. *Bank examiner.* A bank official who doesn't know you is not very likely to contact you with the request that you withdraw money to trap an embezzler. If you get such a call, get the name and number of the "examiner." Phone the bank (at the number listed in the phone directory—not the one the examiner gives you) to confirm the legitimacy of the call, and ask for written documentation on bank letterhead.

3. *Payment up front but no refund policy.* If they can't deliver, you shouldn't have to pay. Don't agree to any terms that say otherwise.

4. *Asking for your credit card or checking account number.* It's often appropriate for you to provide this information, but only when you know the reputation of the firm through personal experience or by confirmation from the Better Business Bureau or other consumer protection agency.

5. *Your signature and bank account number.* In a variation on the above, you'll be asked to provide your signature and bank account number—perhaps even in separate calls, by separate callers—to verify that you're you. If you provide these two bits of assistance, expect someone else to pretend to be you and make a withdrawal from your bank.

6. *City inspector.* A person can identify himself as a city inspector, present an authentic-looking

card, and frighten you with tales of violations you must correct. He can do this to sell you services you don't need, or simply to gain entry into your premises. Contact the department he claims to work for. Get the number not from his authentic-looking card, but from the phone book.

7. *High-pressure tactics.* When you hear "You have to sign now," no you don't. A door-to-door salesman who can't leave literature for you to read, or a time-share agent who expects a signature before showing you the contract, is insulting your intelligence and playing you for a sap.

8. *High profit, no risk.* High profit is never free of risk. If it's such a great deal, why can't the company get financing from a bank or other more traditional lending institution?

9. *Dirtpile scams.* These claims to mine a quantity of dirt "guaranteed" to contain a fortune in mineral ore are generally nothing more than an expensive way to sell you dirt. They will be costly. There may be further processing and extracting fees added later on, and the victim pays them out of fear of forfeiting the investment. Some schemes are backed by glossy brochures and assayer's reports, but the fanciest smokescreen in the world doesn't make them true.

10. *Letters from unknown attorneys.* Legitimate attorneys contact strangers by mail all the time. If you've inherited money from a distant relative, odds are you'll learn about it via mail from the estate's attorney. But any unscrupulous character with a typewriter and a stamp can play on this, send what purports to be an authentic letter, request a fee, and abscond with your money. Be careful not to extend a penny until you first contact your attorney, or the Chamber of Commerce, the Better Business Bureau, and/or local Bar Association for the community in which this attorney claims to work.

11. *Bills of a departed spouse.* Unscrupulous thieves have only to read obituaries to learn of the death of your spouse, and then to present you with a COD package addressed to that name. They hope you'll pay a fee for the worthless or empty box. If a COD package arrives that you weren't expecting, write down the name and address of the company and any identifying numbers, then explain that your spouse has died and you won't accept the merchandise. Contact the company. Describe the action you took. Ask for a copy of the order, saying that you might still be willing to accept the article once you've confirmed that it was legitimate and that it's something you can use.

12. *Loan brokers billing fees in advance.* Be wary of any potential source of financing whose business history cannot be thoroughly and satisfactorily verified. Otherwise, you may pay a fee in expectation of a loan, only to learn later that your application was submitted but you've been turned down.

13. *Investment rollups.* Not every rollup is a deception, but some have turned out to be. If you're asked to combine an investment in your portfolio with a new one, it could mean dumping good money into a failing concern. Moreover, you'll be paying a fee to the party arranging the deal. If you're asked to make the decision, get a second opinion from a qualified, impartial source who doesn't stand to profit from the deal.

14. *New drilling techniques.* Sometimes the technique is pure fantasy. Other times, it's real but the wells don't exist. Like dirtpile scams, these can make mythical bonanzas sound amazingly real, but you'd be better off sinking your funds in fool's gold.

15. *A little cash on good faith.* Anytime a stranger approaches you with found money, a found envelope, or a found suitcase and offers any reason whatever for you to hand over a little money on good faith in exchange for the item, you have a better idea. Suggest that you go together to turn it over to the police. (This scam is also known as the pocketbook drop.)

16. *Phony job offers.* Classified ads boast job opportunities. Callers phone the 900 numbers at several dollars a minute to listen to the names of employment agencies or personnel departments they could have found in any phone book. Or they

call 800 numbers, only to be referred to the 900 numbers. Or they get the information on the 800 number, then later receive an invoice for the service. (If you fall into this and receive an unauthorized bill, don't pay it. Instead, report it to the organizations listed under "What You Can Do" at the end of this chapter.)

17. *I'll help you with your bags.* This can be a lovely, gracious, entirely legitimate gesture. Or it can be a con. A person who offers to put packages in your automobile trunk can flee with them when you step into your car to release the lock. A person who helps you store luggage in a locker can pocket the correct key and hand you the wrong one. When you return to collect your satchel, your key doesn't work and the locker has been emptied anyway.

18. *False affiliation claims.* Just because a salesperson or an ad asserts "fully insured by so-and-so" doesn't make it true. Just because a letter is addressed to "Dear AARP Member" doesn't prove the writer is affiliated with AARP. You'd be doing the insurer or the AARP a favor by calling to confirm the relationship, because either would go to great lengths to silence any bogus claims involving their reputations.

19. *Wireless cable TV investments.* This "no-risk opportunity" to buy into the FCC's lottery for license applications promises gigantic returns on a one-time investment. The trouble is that the investment is substantial, the risks are very real, and the return may never materialize.

20. *Totally free if you buy.* Anyone who gets mail can expect at least one postcard announcing: "You are a guaranteed winner of a car, a fabulous gemstone, or $1,000 cash." Reply, and you'll be asked to buy a vastly overpriced item in order to qualify for the prize. You might buy the item, figuring that its cost is still far less than the value of the prize you've won. But the prize may never arrive. If it does, it's virtually worthless. Or you receive a $200 check to be applied toward purchase, but even after the deduction, the item is overpriced and often junk.

21. *Child support collectors.* Such scams offer to help collect child support. The scammers request a fee. Once it's paid, they phone back *collect* through a third-party billing system, sticking the unsuspecting client with charges of several dollars a minute for the useless call, with no intention of ever acting on your behalf.

22. *Water-testing scams.* There's nothing wrong with a consumer's desire for pure, safe water. Many wonderful devices exist to provide it. But "environment" is one of the top scam buzzwords of the 1990s, and many a promoter offering water-purifying equipment does not have your best interests at heart. Be alert to scare tactics warning you that your tap water is infested, carcinogenic, etc. Realize that if the gadget works, it may be tremendously overpriced compared to what you can buy at any retail outlet. If you're concerned about the quality of your water supply, the Environmental Protection Agency's Safe Drinking Hotline will advise where you can get a list of state-certified laboratories: 1-800-426-4791.

23. *Work at home.* A classified ad stating that you can earn big money by doing work at home is often no more than a way for the company to make money from any caller who dials the 900 number listed in the ad, or a way to sell the caller "raw materials"—or even printed material suggesting that an income can be had by running "Work at Home" ads in newspapers. Notably absent is any ironclad assurance that you will be able to sell the product back to the company once you've completed your end of the bargain.

24. *Mortgage (or other creditor's) change of address.* Don't believe every letter you read. If you receive an official-looking document saying that management of your mortgage (or lease, etc.) has changed hands and that payment should hereafter be forwarded to a new party, get verification. Phone the company of record, and ask for signed authorization on company letterhead. To be doubly safe, speak to and get a letter from the company's attorney, and confirm with the Chamber of

Commerce or Better Business Bureau that the new organization is on the up-and-up.

25. *The catsup drop or mustard drop.* You're walking along. Catsup or mustard splatters on your clothing without warning. Several strangers leap to your aid. One already has tissue out. The others "help" you with your bags. Needless to say, the bags disappear along with the strangers as you come to realize the encounter was no accident.

Adding Insult to Injury

Names and addresses of consumers who fall for one ploy may go onto a "suckers list" which scam artists circulate and share.

What You Can Do

1. If your credit card was involved, stop the charge or request a chargeback.

2. Because an unusually high number of chargebacks to a company is now recognized as the possible indication of a scam, the Federal Trade Commission has required some card processors to investigate merchants with high chargeback rates and to stop processing their sales.

3. This should be further incentive for you to follow through with a chargeback if you're cheated by means of your credit card.

4. If the scam results in an unfair charge on your telephone bill, contact the number appearing on the phone company's statement. Explain your predicament. Credit may be arranged. If it can't, ask to speak to a supervisor.

5. Whether you get a yes or no, ask what steps you can take to pursue the matter.

6. If your money is gone, your only recourse is to work with consumer and law enforcement agencies in hopes that the guilty parties will be stopped. If they're caught, you may be able to recover some or all of your funds. But don't count on it. The best defense against a scam is to be and stay on guard.

7. Report all suspected scams to consumer protection agencies such as these, and ask whether they have similar complaints on file:

- **The attorney general of your state.**
- **The consumer affairs department of your state.**
- **The Better Business Bureau. Contact the local office listed in your phone directory. If the racket is located out of town, get the number of the applicable BBB from the Council of Better Business Bureaus, 703-276-0100.**
- **The Federal Trade Commission, Division of Marketing Practices, 6th and Pennsylvania Avenue, N.W., Washington, DC 20580; 202-326-3128. CC the FTC's Correspondence Branch, at the same address, but the general number is 202-326-2222.**
- **The National Consumer League and Reference Point Foundation has launched the National Fraud Information Center, an 800-number clearinghouse. The service will gather tips from consumers who call 1-800-876-7060, and will pass their findings along to consumer and law enforcement agencies.**
- **The U.S. Postal Service. Contact your local postmaster or Chief Postal Inspector, U.S. Postal Service, Washington, DC 20260-2100; 202-268-4267. The Postal Service is interested in any fraud that relies on the mail, even telephone fraud in which money is sent through the mail, or flyers mailed to solicit for bogus operations.**

▲ *See also* CREDIT CARDS; INVESTMENT BROKERS; 900 NUMBERS; TELEMARKETING; U.S. POSTAL SERVICE; PUBLIC UTILITIES.

Seniors and Elderlaw

An unrelievedly cheerful friend of mine, middle-aged and single, frequents the same neighborhood shops, restaurants, and coffeehouses she's been visiting for the past twenty years. She remembers their employees on holidays, and they, in turn, remember her. This is nice.

But what's nicer is that she's incidentally building a support network of friends, of businesspeople who'll look out for her interests and perhaps intercede with other businesspeople, and act as "gatekeepers" in her later years. She'll do better in those later years than anyone else I know.

This isn't to say that you turn into a different person when you become a senior. Oh, yes, you're wiser, more mature, and have infinite upbeat attributes. Your mind continues to function. You can still balance a checkbook. You're no less than you were thirty years before. It's a national scandal that some storekeepers and clerks will assume a person loses rights because that person is bent by arthritis or happens to have difficulty hearing.

On the other hand, suppose you're retired, or moved, or both. Your support network of friends and associates probably hasn't followed you, so what have you done to replace it? If you and your spouse keep each other company and selectively listen to TV news, you may have allowed yourselves to become less informed than you realize.

For your own protection, you may want to consider the following.

1. Belong to a social group, senior center, community club or service organization, and/or house of worship. In this way, you'll remain informed, and you'll begin a new network of contacts to draw upon when you need advice or assistance.

2. Cultivate friendships with your "gatekeepers." These are the people such as pharmacists and building superintendents who will pay attention to your welfare and will notice when they don't see you around. If you have a problem, they may volunteer to intercede on your behalf.

3. If the time comes when you need help with paperwork, don't be embarrassed to ask. Perhaps you'd rather not go to your children, or don't have children. Truth be told, your fifty-year-old offspring may never have balanced a checkbook or paid an insurance premium. Fortunately, there are affordable personal assistants who specialize in writing checks, balancing checkbooks, and filling out Medicare, Social Security, and insurance forms for seniors. Because the field is relatively young, its practitioners have yet to pin down one generic professional title for what they do. Don't trust the phone book for references in this area. Ask around and be guided by recommendations.

4. Other sources of general advice and referral include your clergyperson, social worker, financial adviser, and doctor.

5. You may also check with support groups for specific diseases, with the social service departments of hospitals and nursing homes, and with any of a number of local agencies—most of which can be found in the yellow pages under the heading "Associations." Among listings to watch for are:

Alzheimer's Association
American Association of Retired Persons
Area Agency (or Council) on Aging
Bar Association (state and/or local)
Children of Aging Parents
Friends and Relatives of Institutionalized Aged
Health Insurance Association of America
National Citizen's Coalition for Nursing Home
  Reform

Social Security Office
Civil Liberties Union
Insurance Commissioner (state government)
United Hospital Fund

6. Find local referrals through local agencies. They'll also provide information on a wide range of general topics. For additional material on issues affecting seniors, write or contact these national agencies:

AARP (American Association
  of Retired Persons)
601 E Street, N.W.
Washington, DC 20049-0002
202-434-2277

National Academy of Elder Law
  Attorneys, Inc.
1604 North Country Club
Tucson, AZ 85716
602-881-4005

National Association of Area
  Agencies on Aging
1112 Sixteenth Street, N.W.,
  Suite 100
Washington, DC 20036
202-296-8130

National Council on the Aging,
  Inc.
409 Third Street, S.W., 2nd Floor
Washington, DC 20024
202-479-1200

National Council of Senior
  Citizens
1331 F Street, N.W.
Washington, DC 20004
202-347-8800

Older Women's League (OWL)
666 11th Street, N.W.
Washington, DC 20001
202-783-6686

7. Visit your library. Look for announcements of free programs about retirement planning and the like. Ask your librarian for referrals and ideas.

8. If you need, or just want to consult, a lawyer, look for one with expertise in what is now being called "elderlaw."

9. Why elderlaw? Although you may be unchanged as an individual when you've reached sixty-five, the same laws that always served you as a citizen may have different implications, and the same decisions you've always made may have different consequences. Besides, you will have new concerns: how to protect your assets if your spouse enters a nursing home; whether you should move to a nursing home, retirement home, or retirement community; when to delegate your power of attorney, and whether to have a "living will"; what to do if you're the victim of age discrimination in employment or housing.

10. Make your plans while you're comfortable and able to get around. For example, if you feel

that you never want to be kept alive by "heroic measures" (if your systems fail and you fall into a "permanent vegetative state"), it isn't enough to advise a few friends. You've got to have a legally acceptable document stating your decision.

11. Choice in Dying, a nonprofit group, can mail you a free form that you can complete and use in your state: 200 Varick Street, New York, NY 10014; 212-366-5540.

12. An attorney who specializes in elderlaw probably doesn't specialize in every area of it. Therefore, look for one with heavy experience in the area that meets your needs.

13. Any of the local agencies above may be able to direct you to one. If you know an attorney personally, even if only socially, ask if he or she can recommend a colleague specializing in elderlaw.

14. As you grow older, chances are you'll find yourself taking more medication. A typical senior is prescribed five different ones, often by different doctors who don't consult with one another.

15. Do yourself and your doctors a favor. When you see yours, bring your pill bottles along. Have the doctor include the information in your file (name and dosage of medication, and prescribing physicians).

16. Don't put off seeing a doctor because you attribute your symptoms to "old age," and don't let the doctor dismiss your symptoms, either. If you've had trouble walking, hearing, chewing your food, or doing anything else, or if you're losing weight unintentionally, mention it.

▲ *See also* DOCTORS; HOSPITALS; INSURANCE; MEDICARE, MEDICAID, AND MEDIGAP; NURSING HOMES; PENSIONS; SOCIAL SECURITY.

Social Security

Social Security has been called the most successful government program in history. Without doubt, it's been the difference between poverty and income for millions of Americans. Granted, it's basic income rather than wealth. And granted, it can tower over you like a huge monster of endless lines and papers if complications arise.

It's the absolute opposite of a mom-and-pop store, often giving the impression that nobody's in charge, nobody knows the rules, and nobody's to blame when everything goes wrong.

But it's there. It's available. You've earned it. If you can't conquer the monster yourself—if illness or age or language barriers prevent you—enlist somebody to give you a hand.

Who Gets What?

1. As soon as you're born, your parents can apply for a Social Security card for you. The hospital usually provides parents with the necessary forms. The number becomes your basic I.D. for the rest of your life.

2. Once you start working, you pay a regular fraction of your wages into Social Security Funds as you go, through withholdings from your paycheck.

3. Your paycheck or stub should show the FICA (Federal Insurance Contributions Act) withholdings paid by you. These go toward Social Security and Medicare.

4. Your employer matches your withholdings by paying equal amounts into the fund.

5. If you're self-employed, you are your employer and (with few exceptions) are required to pay both portions into the fund on a regular basis.

6. If you're among the 95 percent of Americans who qualify, you're entitled to Social Security benefits when you retire or become disabled. Also, your dependents qualify for various benefits through you.

7. Social Security benefits are adjusted for inflation. Increases tied to rising prices are called COLAs (cost-of-living adjustments).

8. You can decide whether your checks will be sent to your home or processed for direct deposit to your bank account.

9. If you choose the direct deposit option, contact the Social Security Administration well in advance if you're planning to change banks or your home address.

10. Social Security laws aren't carved in stone. They change. The best source of the latest information is the Social Security Administration itself. Find it listed in your telephone directory (it will be in the U.S. Government listings under "Health and Human Services"). Contact your local office, or phone the toll-free number, 1-800-772-1213.

11. The line is open from 7:00 A.M. to 7:00 P.M. in all time zones around the country, but the best hours to get through quickly are 7:00–9:00 A.M. and 5:00–7:00 P.M., preferably not during the first week of any month.

Retirement Income

1. The age for qualifying to receive full benefits is currently sixty-five.

2. You can retire earlier, at age sixty-two or older, to receive reduced benefits. For example, by retiring at sixty-two, you'd cut your checks to 80 percent of what you'd get if you'd waited until sixty-five. When you reach sixty-five, and for the rest of your retirement years, the percentage would remain the same. It *would not* become 100 percent when you reach sixty-five.

3. If you work past sixty-five, your benefits upon retirement increase, for each year you continue working up to age seventy.

4. You can work part-time after retirement and still receive your checks. If you're over seventy, you can earn any amount on your own and receive full Social Security benefits. If you're retired, working part-time, and not yet seventy, you can earn up to a certain limit without any reductions in your check. If you go over the limit, you receive benefits for a smaller amount. A call to your Social Security office will tell you what limits and rules currently apply.

5. Bear in mind that if you earn a large enough sum after retirement, a portion of your Social Security benefits may be reduced and taxed at the same time.

6. If you're married, you have a choice of how your spouse will receive retirement benefits. You can be designated the primary worker and receive the maximum benefits to which you're entitled, and your spouse will get an extra one-half of the amount. Or your spouse can retire on his or her own record and Social Security earnings, and get the full entitlement he or she has earned.

7. Because Social Security retirement income is based on the amount paid by you and your employers into the Social Security Fund over your entire career, you'll want to calculate both possibilities to see which pays more. If you and your spouse both earned large incomes, you might do better to request individual benefits. If not, one

and one-half times the primary spouse's benefit might be a better deal.

8. A call to your Social Security Administration can bring you up to date on your figures.

9. If you have a dependent child when you retire, you're entitled to another one-half of your benefit.

10. If you're over sixty, you can phone the Social Security office to learn what you've paid and an estimate of the benefits you've earned so far. Otherwise, request Form SSA-7004-PC, "Request for Earnings and Benefit Estimate," in person or by phone.

11. If you notice discrepancies, follow up right away. Be ready with proof of your claim, such as W-2s and pay receipts. In some cases, the SSA will accept other proof in the absence of contradictory evidence, if it's consistent with the rest of your salary history.

12. Clearly, people can have great years that bear no resemblance to earlier and later wages, they may have discarded their proof, and the company that paid them can be out of business. For this reason, it's important to review your Social Security records every few years; if the SSA made an error, it's much easier to correct while the trail is still hot.

13. If you change your name, or even your job, take the precaution of filing a Request for Earnings and Benefit Estimate. Make sure the SSA transfers everything that's due you.

14. If you receive anything in the mail that offers to obtain this information for you for a fee—coupled with the ominous news that you may have lost your entitlements—contact the SSA. The more frightening it seems, the more likely that it's illegal. The senders may be prosecuted if you report them.

15. Incidentally, Social Security benefits can be garnisheed up to a certain amount (as ruled by the courts, the state, and the federal government) if you fail to make court-ordered child support or alimony payments, and the IRS can issue a levy against them (up to a set amount) to recover back federal taxes you haven't paid.

Survivors' Benefits

If you die and would have been qualified to receive Social Security benefits, your surviving spouse and children (if there are dependent children) should contact the Social Security office to determine what assistance they can expect.

Former Spouses

If you retire and were previously married, your former spouse may be entitled to benefits if the marriage lasted at least ten years, if your spouse hasn't remarried before age sixty, and if other age and income criteria are met. These payments have no effect on the money you and your current spouse receive from the SSA.

Disability Insurance

1. Social Security disability payments are based on your average earnings, and may be reduced if you also receive workers' compensation, benefits received from your state for a work-related disability.

2. To qualify, you need medical records to prove your disability, and the condition must be expected to prevent you from working for at least a year.

3. It's possible to work part-time and still qualify for disability benefits, but there are limits on how much you can earn and your checks may be reduced accordingly.

4. The biggest difference between retirement and disability benefits is that you can plan for retirement: You can start making phone calls way in advance and fill out forms at your leisure. But if you're suddenly injured so severely that you won't be able to return to work, you need instant results from a system not designed for speed.

5. The single most effective step you can take to hurry matters is to research and bring your medical records when you apply. This gives you at least two advantages: The office reviewing your claim has the records faster than when it has to contact your medical sources on its own, and the office will base its decision on material that accurately describes the severity of your condition to your satisfaction.

6. Call before you go. Specify what you have. Ask what you'll need. Raise any questions in advance, to be sure you're prepared. Write down the information you're given. Note the name of the representative who speaks to you, the date, and the time.

7. If you appeal a decision, it may further delay your benefits. At this point—if not before—you'll want to consult any and all advisers available to you, from social workers to senators.

8. Check your telephone directory, government and business listings, for social service and related agencies. Contact them as well as your state and city offices for the disabled (or handicapped).

9. Organizations such as the American Civil Liberties Union (ACLU) and Legal Aid Society can be very helpful and may even initiate a class-action suit if a large segment of the population has the same complaint as you do. (*See* RUNG ELEVEN: CLASS-ACTION SUIT, in Part I.)

Supplemental Security Income

1. Many people entitled to Supplemental Security Income (SSI) never claim it because they aren't aware it exists.

2. SSI provides supplemental monthly help to elderly, blind, or disabled low-income individuals whose conditions keep them out of the work force.

3. State offices of disability determination (look in the government listings for your state, probably within the state department of social services) determine disability claims for the federal Social Security Administration.

4. Eligible individuals can receive both Social Security checks and SSI.

5. Act as you would for disability benefits: Do your research, provide all necessary information as promptly as possible, and contact social service and advocacy groups if it looks as if you won't get the full benefits you deserve.

To Get Answers and to Appeal

1. The free booklet *Social Security: Crucial Questions and Straight Answers* (D13640) is available from the American Association of Retired Persons. Send a postcard to AARP Fulfillment (EE140), 1909 K Street, N.W., Washington, DC 20049.

2. You can go to your local Social Security office. You can write. Or you can phone the 800 number.

3. Surveys have shown that you don't necessarily get identical answers to identical questions from different representatives in different Social Security offices. The safest way to confirm information is to ask several people. Whatever they say, take notes and take names.

4. If their answers don't agree, bring the results of your research to another representative. Ask what technicality or ambiguity would lead to such confusion. If you're happy with the determination, ask to have it in writing.

5. A written answer is more formal than a chat—for better or worse. If it says what you want it to say, hang on to it. If it doesn't, you can't make it go away but you can dispute it.

6. If you act on the basis of wrong information given by a Social Security representative, you stand a better chance of seeing the matter corrected later on if you can provide the name of the person you spoke to and specific details of the conversation.

7. The Social Security Administration has a formal appeals procedure for disputing claims against its various benefits programs. Contact the SSA for instructions relating to your complaint.

8. The National Organization of Social Security Claimants Representatives (19 East Central Avenue, 2nd Floor, Pearl River, NY 10965; 1-800-431-2804, or in New York 914-735-8812) can give you the names of attorneys in your area who specialize in SSA matters and generally work on contingency.

9. If you have an objection to Social Security policies, write a letter to the editor of your newspaper.

10. Write your U.S. senators and congressman. They pass the laws that allocate the funds—and they're in Washington to represent you.

11. Among other important resources and advocacy groups are:

National Alliance of Senior
   Citizens
1700 18th Street, N.W., Suite 401
Washington, DC 20009
(202-986-0117)

National Committee to Preserve
Social Security and Medicare

2000 K Street, N.W., Suite 800
Washington, DC 20006
(202-822-9459)

National Council on the Aging
409 3rd Street, S.W. (No. 200)
Washington, DC 20024
(202-479-1200)

Save Our Security
1331 F Street, N.W.
Washington, DC 20004-1171
(202-624-9557)

▲ *See also* SENIORS AND ELDERLAW; INSURANCE; MEDICARE, MEDICAID, AND MEDIGAP; NURSING HOMES; PENSIONS.

Subscriptions

Your best strategy for subscribing to magazines and newspapers is to work with reputable, accessible operations. Any relationship that begins with a phone call from a stranger at 5:30 P.M.—saying you've "won three free" magazine subscriptions if you agree to pay for "only" four others—has already started off on the wrong foot. Why? An element of deception is involved, the only thing you're likely to get in writing is the bill, and the company doing the calling will probably not be connected with fulfillment or service complaints. Who will? Feel *free* to guess.

Safeguards

1. Expect a printed agreement. It doesn't have to say much, but it must state the number of issues you'll receive and the price you're going to pay.

2. Look for an address and phone number for service complaints. If it's for a local newspaper, look for a local phone number. If it's for a national magazine, certainly you'd prefer an 800 number to a toll number for a subscription office 2,000 miles away.

3. Note the hours for the subscription office. For a newspaper, you need weekend as well as weekday hours, because you want someone to contact if your paper doesn't come (or is incomplete) on Saturday or Sunday.

4. For a magazine, weekend hours are helpful because you may find it easier to make your calls on a nonbusiness day. But if there are no weekend hours, are the weekday hours compatible to yours?

5. If the office is in a different time zone, how do the hours work out for your location?

6. If the information isn't printed, ask for it before you send your check. Write it down where you'll be able to find it.

7. It's permissible and often practical to subscribe to several magazines through one reputable subscription service rather than to have a separate deal with each of them. Just make sure the service is legitimate, and has an address and phone number for complaints.

8. If you aren't familiar with the reputation of the subscription service, phone the Better Business Bureau or the department of consumer affairs in the state or city where the main office is located. Ask if there is a record of complaints against the company and if so, how they were resolved.

9. Keep whatever printed information you receive.

10. Don't pay the same bill twice. As foolish as this may sound, people do. Magazines send so many payment-due notices that people have been known to pay and forget. When another bill comes a month later with UNPAID stamped prominently on the accompanying letter, people imagine that it must have slipped their minds, and they pay again.

11. If you do this and later discover that you did, write the magazine and insist on either a refund or an extension of your subscription. Enclose a photocopy of your canceled check.

12. If you pay by credit card, remember that you can request a chargeback if the publisher fails to deliver the goods.

13. Moreover, if the charge appears on your credit card statement and you're still waiting for your first issue, don't let the figure go unchallenged. You can always have it reinstated if magazines or newspapers start coming. But if you leave the charge too long without question and the goods never arrive, you may go past the deadline for disputing charges.

Free Trials

1. If you subscribe to anything on the basis of a "free" trial offer, keep the entire mailing that explains the terms.

2. If you return a postcard or form, keep a photocopy of it, too.

3. Though the offer may stipulate the opportunity to examine the magazine "free" and direct you to "simply write 'cancel' on the bill if you're not satisfied," don't be surprised if you receive one or more payment-due notices before the first issue arrives.

4. Unless you know you want the magazine sight unseen, don't pay. However, take the precaution of writing to the billing office and stating that you haven't seen your trial issue yet.

5. Include your account number in the letter. Quote the portion of the agreement that guaranteed your trial period.

6. If you get another bill without having seen the magazine, respond again, enclosing copies of the previous correspondence.

7. At any point until you see the stipulated trial issue or issues, you have the option to cancel the subscription. You may wish to state that under the circumstances, you find the operation unreliable and you don't appreciate receiving notices of indebtedness (payment-due notices) before the indebtedness has in fact occurred.

8. Be sure you've kept to the terms of the offer, or you may be obligated for the charge.

9. If the problem persists, read on.

Magazine Complaints

1. If the complaint concerns the contents of the magazine, write to the editorial offices.

2. If you're disputing service, write to or phone the subscription office.

3. If you made the deal with a subscription service, contact the complaint number or address you were given.

4. Sometimes charities raise funds by selling magazines for subscription services. If this was the source of your subscription and if the subscription service doesn't follow through adequately for you, write to the head office of the charity. Explain that you're disappointed, and strongly suggest that the charity sever its ties with the service. CC the president as well as the subscription manager of the service.

5. At this point, the charity might intercede for you—or the service might race to your aid rather than lose an opportunity for future high-volume sales through the charity.

6. If your order was solicited by material which came in the mail ("direct mail"), write to the Direct Marketing Association, 6 East 43rd Street, New York, NY 10017. Because the image of all direct mailers can be hurt by the actions of a few, the DMA will apply pressure on your behalf. Its success rate is impressive.

7. The Magazine Action Hotline, Publishers Clearing House, 382 Channel Drive, Port Washington, NY 11050 (1-800-645-9242, or 516-883-5432), will intervene on complaints about incorrect billings, late arrivals, and the like, whether or not the Publishers Clearing House took your original order.

8. If you wish to discontinue a subscription after several issues, phone to determine the proce-

dure. (If you write, the company may delay correspondence until you've gotten a few more issues, leaving nothing to refund.)

Newspaper Complaints

1. If you don't get what you paid for, insist on knowing what the office intends to do about it. Does the delivery person omit deliveries one or two days a week? Are coupon inserts missing one week, and the TV section the next?

2. Say you are willing to pay only for what you received. Ask what will be done to correct these mishaps in the future.

3. If the office expresses a marked lack of concern that, for example, you received a sale flyer inside a newspaper three days late, write to the owner or manager of the store that ran the flyers. Explain that you were unable to take advantage of the sale because you didn't get the flyer in time, and that the newspaper employees assured you that they're not responsible for timely delivery. Suggest that this carelessness makes the flyers useless, and the store might do better to take its advertising dollars elsewhere. You may want to CC the company's or chain's vice president or director of marketing.

4. CC the publisher of the newspaper and the head of the circulation or sales department.

5. If you're about to cancel a subscription because of faulty service, write to the head of circulation or sales department. Give your reasons. CC the publisher. (The people whose job it is to land your subscription won't be pleased by the ones who drove you to cancel it.)

Who's the Boss?

1. Magazines and newspapers print a column, panel, or box with names, titles, and addresses of key personnel and offices. It's generally but not always toward the front of the publication.

2. Most magazines will give a special address for subscription matters, such as complaints and changes of address. This is often not the address of the editorial offices. Use the correct address. Using any other will only delay your correspondence.

3. If you become angry enough to write the boss, realize that the boss of a newspaper or magazine is the publisher, not an editor or even the editor-in-chief.

▲ *See also* CREDIT CARDS; MAIL ORDERS; TELE-MARKETING.

Supermarkets

Your biggest concern at the supermarket has got to be the safety of the foods you buy. If you see foods on sale at a vastly reduced price because the expiration date is months ago, or conditions of storage or preparation appear to be unhealthy, it's not enough to avoid them for yourself. You ought to report them to authorities, starting with your state or city department of consumer affairs.

You've also got to be on the alert for evidence of *product tampering.* Specifically:

1. It helps to know in advance what the container usually looks like, because you'll be far more likely to notice when an outer seal or wrapper is missing.

2. Does the wrapping seem to have been repositioned or reglued in any way?

3. Is the cap loose?

4. Are there traces of glue or paper that may have belonged to labels or seals?

5. If there's a band around the bottle, has it been broken or stretched?

6. If the jar has a safety button on the lid ("safety button pops up when original seal is broken"), confirm that the button is still down.

7. Presumably, similar tablets in the same bottle should be uniform in size. If they're not, be suspicious. Capsules in a bottle should all be the same size and have the same amount of medication in each one.

8. If the product comes in a metal tube, check both top and bottom for signs of tampering.

9. Be wary of unusual sediment in any liquid.

10. None of these signs proves that tampering has occurred. But any could be a warning signal. Bring them to the attention of the store manager and, if you have any doubts, contact the state or city department of consumer affairs.

11. By the way, if you hope to use a proof of purchase from the packaging for a manufacturer's promotion or rebate offer, make sure the proof is intact. Sad but true, thoughtless shoppers occasionally remove the proofs without buying the product.

Food Labeling

1. The Nutritional Labeling and Education Act of 1990 passed both houses of Congress unopposed, and required certain refinements in labeling. The first phase of the program went into effect in May 1993. Changes include:

2. "Portion sizes" will be made standard for more than one hundred prepackaged foods, meaning that you will no longer have to agonize with mental computations to compare the calories and fat of a one-ounce serving with those of a 1.6-ounce serving.

3. Portion sizes will be made more reasonable. In other words, the manufacturer's idea of a "serving" of pie can't be a pathetic sliver.

4. Health claims such as "low fat," "light," and "cholesterol-free" will be precisely defined by the Food and Drug Administration (FDA). Terms that amount to misleading hype will be eliminated.

5. For answers to questions on nutrition, diet, and product labeling, try the Alberto-Culver Nutrition Information Hotline, 1-800-622-3274.

6. You can also contact city or state health and human services departments.

When You Have to Complain

1. Once you've put safety and health issues to rest, you're not human if you don't turn an eye to pricing. It's not because you consider all supermarkets to be run by con artists and yeggs, but simply that supermarkets by their very nature are open to a remarkable range of possibilities for error. The volume of merchandise is huge and it moves rapidly; clerks and item handlers often work only a few hours a week and it may be their first job, therefore they lack familiarity with the merchandise and procedures; UPC scanners aren't infallible; and there's the occasional assumption by personnel that mistakes are unimportant because per-item dollar amounts are small.

2. What do you do? For one thing, you bone up on state law. In some states, once a food item has been placed on the shelf and offered for sale, the store cannot increase the price by slapping a new sticker over the old one.

3. If this is a law in your state and you see it violated, contact the state department of consumer affairs. Either ask about specific areas that interest you, or request any relevant consumer brochures and leaflets.

4. Ask whether the store can be disciplined, or what steps can be taken, and ask if any report is needed from you.

5. In general, your best defense is to know what the prices are supposed to be. Review store flyers to be sure that you're charged sale prices for sale items.

6. Discourage the clerk from beginning to ring up your order until you can clearly see the prices as they're being entered in the cash register.

7. If you're trying to watch the register, don't feel guilty about discouraging other conversations,

either with the bagger or with a friend who may be shopping with you.

8. If you disagree with a charge, it will most often be faster for you to dispute it before the clerk totals the purchase. Once the total appears, the clerk may simply direct you to the customer service desk, where you might have to wait in another line, or worse, have to ask a half-dozen people when the customer service person plans to return to the post.

9. Register clerks often have quotas. During peak hours, many are required to "move" a set number of people and purchases. For this reason, many do everything possible to rush you through, perhaps starting to ring your order even though you say, "I can't see the register yet," or refusing to correct errors, saying, "I don't have time. If I make a mistake, go to customer service."

10. Encourage cashiers to realize that transactions will go faster if they don't slow *you* down. If items whizzed by too rapidly, double-check them before you pay. If the clerk totaled the order despite your protests, feel free to respond, "Void the order. I'm not interested in doing business this way."

11. Explain that voiding the order is very hard on a clerk's quota.

12. If the clerk insists on a charge which you're sure is wrong, ask for the manager. Then wait for the manager. If it slows the line, that isn't your fault.

13. If the line is long, you'll have to decide whether you want to delay others. You may choose not to. You may want to apologize to them and hold your ground. But you definitely ought to realize that stores sometimes use customers' reluctance to delay others as a tactic to discourage price disputes.

14. If you've gone to the customer service desk and aren't satisfied with the answer you get, ask for the manager.

15. The manager may not satisfy you either. However, most stores have several managers to cover the different shifts. Maybe another manager would have been on your side. Get the names of

the people you speak to, and keep your register receipt, sale flyer, or other substantiation of what you're disputing.

16. Bring these with you when you return to the store. If another manager is on duty, present your case again. If this one agrees with you, suggest that it isn't too late for him or her to make good on the transaction.

17. If your question relates to what could be store policy and if you finally hear the answer you want, either get it in writing or write it down yourself. Note the date, and the name of the person who tells you.

18. If the matter comes up again and is disputed again, state that this was already resolved on such-and-such a date with so-and-so, and you don't appreciate searching the shelves and waiting in line under the impression that a deal will be honored, only to learn that policy is reinvented with each new day.

19. It is always appropriate and permissible to remind store personnel that their sales and promotions are designed to entice customers into the store, not to victimize them with lies and doubletalk. If the impression is given that a certain deal is offered, it's not in the store's best interest to wait until you get to the register to advise you of what the ad would have read if the person who composed it had been paying attention.

20. Never, ever let store personnel embarrass you over the amount you're challenging ("Lady, I can't *believe* you'd make this fuss over 15 cents!"). If the store doesn't want you to care about 15 cents, why does it bother to reduce prices by 15 cents—or less—and claim that a terrific sale is in progress?

21. The next time a clerk says to you, "Okay, I'm wrong. But it's only 10 cents, so let's not bother to correct it," you might reply, "No problem, if it's your 10 cents." Don't be surprised if the reaction you get indicates that the clerk's 10 cents is a far more serious matter than yours.

22. The "manager" often isn't the real manager. In the event of a dispute, find out the name of the single person who runs the operation at that location.

23. Phone or write that person.

24. If you write, include photocopies of register receipts, coupons, flyers, or other documentation with your letter. Name the people you're disputing, and say why.

25. Call the store, or telephone information, for the name of the regional office. Get the name and address of the regional manager. CC your letter to this individual.

26. Local consumer organizations won't worry over a manufacturer's coupon that isn't accepted, but they'll listen to a wide range of complaints. If your supermarket abuses customer trust, report it to the Chamber of Commerce, the Better Business Bureau, and the state or city department of consumer affairs.

27. If meat or poultry is involved, you can file your complaints with the U.S. Department of Agriculture's Meat and Poultry Hotline, 1-800-535-4555, and/or with your state department of agriculture. Report all health-related grievances to the U.S. Department of Health and/or state or city department of health. If you write, CC the store manager and regional manager.

28. If your complaint is against the manufacturer, contact the manufacturer. A usable address should be on the product label, often with an 800 consumer service number. If not, phone 800 Information, 1-800-555-1212, and ask if the company has a toll-free consumer service number.

29. If you're concerned that a product or label may be dangerous, unhealthful, or unfairly promoted to consumers, write your concerns to the American Association of Retired Persons, the American Heart Association, the National Parent-Teachers Association, or other appropriate advocacy groups. CC the manufacturer twice—the customer service department, and also the company president.

30. If you feel strongly enough that a practice or policy should be changed, consider writing a letter to the editor of the area newspaper. Other

shoppers will read your convictions. If they agree, the store may be forced to reconsider.

31. If you paid for the purchase by credit card, bought a defective item, and can't persuade the store to make good, follow the procedures for removing the charge from your credit card account (*see* CREDIT CARDS).

▲ *See also* **PRODUCT LIABILITY AND RECALLS; PROMOTIONAL ITEMS; RETAIL SHOPPING.**

Taxes

By IRS estimates, the country is losing roughly $100 billion a year to tax evasion. Maybe so. But we're also aware that the IRS makes mistakes. Just ask the widow who received correspondence on her late husband's taxes. It included the instruction "Please provide your date of death."

What goes for the IRS applies also to state and local tax agencies. They're capable of error, and although you can't demand value for money the way you can in a supermarket, you have the right to defend your money from other people's mistakes.

In a nutshell, you have the right not to pay more money than required by law.

The guidelines below relate specifically to IRS procedures that can assist in protecting these rights. Like anything else rooted in legislation, they're subject to change. Whole books come out when changes are made, and even accountants can't remember every revision they contain. This section is no substitute for an accountant or a short course in tax preparation. But the underlying approaches aren't likely to change, and can generally be adapted to state and local situations.

The Taxpayer Bill of Rights

Federal legislation assures taxpayers certain rights, which the IRS describes as follows:

1. The right to receive a written notice of levy, no less than thirty days prior to enforcement, which explains in nontechnical terms the key procedures and the administrative appeals and alternatives to levy which are available.

2. The right to bring suit against the IRS for civil damages for certain unauthorized collection actions.

3. The right to make an audio recording or receive a copy of such a recording of an interview for the determination or collection of tax.

4. The right to reasonably rely on written advice of the IRS that was provided in response to a specific written request.

5. The right to representation at any time during these processes by a person who may practice before the IRS, except in certain criminal investigations.

6. The right to file an application for relief with the IRS Taxpayer Ombudsman or Problem Resolution Officer in a situation in which the taxpayer is suffering or is about to suffer a significant hardship as a result of the manner in which the IRS is administering the tax laws.

7. The right to receive an explanation of the examination and collection process and taxpayer rights under these processes before or at the initial interview for the determination or collection of tax.

Take Precautions

1. It's nice to know you can restore your taxpayer's rights when they're violated, but much

nicer not to be put on the spot. If you take certain precautions now, you can either avoid the incident entirely or at least soften the blow when the hammer falls.

2. Keep careful records, not only of your taxes, but also of taxables. Be able to identify and itemize deposits made to bank accounts. Save receipts for deductible items, as well as calendars, appointment books, and journals documenting activities that relate to entries on your tax returns.

3. If you move, familiarize yourself with new state and local tax laws. Even if you've been doing taxes for twenty years, there will be variations. Investigate them long before you have to file.

4. If you move, file a change of address with the IRS (Form 8822: request it by phoning 1-800-829-3676—1-800-TAX-FORM). Although one Tax Court has held that it's enough to show the change on your tax return (such as a 1040), don't count on it.

5. Take due dates seriously. If you must file by a certain date, file by that date.

6. With some taxes, a penalty is levied for each day you're late. To protect yourself from these, consider filing via certified mail, return receipt requested.

7. When you file, write necessary identifying numbers (such as Social Security number or federal I.D.) on the check and forms. Also, indicate which tax you're paying.

8. You may only be aware that one tax is due. But if, for instance, the federal government determines that you owe for something else, your payment may be applied to *it,* leaving interest and penalties to accrue on the tax you think you're paying.

9. Have and use Social Security numbers for your children, particularly if they've received large and otherwise untaxable cash gifts from relatives. Otherwise, the taxing authorities will see the money going into your bank account and want to tax you for it.

10. Proofread all the information that's reported to you and the taxing agencies simultaneously. For example, if an incorrect figure is reported on your 1099 and you use the correct figure on your returns, it won't match what the computers say you owe, and you'll get an official notice.

11. If you use a computer to do your taxes, realize that some programs are better than others at asking the right questions of you. To play it safe, either proofread the returns carefully and knowledgeably or ask your accountant to double-check them.

12. If you use an accountant, proofread everything anyway. Remember that your signature goes on the returns, and you're responsible for any misinformation they contain.

13. An accountant might have to pay penalties for preparing a blatantly unrealistic return that isn't sustainable on its merits, but this doesn't relieve you of your responsibility as a taxpayer.

14. Identify each page of a return with your SSN (Social Security number) and/or federal I.D.

15. If you don't want to force taxing agencies to send you notices of deficiency (correspondence saying you've omitted vital inclusions):

- **Sign your return.**
- **Proofread and double-check to eliminate math errors.**
- **Make sure you haven't entered anything on the wrong line.**
- **Declare your income. Undeclared income is a major red flag.**

Assistance

1. If you want to use the IRS assistance number, 1-800-829-1040, you're most likely to get through between 8:00 A.M. and 9:00 A.M. midweek.

2. Tele-Tax, at 1-800-829-4477, provides recorded messages on more than one hundred subjects, twenty-four hours a day, seven days a week.

3. Numerous helpful publications are available from the IRS. You can request Publication 910 ("Guide to Free Tax Services") by phoning 1-800-829-3676, or you can contact your regional Internal Revenue Service Center noted in the instructions for completing your return.

4. Also available from the same source is Publication 1, "Your Rights as a Taxpayer."

5. Walk-in help is available at local IRS offices.

6. The IRS has informational videotapes that can be borrowed, and offers educational programs for the public to attend.

7. Assistance services are available for people with disabilities, including forms and instructions in Braille, and a TTY number (1-800-829-4059) for hearing-impaired taxpayers who have TV/telephone access.

8. If you suffer a significant hardship, additional assistance is available. Request Form 911, "Application for Taxpayer Assistance Order to Relieve Hardship," or contact 1-800-829-1040.

9. In cooperation with local volunteers, the IRS offers free help in preparing tax returns for low-income and elderly taxpayers through VITA (Volunteer Income Tax Assistance) and TCE (Tax Counseling for the Elderly).

10. U.S. taxpayers abroad may write for information to Internal Revenue Service, Attn: IN:C:TPS, 950 L'Enfant Plaza South, S.W., Washington, DC 20024, or can contact the U.S. embassy for information about forms and services.

11. For assistance with state and local taxes, consult your telephone directory; look in the government listings for your state or city.

12. Local and state assistance may be available from your bank and your accountant. Also, inquire at schools, libraries, and houses of worship to learn what free programs or preparation services may be offered in your area.

If You Don't Get Your Refund

1. If you're due a refund and you don't receive it within eight weeks, follow up by phoning the TeleTax number or 1-800-829-1040.

2. If the IRS reduces your refund because you owe a debt to another federal agency (or child support), the IRS must notify you.

If You Discover an Error After You've Filed

1. IRS Form 1040X allows you to amend a previously filed tax return.

2. Occasionally, you'll become aware of information that wasn't available when the taxes were filed. Or perhaps a new ruling has gone into effect and has retroactive consequences.

3. File an amended return whether you discover you've misreported something and owe the government money, or money is owed to you.

Problem Resolution

1. The number of the IRS Problem Resolution Office appears in the instructions for Form 1040, or can be found in the U.S. Government listings in your telephone directory. If you can't find the number, phone 1-800-829-1040.

2. Keep records of every conversation you have with a tax office representative: date, name of the party, what you were asked, what examples you gave, and what you were told.

3. Complaints, including about the conduct of IRS employees, can be brought to the individual's supervisor, or to the district director or service center director for your area IRS.

If You Can't Pay

1. File no matter what. The penalty for not filing is higher than the penalty for filing without sufficient payment attached.

2. Don't convince yourself that you can put off paying by getting an extension on filing. Your taxes are due by the due date. If they're not paid on time, they'll generate interest and penalties.

3. If you can't pay, contact your area IRS Problem Resolution Office. Explain your situation and ask to arrange installment payments.

4. In doing so, be prepared with a valid reason why you can't pay. If you have a CD coming due and you'd prefer not to cash it prematurely, the IRS won't be very understanding. But if a sudden reversal has left you strapped (hardship, illness, unemployment), it's inclined to be sympathetic.

5. Once you accept an installment schedule, don't miss a payment. If a new problem prevents you from paying promptly, discuss it with your revenue officer.

6. Following review of your current finances, the IRS may change your payment agreement: "We will notify you thirty days before any change to your payment agreement and tell you why we are making the change."

7. To avoid the complications of an installment agreement, look into the possibility of borrowing the money from a bank. Even if the IRS agrees to an installment, your overhead on the arrangement may add up to more than the interest a bank would ask.

If You Get an Official Letter

1. Don't ignore it, but don't panic either.

2. If you're required to respond, respond.

3. If you have any doubts whatsoever, and often if you don't, consult your accountant. If you answer it on your own, provide your accountant with copies of any correspondence.

4. Don't assume the letter is correct. When you receive a letter (or refund check for an unexpected amount), check the figures against your return.

5. If you get a refund that you wanted to credit to upcoming taxes but decide to cash it instead, *first* talk to your accountant. Under no circumstance should you leave your accountant believing that the money's in the IRS piggy bank when in fact it's in your pocket.

6. Whatever communication you receive, it will indicate a response procedure. You may feel comfortable phoning. But you're better protected if you write and keep a copy of the correspondence, proof that you responded.

7. Don't mail originals of attachments if you can send copies.

8. If you're enclosing several exhibits, identify each separately with your SSN, federal I.D. and whatever other number is assigned to the correspondence. In your cover letter, refer to each exhibit, as in "I am sending you (1) a photocopy of the canceled check, front and back, (2) a photocopy of . . ."

9. Realize that if you don't file when you're supposed to, and if you don't pay taxes that are due, you're breaking the law. Your property can be seized and sold.

10. If your property is sold, you have certain protections. For example, you can continue to receive unemployment and workers' compensation benefits, and if your house is sold, you may compel the purchaser to sell it back to you within 180 days for the purchase price plus stipulated interest.

11. If you receive an Audit Notice, keep reading.

If You're Audited

1. The Taxpayer Compliance Measurement Program is responsible for the auditing of randomly selected returns. Yours may be one of them. If it is, the procedure may be extremely detailed or, if your records are in excellent shape, essentially routine.

2. Be prepared. Your big allies will be credibility and consistency. If your documents have been well kept and methodical, the examining officer is more likely to believe you when you're questioned.

3. Be creative, but don't invent. For instance, if you subscribe to a magazine for professional reasons and can't find the subscription invoice, bring the magazine with your address/subscription sticker on it. But don't falsify subscriptions that you never had.

4. You stand a better chance of being audited if your claims go far beyond the norm, such as a

$20,000 gift to charity or golfing expenses as a business deduction. This doesn't mean you have to back down. It just means that you've got to be able to prove and document your contentions.

5. You can have assistance, such as your accountant or spouse, present at an audit. But bear in mind that your accountant may want to bill you for the time.

6. If your accountant has a solid reputation with the tax office, it may be to your advantage to stay home. In this way, the accountant can do your negotiating for you, and you can't be caught off guard by an unexpected question.

7. If the IRS wants to conduct a field audit, it means the agent wants to come to your home or workplace. Unless the agent specifically needs to see the site to verify items on a return, you can ask your tax adviser or accountant to take your records to his or her office, and hold the audit there.

8. Audits generally relate to particular questions: You're asked to bring certain records that will support entries that are identified to you.

9. If the examiner waits until you're in an IRS office to raise further questions and require additional documents, you may wish to report it to a supervisor. The examiner will have to substantiate the request.

10. If an examiner appears and says, "I'm a special agent," it may have to do with criminal proceedings—in which case, speak to an attorney before continuing with the audit.

11. Whatever the agent determines, you'll receive an audit report.

12. If tax is deemed to be due, you can discuss it with the agent's superior.

13. If the superior agrees with the agent, you'll receive notice that you have thirty days to take your case to the IRS Appeals Division.

14. Request the auditor's examination notes from the Disclosure Office of your local IRS district office.

15. See below.

You Can Appeal Findings

1. The IRS may cancel or reduce (abate) certain penalties if you can show reasonable cause for your error—for instance, if you can prove you were given wrong advice by an IRS employee.

2. Speak to the Problem Resolution Office. Also, request Publication 5, "Appeal Rights and Preparation of Protests for Unagreed Cases," available by request from 1-800-829-3676.

3. If you disagree with that decision or any decision, you have options for appeal.

4. You might want to discuss this step with a trusted adviser before launching a full-scale attack. After all, you'll be calling attention to your tax history. If your record-keeping has been substandard, it's conceivable you'd be better served by letting the matter rest.

5. If you decide to go ahead and you've paid the judgment and believe it's incorrect, file a claim for a refund.

6. If the claim is disallowed, approach the Appeals Office.

7. If you don't accept the Appeals Office's decision or it doesn't act on your claim within six months, you may take the case to the U.S. Claims Court or U.S. District Court.

8. If you haven't paid the disputed tax, you can take the matter to Tax Court. There are limitations. There is a filing fee. And if you lose the judgment, interest is retroactive from the date the taxes were originally due (not the date of the Tax Court's decision).

9. Because it's a court with a busy calendar, cases don't come up right away. However, the Small Case Division of the Tax Court (for disputes up to $10,000) is faster and more informal than regular Tax Court.

10. Disputes are often settled before trial, on the way to court.

11. If yours isn't, go prepared. Bring proof, photographs, witnesses. Don't assume that the IRS will have anything simply because you've

already sent it. Bring any documentation or diary entries of conversations you've had with IRS representatives.

12. If you wish to file, contact the Clerk of the Court, U.S. Tax Court, 400 Second Street, N.W., Washington, DC 20217.

Telemarketing

Here's the deal. Imagine that you're in a store, a salesman strolls over to you to pitch an overpriced product you had no intention of wanting, then offers to go to the back room to get it for you for the price plus a $50 agent's fee. Incidentally, as soon as he starts for the back room, you have no way out of the arrangement. You don't get to inspect the product first.

There are a half-dozen things wrong with this, so you'd never fall for it, right? But each year, consumers given the same set of enticements are tele-swindled out of more than $1 billion, according to FTC figures. And these customers don't even get to walk into the store—or have any real reason to believe the store exists.

Not that all telemarketing is dishonest. It's a legitimate way of doing business to the tune of $100 billion annually. But what about the bad apples? How do they get away with it? They call, announce to you with bubbling enthusiasm that you're entitled to a windfall or remarkable opportunity, perhaps they even prod over and over, "Aren't you happy? Aren't you excited?"—then proceed to work the following angles.

They Offer Unbelievable Investments or Merchandise

- **A free vacation.**
- **A free car.**
- **Time shares at a monumental bargain.**

- **Shares in a gold mine that pays 20 percent interest.**
- **A small fortune left to you by a distant relative.**
- **Free subscriptions.** *All* **you have to do is subscribe to several others (that you'll never read either) at full price.**

They Disguise Their Source of Profit

1. They won't tell you if the merchandise is nonexistent, junk, or selling for twice its worth—thereby leaving them a huge markup.

2. They may ask for a "handling fee," "registration fee," "agency fee," or the like, any one of which can be higher than the value of what you're getting.

3. In other words, you can get a "free vacation including hotel" for a "small $400 service fee to our agency, which you understand has been hired by the company giving away this great gift, but the vacation is worth $1,000"—but you get no vacation, or a vacation loaded with hidden charges once you reach your destination, or a vacation you wouldn't wish on your worst enemy. Often there are so many restrictions bound into the package that it's impossible to meet them, and impossible to get your money back.

4. Any time you can be enticed into returning a call, remember that the return call appears on your phone bill and the fee might knock your

socks off. With many 900-number operations, their profit is derived from $5 a minute (and up) for the return phone call (*see* 900 NUMBERS).

5. Some callers will sink to the low level of milking your charitable instincts. An opportunity to contribute to AIDS organizations, the homeless, or the troops overseas may be an outright lie.

6. By giving themselves a fancy name or a name that sounds very similar to that of a highly regarded institution, they can appear to be something they're not. To fabricate an example: a call from the President of the United Stats would not be the same as one from the President of the United States.

They Might Throw in a "Free" Gift

1. A free television set might be a tiny one that requires an expensive battery pack (to be bought separately by you, of course).

2. A free car phone might be a cheap phone shaped like a car.

3. A free motorboat might be an inflatable raft propelled by an eggbeater-like device you hang over the side and operate by hand.

What You Can Do

1. Listen critically. If the offer sounds too good to be true, it probably is. Remember that you can't inspect merchandise over the phone.

2. Be extremely cautious of any unsolicited caller who wants to bill your credit card. You have no control of the amount the company can claim you owe, although you can contest the charge (*see* CREDIT CARDS). Or maybe you were called *just* to get your credit card number . . . and the whole conversation is a pretext for obtaining it.

3. Even if *you* place the call, giving your credit card number can be risky. Don't doubt for a minute that the claim will be presented to your card company right away. But you could wait months (or forever) for your order to be filled.

4. Weigh the value of giving *any* personal information to unsolicited callers. If you give your address followed by the warning "Don't send a salesman by—I'll be on vacation for two weeks," you may be advising a criminal when to stop by and rob you silly. If you give your address, it's *never* a good idea to let the caller know you live alone—no matter how cleverly the attempt to discover this is disguised.

5. Never be pressured to make a decision on the phone. Ask to see something in writing. Ask what recourse you have if you're dissatisfied. Ask for the phone number of the company. Ask for an address.

6. Bear in mind that even when you're given this information freely, it's subject to change. Or it could be the address of the "agent" or "packager" or some other term, tipping you off to the fact that if you encounter a problem down the road, each arm of the operation will shunt you off to another in a runaround that can be endless: "That's not our responsibility. Write to the packager. . . . Write to the clearinghouse. . . . Write to the supplier. . . ."

7. Remember that swindlers are in the business of swindling. If they've done their homework, they're armed with convincing replies. It doesn't make them true. Con artists glibly quote phony laws to bolster their credibility. "You have sixty days' full protection under the Congressional Universal No-Fault Consumer Protection Act" only works if such an act exists. It doesn't.

8. A variation on phony laws is to twist actual laws. An encyclopedia salesman might claim the purchase "is deductible as an educational expense on your taxes." Certainly it's legal to deduct for legitimate educational expenses, but at best, a small fraction of the cost of the books might under some circumstances be deductible to a limited degree over a period of time. Worse, if misinformation leads you to report wrongful deductions on your taxes and they're disallowed, your telemarketer won't pick up the bill for interest and penalties. You will.

9. If it's an investment proposal and it interests you, find out if the caller is licensed and has a clean record, and whether the investment program is registered. In some states, registered telemarketers are required to post substantial bonds.

10. The number can be found in your phone directory, or from the National Association of State Securities Administrators and/or North American Securities Administrators Association in Washington, DC, 202-737-0900.

11. The self-regulatory National Futures Association monitors registered individuals and brokers dealing in commodity futures: 200 W. Madison Street, Suite 1600, Chicago, IL 60606; 1-800-621-3570, or 1-800-572-9400 in Illinois.

12. If it's an offer of a noninvestment nature, ask for the name of the community in which the organization does business. Contact the Chamber of Commerce or Better Business Bureau in that community. The Council of Better Business Bureaus, 703-276-0100, can provide the numbers of out-of-state BBBs.

When It Doesn't Work

1. Hanging up will usually be the end of it. But be sure you hang up before you've given away any information that can be used against you.

2. In this age of "random dialing," computers can generate an infinite number of combinations and dial them, enabling either a telemarketer or a recording to take over when you answer. If you have an unlisted number, you're as likely to be called by random dialing as anybody else, because the computer doesn't know you're unlisted; it just puts numbers together. If your answering machine answers, the recording may proceed to its spiel without losing a beat.

3. If you come home to one of these messages on your answering machine—such as "Call back and we'll give you a free watch"—don't return the call unless you're prepared to pay fat rates for the phone call itself. The company is required to advise you in advance of the charges, but this is usually the part of the recording that's garbled. (*See* 900 NUMBERS.)

4. If you hang up on a computer message, it may continue to tie up your line until the pitch is completed. The Federal Communications Commission (FCC) considers line-seizing illegal. Report incidents to the FCC (202-632-7553) when they occur, and ask what steps you can take.

5. Some states have made it illegal to automatically transmit unsolicited recorded telephone or fax messages offering to sell services or goods.

6. If you've been bothered or swindled by a telemarketing operation, file your complaint with the Better Business Bureau, the FCC, the FTC, and the Alliance Against Fraud in Telemarketing, 815 15th Street, N.W., Suite 516, Washington, DC 20005; 202-639-8140. They may be able to offer immediate assistance. If not, your complaint will be added to their files and may be the basis for subsequent legal action.

7. To have your name removed from calling lists, contact the Telemarketing Preference Service, Direct Marketing Association, 6 East 43rd Street, New York, NY 10017. This won't eliminate randomly dialed calls, but it ought to reduce the frequency of invasions of your privacy.

8. In instances of fraud, report the matter to your state attorney general and state or city department of consumer affairs. If the company operates from out of state, you will be referred to the appropriate office.

9. An enraged Boston attorney won an injunction against a telemarketing company, only to receive calls from different companies the following week. Back to court he went. So yes, it is possible to secure injunctions against telemarketers. But if you do, it may be debatable whether the victory was worth the time it took.

10. People have been known to take civil action, and to recover damages plus costs and a reasonable attorney's fee. Jurisdictions may be limited to callers located within your own state.

11. Because much of the technology is so new, laws that should be passed haven't been passed yet. The consumer protection agencies named

above can advise you of late-breaking developments. But remember, as soon as laws are passed, new ways around them are born. As telephone rates plunge, it's increasingly cost-effective for companies to operate from states whose laws haven't caught up with the times, and even from overseas, where jurisdiction is fuzzy.

12. So above all, keep reminding yourself how hard it will be to get your money back if you're bilked. Do you know where the office is? Maybe you can storm in, demand satisfaction, and receive it. But offices can be moved. Do you have the number? Maybe you can phone and persuade the company that there are laws against their evil practices. But numbers can be changed or disconnected.

13. Maybe you'll be the exception. Maybe this too-good-to-be-true offer is every bit as good as it sounds. Maybe your ship has come in! *But* never forget: The tele-scammers' strongest weapon is the possibility that you'll think exactly that.

▲ *See also* CREDIT CARDS; INVESTMENT BROKERS; 900 NUMBERS; PUBLIC UTILITIES; SCAMS.

Tours

A great deal of consumer law hinges on reasonable expectations. For instance, you can reasonably expect that a coffee mug won't shatter on contact with boiling water. You can reasonably expect that the moisture in bread won't be enough to electrocute you on contact with a toaster.

Your expectations for a tour need be no less reasonable. The tour company protects itself with a brochure clearly enumerating the items covered by the package price and those not. Read it and understand what's excluded. By implication, anything not specified is also excluded.

Phrases in tour brochures may be so deceptively upbeat that neither the consumer nor the travel agent can properly interpret them. Add to this the fact that anything written abroad may have been produced by people who use English words differently than we do, and it's obvious that confusion can occur. For instance, "European Plan" (EP) denotes a room without meals in the United States but in Europe usually suggests that breakfast is included. A leaflet defining popular tour terminology is available free from Trafalgar Tours, 11 East 26th Street, Suite 1300, New York, NY 10010.

Realize that a bare-bones bargain tour may not be any cheaper in the end because if, for example, ground transfers between hotel and airport aren't covered, you may be stuck for large cash outlays en route. Don't be surprised if they're unreasonably inflated, because people charging them may surmise that you're over a barrel.

Once you've begun the tour, a certain take-it-or-leave-it reality is thought to prevail. In other words, if you find the tour guide, or the route, or the service intolerable, you're expected to believe that you can't do much in the way of making other arrangements unless you simply want to forfeit the cost of the trip and leave. This means that, as always, you should do your homework before making a financial commitment; you should arm yourself with certain addresses and phone numbers before you leave home; and you should register accurate complaints with the proper parties as soon as possible.

Questions to Ask

1. Review an assortment of brochures, and solicit word of mouth from your friends.

2. List your vacation goals, and either discuss them one by one with your travel agent or compare them point for point with a selection of brochures.

3. Ask what's included in the price. If airfare is included, is it from your city, or is it from a distant airport? Are there service charges? Taxes? Airport taxes? Airport transfers? Is the price for land only?

4. What airlines does the tour operator use? (If you belong to a frequent flyer program, can you apply the mileage to your account, and if so, how?)

5. What meals are included?

6. Is the room rate based on double or single occupancy?

7. What's the refund policy?

8. What assurances are offered?

9. What phone numbers does the tour operator provide, and what procedures does it recommend if a complaint should arise?

10. Is the operator an active member of the United States Tour Operators Association (USTOA)? There is absolutely no evidence that nonmembers provide less worthy tours, but active members do participate in the USTOA Consumer Protection Plan, which may reimburse consumers in the event of member bankruptcy, insolvency, cancellation by the company, or total nonperformance.

11. To become an active member, a tour operator must have eighteen references from industry sources and financial institutions, must have been in business at least three years under the same management and/or ownership in the United States, and must carry a minimum of $1 million professional liability insurance and furnish USTOA with a $250,000 indemnity bond or equivalent security to protect consumers against losses of tour payments or deposits as a result of bankruptcy or insolvency.

12. Active members subscribe to USTOA's code of ethics and standards.

13. Claims in cases of bankruptcy or insolvency can be filed on forms from the USTOA, 211 East 51st Street, Suite 12B, New York, NY 10022; 212-750-7371.

14. Other complaints can be directed to the USTOA at the same address and phone number.

15. The National Tour Association (NTA), 546 East Main Street, Lexington, KY 40508, 606-226-4444, offers similar services and attempts to reach resolutions between members and their clients.

16. The Consumer Affairs Department of the American Society of Travel Agents, 1101 King Street, Alexandria, VA 22314, 703-739-2782, will try to resolve disputes for consumers and member travel companies.

17. Your local Better Business Bureau or Chamber of Commerce may be able to tell you if complaints have been lodged against your travel agency, but they aren't in any position to comment on tour operators in other towns, regions, and states. On the other hand, you can contact the BBB or Chamber of the city in which the tour operator's offices are located.

On the Road

1. *If* you've done your homework and know your options, you may have more leverage en route. If you're familiar with the recourse you'll have at home, that too may strengthen your bargaining position.

2. If you have the number of your travel agency and the country and main U.S. office of the tour company, phone, stating your objections. The company certainly has the ability to replace an unsatisfactory guide or to put pressure on a surly hotel staff. This brings us back to reasonable expectation. If you tear your skirt every time you use a chair or the windows have no screens, don't wait until you get home to raise a commotion. Ask if the tour company can correct the problem before the rest of your trip is ruined and how it intends to make reparations, and demand some assurance that it will at the very least attempt to correct these horrors in future.

3. Take photographs or, better yet, use your videocamera. If you record your difficulties, you can use the pictures later to substantiate your complaint when you get home. You can also call the local TV action reporter. Good video coverage of a miserable trip plays very well during tourist

season, and the station will probably thank you—perhaps even remunerate you—for your efforts.

4. Save receipts for any expenses you incur as a result of the tour company's failure to provide promised service.

When You Get Home

1. If you've paid by credit card and if you feel the trip was misrepresented to you, write your credit card company when you receive the statement. Explain your reasons for disputing the charge.

2. It's possible that some extra service included with your credit card has insured or otherwise protected your trip. Reread the terms of the original offer, and ask your card company.

3. Whether or not you complained from the road, follow up when you get home. If you write the tour operator, CC your travel agent if you used one, and CC the Chamber of Commerce, the Better Business Bureau, and the state or city department of consumer affairs in the tour operator's area.

4. Provide photocopies of any evidence that the travel contract was breached—receipts, photos, and so on.

5. If you traveled abroad, travel agencies and tour operators may hide behind an ignorance of foreign laws, taxes, and customs. However, it is a reasonable expectation that any company operat-

ing in a foreign country will be informed of these matters. Furthermore, they can only plead ignorance once. If you put them on notice that certain things went wrong, and if you file with the various consumer organizations noted above, it will be considerably more difficult for the travel agent or tour operator to plead ignorance in the future.

6. Write to the Ombudsman, *Condé Nast Traveler,* 360 Madison Avenue, New York, NY 10017. If your problem would interest readers, this columnist makes suggestions in the magazine and attempts to resolve your dispute with the company.

7. If you feel so strongly about the inadequacy of the tour that you want to issue a warning to other consumers, write to the travel editors of big-city newspapers. They may research your letter and carry it in their columns. They may even try to intervene on your behalf.

8. If a large tour operator has behaved horribly in a way that's involved numerous travelers, consider a class-action suit. (*See* RUNG ELEVEN: CLASS-ACTION SUIT, in Part I.) You may be able to convince the tour operator's customer service person that if a suit is initiated and grounds seem sufficient, the costs to the company could be enormous—and really, it would be so much easier simply to appease you.

▲ *See also* AIRLINES; CREDIT CARDS; HOTELS; PUBLIC TRANSPORTATION.

U.S. Postal Service

"Postal Service" has been labeled a contradiction in terms, and more than a few stations have the reputation of behaving like the only game in town. But with faxes and rival delivery systems, the pressure is on for all of them to act like highly competitive corporations. There's even a quality improvement program in effect, SET (Striving for Excellence Together).

Other evidence can be detected, in the form of helpful flyers distributed in literature racks, increased opportunities to buy stamps and obtain simple services without waiting in line at the post office, and a chain of command that has new incentives to respond to disgruntled consumers.

If You Want Service

1. It's helpful to clarify the sort of service you're getting. For instance, Priority Mail offers "quick two-day delivery between all major business centers in the U.S.," but if it takes a Priority Mail letter two weeks to get from Los Angeles to Miami, you'll be told, "We don't say the service is guaranteed."

2. Do you want to know if it's guaranteed? Then ask, "Is this a guarantee?" Don't assume.

3. Ask at the counter. Better yet, phone in advance. Be specific and comprehensive in your questions: "Do I need identification to pick up the package you're holding for me? This is what I have. Will you accept it? Thank you. May I have your name, please?"

4. If you arrive and suddenly an extra condition is imposed, refer to your earlier conversation. Don't let the clerk wave you away. Hold your ground. Name your source.

5. If the clerk won't help, ask for the superintendent, a supervisor, or a customer relations representative.

6. Don't be surprised if you're told that person is out to lunch, at any hour of the day. Get the name of the person who tells you.

7. If this occurs, follow up as soon as you can with a phone call to the head of the branch, who might very possibly tell you, "That would never happen. Someone in a supervisory capacity is always on duty." Swell. You were either purposely or unintentionally misled. Name the person who misled you. Then restate your original complaint.

8. The reason you need to report the incident quickly is that you don't want the superintendent to say, "There's nothing I can do about it now. I can only counsel or discipline an employee immediately after the problem occurs."

9. Remind the superintendent that you wanted to act immediately, but you were refused assistance. Surely you would have stayed to finish your business if you'd been allowed. Instead, you've been inconvenienced by having to make a wasted trip to the post office.

10. Unlike private industry, the post office won't be able to appease you with free merchandise. But you can ask what steps will be taken, and what you can do to avoid repetition of your difficulties.

11. If the supervisor or superintendent seems to be dismissing you, find out if the branch is a substation of a larger office. If so, complain to the supervisor there. CC the head of the branch office.

12. Like private industry, the Postal Service has consumer affairs representatives. Check your telephone directory (in the U.S. Government listings) and call the main office nearest you to learn the complaint procedure.

13. Headquarters for the U.S. Post Office, Office of Consumer Affairs, is 475 L'Enfant Plaza, S.W., Washington, DC 20260; 202-268-2283.

14. Complaints about fraudulent or obscene mail should be directed to your local postmaster or Chief Postal Inspector, U.S. Postal Service, Washington, DC 20260-2100; 202-268-4267.

15. Incidentally, complaint forms should be available from your post office. If you don't see any, ask for them.

16. Some communities have Customer Advisory Councils to act as liaisons between customers and the Postal Service. Ask your local (or main) post office if one exists for your neighborhood. You may want to volunteer to join it. You can certainly advise the council of your suggestions and concerns.

17. If the problem has to do with lost mail which has been insured, registered, or indemnified in some other way, follow the steps outlined in the chart on page 233 to trace the item and/or be reimbursed.

18. To avoid having your first-class mail returned, it pays to keep these standards in mind:

- **Pieces are prohibited from the mails unless they are rectangular in shape and at least 3½ inches high and at least 5 inches long (although keys and identification devices are exceptions that don't have to conform to these restrictions).**

- **Pieces greater than ¼ inch thick can be mailed even if they measure less than 3½ by 5 inches. But at the same time, first-class mail (except presorted first-class and carrier-route first-class) weighing one ounce or less is nonstandard and subject to a 10-cent surcharge in addition to the regularly applicable postage if it is longer than 11½ inches, taller than 6⅛ inches, or thicker than ¼ inch, or if the length divided by the height is not between 1.3 and 2.5. No fooling! (Who could make this up?)**

Checklist for Filing Domestic Indemnity Claims

ACTION	INSURED	COD	REGISTERED	EXPRESS MAIL	EXPRESS MAIL COD
			TYPE OF MAIL		
Complete Form 565			✓		
Complete Form 3812	✓	✓			
Complete Form 5690				✓	✓
File Immediately if Damage or Partial Loss	✓	✓	✓	✓	✓
File after 7 Days				✓	
File after 15 Days			✓		
File after 30 Days (45 if sent SAM or PAL) (75 Days if sent surface to an APO, FPO, or outside our 48 states)	✓				
File after 45 Days		✓			✓
File Within 90 Days from Date Article Was Mailed				✓	✓
File Within 1 Year from Date Article Was Mailed	✓	✓	✓		
File at Any Post Office	✓	✓	✓	✓*	✓*
If Complete Loss, Only Sender May File		✓	✓	✓	✓
If Claim is for Damage or Partial Loss, Either Sender or Addressee May File	✓	✓	✓	✓	✓
Submit Original Mailing Receipt	✓	✓	✓	✓	✓
Submit Evidence of Value	✓	✓	✓	✓	✓
Submit Proof of Loss	✓		✓		
Submit Article, Container, Wrapper, and Packaging, if Damage or Partial Loss	✓	✓	✓	✓	✓

If for the complete loss of Express Mail, the claim must be filed at the post office where the article was mailed.

VAT (Value-Added Tax) Abroad

Here's a bonus, maybe better than getting what you pay for, because this one's a case of getting back money if you paid too much. It applies to purchases made abroad when a value-added tax has been passed on as part of the price.

The value-added tax is a sort of middleman's tax, levied on the business that turns a raw material such as fabric into an item such as a dress. Businesses generally recover this expense by upping the cost of the finished products.

If you buy certain durable goods abroad, the VAT can account for more than one-quarter of your bill. But if you're planning to take your acquisitions home with you, you may be entitled to a refund (less service charge).

To Get a Refund

1. Confirm that the store participates in the program. A sign may advertise the fact. If you don't see a sign, ask.

2. Establish the manner in which the refund will reach you. If the store can direct your credit card company to credit your account, it may be handiest to pay by card.

3. If the payment will be by card, suggest that the store write two slips: one for the cost of the purchase with the VAT amount deducted, and the other for the balance. Many stores will put the first through immediately, then wait a week to ten days to receive your validated customs exit documents. When the documents arrive, they tear up the second slip.

4. If this approach is taken but the second charge nevertheless appears on your credit card statement, it will be easier to dispute. Write your explanation to the card company, attaching photocopies of your supporting documents.

5. If you don't have a card or if the store won't accept your card, see if the parcels can be sent to your home address. If they can, urge the store to deduct the VAT on the spot—because if it makes the direct shipment without deducting the tax, your rebate might be overlooked and therefore only recoverable after lengthy correspondence.

6. Determine and corroborate the rules in effect for the country you're visiting. For instance, do packages have to remain sealed until you reach Customs?

7. Carry your passport when you shop. The store will need to see it before handing over the refund form.

8. Ask exactly how you're to use the form. Does Customs stamp it when you leave the country? Do you send it back to the store? To a particular department of the store? To a business office at another address? It's much easier to get your answers face to face than to try to resolve the matter by correspondence after you get home.

9. Expect to spend more time at Customs than a fellow traveler with nothing to declare, and have your refund form with you. The form won't do

you any good stashed away in a suitcase that's already on the plane.

10. Double-check the rest of the procedure with the Customs agent. Should the form be stamped? Where's the nearest mailbox so you can post the form to the correct address before your departure?

11. Inquire how long the refund should take to process. Keep your paperwork in case the time comes and goes without a refund. If necessary, follow the instructions for following up.

Warranties

Unpacking your newly bought merchandise can be a pain after you get it home. Too much paper. Too much plastic. Too much Styrofoam. Too much box. But be careful not to throw *too much* away in your zeal to tidy up. You'll certainly want to keep your warranty. There may be a postcard for you to complete and mail to the manufacturer. And there may be instructions that if you need to return the merchandise, you have to use the original carton. Pay attention to these details if you want to save trouble later on.

Concerning the warranty itself, you might want to designate one folder in your home office and keep all your warranties there. Keep with it a record of the date of purchase, the date the postcard was returned (if applicable), any print advertising that might have described the terms of sale, and any notations concerning service if service needs arise. If certain commitments are made on the box and you decide not to keep the box, at least photocopy the portions where the promises are made.

There are a variety of warranties covering new merchandise, with some differences between states, and many similarities in accordance with the Uniform Commercial Code and the Magnuson-Moss Warranty Act.

Implied Warranties

1. Based on common law and established by almost all states under Section 2-314 of the Uniform Commercial Code, the Implied Warranty of Merchantability says that stores in business to sell a particular product promise that the product is fit to sell. If you buy a toaster that doesn't toast or an air conditioner that just hums, the seller has breached the Implied Warranty of Merchantability.

2. The Implied Warranty of Fitness for a Particular Purpose, under Section 2-315 of the Uniform Commercial Code, says that if a merchant promises a product can be used for a specific application, the merchant is bound by that promise. If the salesman tells you that the air conditioner can cool your huge, steamy attic and you learn later that it's useless except in a small office, he has breached the Implied Warranty of Fitness for a Particular Purpose.

3. Implied warranties aren't in writing and are considered to be in force unless the seller conspicuously advertises the product for sale "as is."

4. In some states, stores aren't permitted to sell new merchandise on an "as is" basis.

5. Even if a product is bought "as is," if it proves harmful, the seller and/or manufacturer may still be liable under product liability requirements.

6. Consumers generally have four years to enforce implied warranty claims. This doesn't mean the product has to last for four years, but it should have a normal durability, and if it doesn't, state statutes of limitation generally give you four years after date of purchase to demand satisfaction.

7. If you feel that an implied warranty has been breached, phone the store and explain the prob-

lem. Name the warranty in question. Cite the appropriate section of the Uniform Commercial Code. Show that you've done your homework and you know your rights.

Express Warranties

1. Express (meaning "expressly stated," not "fast") written warranties can be offered by the manufacturer or the merchant or both. Under the federal Magnuson-Moss Warranty Act and the FTC rules adopted to clarify compliance, manufacturers and sellers have certain obligations to product consumers.

2. No business is required to offer a written warranty. If you buy a product without any written warranty, you may have only implied warranties to protect you. But if the product additionally has a written warranty, you can expect further protection.

3. According to the FTC's Rule on Disclosure of Written Consumer Product Warranty Terms and Conditions (the Disclosure Rule), every written warranty for a consumer product costing more than $15 must spell out in a single, clear, easy-to-read document (a) what the warranty covers and excludes, (b) the period of coverage, (c) how problems will be addressed if they occur and who will be responsible for the charges, (d) how consumers can get warranty service when needed, and (e) the application of state law.

4. Read the terms and conditions. What in fact is covered? Does coverage begin after installation, or as soon as the item leaves the store? If it doesn't work, will the seller/manufacturer replace it, repair it, or give a refund or a credit? Are consequential damages covered (in other words, if a refrigerator fails, who pays for the food)? Are incidental damages covered (if, for instance, you lose income because you have to take time off from work)?

5. If warranty terms may not apply in your state, the document has to say so; for example, the sentence, "Some states do not allow limita-

tions on how long an implied warranty lasts, so the above limitation may not apply to you," might appear.

6. With some exceptions, tie-in sales provisions aren't permitted. This means that, for example, the warranty for a tape recorder can't be tied in to your using only a specific brand of tape. Such provisions can be included only if the FTC has been convinced that the product won't work properly with any other brand.

7. Make no mistake. The FTC doesn't say that the product *must* be replaced, or that you *must* be compensated for spoiled food, or that you *must* be covered for missed work. It only says that the warranty must state what the manufacturer and/or seller is prepared to do and how you can avail yourself of these services.

8. If you fail to read the warranty, don't blame anybody but yourself. However, if the warranty is breached, you have very definite remedy under the law.

9. For every consumer product costing more than $10, the Magnuson-Moss Warranty Act says that the warranty should have a title identifying the coverage as either *full* or *limited*.

10. Limited warranties must specifically state the limitations, but they can't override state law. For example, they can't take away any implied warranty that pertains, though they can restrict the duration of the implied warranty to the duration of the limited warranty.

11. Full warranties meet these criteria:
- **They don't limit the duration of implied warranties.**
- **They extend warranty coverage to whoever owns the product during the warranty period (in other words, the recipient of a gift as well as the person who bought it).**
- **They provide warranty service without charge, including free shipping.**
- **They will replace or issue a refund for a product that isn't fully repaired after a reasonable number of tries.**
- **They don't impose extra duties on a customer as a condition of receiving warranty service.**

If a warranty is entitled "Full Warranty," it must deliver according to all of these terms.

12. A "multiple warranty" can be part full, part limited, provided that it identifies which part is which.

13. The FTC Rule on Pre-Sale Availability of Written Warranty Terms says that written warranties on consumer products costing over $15 must be available for customers to read before purchase. In a store, these must be accessible at the point of sale. They include any written warranties from the manufacturer plus any written warranties offered by the seller.

If You Have a Problem

1. Better safe than sorry, so try all the features of the product well within the warranty period. This way, you'll be able to seek satisfaction before your coverage runs out.

2. If you discover a problem, reread your warranty. If your seller and manufacturer each extended a warranty, read both. Find out exactly what commitments were made, and follow the procedure given. Under the FTC Disclosure Rule, all written warranties must detail this procedure.

3. If you purchased the item with a credit card, it may be appropriate for you to cancel the charge, or to request a chargeback.

4. Some credit cards offer additional product warranties as a service to cardholders. Read the agreement to see what coverage you have.

If You Have to Fight

1. If you followed the detailed procedure but weren't satisfied, speak to the store manager.

2. If appropriate, contact the consumer relations department of the manufacturer.

3. If you saved your print advertising, look it over. Were particular features promised? Did the seller or manufacturer make any commitments that you'll want to apply?

4. Cite the Magnuson-Moss Warranty Act. Explain that Congress passed it to permit consumers to compare warranties before purchase, and that you did in fact waste your time and base your spending on a comparison of warranties. To put it simply, you find it outrageous that the company misrepresented its warranty, thereby extracting money from you with false promises. Before purchase, you had the option of buying another product. But now you cannot unspend your money, so it's up to the company to make good on its promise.

5. Your warranty may explain a mechanism, such as an outside panel or a company department, for resolving disputes based on the Magnuson-Moss Warranty Act. If it does, the mechanism must, among other obligations, be (a) free to customers, (b) large enough and sufficiently funded to resolve matters quickly, (c) free of influence from the disputing parties, (d) follow written procedure, (e) inform both parties of its decision and its reasoning within forty days, and (f) be audited annually for compliance.

6. If such a mechanism exists and you're not satisfied with its findings, the decisions aren't binding. You can still go to court.

7. Congress intended the Magnuson-Moss Warranty Act to encourage companies to settle product complaints with minimal delay and expense to the purchaser. If you feel you have no remaining remedy other than a lawsuit, explain that neither the delay nor the expense has been minimal.

8. Add that if you go to court and prove an implied or written warranty has been breached, it's a violation of federal law, and the Magnuson-Moss Warranty Act enables you to recover court costs, including lawyer's fees.

9. At this point, the seller may be more than willing to replace your air conditioner, or the

manufacturer may find it cost-efficient to give you a better appliance for making toast.

10. If the seller lets you down, report it to the head office, the Chamber of Commerce, and the Better Business Bureau. If the product was at fault, notify the Correspondence Branch, Room 692, FTC, 6th Street and Pennsylvania Avenue, N.W., Washington, DC 20580.

▲ *See also* APPLIANCES; CREDIT CARDS; GUARANTEES; RETAIL SHOPPING.

Workplace

You pay for your rights in the workplace with the time you put into your job—and whenever there's money involved in a deal, there's always the risk of losing it.

A smart consumer can take the same skills that work in a retail store or an automobile showroom and apply them to a bad job situation. Here are guidelines for translating those talents. Not surprisingly, they rely on research and preparation as much as on knowing how to complain.

Prepare for the Worst

1. In the best of all possible worlds, something can go wrong with a job. Even if everybody gets along with everybody, a company can go out of business. Even if the company is turning huge profits, calamity can strike, and you can find your job in jeopardy.

2. It certainly isn't advisable for you to walk around spouting doom. Chicken Little squawking that the sky is falling is nobody's idea of a party animal. But if you lay calm, rational foundations in advance, you'll be better prepared if the sky just happens to drop on your head.

3. When you start a job, ask for an employee handbook if your company issues any. If not, attempt to get an accurate statement of what employees will receive in the way of vacation, personal and sick days, health coverage, profit-shar-

ing arrangements, retirement benefits, financial services, and employee assistance programs (see below). Write down what you're told.

4. Is sick leave unpaid if it comes just before or after a vacation? Is a doctor's statement required? To whom do you report if you're sick and can't get to work?

5. It's not enough to know what you'll get. Make sure you know how it will be provided. To receive medical coverage, what forms would you fill out? When you're ready to take your vacation, how much notice should you give?

6. Ask how you'll know if the information is changed or updated. If you get updates, file them with your records.

7. With or without an employee handbook, you're entitled to ask to have the terms of your health and retirement packages in written form, as an agreement that would be considered legally binding.

8. If you'll be enrolled in a pension, profit-sharing, or similar program, ask what sort of reports and statements you'll receive, and on what schedule. Find out the name, number, and address of the person you can contact if questions or problems come up (see PENSIONS).

9. If the company is large enough to have a human resources (or personnel) office or a benefits department, call or stop by to research the various savings, mortgage assistance, and credit union options open to you.

10. Ask whether the company will pay for courses to continue your job-related education. If there's an aspect of business that you've meant to learn—such as computers—try to persuade your employer to pick up the tab. Then if you leave or lose your job, you'll have more to offer at your next interview, and you might make contacts you can tap later on.

11. Does the company have a procedure for performance evaluations? Read and understand it before you go in for one.

12. Study the employee handbook and observe the chain of command. Who's in charge of what, and of whom? Is there a risk manager? A safety manager?

13. Pay attention when people tell stories about their own job disputes. Was some manager particularly helpful? Was another unusually uncooperative? Did a union become involved? Does the company have an internal policy for mediation or arbitration?

14. Basically, you want to analyze policy and past history to come up with the correct procedure for contesting or reacting to a decision—whether the decision is that you're fired, or that you've got to do something you don't want to do.

15. Documentation is invaluable in any dispute. If you've been injured by a safety hazard that a dozen people reported over two years' time, your best ally is a running record of when it was reported and who filed the reports. Or if a supervisor suddenly criticizes your every move, your best defense is a journal of previous discussions in which your performance was praised and you were specifically instructed to do what you're now blamed for doing.

16. Don't rely on other people to keep your records. Complaints about a safety hazard may not be documented anywhere else. The times your supervisor applauded your efforts may never turn up in a formal evaluation.

17. Your employer is probably required by law to keep you informed of safety plans, workers'

compensation policies, and the like. Often, posters must be displayed or training sessions offered. Make a note if posters are removed and not replaced. Keep a record of employee-oriented classes you attend.

18. If you're injured because you weren't informed—if labels were removed, or if you were never properly taught to use equipment—your position is much stronger in the eyes of the law and insurers.

19. There are federal, state, and local laws to protect you. Phone the U.S. Department of Labor and/or the equivalent department of your state or city government to learn what they are. But remember that laws can be changed.

20. Your best advantage in knowing the law may be that you can warn an employer who's breaking it. Though excellent laws exist, you've got no guarantee that they'll be enforced soon enough to rescue you. Understaffed government agencies may be slow to respond. If regulations exist but lack specific standards, you may have to wait for a court to interpret them. For example, if emergency exits must be "readily accessible" by law, do they have to be in every room? On every floor? Who decides?

21. State and city standards are set by governments anxious to attract and retain industry. Particularly when the economy is bad, enforcement agencies may relax the burdens on businesses though workers could suffer as a result.

22. Realize that many laws apply only to operations of a certain size or don't apply at all to some kinds of employers (such as federal, state, and local governments!).

23. If you intend to charge a company with breaking a law, consult with an informed legal adviser first. It doesn't have to be a lawyer, but it should be someone who can tell you exactly where you stand.

24. Don't wait until you're leaving a company to begin to prepare. It's a good idea to have copies of the employee handbook and the company

directory and a photocopy or other record of your personal Rolodex *at home.*

Employee Assistance Programs

1. Employee Assistance Programs—EAPs—can be wonderful free resources. Fifty years ago, they focused on rehabilitating employees who had drinking problems. Today, depending on your company's arrangement with them, you might have access to free counseling on employment matters, care for children and elderly dependents, even stress and weight-control counseling.

2. When your employer contracts with an outside firm specializing in employee assistance programs, you have access to a larger pool of experts than most small or medium-sized companies could afford to put on staff.

3. Some EAPs have staff attorneys to help you with legal advice.

4. Members of your immediate family may be eligible for EAP assistance.

5. If confidentiality concerns you, ask if you can have a phone conversation without revealing your name.

6. Depending on the nature of your discussion, you might want to clarify in advance whether the subject will be kept confidential from your employer. If you can't be assured that it will, you may want to contact the state or city department of labor to see if this is acceptable under the law.

7. Before using any services, confirm with the company and with the EAP representative that there won't be a charge.

8. If you're referred to an outside professional, determine whether part or all of the cost is covered by your employer. If not, who pays, and how much will it be?

If You're Injured

1. Know what company policy is and follow it to the letter. If you're required to report the incident to guarantee coverage, don't delay.

2. If you're a union employee, report it to the union. If you have any doubts about what to do, call the company's human resources or personnel department. Speak to your supervisor. Reread the employee handbook. It isn't enough just to report an injury; you have to report it correctly.

3. What's the procedure for obtaining treatment? What paperwork do you need? What are the deadlines for completing it? What kind of approval do you need to be sure the doctor you see will be reimbursed?

4. Workers' compensation (state benefits for employees injured on the job) ought to be available, and shouldn't be related to assigning blame. Your state or city department of labor will have information for you. Posters may be on display in your place of business.

5. What are the limits to your coverage? Will you be paid for time lost from work? For how long? If it's time to come back to work and you don't feel you're fully recovered, what are your options?

6. If you disagree with the findings, the coverage, or the limits, how can you appeal? Don't just take your company's word for it. Ask the state or city department of labor.

7. Definitions of job-related injuries are expanding. Some states recognize stress as a fair claim. But if you abuse the law—inaccurately claiming a string of stressful cruelties—you'll lose your case and brand yourself as a risky person to hire.

8. When the same task is performed again and again, day after week after month, it may lead to physical damage such as swelling of the wrist. This is known as a repetitive strain injury, and may be covered by workers' compensation or your company's insurance.

9. Some injuries have extra coverage because they fall under special laws. For example, if you're hurt in a fire because your company didn't obey fire codes, not only do you have a valid case, but the company is doubtless subject to fines.

10. According to the federal Hazard Communication Standard, you have a "Right to Know" what hazards you face on the job and how to protect yourself against them.

11. Hazardous chemicals should be labeled by manufacturers, alerting you to possible dangers and how to deal with them. Additionally, a Material Safety Data Sheet (MSDS) for each chemical used should be on file in your workplace. The MSDS should identify ingredients, describe emergency response techniques, and provide a name, address, and emergency phone number of the manufacturer.

12. MSDS information should be on hand not only for products that can cause accidents, but also for chemical substances that may endanger you over long periods of exposure.

13. Keep records of any time you're denied access to the information. If you're scheduled to attend a training session and you miss it, make an effort to get to another one. If your employer prevents you from going, document the circumstances.

14. The federal Occupational Health and Safety Administration (OSHA) is concerned with all safety conditions, ranging from chemical and electrical safety to transmission of tuberculosis and AIDS. MSDS violations are an OSHA issue.

15. Check your telephone directory for the regional OSHA office (look in the U.S. Government listings, or consult telephone information). Not every state has its own OSHA office. For instance, Vermont's regional office is located in Boston. If you want to protect yourself while reporting a suspected violation, you can request that your name be withheld.

16. An OSHA investigator may respond very quickly, showing up at your workplace and slapping your boss with a huge fine.

17. Violations can be in fact or in record-keeping. It's especially serious if your employer willfully exposes workers to potentially harmful situations.

18. Don't expect OSHA to prosecute a case for you. Simply understand that no business wants to be on the losing end of a battle with OSHA. Point out to your employer that fines are high, investigations can be rigorous, and criminal penalties have been imposed. Particularly if you've kept a record of past reports that the hazard existed, you'll be able to argue more persuasively for the additional time or compensation you request.

19. If the violation is significant, a local TV or newspaper action reporter may be interested in covering it. If the possibility of OSHA repercussions didn't get your company's attention, perhaps the thought of headlines will.

20. If you've been seriously injured, speak to a lawyer and to the state or city department for the disabled (*see* DISABILITIES).

21. Social Security extends some coverage to people disabled on the job (*see* SOCIAL SECURITY).

22. *Never* sign a waiver or release following an accident until you've spoken to a trusted adviser. *Never* settle for what seems like a reasonable arrangement without investigating whether you may be more severely injured than you realize.

Job Discrimination

1. If you believe you've been discriminated against, either on the job or while looking for one, find out if the company has a written policy on discrimination issues. But even if it does, you may feel uncomfortable about seeking protection under it.

2. Nevertheless, see what the policy says. Ask workers if they've had any experience with it. You may want to ask friends, a clergyperson, or a lawyer for advice.

3. If you can't afford a lawyer but need legal assistance, contact the local Legal Aid Society for guidance and referrals to qualified, affordable help.

4. The Equal Employment Opportunity Commission (EEOC) is the federal civil rights agency established to investigate charges of discrimination based on race, color, religion, sex, national origin, age, and disability. Contact its local or state office for information (look in the govern-

ment listings for your city or state). If you want to file a claim, ask about the procedure.

5. You'll have a better case if you can *prove* bias. If you've kept documentation of a pattern—derogatory remarks and prejudicial treatment aimed at you *and others* of the same race, color, religion, sex, national origin, age, or disability—your complaint is less likely to be rejected. Otherwise, expect your employer to argue that you got the treatment you deserved because you were an incompetent worker.

6. The EEOC may investigate, urge arbitration, and, if the claim is found to have merit, provide relief through settlement.

7. Because employment discrimination is a civil rights issue, a number of advocacy groups and government agencies are available to you. Start by contacting the state and city department (or division or commission) of human rights (look in the government listings for your state and city). Ask for guidance and referrals. Also check your directory business listings under a heading appropriate to your problem. For instance, if the issue is sexual harassment, see if there are listings under "Women's Advocacy Groups" or a similar heading.

8. Among federal laws written for your protection are:

- **Title VII of the Civil Rights Act of 1964, forbidding job bias on the basis of race, color, sex, religion, and national origin.**
- **Section 510 of the Employee Retirement Income Security Act, forbidding discrimination on the basis of a person's entitlement to pension benefits.**
- **Age Discrimination in Employment Act of 1967, forbidding job bias against people forty years old or older.**
- **Americans with Disabilities Act of 1991, forbidding job bias for reasons of disability.**

9. The laws of your state and municipality may broaden this to include marital status, history of mental disorder, sexual orientation, liability for service in the Armed Forces, and other considerations.

Warning Signals

1. Sometimes people are eased out of a job for good cause. Sometimes they're fired unfairly. If you report a violation to OSHA, complain about sexual harassment, or behave in a way that unjustly leads to your dismissal, don't think your employer will admit that you were made to leave for all the wrong reasons. Rely on your records for proof, not on your boss.

2. Be prepared before you hear the news. Have copies of your employee handbook, company directory, and Rolodex at home. Have easy access to your documentation.

3. If you did your job the way you were told to do it, your employer is on weak ground. The best way to substantiate that you did your job as directed yet were criticized for it is to document the times it happened.

4. If your company conducts regular performance evaluations, know the procedure before you sit down to one. Know whether the employee has to sign a review before it's considered complete, and whether you're entitled to time (or overnight, or longer) to formulate a response before signing.

5. If you've been expecting trouble, you may want to have your response handy and ready to attach to the evaluation form. It will be more carefully thought out than if you'd been caught off guard, or forced to comment on short notice.

6. If the review is unfavorable, make notes. If your supervisor asks why you're taking notes, say, "I want to go over this later to be sure I understand." If you're given ambiguous or conflicting directives, ask for clarification. The person conducting the review has an obligation to make sense. If his or her clarification doesn't clarify anything, indicate that it's still unclear. Then jot down a reminder of this exchange. Your job may be at stake.

7. If you're told to do something in a way that's bound to backfire, you may want to reply along the lines of "I've avoided doing that because if I do, so-and-so will happen. Of course, if you want

me to, you're the boss and I'll do as you request. But if I follow your guidelines and my performance suffers, I hope you'll appreciate that it's not an indication of my inability to do the job, but rather of my willingness to cooperate."

8. If you're assigned to tasks for which obstacles stand in the way and the obstacles aren't under your control, say so. Ask what kind of commitment your supervisor will make to remove them. Carefully document this portion of the discussion.

9. In the case of a bad grade, is the supervisor giving it to you, or to himself or herself? If you're told to do things in order of importance but the supervisor refuses to commit to what's important, can you be held responsible for prioritizing? State this courteously but for the record. As a rule, if your job gets in the way of your doing your job, you're not at fault—the job is. Suggest that you'd be happy to cooperate with any effort to redesign the job. Make notes of what is said.

10. Be aware of possible clues that your supervisor doesn't know what it means to conduct an evaluation. Document the clues, not your feelings. "She was on a power trip" is useless. But "She called me a lazy idiot, then said, 'Don't take this as personal criticism' " would demonstrate that your evaluation was prepared by a person of questionable competence (or even by a lazy idiot on a power trip).

11. Ask what will be expected of you before the next review and how your improvement will be evaluated.

12. Whether the evaluation is good or bad, ask if you can make a photocopy. Keep it for your records.

13. Don't fall into the trap of thinking everything is fine. If your current supervisor adores you and gives glowing reviews, that's terrific. But what if your supervisor is replaced by someone who wants to hire his or her cousin for your job? This new supervisor may say you're impossible, but your past evaluations will prove otherwise.

14. Know the procedure for disputing a review. Speak to your union steward or personnel office. Is mediation or arbitration appropriate?

15. Whether for an evaluation or another issue, it's usually a bad idea to go over your supervisor's head without first exhausting every opportunity to reach accord with your supervisor. Document your efforts to work things out.

16. There are times when your supervisor will be a total brick wall and you have no choice but to talk to someone else. Before you do, investigate the chain of command and the proper procedure.

17. Begin your remarks with a reference to the fact that you really tried to deal with your supervisor on this, but you were repeatedly ignored. If a fellow employee had repeatedly complained to you about your work and you consistently ignored the person, surely it would be acceptable for the employee to speak to your supervisor. Now you find yourself in the same awkward position in having to speak to your supervisor's supervisor. You'll sound more professional if you say you regret having to.

18. Don't come on like a rebel or a whiner when you speak to your boss's boss. Express your loyalty to the company and its resources; you want the company to get maximum effectiveness from those resources, even when one of them is you.

19. Ask your boss's boss what the next step will be, and whether the matter will be discussed with your supervisor.

20. Document the conversation.

Parting Shots

1. If you sense that your position is in trouble, talk to a lawyer or trusted adviser. Find out what you can be pressured into signing. Otherwise, when someone informs you that you're fired and you'd better sign the waiver right away or lose your severance and benefits, you won't know where you stand.

2. Reread your employee's handbook when you see the danger signs. What kinds of warnings are required before dismissal? If you're fired, be sure to ask why. Feel free to take notes.

3. If you want to keep a job, your documentation will come in handy. Speak to your union steward or designated person and the personnel office to find out how you can challenge your termination.

4. If you can't win the argument to let you keep your job, or if you have no interest in working for a company that just fired you, your documentation is still important. Use it to demonstrate that you were fired for reasons of the company's convenience, not because you performed inadequately.

5. Ask to see the information in your personnel file. Many but not all states have laws empowering you to do this. Make notes of what you see. If there's not a negative word in the folder but the company later contests your right to unemployment benefits because you were fired "for cause," it's helpful to produce your proof that cause didn't appear in the file until after you were gone.

6. Being fired isn't the end. Is it effective immediately? Even if you're told to leave immediately, resist finality at this point. Try to keep the door open to follow-up discussion about the terms of your departure. If possible, set a meeting.

7. After being fired, you may be escorted to your office and told, "Remove just your personal effects. We'll look through your papers and Rolodex after you leave, and mail them to you if we decide they're not company property." The procedure is increasingly common and hard to prove illegal (unless the employer asks you to leave your wallet and clothes behind). Your best defense is to have copied important information (such as Rolodex entries) in advance.

8. Even this isn't the end.

9. If you've worked at a company and have been fired for no fault of yours (and often if you were in error too), you've earned certain financial entitlements, as well as definite rights.

10. The better your documentation, the better your chances for negotiating terms *on your terms.* Among requests to consider: extended severance, continued health insurance at the company's expense, placement counseling and résumé assis-

tance, and access to office equipment such as copiers, computers, and the fax while you search for your next job.

11. If a legal issue is conceivably involved, rest assured your company doesn't want to be sued for unfair termination. Use this in negotiating the best possible separation deal, but avoid being so obnoxious about it that your employer says, "Go ahead, smartie, take us to court." If you go to court, the case could drag on for years, while you fall back on your savings.

12. Keeping this in mind, realize that by law, you can't be forced into early retirement against your will. If you are, it may be a case of age discrimination and, as such, of interest to the Equal Employment Opportunity Commission (discussed above under the head "Job Discrimination"). Contact the EEOC and organizations such as the American Association of Retired Persons (AARP) for guidance.

13. For terminations involving other types of discrimination, also see "Job Discrimination" above.

14. In some instances, being fired constitutes a breach of contract. Some states include employee handbooks and promises made by employers in the definition of a contract. Mentioning this may strengthen your hand in negotiating severance and benefits.

15. If you resign, you usually don't have much to negotiate. Your employer says, "If you don't like it, leave." You say, "Well then, goodbye."

16. An exception might be if a contract has been breached. Another might occur if you've been the victim of constructive discharge, which is when an employer deliberately makes working conditions so miserable that the employee is forced to quit. Constructive discharge coupled with discrimination may improve your negotiating position.

17. If you're going to quit and think you're entitled to unemployment benefits, think again. Don't just take the word of people who left in the past. Your state's rules are subject to a degree of interpretation, sometimes depending simply on the state's ability to pay benefits. Call the state depart-

ment of labor or your state's unemployment compensation division if it's separate from the department of labor to ask what your entitlements are.

18. What does and doesn't qualify for unemployment benefits? How do you apply? Once benefits begin, what must you do to keep collecting? What job searches are you required to conduct? What sort of employment must you accept? (Does it have to be in your own line? Could you be required to take a salary cut?) How long will benefits last? What would interrupt them or cut them off?

19. Follow up with your company's benefits officer or other appropriate person in the human resources or personnel department. Has your paperwork been processed? What information is required from you? What must you do or continue to do to receive what you have coming to you— severance, profit-sharing, early retirement benefits, whatever? What names, addresses, and phone numbers will you need if problems arise?

20. During and after the job, deadlines will apply. Find out what they are and observe them meticulously. If you miss a deadline, you may forfeit your rights.

21. Your health benefits may be covered under the Consolidated Omnibus Budget Reconciliation Act of 1986, or COBRA (*see* INSURANCE, Health Insurance). But your company may offer a better package than COBRA requires. Ask for a Summary Plan Description that spells it out for you.

When It's Finally Over

1. Keep a record of what benefits you receive and when. Have phone numbers and addresses, preferably 800 numbers for out-of-state offices. If checks regularly come from the same bank, note the contact for the bank. The more you know, the more you have to work with if checks are delayed or stop coming.

2. If you have a dispute over earned income, contact your state department of labor, which

should have a division of labor standards or a related division.

3. Watch newspaper classified ads and talk to your union and trade or professional association to learn of job opportunities. Check local newspapers and bulletin boards for notices of seminars offered by adult education programs and community service groups. Some may help you with your job-search techniques (such as writing résumés), while others improve your on-the-job skills (such as using computers or taking shorthand).

4. If you went to college, your alumni association may provide placement services.

5. Attend as many different meetings of as many different groups as you can: conventions, seminars, community social hours, high school and college reunions. The more you mingle, the more opportunities you have for networking.

6. Career counseling and employment placement agencies are listed in the business section of your telephone directory. Though the best are excellent, be sure you know what you're getting before you go, and whether there's a fee.

7. If you're going to spend money, get a recommendation or reference first. Why throw away money on someone who can't help you?

8. If you feel you've been defrauded by an employment counseling service—for instance, if you pay a fee and the counselor skips town—the National Consumer Fraud Task Force would be interested in hearing about it: P.O. Box 402036, Miami Beach, FL 33140; 305-532-2607.

To Complain

1. If your company's policies are unfair to you, are they unfair to other employees too? Ask other employees. What are they and their unions doing about it?

2. If your company is violating a law, contact one of the agencies such as EEOC or OSHA, discussed above.

3. If a small employer has unethical practices and expects you to follow them, speak to your state department of labor and the local Chamber of Commerce and Better Business Bureau. Your concerns may also interest local newspapers and radio and TV stations.

4. You can do the same if a large employer is at fault. If the employer is large enough, its abuses might affect the entire community and therefore concern local and state elected officials. Call their offices and let them know why you think they should become involved.

5. If laws should be changed, call or write your legislators. Urge them to take action.

6. If hearings are held, attend them. Make your presence felt. Make your feelings known. Show your lawmakers that the outcome matters to you.

Other Resources

This list barely scratches the surface of advocacy groups that may be able to support you with facts, guidance, and referrals. Don't stop here. Check your telephone directory and library for the organizations best suited to your needs. Look under specific topics or the general headings "Associations" and "Social Services."

American Association of Retired
  Persons
601 E Street, N.W.
Washington, DC 20049
202-434-2277

American Civil Liberties Union
132 West 43rd Street
New York, NY 10036
212-944-9800

Equal Rights Advocates
1663 Mission Street, Suite 550
San Francisco, CA 94103
415-621-0672

National Council on the Aging
409 3rd Street, S.W., No. 200
Washington, DC 20024
202-479-6665

National Legal Aid and Defender
  Association
1625 K Street, N.W., 8th Floor
Washington, DC 20006
202-452-0620

▲ *See also* DISABILITIES; DOCTORS; HOSPITALS; INSURANCE; PENSIONS; SOCIAL SECURITY.

Additional Consumer Resources

American Apparel Manufacturers Association

Director, Education and
  Conventions
2500 Wilson Boulevard, Suite 301
Arlington, VA 22201
703-524-1864
Membership: Manufacturers of clothing.

American Arbitration Association

Public Relations Director
140 West 51st Street
New York, NY 10020-1203
212-484-4006
Private, nonprofit organization with 35 regional offices across the country. Provides consumer information on request. Check local telephone directory for listing. If there is no office in your area, write or call the office listed above.

American Automobile Association AUTOSOLVE

1000 AAA Drive
Heathrow, FL 32746-5064
1-800-477-6583
Third-party dispute resolution program for Toyota, Lexus, Hyundai and Subaru in selected areas of the United States.

American Bar Association

Standing Committee on Dispute
  Resolution
1800 M Street, N.W., Suite 790
Washington, DC 20036
202-331-2258
Publishes a directory of state and local alternative dispute resolution programs. Provides consumer information on request.

American Collectors Association

Executive Vice President
4040 West 70th Street
P.O. Box 39106
Minneapolis, MN 55439-0106
612-926-6547
Membership: Collection services handling overdue accounts for retail, professional and commercial credit grantors.

American Council of Life Insurance

Information Department
1001 Pennsylvania Avenue, N.W.
Washington, DC 20004-2599
1-800-942-4242 (8 A.M.–8 P.M.
  EST, M–F)
Membership: Life insurance companies authorized to do business in the United States.

American Gas Association

Director of Consumer Affairs
1515 Wilson Boulevard
Arlington, VA 22209
703-841-8583
Membership: Distributors and transporters of natural gas.

American Health Care Association

1201 L Street, N.W.
Washington, DC 20005-4014
202-842-4444
1-800-321-0343 (publications only)
Membership: State associations of long-term health care facilities.

American Hotel and Motel Association

1201 New York Avenue, N.W.,
  Suite 600
Washington, DC 20005-3931
Written inquiries only.
Membership: State and regional hotel associations.

American Institute of Certified Public Accountants

Director, Professional Ethics
  Division
1211 Avenue of the Americas
New York, NY 10036-8775
212-575-6209

Membership: Professional society of accountants certified by the states and territories.

American Newspaper Publishers Assn. Credit Bureau Inc.

P.O. Box 17022
Dulles International Airport
Washington, DC 20041
703-648-1038
Investigates fraudulent advertising published in newspapers.

American Orthotic and Prosthetic Association

1650 King Street, Suite 500
Alexandria, VA 22314-1885
703-836-7116
Represents member companies that custom-fit or manufacture components for patients with prostheses or orthoses.

American Society of Travel Agents, Inc.

Vice President, Consumer Affairs
P.O. Box 23992
Washington, DC 20026-3992
703-739-2782
Membership: Travel agents.

American Textile Manufacturers Institute

Director, Communications
   Division
1801 K Street, N.W., Suite 900
Washington, DC 20006
202-862-0552
Membership: Textile mills which produce a variety of textile products, e.g., clothing, using natural and man-made fibers.

Automotive Consumer Action Program (AUTOCAP)

Manager, Consumer Affairs
8400 Westpark Drive
McLean, VA 22102
703-821-7144
Third-party dispute resolution program administered through the National Automobile Dealers Association. Consumer information available on request.

BBB AUTO LINE

Council of Better Business
Bureaus, Inc.
4200 Wilson Boulevard, Suite 800
Arlington, VA 22203-1804
703-276-0100
Third-party dispute resolution program for AMC, Audi, General Motors and its divisions, Honda, Jeep, Nissan, Peugeot, Porsche, Renault, SAAB and Volkswagen.

Better Hearing Institute

P.O. Box 1840
Washington, DC 20013
703-642-0580
1-800-EAR-WELL
Membership: Professionals and others who help persons with impaired hearing. Provides voluntary mediation between consumers and hearing aid dispensers.

Blue Cross and Blue Shield Association

Consumer Affairs
Metro Square—Phase II
655 15th Street, N.W., Suite 350F
Washington, DC 20005
202-626-4780
Membership: Local Blue Cross and Blue Shield plans in the United States, Canada and Jamaica.

Boat Owners Association of the United States (BOAT/U.S.)

Administrator, Consumer
   Protection Bureau
880 South Pickett Street
Alexandria, VA 22304-0730
703-823-9550
Consumer Protection Bureau serves as a mediator in disputes between boat owners and the marine industry. BOAT/U.S. also works closely with the U.S. Coast Guard to monitor safety defect problems.

Carpet and Rug Institute

Director of Governmental Affairs
1155 Connecticut Avenue, N.W.,
   Suite 500
Washington, DC 20036
Written inquiries only. Membership: Manufacturers of carpets, rugs, bath mats and bedspreads; suppliers of raw materials and services to the industry.

Cemetery Consumer Service Council

Assistant Secretary
P.O. Box 3574
Washington, DC 20007
703-379-6426
Industry-sponsored dispute resolution program. Other consumer information about cemetery practices and rules available on request.

Children's Advertising Review Unit (CARU)

Council of Better Business
   Bureaus, Inc.
845 Third Avenue
New York, NY 10022
212-754-1354
Handles consumer complaints about fraudulent and deceptive advertising related to children.

Chrysler Motors Customer Relations

National Office
26311 Lawrence Avenue
Center Line, MI 48288
1-800-992-1997

Department of Defense

Office of National Ombudsman
National Committee for Employer
  Support of the Guard and
  Reserve
1555 Wilson Boulevard, Suite 200
Arlington, VA 22209-2405
703-696-1391
1-800-336-4590 (outside DC)
*Provides assistance witn
employer/employee problems for
members of the Guard and Reserve
and their employers.*

Direct Marketing Association (DMA)

Director, Ethics and Consumer
  Affairs
6 East 43rd Street
New York, NY 10017-4646
*Written complaints only. Membership: Members who market goods
and services directly to consumers
using direct mail, catalogs, telemarketing, magazine and newspaper
ads, and broadcast advertising.*

*DMA operates the Mail Order
Action Line, Mail Preference Service
and Telephone Preference Service.*

*For problems with a mail order
company, write:*
Mail Order Action Line
6 East 43rd Street
New York, NY 10017

*To remove your name from a direct
mail list, write:*
Mail Preference Service
P.O. Box 3861
Grand Central Station
New York, NY 10163

To remove your name from a telephone solicitation list, write:
Telephone Preference Service
6 East 43rd Street
New York, NY 10017

Direct Selling Association

Code Administrator
1776 K Street, N.W., Suite 600
Washington, DC 20006-2387
202-293-5760
*Membership: Manufacturers and
distributors selling consumer products door-to-door and through
home-party plans.*

Electronic Industries Association

Executive Director, Consumer
  Affairs
2001 Pennsylvania Avenue, N.W.,
  10th Floor
Washington, DC 20006
202-457-4977
*Complaint assistance program, consumer education, etc. concerning
televisions, videocassette recorders
and other video systems, audio
products, personal computers and
communication electronic products.*

Ford Consumer Appeals Board

P.O. Box 5120
Southfield, MI 48086-5120
1-800-392-3673

Funeral Service Consumer Arbitration Program (FSCAP)

1614 Central Street
Evanston, IL 60201
1-800-662-7666
*Third-party dispute resolution program sponsored by the National
Funeral Directors Association.*

Hearing Industries Association

President, Market Development
1255 23rd Street, N.W.
Washington, DC 20037-1174
202-833-1411
*Membership: Companies engaged in
the manufacture and/or sale of electronic hearing aids, their components, parts and related products
and services on a national basis.*

Home Owners Warranty Corporation (HOW) Operation Center

P.O. Box 152087
Irving, TX 75015-2087
1-800-433-7657
*Third-party dispute resolution program for new homes built by
HOW-member home builders.*

Insurance Information Institute

Manager, Consumer Affairs and
  Education
110 William Street
New York, NY 10038
1-800-942-4242
*National Insurance Consumer
Helpline is a resource for consumers
with automobile and home insurance
questions. The Helpline is open
Monday through Friday from 8
A.M. to 8 P.M.*

International Association for Financial Planning

2 Concourse Parkway, Suite 800
Atlanta, GA 30328
404-395-1605
*Membership: Individuals involved in
financial planning.*

Major Appliance Consumer Action Panel (MACAP)

20 North Wacker Drive
Chicago, IL 60606
312-984-5858
1-800-621-0477
Third-party dispute resolution program of the major appliance industry.

Monument Builders of North America

Executive Vice President
1740 Ridge Avenue
Evanston, IL 60201
708-869-2031
Membership: Cemetery monument retailers, manufacturers and wholesalers; bronze manufacturers and suppliers. Consumer brochures available on request.

Mortgage Bankers Association of America

Media Relations Coordinator/
   Consumer Affairs
1125 15th Street, N.W., 7th Floor
Washington, DC 20005
202-861-1929
Membership: Mortgage banking firms, commercial banks, life insurance companies, title companies, and savings and loan associations.

National Advertising Division (NAD)

845 Third Avenue
New York, NY 10022
212-754-1320
A Division of the Council of Better Business Bureaus, Inc. Handles consumer complaints about the truth and accuracy of national advertising.

National Association of Home Builders

Director, Consumer Affairs/Public
   Liaison
15th and M Streets, N.W.
Washington, DC 20005
202-822-0409
1-800-368-5242 (outside DC)
Membership: Single and multifamily home builders, commercial builders, and others associated with the building industry.

National Association of Personnel Consultants

3133 Mt. Vernon Avenue
Alexandria, VA 22305
703-684-0180
Membership: Private employment agencies.

National Association of Securities Dealers, Inc.

Consumer Arbitration Center
33 Whitehall Street, 10th Floor
New York, NY 10004
212-858-4000
Third-party dispute resolution for complaints about over-the-counter stocks and corporate bonds.

National Association of Trade and Technical Schools

Accrediting Commission
2251 Wisconsin Avenue, N.W.
Washington, DC 20007-4181
202-333-1021
Written inquiries only. Membership: Private schools providing job training.

National Food Processors Association

Government Affairs
1401 New York Avenue, N.W.
Washington, DC 20005
202-639-5939
Membership: Commercial packers of such food products as fruit, vegetables, meat, poultry, seafood, and canned, frozen, dehydrated, pickled, and other preserved food items.

National Futures Association

Manager, Compliance
200 West Madison Street
Chicago, IL 60606-3447
312-781-1410
1-800-621-3570 (outside IL)
Membership: Futures commission merchants; commodity trading advisers; commodity pool operators; introducing brokers; and brokers and associated individuals.

National Home Study Council

Executive Director
1601 18th Street, N.W.
Washington, DC 20009
Written inquiries only. Membership: Home study (correspondence) schools.

National Tire Dealers and Retreaders Association

1250 Eye Street, N.W., Suite 400
Washington, DC 20005
202-789-2300
1-800-876-8372
Membership: Independent tire dealers and retreaders.

National Turkey Federation

Department of Consumer Affairs
11319 Sunset Hills Road
Reston, VA 22090-5205
Written inquiries only. Membership: Turkey growers, turkey hatcheries, turkey breeders, processors, marketers, and allied industry firms and poultry distributors.

Photo Marketing Association

Executive Director
3000 Picture Place
Jackson, MI 49201
Written complaints only. Membership: Retailers of photo equipment, film, and supplies; firms developing and printing film.

The Soap and Detergent Association

Director of Consumer Affairs
475 Park Avenue South
New York, NY 10016
212-725-1262
Membership: Manufacturers of soap, detergents, fatty acids, and glycerine; raw materials suppliers.

Tele-Consumer Hotline

1910 K Street, N.W., Suite 610
Washington, DC 20006
202-223-4371 (voice/TDD)
Provides information on special telephone products and services for persons with disabilities, selecting a long distance company, money-saving tips for people on low income, reducing unsolicited phone calls, telemarketing fraud, dealing with the phone company, and other issues. All telephone assistance and publications are free of charge, and Spanish-speaking counselors are available.

Toy Manufacturers of America

Communications Director
200 Fifth Avenue, Room 740
New York, NY 10010
212-675-1141
Membership: American toy manufacturers.

U.S. Tour Operators Association (USTOA)

President
211 East 51st Street, Suite 12-B
New York, NY 10022
212-944-5727
Membership: Wholesale tour operators, common carriers, suppliers and providers of travel services.

Glossary

The language of consumerism is the language you use every day, with an occasional word that has a unique meaning in a different context, and with an occasional unfamiliar word.

Don't be daunted, but more than that, don't gloss over a word you don't understand. Don't assume you know what it means if you're not sure. Never decide it doesn't matter. And never, ever sign anything that isn't crystal clear to you—even if it means asking the seller to write an explanation which you will both also sign and make part of the formal agreement.

Among the words you'll doubtless encounter:

affidavit: A sworn written statement, especially one made by oath before an authorized official.

boilerplate contract: The standard contract as it comes from the company, before negotiation. Usually a boilerplate will be as favorable as legally possible to the company. Therefore, anything you can negotiate beyond it will be a definite plus.

bond: An agreement, such as by an insurance company, to pay out financial obligations to others (within stated limits) if the bonded individual or company becomes unable to pay them.

cc: When this abbreviation appears in the lower left-hand corner of a letter, it is followed by a colon and a name or names and it means copies (originally, carbon copies) have been forwarded to the parties named. It serves to put the recipient of the letter on notice that others (supervisors, consumer agencies, state senators, the FTC, whatever) are receiving copies. When sending the copies, you may send them with a separate cover letter to each CC'd party, or simply put a check mark by the name getting the copy, and pop the copy into an envelope.

class-action suit: A lawsuit in which one or more persons (such as lawyers, or an attorney general) represent a group too large for separate suits to be instituted by each member of the group (class). *See* RUNG ELEVEN: CLASS ACTION SUIT, in Part I.

coinsurance: This is an insurance term meaning that you and your insurer share expenses when you receive a bill for medical service. For instance, if your coinsurance is on an 80-20 basis, your insurer picks up 80 percent of the cost (frequently up to a certain amount, after which other conditions may apply) and you pay the remaining 20 percent.

cooling-off period (for contracts): Various periods, as defined by law, during which you can decide to cancel a contract even though you've already signed it.

deductible: This insurance term means that benefits are paid after the deduction of an amount (usually per-claim or annual) stated in the policy.

dunning letter: A letter demanding payment for a debt or alleged debt (*see* DEBT COLLECTORS).

endorsement: An addition to a contract or insurance policy that increases, decreases, or otherwise alters the terms of the document. Also called a rider.

first-dollar coverage: This insurance term means that there are no deductibles for the policyholder to pay. Coverage begins with the first dollar of expense that the insured party incurs.

fulfillment house: A company formed to fulfill other companies' offers by, for instance, processing coupons and shipping merchandise. When you respond to a promotion, the address you use is usually not that of the company making the offer, but of its fulfillment house. If you use the address later to write to the company itself, your letter will not be answered and may not be forwarded either.

grace period: With an insurance policy or other agreement in which regular payments are due, this is the stated period after payment-due date (usually thirty-one days) during which the agreement will remain in force. However, don't expect to buy a month's free ride. You must pay within the grace period, and when you do, your money will be applied for the period beginning on the original due date.

guarantee: An agreement to make good on a faulty product or service (*see* GUARANTEES).

guaranty: An undertaking to answer for another party's debt, such as when a state sets up a guaranty fund to protect home builders if a contractor goes out of business.

hold harmless: When a contract states that somebody will be held harmless if certain events occur, it means the person won't be responsible for repairs, damages, or other consequences.

lien: A ruling to control or enforce a charge against real or personal property until the owner has satisfied a debt or claim. For instance, if you can't pay your taxes, the IRS can put a lien on some of your property, preventing you from selling it and—if you don't meet your tax bill—allowing the IRS to sell it to raise the money (*see* TAXES).

rider: An addition to a contract or insurance policy that increases, decreases, or otherwise alters the terms of the document. Also called an endorsement.

settlement: When plaintiff and defendant reach an agreement out of court.

subpoena: The document instructing a person or business to appear in court as a witness. A subpoena may also be used to demand that documents be presented in court.

warranty: A statement that something is as it is promised to be, and will be repaired or replaced, or another corrective action taken, if it isn't (*see* WARRANTIES).

Word Confusions

When speaking or writing about your complaint, be careful in your use of certain phrases that can have more than one meaning. Make sure that your statements can't be interpreted to commit you to more than you intend. When in doubt, clarify. For instance:

liable *vs.* liable: It can mean there's a fair chance that you'll do something—or that you are legally and financially responsible for it.

on time *vs.* on time: If you agree to pay something on time, you might be agreeing to pay it by a specified date—or in installments.

responsible *vs.* responsible: If you're responsible for something, you may simply be the person who did it—or you may be financially responsible for its consequences.

Index